CONFLICT & SECURITY IN AFRICA

T0313511

 African Readers

Series Editors:

Tunde Zack-Williams
Professor Emeritus in Sociology, University of Central Lancashire

Ray Bush
Professor of African Studies and Development Politics, University of Leeds

The Politics of Transition in Africa
   Giles Mohan & Tunde Zack-Williams (eds)

Conflict & Security in Africa
   Rita Abrahamsen (ed.)

CONFLICT & SECURITY IN AFRICA

Edited by

RITA ABRAHAMSEN

Professor, Graduate School of Public
& International Affairs
University of Ottawa

Published in association with

James Currey
is an imprint of Boydell & Brewer Ltd
PO Box 9
Woodbridge, Suffolk IP12 3DF (GB)
www.jamescurrey.com

and of

Boydell & Brewer Inc.
668 Mt Hope Avenue
Rochester, NY 14620-2731 (US)
www.boydellandbrewer.com

British Library Cataloguing in Publication Data
A catalogue record is available on request from the British Library

ISBN: 978-1-8470-1-078-0 (James Currey cloth)

The publisher has no responsibility for the continued existence or accuracy of URLs for
external or third-party internet websites referred to in this book, and does not guarantee that
any content on such websites is, or will remain, accurate or appropriate.

Papers used by Boydell & Brewer are natural, recycled products
made from wood grown in sustainable forests

Typeset in 10/11pt Photina MT
by Avocet Typeset, Somerton, Somerset
Printed and bound in Great Britain by
CPI Group (UK) Ltd, Croydon CR0 4YY

Contents

5

Oil as the 'Curse' of Conflict in Africa:
Peering through the Smoke & Mirrors
CYRIL OBI (37 (126) 2010)

6

Defence Expenditures, Arms Procurement & Corruption
in Sub-Saharan Africa
SUSAN WILLETT (36 (121) 2009)

Section Two:
Global Security Governance

7

Somalia: 'They Created a Desert & Called it Peace(building)'
KEN MENKHAUS (36 (120) 2009)

8

The Burundi Peace Negotiations: An African Experience
of Peace-Making
PATRICIA DALEY (24 (112) 2007)

9

Blair's Africa: The Politics of Securitisation & Fear
RITA ABRAHAMSEN
(*Alternatives* 30 (1) 2005)

Contents **vii**

Preface

Conflict and Security in Africa is the second in the series of the Review of African Political Economy (ROAPE) Readers. The series is assembled in response to requests from colleagues and activists working within and beyond the continent. Subscribers to ROAPE were increasingly requesting that specific articles in the journal be available in another format, especially for teaching and advocacy work. The popularity of the first volume, *The Politics of Transition in Africa*, edited by Giles Mohan and Tunde Zack-Williams has encouraged members of the editorial working group to proceed with volume two. The Readers will ensure that there is continued access to relevant material not just for students and teachers but also for grassroots activists.

The Readers do not seek to present a comprehensive overview of a discipline or sub-field. Rather we have brought together articles that reflect the way contributors to ROAPE have interpreted and transformed these debates. The journal, which began in 1974, is committed to a practical politics, which is not simply tied to the more rarefied world of academic debates. It continues to maintain its identity and remains true to its founding goals of providing radical political economy analysis of inequality, oppression and power in Africa in the context of capitalist globalisation. The material for the Readers comes mostly from issues of ROAPE.

The first volume in the Series was published by James Currey and Africa World Press. We are happy that the collaboration with James Currey (now an imprint of Boydell and Brewer) can continue for the second and future volumes in the Series. *Conflict and Security in Africa* addresses a most topical subject given the ongoing war on terrorism and western interventions in Libya, Côte d'Ivoire and Mali.

Tunde Zack-Williams
Ray Bush
Series Editors

Notes on Contributors

Rita Abrahamsen is a Professor in the Graduate School of Public and International Affairs at the University of Ottawa. She is the author (with M.C. Williams) of *Security Beyond the State: Private Security in International Politics* (Cambridge University Press, 2011) and *Disciplining Democracy: Development Discourse and the Good Governance Agenda in Africa* (Zed Books, 2000). She is currently joint-editor of *African Affairs*.

Richard Banégas is a Professor in Political Science and Maitre de Conférences des Universités at the Université de Paris I – Sorbonne. He is currently the editor of *Politique Africaine*. He is the author of *La Démocratie 'à pas de caméléon': Transition et Imaginaires Politiques au Bénin* (Karthala, 2003) and numerous articles on Côte d'Ivoire.

Patricia Daley is a Lecturer in Human Geography at Oxford University. She is the author of *Gender and Genocide in Burundi: The Search for Spaces of Peace in the Great Lakes Region* (James Currey, 2008). She has published widely in academic journals such as *Review of African Political Economy*, *Political Geography* and *Third World Quarterly*.

Franklin Graham holds a PhD in Geography from West Virginia University. He has conducted research on changes in pastoral livelihoods in northern Mali and northern Niger, and the consequences of sedentarisation among pastoral communities in the Western Sahara territory of Morocco.

Patrick B. Johnston is an Associate Political Scientist at the RAND Corporation. His research interests include insurgency, political economy, and conflict resolution. His work has been published in many academic journals, including the *American Economic Review*, *International Security*, *Security Studies* and *Studies in Conflict & Terrorism*.

Musambayi Katumanga is a Professor of Political Science at the University of Nairobi. His research has focused on violent insurgency movements. He has consulted extensively for the African Union, the Intergovernmental Authority on Development, and the United Nations on security sector reforms in Africa.

Ken Menkhaus is Professor of Political Science at Davidson College. His research focuses on politics of development, peace operations, state failure, state-building, and political Islam in the Horn of Africa. He has served as special political advisor to the United Nations mission in Somalia. He has published widely in academic journals including *International Security*, *African Affairs* and *International Peacekeeping*.

Cyril Obi is the Program Director of the Africa Peacebuilding Network (APN) of the Social Science Research Council (SSRC). He is the editor (with S. Rustad) of *Oil and Insurgency in the Niger Delta: Managing the Complex Politics of Petro-Violence* (Zed Books, 2011), and has published widely in academic journals on African politics.

William Reno is a Professor of Political Science at Northwestern University. He is author of *Warlord Politics and African States* (Lynne Rienner Publishers, 1998), and *Warfare in Independent Africa* (Cambridge University Press, 2011). His research focuses on the role of violence and patronage networks in the political strategies of African state regimes and the rise of armed conflict.

Carol B. Thompson is a Professor of Politics and International Affairs at the Northern Arizona University. Her research interests include agricultural and environmental development policy in Africa. She has published in many research journals including *New Political Economy, Review of African Political Economy* and *Global Environmental Politics.*

Theodore Trefon holds a PhD from Boston University. He is the author of *Congo Masquerade: The Political Culture of Aid Inefficiency and Reform Failure* (Zed Books, 2011). He heads the Contemporary History Section of the Belgian Royal Museum for Central Africa and is Adjunct Professor of International Relations at Boston University, Brussels.

Michael Watts is a Professor of Geography at the University of California, Berkeley. His most recent research has focused on the violent political economy of Nigeria's oil industry in the Niger Delta. He is author of *The Curse of Black Gold* (Powerhouse Press, 2008) and co-editor of *Global Political Ecology* (Routledge, 2010 with P. Robbins and R. Peet).

Susan K. Willett was an expert in the economics of defence policy. She acted as a UN elections monitor in several post-conflict countries. She held positions at the Copenhagen Peace Research Institute and the United Nations Institute for Disarmament Research. Her research has been published in many academic journals including *Survival, Review of African Political Economy* and *International Peacekeeping.*

Permissions:

Rita Abrahamsen 'Blair's Africa: The Politics of Securitisation and Fear', *Alternatives* 30 (1) 2005: 55–80. By permission of Sage Publications.

Richard Banégas 'Côte d'Ivoire: Patriotism, Ethno-Nationalism and other African Modes of Self-Writing', *African Affairs* 105 (421) 2006: 535–552. By permission of Oxford University Press on behalf of the Royal African Society.

1

Introduction: Conflict & Security in Africa

RITA ABRAHAMSEN

More than any other part of the globe, Africa has in the post-Cold War period been associated with conflict, insecurity and human rights atrocities. In the 1990s, Robert Kaplan's (1994) nightmare vision of 'the coming anarchy' epitomised the continent's perceived affinity with ethnic hatred, senseless violence and environmental dystopia. Two decades later, Pulitzer prize-winning journalist Jeffery Gettleman painted a similar picture, despairing that the continent's wars 'never end' but spread 'like a viral pandemic', making 'quiet places' like Tanzania 'the lonely exceptions' in Africa (Gettleman 2010). In academic and policy-making circles, conflict and insecurity have also come to occupy centre stage, with resource-hungry warlords and notions of 'greed' and 'grievance' playing key explanatory roles. Following the attacks of September 11, 2001 and the ensuing global war on terror, Africa has become increasingly embedded within discourses and policies of security, amidst mounting concern that the continent's so-called 'ungoverned spaces' will provide safe havens for terrorists intent on destroying Western civilization. In this environment, development and security policies have converged. The World Bank's 2011 *World Development Report* on Conflict, Security and Development is one of the latest articulations of this security/development nexus, describing a cycle of repeated violence in fragile states whose 'territories can become breeding grounds for far-reaching networks of violent radicals and organized crime' (2011:xi).

There are thus good reasons for this Reader on 'Conflict and Security'. The *Review of African Political Economy* has engaged with issues of war and insecurity on a regular basis, analysing ongoing conflicts and often challenging predominant modes of interpretation. True to its commitment, the journal has warned against simplistic and essentialist explanations and instead drawn attention to the complex political economies of inequality, exploitation and oppression associated with the continent's integration into the global capitalist order. The journal has also systematically reminded readers of the powerful outside interests involved in African conflict environments, thus refuting any explanation centred solely on the deficiencies of domestic political arrangements. This Reader offers a rich *tour d'horizon*, drawn from more than 20 years of debate and analysis, and while making no claim to comprehensiveness the selected articles provide a uniquely wide-ranging, yet critical library that casts new light on conflict and security on the African continent and that showcases the *Review*'s contribution to these debates. To contextualise the articles, this introduction provides a broad overview of the changing history of conflict and insecurity on the continent, demonstrating the need to take account of global political transformation and to analyse African security in a global perspective.

This is further developed in the second part of the introduction, which highlights the need for a systematic global political economy of African conflict and security.

The changing forms of conflict and security

In the Western imaginary, Africa has arguably always occupied a space of horror and violence. Much has been made of Joseph Conrad's depiction of the *Heart of Darkness*, but the association of the continent with barbarity and bloodshed is not the exclusive domain of fiction or history but has been a mainstay of scholarly and policy debates from independence to the present. There is of course no denying that Africa has had, and still has, more than its fair share of wars and atrocities, many of which are covered in this Reader, but the danger of a master narrative of violence is that we lose sight of differences and nuances, as well as of change and its dynamics. Put differently, blinded by the perception of seemingly endless wars and pervasive insecurity, we neglect both the specificity of individual conflicts and the manner in which patterns of conflict have changed in numerous and significant ways.

At the outset, the most important recent change to note is that warfare has declined on the continent. While conflicts and their casualties are notoriously difficult to measure, recent analyses suggest that, consistent with global trends, the signs from Africa are encouraging (Straus 2012; Williams 2011). Focusing on the changing patterns of political violence, Scott Straus (2012) demonstrates that, large-scale mass killings of civilians, including genocide, are on the decline in Africa and that large areas of the continent are stabilising. His analysis also shows that although about thirty countries in sub-Saharan Africa – or around 65% of all states in the region – have experienced an armed conflict since independence, Africa is no more violent than many other world regions, and that the continent cannot claim to be the world leader in either the frequency or duration of major forms of political violence such as warfare or mass killings. In other words, when analysed alongside other world regions, Africa does not appear as uniquely violent or qualitatively distinct.

That said, it cannot be denied that conflict and insecurity remain all too frequent in many countries and areas, but the situation is far from static and there are important changes to the patterns of conflict. In particular, several authors (Reno 2011; Straus 2012; Williams 2011) have noted the shifts associated with the end of the Cold War, which facilitated the closing of some long-standing conflicts while precipitating the proliferation of so-called 'new wars'. More recently, novel forms of conflict seem to be emerging, while the new scramble for resources, combined with the war of terror, can be seen to indicate a return of geopolitics and a new militarisation of relations with the continent. These historical changes in the continent's security landscape are discussed in more detail in the remainder of this section.

The Cold War is in many ways a misnomer when applied to Africa, as superpower rivalry on the continent, and in the South more generally, frequently involved active and prolonged proxy warfare (Westad 2005). During this period, policy towards the continent was predominantly guided by strategic, geopolitical considerations, as the East and the West supported various African regimes as part of their ideological power struggle to secure allies and spheres of influence. The United States, the Soviet Union and their respective allies were major sources of funding for both insurgents and states, and weaponry, military training, ideological inspiration, and diplomatic support were provided as part of the struggle for dominance and influence. As William Reno comments, 'considerable rebel effort went into deciding what kind of image to present to the rest of the world... Americans looked for evidence that anti-colonial rebels were willing to sideline radical leaders, while Soviet officials sought reliable socialists' (2011:26). Some of the continent's most brutal dictators were kept in power because of their function as bulwarks against communism, the most notable being Mobutu Sese Seko in Zaire. Others fell in military coups, sponsored or encouraged by foreign powers, often as policies appeared to be leaning towards the East. While the Cold War may have kept some conflicts in check, by preventing their escalation to inter-state wars and supporting the coercive capacities of states, it also fueled some of the region's most long-standing conflicts. Angola and Mozambique are telling examples of conflicts that could not be resolved under conditions of superpower rivalry, and where local human suffering was exacerbated by geopolitical battles.

In this perspective, the tripartite agreement between South Africa, Cuba and the Soviet Union in December 1988 marks a milestone in the retreat of Cold War politics in Africa, as it enabled military disengagement from Angola as well as the independence of Namibia. The agreement was brokered by the Soviet Union and the US, and was the first attempt at superpower co-operation to end the Cold War on the continent (O'Neill and Munslow 1995; Cohen 1995). The Gorbachev regime shortly afterwards informed President Mengistu that Ethiopia could expect no more arms shipments, and by 1990 the Soviet Union had extricated itself from military involvement in Africa (Light 1991; 1992).

With the decline of superpower rivalry, Africa lost much of its strategic relevance. In the words of Samuel Decalo, 'African states were transformed from Cold War pawns into irrelevant clutter' (1992:17). No longer fearful of losing allies to Communist expansion, the US and other Western states gradually disengaged from the continent. Following the collapse of the Soviet Union, the US reduced or eliminated military aid to long-term friends like Kenya, Somalia, Liberia, Chad and Zaire. American aid missions and intelligence posts were closed, as personnel was redirected to new priority assignments in Eastern Europe (Bratton 1994). Britain also closed several embassies, and France signaled a more hands-off approach when declining to send troops to stop an army and police mutiny in Côte d'Ivoire in 1990.

At this point, states that had survived in part on external support became more vulnerable to domestic revolt and civil war, and subsequent developments in Mengistu's Ethiopia, Siad Barre's Somalia, Samuel Doe's Liberia and Mobutu's Zaire, to mention but a few, must be understood in the context of their disappearing status as clients in a bipolar world. The loss of strategic relevance often coincided with a worsening economic crisis and increased pressures for democratisation. Not only did donors redirect their aid towards governance projects involving support for elections and local government, but overall official development aid to sub-Saharan Africa declined by 21% in real terms from 1990 to 1996 (Riddell 1999). In the face of dwindling military and economic resources, many centralised patronage networks collapsed and ruling coalitions fragmented.

Not surprisingly, therefore, the immediate aftermath of the Cold War saw an increase in conflict and insecurity, with the number of civil wars peaking in the early 1990s (Straus 2012). In Sierra Leone a bloody civil war raged from 1991 to 2002, in neighbouring Liberia Charles Taylor unleashed a reign of terror, while at least 700,000 perished in Rwanda's genocidal violence. Labelled 'new wars' (Kaldor 1999), post-Cold War conflicts are frequently described as significantly different from previous conflicts, in terms of their character and objectives, as well as their brutality: warlords and drugged-up thugs, fighting for diamonds and self-enrichment, are juxtaposed to freedom fighters motivated by ideology and political justice. This new war thesis is sometimes captured in an opposition between 'greed' and 'grievance' (Collier and Hoeffler 2001), giving little room for the more complex social and political causes and dynamics of post-Cold War conflicts.

The enduring imagery and impact of this violent period in Africa's history risk obscuring the fact that many of these conflicts have now come to an end: Sierra Leone has been peaceful since 2002, Liberia has elected the continent's first woman president, and Rwanda consistently boasts one of the continent's highest growth rates. To be sure, challenges endure. In Rwanda, a creeping authoritarianism is cause for unease (Reyntjens 2011), while high poverty rates, inequality and youth marginalisation continue in both Sierra Leone and Liberia. Other conflicts persist: Somalia has been without a central government since 1991, with large parts of the territory ravaged by hunger and competing militias. Military interventions by neighbouring states, encouraged by foreign powers, and an AU peacekeeping mission, underline the regional dimensions of the conflict. Conflict in the Democratic Republic of the Congo escalated into a complex form of inter-state war, with six countries involved at its height. As many as five million people may have died in the war, and conflict and insecurity still linger, especially in the Kivus. In Africa's newest state, South Sudan, there is at best a fragile peace.

There are also other changes in the security landscape. Straus (2012) has noted the increasing frequency of electoral violence associated with the return to multi-party competition. While democracies are traditionally perceived as more peaceful than authoritarian regimes, political competition can increase the temptation towards ethnic mobilisation. While most African elections are relatively peaceful, the violence that killed over 1,000 people and displaced at least 350,000 after the 2007 Kenyan elections serves as a salient reminder of the havoc that can be unleashed in the wake of the ballot. Violence has also accompanied elections in Zimbabwe, Côte d'Ivoire and Nigeria, with politicians manipulating ethnic sentiments and notions of belonging as a means of capturing or maintaining political power. Often such electoral violence, although expressed in ethnic terms, intersects with more material local concerns of access to land and other livelihood resources, rendering simplistic narratives of ethnic essentialism largely invalid (Bekoe 2010). As Richard Banégas shows in his contribution to this Reader, in Côte d'Ivoire ultra-nationalist narratives of belonging were also a means for youth to assert their autonomy as individuals, where the politics of identity intersected in numerous ways with material struggles and international relations.

Another significant change in Africa's post-Cold War security landscape appears to be an increase in religious fundamentalist and terrorist violence, aligned in various ways to global struggles against Western hegemony. The long-standing warfare of *al-Shabab* in Somalia, the rise of *al-Qaeda in the Islamic Maghreb* (AQIM), and the 2012 insurgency in Mali all seem to suggest that fundamentalist violence is spreading across the continent. Boko Haram, with its chilling translation 'Western education is forbidden' and violent attacks on Christians, police stations and aid workers in Nigeria, similarly seems to indicate a rise in religious intolerance and violence. Both the religious and the global dimensions of these conflicts merit careful investigation. Historically, religion has played a relatively minor role in African conflicts, leading Gerri ter Haar and Stephen Ellis to conclude that 'Properly speaking, there are no religious wars in Africa south of the Sahara' (2004:106–7; see also Williams 2011). This is, of course, not to say that religious beliefs have not been crucially important in warfare; in both Liberia and Sierra Leone belief in the power of the spirit world shaped the behaviour of combatants and hence the pattern of warfare (Ellis 1999; Richards 2006), but religion was not the cause of warfare. Instead, in Africa's past, what appeared at first sight to be clashes between religions were instead intimately connected to struggles between elites for political and material power. This, for example, has traditionally been the case in northern Nigeria, and in today's Mali the long-standing struggles of the Tuareg populations for recognition and autonomy intersect with fundamentalist agendas. The manner in which contemporary religious violence is simultaneously entangled with articulations of local elite competition and global jihadist struggles accordingly requires careful and systematic investigation.

By the same token, the global dimensions of contemporary conflicts are far from straight-forward. On the one hand, the trans-boundary character of recent violence is not in doubt. AQIM is now believed to operate across the Sahel, in Algeria, Niger, Mauritania and Mali. *Al-Shabab* has launched attacks in both Kenya and Uganda, while fighters from Algeria, Mauritania, Nigeria and Sudan, amongst others, are reported to have joined the Islamist movements in Mali. Further transnational dimensions are provided by the intervention forces of France, ECOWAS, and other Western countries, whereas in Somalia AU troops have been supported by both Western and neighbouring states. On the other hand, the relationship of recent conflicts to global terrorist networks needs to be treated with caution. The current fear of Islamist fundamentalism immediately escalates local conflicts to the global arena, as testified by Boko Haram's designation as a 'national security threat' by the US. This global climate of fear in turn allows insurgents access to a global discourse of power, and can give governments an almost blanket approval for violent oppression – even of legitimate opposition and protest. The result could be not only an increase in violence and insecurity, but also a restriction of political space under the cover of security and the global war on terror. As Franklin Charles Graham's contribution to this Reader shows, abductions, kidnappings and killings in the Sahel are also part of local struggles, concerns and grievances and cannot be reduced to their global jihadist dimensions. That said, there can be little doubt that the emergence of fundamentalist groups adds a new and often volatile ingredient to conflict in parts of Africa, and there is a pressing need for systematic, empirical investigations of the continent's material, ideological and normative links to global terrorist networks of violence. In doing so, however, care is needed to avoid further securitisation of the continent (see my contribution to this volume).

It is by now well-established that the heightened concern with international security since September 11, 2001 has significantly changed the Africa policy of most donor states. As President George W. Bush declared, September 11 'taught us that weak states, like Afghanistan, can pose as great a danger to our national interests as strong states... poverty, weak institutions, and corruption can make weak states vulnerable to terrorist networks and drug cartels within their borders' (Bush 2002). Nearly a decade later, President Obama echoed the same sentiment, stating that 'extremely poor societies... provide optimal breeding grounds for disease, terrorism and conflict' (*The Economist* 2010). Following this logic, Africa's conflicts and poverty are no longer simply problems of development, but threats to the stability and prosperity of Northern countries. Hence, Africa is increasingly discussed in security terms, its so-called weak and fragile states perceived as dangerous and ungoverned spaces threatening the welfare and survival of the more ordered parts of the world.

The result has been a re-alignment of security and development policies, and one of the characteristics of contemporary development aid is an unashamed acknowledgement by donors that aid must serve their national security interest. Whereas in the past such geopolitical motivations were dressed up in a humanitarian language, today the straightforward assumption is that 'development and security goals can be pursued in a mutually reinforcing way' (DFID 2005:13). Geopolitics has thus returned in full force, with more funding for security and a clear reallocation of resources towards countries considered important in security terms. For example, a full 30% of British official development assistance is now directed towards fragile and conflict-affected states (UK Government 2010:44), and Ethiopia and Nigeria – two strategic allies – are the top recipients of UK bilateral aid, whereas poor countries like Burundi and Niger have been cut from the list of recipients.

The number of security and military assistance initiatives has also proliferated. The most extensive and controversial of these is AFRICOM, the US Africa Command authorised by President Bush in December 2006. According to its mission statement, the 'Africa Command protects and defends the national security interests of the United States by strengthening the defense capabilities of African states and regional organisations and, when directed, conducts military operations, in order to deter and defeat transnational threats and to provide a security environment conducive to good governance and development' (AFRICOM 2012:1). Since its formation, AFRICOM's activities and budget have expanded significantly. In East Africa, the command supports the Combined Joint Task Force – Horn of Africa (CJTF-HOA). The Pan-Sahel Initiative expanded into the Trans-Saharan Counter-Terrorism Initiative (TSCTI) in 2005, raising the number of countries involved from four (Mauritania, Mali, Niger and Chad) to nine with the inclusion of Senegal, Nigeria, Morocco, Algeria and Tunisia. There is also the Partnership for Regional East African Counter-Terrorism (PREACT), as well as the Africa Partnership Station, focused on enhancing maritime security in the Gulf of Guinea (AFRICOM 2011), to mention but a few. Overall, the Obama administration has continued the militarised policies towards Africa, and even expanded some (Volman 2005; Wiley 2012). Arguably, then, Africa has regained much of its strategic importance, and now serves as a key battleground in the war against terrorism. The implications of this for the future of conflict and security on the continent are as yet unclear, but there can be little doubt of their significance.

As this brief overview illustrates, there is nothing static about Africa's history of violence. Instead, what emerges is a dynamic and ever-changing picture, where the forms of conflict and insecurity are intimately related to transformations in global politics. This in turn points towards the importance of developing an international political economy of conflict and security, a topic that is close to the heart of the *Review of African Political Economy*.

Towards an international political economy of conflict and security

Arguably, two weaknesses have plagued approaches to conflict and security in Africa. The first is a form of cultural essentialism, where conflict is seen as the outcome of African cultures and fixed, primordial identities and ethnicities. While rarely expressed as forcefully as in Kaplan's 'The Coming Anarchy', essentialist attitudes continue to inform and underpin much contemporary commentary on African conflicts.[1] The second weakness is a form of economic reductionism, where conflict is regarded as the outcome of economic opportunities and rational decisions. This approach, epitomised above all by the 'greed and grievance' debate, has become increasingly hegemonic and influential in academic debates and in international policy (as evidence, for example, by the predominance of economistic references in the 2011 *World Development Report*). Often masquerading as a form of political economy, it is important to underline the economism of this approach so as to differentiate it from the perspectives adopted in this Reader.

At their most populist and unrefined, economistic approaches reduce the causes of conflict to a question of either political grievances or economic greed. Since political grievances are present virtually everywhere, but only a few countries suffer from civil war, it is concluded that conflict is caused primarily by economic opportunities, or greed. The presence of lootable resources such as oil and diamonds are key 'greed variables', whereas political factors such as exclusion and repression are found to be of minimal importance. African conflicts thus frequently appear as a form of criminal activity, instigated by greedy, self-interested warlords and perpetrated by poor people who because of their poverty have little to lose from engaging in violence. Although the greed versus grievance approach has been somewhat modified in recent years, and now places less emphasis on economic motivation, conflict is still explained in terms of opportunity structures rather than politics (Collier et al., 2009).

While this approach is not entirely without insights, it is, as Christopher Cramer concludes in his incisive critique, 'extremely reductionist, highly speculative and profoundly misleading' (2002:1849). In the parsimonious universe of neoclassical economic theories of conflict, people are reduced to rational calculating individuals, stripped of their social relations, their cultural identities, their histories – the very things that make them human. Even when the analysis is structured in more complex ways than the greed/grievances opposition allows for, methodological individualism and rational choice cannot capture the empirical specificities and social universes in which conflicts take place. Thus reduced to 'homo economicus', people's conflictual behaviour becomes a simple function of self-interested greed, allowing for a depoliticisation of African conflicts as

---

[1]   For a critical review of Kaplan's cultural essentialism, see Englund (1996).

criminal and deviant. Put differently, economic rather than political variables are seen as sufficient to explain the actions of often alienated and excluded youth seeking jobs, education and social recognition. Against this imperialism of economic approaches, Cramer (2002) calls for 'an analytical liberation struggle' and this Reader is intended as a contribution to this struggle for a proper political economy of the dynamics of security and insecurity.

As a point of departure, a political economy approach recognises a much more complex universe of actors and causal factors, expanding the analysis both geographically, methodologically and epistemologically. In common with the discipline of economics, a political economy approach places the materiality of conflicts centre stage and also assigns a leading role to natural resources. But the similarities end here. While there is no disputing the centrality of natural resources to many post-Cold War conflicts – timber in Liberia, diamonds in Sierra Leone, oil and diamonds in Angola, minerals in the DRC – the mere presence of resources does not cause warfare (Cramer 2002; Williams 2011). Natural resources may finance and sustain conflict, but this is not to say that they were the original cause of conflict or that the conflict is about resources. Conflicts are much more multi-dimensional than the single narrative of resources allows for, with conflicts within conflicts, different motivations, and constantly evolving agendas. In Sierra Leone, for example, diamonds may have sustained the decade-long civil war, but its root causes were both much more complex and more mundane than the fascination with 'blood diamonds' suggests. Rather than a simple story of greed and illegal diamond trade, the war was in part a revolt against oppressive agrarian structures (Mokuwa et al., 2011). Many young men participated in the civil war in order to escape the rural structures that trapped them in slave-like conditions, dependent upon larger farmers and unable to find legal marriage partners. The RUF allowed young men to break free from these restrictive customary institutions (*ibid.*), and while they may have ended up digging for diamonds, this was much more than simply a 'new war' fought with economic rather than political objectives. Similar motivations have been documented among young men participating in Zimbabwe's liberation war (Kriger 1992), while in the DRC there is much to suggest that the mining of precious metals and minerals is part of the dynamics of conflict, but not the main cause – and certainly not the only cause – of the long-standing violence. Instead, complex struggles over access to land, disputes over traditional and administrative power, and conflict over local resources such as cattle and charcoal are crucial (Autesserre 2012).

A political economy approach thus dispenses with the distinction between 'greed' and 'grievance', which obscures and overlooks any relationship between the two. It is precisely in this relationship that we can begin to open up the political economy of conflict: How and under what circumstances can political grievances be seen to lead to particular forms of violent behaviour, and how and when are leaders able to mobilise and manipulate the grievances of others? To answer such questions we require a much more fine-grained analysis that not only includes the means of paying for the war effort (resources), but also a careful investigation of people's shifting relationships to their material surroundings and means of livelihood. This requires attention to capital and capital accumulation, as well as to class formation and shifting class relations. From this perspective, civil war cannot be reduced to a question of rational calculation and individual choice. Instead, it must be recognised that, while agency matters and individuals do act on economic incentives, they do so, to paraphrase Marx, in conditions that are not of their own choosing.

More often than not, the conditions of contemporary conflict are global in character and a full analysis hence needs to include a broader set of actors than commonly found in the economists' tale. These accounts are strangely silent on the global dimensions of Africa's conflicts, and the involvement of transnational corporations is almost absent from their causal explanations. When the corporations do appear, it is in terms of trade in 'conflict diamonds' and 'conflict minerals', which can be regulated and fixed through legal provisions and certification schemes. The effect is not only that conflict appears as 'African', contained within its geographical territory, but also as an aberration from the normal functioning of global capital. As many of the contributions to this Reader show, however, African conflicts cannot be understood in isolation from the global but are instead intimately linked to the interests and activities of transnational capital. In this sense, the battlefields stretch from South Kivu to London, from Juba to Beijing, and from the Niger Delta to Texas, forming an integral part of the global economic system.

The global dimensions of war and insecurity also include broader transformations of governance, taking place at the level of ideology, ideas and norms. Most notably, perhaps, the move towards neoliberal modes of governance, including privatisation, outsourcing and downsizing, has given rise to a plethora of private, non-state security actors that are now closely involved in African security, be it in the form of private soldiers, military contractors, commercial security companies or vigilantes (see Abrahamsen and Williams 2008; 2011). The dynamics of conflict cannot therefore be contained within national boundaries, but are part of complex global networks or security assemblages.

A key player in these global security assemblages is the development aid and relief industry. While couched in the language of humanitarianism and peace, relief and development interventions have frequently – if inadvertently – helped reproduce violence and conflict in numerous and different ways (de Waal 1997; Duffield 2001; Keen 2008). Not only can aid provide resources for both rebels and regimes, enabling them to continue their violent campaigns, but it can also fuel war economies and lead to further militarisation as relief agencies themselves hire armed guards to protect their operations. Development aid and humanitarian assistance thus become embedded in the logic of conflict, and their impact cannot be abstracted from conflict dynamics. Similarly, the more long-term effects of development aid cannot be ignored; as both William Reno's and Patrick Johnston's contributions to this Reader show, the civil wars in Sierra Leone and Liberia unfolded after the central state apparatus had been significantly weakened as a result of structural adjustment programmes imposed by the World Bank and the IMF. Similar long-term effects of the economic restructuring of the state have been observed in other conflicts, including the genocide in Rwanda (Storey 2001; Hintjens 1999). In this Reader, both Ken Menkhaus and Patricia Daley show how international peace-building interventions impact on the security situation, and not always in the manner intended. In this way, the political economy of conflict and security stretches beyond the geographical confines of the continent itself, and includes a broader set of actors, ideologies and norms than those immediately present in the theatre of war.

One of the analytical advantages of a broader, more complex political economy focused on changing structural and social relations is that conflict appears less as a breakdown or failure and more as an intrinsic part of socio-economic systems. As argued by close observers of African conflicts, peacetime and wartime are not necessarily all that different (Keen 2001; Richards 2005). In the words of Krijn Peters and Paul Richards, 'armed conflict is at times no more than an intensification of structural violence present in "peaceful" society' (2007:451). It may thus be more instructive to speak of a 'war-peace continuum' (Richards 2005), where the factors that lead to violence have to be analysed in their long-term, sociological context. Such an approach poses challenges both to our methodologies and our moralities. Methodologically, the study of war (as opposed to peace) counts battle deaths, and the number of violent deaths resulting from low-level violence and crime is not included in the statistics. But widespread violence frequently persists after war, and in some societies, violence is routinised and pervasive, without ever being part of a conventionally defined war. In South Africa, for example, murder claimed 15,609 lives in 2011, or 43 lives a day, which is equivalent to some of the continent's most brutal civil wars (Parker 2012). Other forms of violence, such as domestic violence, may see relatively little change from war to peace (or may even increase in peacetime), and women's sense of security and the risks to their lives may hence be unaffected by a change from war to peace. Methodologically, then, the distinction between war and peace can give an illusion of peace after war, a morally comfortable universe where what peace research once termed the structural violence of inequality and repression continues to claim lives in its steady, but hidden ways (Galtung 1969). We thus need a political economy not only of war, but of (in)security.

Security, however, is not an objective condition, nor is it a social good that is equally shared in society. From a radical political economy perspective, security can come at the expense of social justice and serve to maintain and reproduce existing inequalities and divisions. Fear of crime leads the rich and the middle classes to retreat to their fortified enclaves of work and leisure, leaving the poor to increasingly neglected downtown areas. The turn to private security solutions can cement such inequalities, thus acting in a socially conservative manner. In post-conflict situations, international peace builders and development organisations prioritise stability following the mantra of 'no security, no development'. Frequently, this focus on stability allows existing elites to recapture their positions of power and influence, reproducing the existing social structure of exclusion and privilege (see Daley, this volume; Curtis 2013; Labonte 2012). A political economy of security may thus lead to some morally uncomfortable insights and conclusions, unsettling easy assumptions of a clear link between security, development and social justice.

This Reader contributes to the study of the global political economy of conflict and security. The first section, 'Global Economies, State Collapse and African Conflicts', covers some of the continent's main post-Cold War conflicts and demonstrates their global connections. The articles also discuss the so-called 'resource curse', as well as the global arms trade, and reveal the complexities of the relationship between the economic and the political. The second section focuses on security as part of post-Cold War global governance, and discusses the effects of liberal peace building as well as the link between development assistance and the 'war on terror'. The final section, entitled 'Cultures of Conflict and Security', examines life as it continues in conditions of war and insecurity. It shows how 'there is order in the disorder' (Trefon, this volume), and also how insecurity reconfigures urban space, and transforms social order, identities and authority. Taken together, the chapters provide a comprehensive, empirically rich and nuanced overview of key aspects of Africa's post-Cold War security landscape, and also demonstrate the analytical advantages of a global political economy approach centred on specific and changing structural, historical and social conditions and relationships.

References

Abrahamsen, Rita and Michael C. Williams. 2008. Public/Private, Global/Local: The Changing Contours of Africa's Security Governance. Special Issue *Review of African Political Economy* 35(118).
———— 2011. *Security Beyond the State: Private Security in International Politics.* Cambridge: Cambridge University Press.
Autesserre, Séverine. 2012. Dangerous Tales. Dominant Narratives on the Congo and Their Unintended Consequences. *African Affairs* 111(443):202–222.
AFRICOM. 2011. Statement of General Carter F. Ham, USA Commander, United States Africa Command before the House Armed Services Committee. 5 April.
AFRICOM. 2012. Posture Statement of U.S. Africa Command before the House Armed Services Committee. Statement of General Carter F. Ham, USA Commander, 29 February.
Bekoe, Dorina. 2010. Trends in Electoral Violence in Sub-Saharan Africa. Peace Brief 13. United States Institute of Peace. www.usip.org.
Bratton, Michael. 1994. Internal versus Domestic Pressures for 'Democratization' in Africa. Presented at the conference 'The End of the Cold War: Effects and Prospects for Asia and Africa'. School of Oriental and African Studies, London.
Bush, George W. 2002. *The National Security Strategy of the United States of America.* Washington, DC: Whitehouse.
Cohen, H.L. 1995. Political and Military Security. In *Africa in World Politics: Post-Cold War Challenges,* eds. John W. Harbeson and Donald Rothchild. Boulder, CO: Westview Press.
Collier, Paul and Anke Hoeffler. 2001. *Greed and Grievance in Civil War.* Washington, DC: World Bank
Collier, Paul, Anke Hoeffler and Dominic Rohner. 2009. Beyond Greed and Grievance: Feasibility and Civil War. *Oxford Economic Papers* 61(1):1–27.
Cramer, Christopher. 2002. Homo Economicus Goes to War: Methodological Individualism, Rational Choice and the Political Economy of War. *World Development* 30(11):1845–1864.
Curtis, Devon. 2013. The International Peacebuilding Paradox: Power Sharing and Post-Conflict Governance in Burundi. *African Affairs* 112(443):72–91.
Decalo, Samuel. 1992. The Process, Prospects and Constraints of Democratization in Africa. *African Affairs* 91(362):7–35.
DFID. 2005. *Fighting Poverty to Build a Safer World: A Strategy for Security and Development.* London: Department for International Development.
de Waal, Alex. 1997. *Famine Crimes: Politics and the Disaster Relief Industry in Africa.* Oxford: James Currey.
Duffield, Mark. 2001. *Global Governance and the New Wars.* London: Zed Books.
Ellis, Stephen. 1999. *The Mask of Anarchy. The Destruction of Liberia and the Religious Dimensions of an African Civil War.* London: Hurst.
Ellis, Stephen and Gerrie ter Haar. 2004. *Worlds of Power: Religious Thought and Political Practice in Africa.* Oxford: Oxford University Press.
Englund, Harri. 1996. Culture, Environment and the Enemies of Complexity. *Review of African Political Economy* 76:179–188.
Galtung, Johan. 1969. Violence, Peace, and Peace Research. *Journal of Peace Research* 6(3):167–191.
Gettleman, Jeffrey. 2010. Africa's Endless Wars: Why the Continent's Wars Never End. *Foreign Policy* 178 (March/April):73–5.
Kaldor, Mary. 1999. *New and Old Wars:Organized Violence in a Global Era.* Palo Alto, CA: Stanford University Press.
Kaplan, Robert. 1994. The Coming Anarchy: How Scarcity, Crime, Overpopulation, and Disease is Rapidly Destroying the Social Fabric of Our Planet. *Atlantic Monthly* February:44–76.
Keen, David. 2008. War and Peace: What's the Difference? *International Peacekeeping* 7(94):1–22.

———— 2008. *Complex Emergencies*. Cambridge: Polity.

Hintjens, Helen. 1999. Explaining the 1994 Genocide in Rwanda. *Journal of Modern African Studies* 37(2):241–286.

Kriger, Norma J. 1992 *Zimbabwe's Guerilla War: Peasant Voices*. Cambridge: Cambridge University Press.

Labonte, Melissa T. 2012. From Patronage to Peacebuilding? Elite Capture and Governance from Below in Sierra Leone. *African Affairs* 111(422):90–115.

Light, Margaret. 1991. Soviet Policy in the Third World. *International Affairs* 67(2):263–280.

———— 1992. Moscow's Retreat from Africa. *Journal of Communist Studies* 8(2):21–40.

O'Neill, Kathryn and Barry Munslow. 1995. Angola: Ending the Cold War in Southern Africa. In *Conflict in Africa*, ed. Oliver Furley. London and New York: I.B. Tauris.

Mokuwa, Ester, Maarten Voors, Erwin Bulte, and Paul Richards. 2011. Peasant Grievance and Insurgency in Sierra Leone: Judicial Serfdom as a Driver of Conflict. *African Affairs* 110(440):339–366.

Parker, Faranaaz. 2012. Crime Statistics Show Marginal Improvement. *Mail and Guardian*, South Africa. 20 September. www.mg.co.za.

Peters, Krijn and Richards, Paul. 2007. Understanding Recent African Wars. *Africa* 77(3):442–454.

Reno, William. 2011. *Warfare in Independent Africa*. Cambridge: Cambridge University Press.

Reyntjens, Filip. 2011. Constructing the Truth, Dealing with Dissent, Domesticating the World: Governance in Post-Genocide Rwanda. *African Affairs* 110(438):1–34.

Richards, Paul. 2006. Accidental Sects: How War made Belief in Sierra Leone. *Review of African Political Economy* 33(110):651–663.

———— 2005. New War. An Ethnographic Approach. In *No Peace, No War*, ed. Paul Richards. Athens, OH and Oxford: Ohio University Press and James Currey.

Riddell, Roger. 1999. The End of Foreign Aid to Africa? Concerns about Donor Policies. *African Affairs* 98(392):309–35.

Straus, Scott. 2012. Wars Do End! Changing Patterns of Political Violence in Sub-Saharan Africa. *African Affairs* 111(443): 179–201

Storey, Andy. 2001. Structural Adjustment, State Power and Genocide: The World Bank and Rwanda. *Review of African Political Economy* 28(89):365–385.

The Economist. 2010. Exploding Misconceptions. December 16. www.economist.com.

UK Government. 2010. *Securing Britain in an Age of Uncertainty. The Strategic Defence and Security Review*. http:/www.official-documents.gov.uk

Volman, Daniel. 2005. US Military Involvement in Africa. *Review of African Political Economy* 32(103):187–189.

Westad, Odd Arne. 2005. *The Global Cold War: Third World Interventions and the Making of our Times*. Cambridge: Cambridge University Press.

Williams, Paul D. 2011. *War & Conflict in Africa*. Cambridge: Polity.

Wiley, David. 2012. Militarizing Africa and African Studies and the US Africanist Response. *African Studies Review* 55(2):147–161.

World Bank. 2011. *World Development Report 2011: Conflict, Security and Development*. Washington, DC: World Bank.

2

Ironies of Post-Cold War Structural Adjustment in Sierra Leone

WILLIAM RENO (1996)

Africa's creditors stress 'capacity building' measures to strengthen bureaucratic effectiveness to reverse economic and political decline (Dia 1993). World Bank officials point to the East Asian example of success in using government policies and institutions to promote 'market friendly' growth policies insulated from the pressures of clients demanding payouts as a positive example for Africa (World Bank 1993a). Analysts recognise, however, that decades of patron-client politics and intractable rent-seeking behaviour (the use of state resources for personal gain) among state officials limit short-term prospects for increasing revenue collection. With little internal financing for market-boosting policies, World Bank programmes prescribe extensive civil service layoffs. Subsequent reductions in unproductive expenditures will reduce corruption, balance national budgets and remove obstacles to private market growth. Economic growth will in turn produce a class of entrepreneurs to demand more policies and slimmed-down bureaucracies to enhance economic efficiency. This 'growth coalition' will identify their interests with those of cost-effective technocratic administrators (World Bank 1994a:10–13).

Meanwhile, reform programmes stress the role of foreign investment in generating reliable, politically insulated revenues, especially where domestic public and private investment is limited. A recent World Bank report recommends privatisation and commercialisation of customary state activities where scarce revenues and political entanglements make technocratic reform unlikely (World Bank 1994b:22–51). It argues the advantages of private contractors taking direct responsibility for state services, especially in public works and utilities that are crucial to attracting more foreign investors and supporting local entrepreneurs.

Sierra Leone's recent World Bank agreements resemble other African government creditor arrangements in which state services are to be taken over by private commercial operators (Sierra Leone 1995). Sierra Leone's multilateral lenders, led by the World Bank, propose that private operators be found to run state services for a profit. A strong profit motive will encourage them to become vigorous collectors of fees and taxes in contrast to corrupt civil service employees under the influence of powerful interests. Services rendered in this fashion will thus be politically immune from patronage politics. Meanwhile, civil service employment can be more safely pruned in agencies that are no longer needed to perform crucial functions (Kessides 1993).

But World Bank-sponsored reforms in Sierra Leone in the 1990s have produced outcomes contrary to the goals of building bureaucratic efficiency. Foreign investors and contractors did efficiently perform state functions formerly reserved for corrupt bureaucracies. Creditors and rulers benefited from more predictable revenues. Rulers, however, used foreign firms to consolidate their power and fend off sudden increased threats from political rivals. Sierra Leone's rulers engaged foreign firms for profit and as partners to wage war against opponents and limit rivals' independent access to wealth and weapons.

The Sierra Leone case illustrates how the post-Cold War milieu of patrimonial collapse and creditor-sponsored reform does not necessarily favour efficiency or any official commitment to development. Instead, local innovations and adaptations of 'reform' leave rulers free to destroy state agencies, to 'cleanse' them of politically threatening patrimonial hangers-on and use violence directly to extract resources from people under their control. 'Reform' in this manner destroys bureaucratic means of exercising power and provides alternative means of control that encourages hardpressed rulers to mimic the 'warlord' logic characteristic of many of their non-state rivals. Rather than marginalising local economies from global commerce (Kaplan 1994) or signalling 'state failure' and anarchy (Zartman 1995), this process promotes stronger global ties between troubled patrimonial African political economies and the world economy. The adaptive strategy receives a boost from post-Cold War global shifts in external resources available to weak state leaders. To the extent that the same shifts aggravate internal political crises, they provide a further incentive for rulers to innovate and experiment with new ways of exercising power.

Regime security and post-Cold War reform

Sierra Leone's rulers faced intense pressures to comply with creditor demands to reduce expenditures and government employment. In return, good relations with multilateral creditors brought the promise of loans and debt rescheduling, worth about $500 million since 1992, or about 80%of GNP. Occupants of State House appeared to have no real option but to comply with creditor demands. As among ruling circles in other deeply creditor-dependent and internally weak African states such as Mozambique, Angola and Guinea, Sierra Leone's rulers faced a growing list of economic and political conditions for loans. Nonetheless, they have to continue appeasing creditors to get loans to buy off loyal associates and fend off internal rivals.

At first glance, these developments appear to leave such ruling groups little leverage as external resources needed to manage internal threats dwindle or come with more stringent conditions (Ayoob 1995; Job 1992). The end of the Cold War fundamentally changed the nature of relations between patron-client politics in Africa and major powers outside Africa. Formerly, rulers could expect some external resources in return for their political support of Cold War patrons (David 1991). Global definitions of 'good citizenship' also entitled rulers to limited resources from old colonial masters and great powers. Post-Cold War decreases in these resources, coupled with high costs of continuing internal patron-client politics and mounting debt, leave rulers increasingly 'hemmed in' (Callaghy and Ravenhill 1993).

These global shifts disrupt internal patron-client networks. Rulers in states lacking effective bureaucracies, and who are surrounded by newly marginalised but still expectant clients, face contradictory pressures. Layoffs of public sector employees in return for loans or creditor leniency – in the case of Zaire, for example, recent austerity plans foresee public employment dropping from 600,000 to 50,000 – risk creating legions of disgruntled former beneficiaries of state largesse. Suddenly shrinking state employment creates opportunities for enterprising strongmen to find allies among the discontented job-leavers. Post-Cold War growth of small arms trade in Africa increases the security threat to incumbent leaders from these marginalised groups (Klare 1995). As the 1994 coup in Gambia demonstrated, newly marginalised clients can team up with those at the periphery of the collapsing political system. In this case, unhappy public sector employees found common cause with armed youth from the capital city's shantytowns. The global spread of illicit trade, a consequence of political changes elsewhere, has given political outsiders additional ways to collect resources free from the direction of State House.

Yet continuing to distribute state resources to supplicants promises to accelerate economic decline and further alienate foreign supporters. Even if resources are found to rebuild institutions of government, this too is an unappealing strategy once patronage networks begin to detach themselves from central control. Increasingly independent strongmen can use effective bureaucracies to challenge rulers shorn of patronage resources in the name of efficiency (Migdal 1988). The success of Captain Valentine Strasser's April 1992 coup d'état in Sierra Leone underscores the peril of strengthening state agencies. The decision of his predecessor, Joseph Momoh, to build up army strength to counter a 1991 invasion from Liberia and the concurrent Sierra Leonean insurgency exposed his inability to retain a grip simultaneously on the state and on patron-client organisations. The shrinkage of patronage rewards, the deinstitutionalisation of civilian agencies of the state and Momoh's very limited public support stripped him of the resources he needed to balance opposing forces and impose his own control over them. Momoh's failure may have been very instructive to the man who deposed him.

Struggling to survive, Strasser tried new techniques, seized opportunities as they appeared, incorporated new social actors into his ruling coalition and reincorporated old ones on new terms. Seen in this light, bureaucratic collapse is not simply 'state collapse,' but rather a reconfiguration of political authority compatible with exogenous and internal post-Cold War shifts. Ironically, creditor pressures provided an incentive for Strasser to experiment with forms of social control while intentionally destroying state agencies. The Sierra Leone case illustrates that considerable agreement exists between creditors and rulers of weak states that government institutions ought to be pruned drastically. Both desire to extract state officials and their associates from the framework of patron-client politics. Creditors regard this exercise as a revenue-saving and efficiency measure since, as one local representative put it, 'it destroys bureaucracies that do not work anyway. If we give them the money for such purposes, they just waste it' (interviews with Freetown informants, 1995). Rulers view it as a means of reducing threats to their internal security. Yet the dilemma remains for the ruler: How can angry clients cut off from rewards be disciplined in the absence of significant formal state institutions, while still appeasing creditors? How can revenue be raised without the means to mobilise resources and promote development in any meaningful sense?

The key to a viable non-bureaucratic strategy lay in Momoh's, but especially Strasser's use of foreign firms and contractors as surrogates to help enforce discipline among those no longer included in patronage networks and intensifying links to external resources. Their dilemma centred on how to accumulate resources and concentrate coercive capabilities without losing control to bureaucracies or strongmen who had developed their own perspectives and posed a threat to the incumbent ruler. One option was to find other external allies to balance against strong rivals. Foreigners have the critical feature of posing a tangible counterweight under presidential control to state bureaucracies and increasingly autonomous strongmen. More recently, the foreign firms that creditors and 'reformers' court helped Strasser freeze competition among rivals with himself at the top. Control over resources with their help was used to solidify his position as a powerbroker to the country's population.

Momoh's and Strasser's strategies illustrate how crisis-managing rulers of very weak states find significant latitude to manipulate and reinterpret externally imposed rules to achieve these aims, while limiting the impact of fragmented patronage networks. Reconfigured political control raises doubts about assumptions that economic liberalisation reinforces political liberalisation (Hyden and Bratton 1992). It also suggests that political control is pursued in spheres that others recognise as 'private' but are in fact integral to the exercise of rulers' power. Distinctions between state and society, recently fashionable in 'governance' approaches to political change in Africa, become less clear. The label of autonomy is difficult to attach to nominally private firms that are integral partners in a reconfigured system of rule. This also means that the growth of 'private' businesses that are thought to limit the reach of predatory regimes in places like Zaire, Nigeria and Sudan can, however, extend their reach in non-bureaucratic ways.

Manipulating reform to centralise political control

Sierra Leone's heads of state have long understood the wide range of benefits of cooperation with foreign partners. Before he stepped down in Momoh's favour in 1986, President Siaka Stevens built a network of loyal politicians organised along commercial, especially illicit, diamond mining opportunities that he financed with profits from state-run diamond mining operations that he then converted to personal use (Reno 1995a:105–12)

Lebanese traders and diamond dealers provided him with links to international markets. By the mid-1980s 'official' smuggling accounted for at least 80% of the country's diamond exports, normally the country's largest source of trade income (*Ibid.*). Political control in this context rested upon manipulation of trade and those involved in it rather than the development of production with support of a bureaucratic state that would be less discriminating in providing benefits. At first, foreign loans with relatively lenient conditions and even private credits arranged through Lebanese middlemen helped Stevens to weather a general economic downturn and still provide benefits to his associates and followers (World Bank 1985).

Momoh inherited these entrenched political – commercial networks when he rose to power in 1986. He initially set out to establish himself as a magnate in the image of Stevens. But Stevens chose Momoh as a successor precisely because Momoh lacked personal control over Stevens' established political allies, their partners and their source of income. Just as Stevens stepped down in 1986, multilateral creditors stiffened performance criteria for further loans. Momoh turned to foreign collaborators, including among them two Israeli diamond mining companies, in an attempt to contest politicians' control of diamond resources. Bereft of easy access to foreign loans, Momoh's aim was to suffocate the increasingly autonomous diamond trading of local strongmen and make it possible to allocate mining opportunities according to his own clientelist priorities.

Momoh's eventual failure to accomplish this task highlighted the internal vulnerability of his regime, especially in 1988–89 as unruly strongmen resisted his efforts to control illicit trade. Momoh's ineffectiveness then became apparent to his associates. The worsening economy and Momoh's attempts to make up for lost diamond resources through distributions of dwindling state resources to his own clients further alienated already wary creditors. Pressure from creditors and mounting economic problems seemed to make economic austerity and administrative reform inescapable by the late 1980s. Creditors also balked at offering finance simply to enlarge Momoh's patrimonial potential, reiterating concern 'over Sierra Leone's continued failure to fulfil its financial obligations to the Fund' (IMF 1989:27).

Creditor officials in Sierra Leone made clear their concerns that corrupt state agencies were to blame for Momoh's inability to sustain even minor reforms. Delegations of high-level 'technocratic reformers' were flown off to Ghana after 1989 to observe how massive cuts in public sector employment, centralised command over policy and pruned state responsibilities were boosting economic growth there. Sierra Leone's agreements with the International Monetary Fund (IMF) and World Bank in 1991 stressed that loans would be contingent on State House commitments to dismantle a public sector deemed responsible for inefficiency and unproductive spending. To those who evaluated state agencies against their formally stated functions, state officials did not appear to do much in Sierra Leone except waste revenues. Social spending was in a state of collapse, standing at just 15% of its level of a decade earlier. Revenue collections had also decreased, from 30% of GNP in 1982 to about 20% of a smaller 1992 GNP (Bank of Sierra Leone 1994). The harshness of required austerity amidst crisis seemed to indicate that Sierra Leone's leaders had either little leverage or little room for manoeuvre in negotiating a reform programme that would further dismantle patronage networks and increase the President's internal security dilemma. Following the example of Ghana (World Bank 1993b:55–9), dismissals reached 15,000 personnel, or 40% of total state employment, by 1994. Seen in the context of the larger economy, this affected 30% of the country's salaried labour force (Economist Intelligence Unit 1994:16).

Dismissals produced an additional benefit for creditors by destroying inefficient state-owned enterprises. Local representatives of creditors had regarded privatisation exercises in the 1980s with suspicion, since most 'privatised' companies came under the control of insiders and powerful politicians. These firms then remained dependent upon state largesse of one sort or another. At the time, Momoh had little choice but to provide inherited client politicians with easy access to credits in exchange for loyalty, a major cause of serious inflation and credit scarcity for the country's few independent entrepreneurs. The subsequent dismantling of the public sector, however, did not condemn Momoh's regime. By shutting off autonomous accumulation, it strengthened the hand of the President, who struggled to assume a position as principal distributor of resources. World Bank demands thus helped the President gain a freedom of action with respect to a political class and bureaucracy that were cutting loose from the centre and were operating independently at the expense of a runaway official debt. World Bank officials quickly stressed the importance of 'regularising revenue collections' within this policy milieu. Accordingly, creditors supported the arrival in 1991 of a German firm, Specialist Services International (SSI), to operate ports and collect customs, and British-owned Marine Protection Services of Sierra Leone (MPSSL) to police and collect royalties from the country's offshore fisheries. Creditors concluded that foreign firms with few local political connections represented the best prospect of eventually clearing Sierra Leone's debt arrears, restoring fiscal solvency and eliminating corruption. Specialist Services International and MPSSL offered Momoh the opportunity to deny subordinates an opportunity to acquire foreign exchange independently of the President's favour, even if the foreign operations produce little revenue for local use beyond paying creditors. These arrangements also indicate the extent to which creditors are reluctant to include agencies of 'the state' and its corrupt officials in any project of 'capacity building'. Creditor and debtor both share suspicions that formal state institutions promote centrifugal forces that weaken central control.

Diamond mining, at one time contributing 70% of state revenues, presented Momoh and creditors with their greatest problem and potentially their greatest reward. As Momoh's regime struggled to repair relations with creditors, local IMF officials stressed the need to find a foreign investor able to 'regularise' diamond mining and mineral revenue collection. Reformers proposed attracting foreign firms with the promise of exclusive mining rights to a significant portion of the diamond region. A Dallas-based firm, Sunshine Broulle, showed some interest in 1991–92, but withdrew as rebel incursions in the diamond fields grew worse. The firm made tantalising offers to provide its own security force and take on some local social service burdens (National Diamond Mining Corporation 1990). Momoh recognised an opportunity forcibly to marginalise his political rivals and redirect foreign exchange away from them without fielding a politically vulnerable and costly security force of his own.

Sierra Leone's creditors sought a diamond mining company to accomplish in diamond mining areas what US-owned Sierra Rutile was doing around its titanium ore mine. Sierra Rutile controls a 224-square-mile concession. Until rebel attacks disrupted mining in 1995, it was a major source of foreign exchange for debt service. The company provided additional social services for families living in the concession area. Thus released from any obligation to use state agencies to raise tax revenue or provide social services, Momoh could still benefit from the foreign firm's success at accumulating wealth. Equally important, he could deny resources to his rivals and devote more of his energies and meagre resources to battling with his political enemies.

The collapse of the Sunshine Broulle deal contributed to Momoh's rising security threat, however. As the rebel war intensified and unruly clients, including army commanders, continued to divert state resources, troops went unpaid.

Allegations circulated in Freetown that individual commanders mined diamonds with army machinery and were using pay meant for soldiers to finance their operations. The allure of diamond wealth, the scarcity of state resources for patronage rewards and Momoh's inability to control strongmen created a situation in which the country's patronage networks were dividing into distinct rival factions as in neighbouring Liberia. Like Liberia's civil war, the collapse of a creaky patronage system spun off independent operators whose political and financial appetites could no longer be satisfied at the centre. Politicians and military commanders increasingly resembled warlords, using their own control of violence to accumulate resources and reward their own followers.

Momoh's experiment was cut short when the unpaid 27 year-old Captain Strasser and his comrades deposed Momoh in April 1992. This coup demonstrated the risk of maintaining a bureaucratic organisation that allowed individuals enough autonomy to build their own followings. Upon assuming control of State House, however, Strasser found himself facing the same pressures that had confronted Momoh. Meanwhile, rebel attacks spread. By 1993, rebels and military units that collaborated with rebels occupied much of the eastern third of the country. They controlled the country's primary source of mineral and agricultural exports and by 1995 they threatened Freetown itself.

Centralising control though privatising war

Strasser continued Momoh's strategy of fighting rebels with state military force. But as enlistment crept up to 14,000, at least triple pre-war figures, the revenue crunch, officer indiscipline and soldier defections continued to hobble the fighting effort. The institutional approach contributed to Strasser's more menacing internal security situation. Already half of state revenues were devoted to the war effort. Yet it was too risky to alienate creditors by shifting all available revenues to the war effort at the expense of debt service obligations; past cooperation had translated into Paris Club debt reductions and subsequent multilateral and bilateral assistance. A recent account estimates that US food assistance benefited a third of the country in 1994, further releasing Strasser from the need to build effective bureaucracies to provide social services (Shiner 1994). European Community grants were rebuilding power-generating capability in Freetown. More assistance was promised to help with resettling refugees – about a third of the country's population – uprooted by the war.

DeBeers' interest in a diamond mining concession offered Strasser a chance to improve upon his predecessor's strategy. Like Momoh, Strasser had compelling internal security reasons to remove interlopers from the diamond fields. The pressures he faced, however, were more intense, namely the occupation of mining areas by rebels, many of whom included miners who considered themselves exploited under old politician-run operations and disobedient strongmen. Some strongmen, including army commanders, refashioned themselves as 'warlords', leading youthful miners, rebels and soldiers (who, when collaborating with rebels, are known locally as sobels) in independent mining operations. The political unreliability of the army made a conventional state institutional strategy of regaining control unappealing. DeBeers also required assurances that independent operators would not poach local diamonds and disrupt its own operations, a condition that Strasser's state agencies could not fulfil. At the same time, the company needed a juridically recognised interlocutor capable of respecting its contract rights in mining areas. Accordingly, foreign firms could use state sovereignty to gain preferred access to resources and evade regulations elsewhere. Strasser's regime could share the benefits of partner firms' commercial success while maintaining the outward appearance of international standards of sovereignty.

Strasser's innovation lay in extending collaboration with foreign firms to include military combat. As with efforts to re-centralise accumulation, foreigners proved useful as reliable collaborators against internal rivals. Strasser's first opportunity appeared among about 800 Nigerian troops to help battle with rebel forces. Ties with these forces were solidified with the 'privatisation' of several agricultural and logging operations in the south and east of the country under Momoh, again denying autonomous sources of accumulation to local rivals and potential rivals in that sector of the economy. Finances and domestic politics in both countries, however, limited Nigerian troop deployment. Experiences in Liberia also indicate that Nigerian commanders extend their commercial dealings to contending factions and stake out their own commercial turf (Ellis 1995). Strasser's best hope lay in hiring reliable outsiders to support him in his war with foreign-based rebels and internal rivals. A precedent for this already existed in arrangements with Sierra Rutile to police its own concession area, by 1994 the country's largest source of foreign exchange under State House control. Sierra Rutile showed the way further when it hired Frontline Security Services to take direct responsibility for protecting its lease area. Accordingly, Strasser's government hired another British firm in late 1994, Gurkha Security Guards, Ltd., to help regain control over economically viable parts of the country. Freetown street rumour identifies DeBeers as the bankroller of this operation, though this allegation is not proven (Thomas 1995).

This strategy of using foreign mercenaries and advisors as a replacement for the national army has become more acceptable to outsiders in the wake of the Cold War. United Nations experiences in Bosnia and Somalia make clear that crisis management will have to be centred in Freetown. Outsiders may be more tolerant of how this is accomplished, since most recognise that 'rebel' forces often turn out to be renegade military units and followers of rival politicians. They were aware that Strasser's defeat would have drawn factional fighting into Freetown itself. Were this to occur, aid organisations would find fighting among members of the old patrimonial elite coalition similar to that around Mogadishu. Creditors and interested governments ultimately supported Strasser's policy of contracting out customary core functions of the state to potentially undesirable groups. They recognised that the alternative – protracted struggle amongst competing factions – would be a less desirable outcome. Outsiders interested in fostering accumulation – creditors for debt servicing, foreign firms for profits – recognised that centralised control is critical for keeping interlopers from disrupting the flow of diamonds. Ironically, foreigners interested in reinforcing a standard of sovereign behaviour needed Strasser as an interlocutor of Sierra Leone's relations with the rest of the world, despite his divergence from classically 'statist' concerns. They preferred to negotiate debt repayment with Strasser rather than to have to confront illiterate young men who loot for a living and faction leaders who articulate no political programme.

Gurkha Security Guards worked within Strasser's formal state structure, coordinating their efforts with the army, virtually the only major functioning state agency. The Gurkhas' experience highlighted the extent to which the Strasser regime had become separated from and at odds with the dwindling formal institutions of the state. This became apparent when rebel forces killed the Gurkhas' American commander and Strasser's aide de camp in well-coordinated attacks. Freetown observers suspected that the attack was the result of inside information. The murder of a Ukrainian helicopter pilot inside Army Headquarters in Freetown a month later confirmed the threats to Strasser lurking in the highest reaches of the state's institutions. So dire were the implications of this murder that Strasser's spokesmen dismissed it as a suicide over a love affair gone sour.

Executive Outcomes, a Pretoria-based company, replaced the British firm in 1995. This contractor, employing South African veterans of combat in Angola and Namibia and former Rhodesian Selous Scout anti-insurgency experts, worked exclusively with their State House employer. According to informants in Freetown, unlike their Gurkha predecessors, Executive Outcomes employees identified Sierra Leone army personnel as potential enemies, and made clear their intentions to shoot army personnel encountered as they battled with rebels. This policy suited State House, which identified elements of the army as hostile to Strasser's efforts to control the country's resources. Executive Outcomes' strategy also produced quick results, delivering the main mining areas to State House control in July, 1995, ridding it of both rebels and 'sobels' attached to the military.

Executive Outcomes' success highlighted a new commercial network. The firm's parent corporation, the South African-based Strategic Resources, has links to Branch Mining, a diamond mining firm that moved into Sierra Leone in August 1995 in a joint venture with the Sierra Leone government. It is possible that this mining firm footed Executive Outcomes' bill in expectation of future diamond mining profits. If so, this contact would be useful for exploiting DeBeers' anxieties over newcomer influence in the Sierra Leone diamond industry. It is also significant that Executive Outcomes' ties to this enterprise indicate that firm's quasi-commercial character, an involvement in Sierra Leone that extends beyond their primary role as supposedly politically uninvolved mercenaries. The company may bring additional commercial benefits, paralleling its move into trucking and construction industries in the territory of another customer, the Angolan government (Thomas 1995; McNallen 1995).

Strasser's strategy also had its drawbacks. His collaboration with foreign firms forced him into a position where his partners could compel him to continue fighting rebel forces rather than moving towards negotiations, as some foreign advisors were recommending. Moves to start peace negotiations that became apparent in December 1995 made hard-line military factions that also benefited from collaboration with foreigners anxious about the threat of peace. They feared that negotiations with rebels would create political pressure to expel Executive Outcomes and the possibility that they might be excluded from lucrative deals with foreign firm-mercenary partners. In January 1996 one such hard-liner, Strasser's second-in command Julius Maada Bio, launched a successful palace coup. Strasser was shuffled off to Guinea, but his arrangements with foreign firms continue under Bio's administration. This latest coup shows, however, that the innovating rulers' strategy attracts its own followers who are willing to act to maintain the strategy for their own profit.

Exploiting dependence

Sierra Leone's rulers have compensated for their problems of autonomy and power by intensifying their exploitation of dependence and employing conscious strategies that will secure links to the global economy. This process may be mistaken for societal 'disengagement' where this involves informal and illicit trade and undercuts formal bureaucratic organisation and abjures state mobilisation of society. One scholar notes that 'societal disengagement would, if carried out to its logical conclusion, result in the dissolution of the political community – as it has done in contemporary Somalia and Liberia' (Rothchild 1994:202). This interpretation presupposes what African states should be, not what African political authority actually exists. Predictions of anarchy and collapse in other very weak African states (Kaplan 1994) are more properly understood as laments for what Africa is not rather than accurate descriptions of post-Cold War reconfigurations of political authority.

The Sierra Leone case illustrates the methods of exploiting dependence. Foreign firms, mercenary troops, anxious creditors and aid organisations all have contributed resources that sustained State House without formal state agencies. A different kind of political authority has taken shape. Bounded territoriality has become less significant where the targets of control are people and economically useful areas. Sierra Leone's rulers and foreign partners have safely ignored economically unviable areas of the juridical state which are not likely to lodge rivals or provide political resources. Authority constructed in this way abjures conventional state definitions of a public realm and any commitment to serve it.

This process of exploitation has been determined by several factors peculiar to the Sierra Leone case. The availability of resources that are attractive to outsiders, especially diamonds, creates opportunities for Sierra Leone's rulers to experiment with alternative means of exercising power. The country's demography plays a role in shaping strategies, insofar as control over people and trade replaces territorial definitions of sovereignty. President Strasser's, and now President Bio's capacities to influence population mobility, especially in their struggle to control illicit mining and army marauding, has contributed to their accumulation of wealth and enhanced their appeal to foreign collaborators. Finally, the capacity of societal groups to resist or negotiate has influenced the configuration of the new ruling coalition. For example, Strasser struggled to control strongmen. But to do so, he appealed to impoverished, unemployed youth who otherwise find that they have little to lose in taking up an occupation of looting or illicit mining. Accordingly, Strasser attempted to portray himself as 'The Redeemer', paying respect to youths' political aspirations. Strasser's own youth – he took power at age 27 – and his sponsorship of Freetown street art containing nationalist or other overt political themes initially contributed to his consolidation of power (Opala 1994).

Ultimately, however, Strasser's capacity to sustain mass appeals was undermined by material scarcity. Patronage on the Cold War scale is no longer feasible. Given the imperative to suppress threats among strongmen and in state agencies, development, as most Sierra Leoneans understand it, is an even more remote possibility. The key to the viability of Strasser's strategy centred on resolving the problem of exit and resistance in a setting of scarcity where power undermines continuity and calculability. Here lies the special role of the contractor, which marks a fundamental shift in the rules of African weak state politics. State power in the post-colonial era rested upon expectations of entitlements from external patrons. Post-Cold War interstate norms, creditor demands and rising internal threats push rulers of weak states to appeal to external partners who expect to make a profit in exchange for services rendered and risks incurred. This basis for collaboration intensifies exploitative relations to subjects and further removes political authority from them.

This shift, made more likely by structural adjustment programme requirements of civil service layoffs, commercialisation of state functions and preference for foreign investors, bears little resemblance to catechisms of 'governance'. It also reduces the probability that there will develop a class of entrepreneurs whose interests will be distinct from and enforceable against those of the state. Instead, relations between state power and commerce resemble the colonial catechism of *mise en valeur*; an alien authority that supervises a society and uses labour and control over commerce to discipline subjects. Those who do not take part in accumulation on the ruler's terms are punished. Exit of non-productive members of society is not a serious threat. Limiting active economic evasion becomes a major preoccupation of rulers and their foreign partners, however. To the extent that control can be mapped, it traces an archipelago of economically useful people and regions. In such a setting, material bases of a 'civil society' capable of addressing rulers and defending producers' interests are unlikely to develop.

This shift is not limited to Sierra Leone. It reflects a change in African states' positions in the post-Cold War global economy. A striking feature of contract firms that differentiates late twentieth century developments from charter company colonialism centres on their origins. Many collaborating firms hail from political establishments in relatively weak states that are themselves managing internal pressures and external constraints. For example, Nigeria's military rulers find new ways of extending patronage rewards to a slimmed-down elite network through exploiting commercial opportunities associated with army interventions in Liberia, Sierra Leone and Gambia. Financial sector 'reform' unleashes some Nigerian banks to provide services for all sorts of trade in West Africa that larger and more established banks avoid (Reno 1995b).

Surely Executive Outcomes' success in Sierra Leone benefits other South African enterprises interested in extending their investments in an underexploited region. As one South African political scientist noted of sub-Saharan Africa, 'we are not going to get much from Washington, or Paris or London. This is where our future lies' (French 1995). Local leaders may be able to exploit these newcomers' advances. A French newsletter, for example, warns of 'aggressive financial, industrial and commercial competition, in particular by Anglo-Saxons and Japanese, in league with South African firms' (*Lettre d'Afrique*, June 1994). There are already indications that Zaire's President Mobutu, a master at replacing bureaucratic with commercial control, attracts increasing attention from French commercial and diplomatic interests fearful of rivals' roles in Mobutu's political-commercial strategy of weathering the demise of his state's formal institutions. In a very real sense, African economies do not face increasing marginalisation from the Cold War's end. They continue to be engaged in the global economy, albeit now in more unconventional and violent ways. The way in which this comes about signals the emergence of a new division of labour that reflects a hierarchy of real power capabilities among increasingly heterogeneous African states.

References

Parts of this article are based upon interviews conducted during field research in West Africa.

Ayoob, Mohammed. 1995. *The Third World Security Predicament.* Boulder, CO: Lynne Rienner.

Bank of Sierra Leone, *Economic Review,* Freetown: Bank of Sierra Leone, various issues.

Callaghy, Thomas M. and John Ravenhill. 1993. *Hemmed In: Responses to Africa's Economic Decline.* New York: Columbia University Press.

David, Steven R. 1991. Explaining Third World Alignments. *World Politics* 43: 233–56.

Dia, Mamadou. 1993. *A Governance Approach to Civil Service Reform in Sub-Saharan Africa.* Washington, DC: World Bank.

Economist Intelligence Unit. 1994. *Country Profile: Ghana, 1994–95,* London.

Ellis, Stephen. 1995. Liberia 1989–1994: A Study of Ethnic and Spiritual Violence. *African Affairs* 94(375): 165–97.

French, Howard. 1995. Out of Africa, Progress. *New York Times,* 6 July.

Hyden, Goran and Michael Bratton. 1992. *Governance and Politics in Africa.* Boulder, CO: Lynne Rienner.

International Monetary Fund. 1989. Sierra Leone – Staff Report. Washington, DC: IMF.

Job, Brian L. 1992. *The Insecurity Dilemma: National Security in Third World States.* Boulder, CO: Lynne Rienner.

Kaplan, Robert. 1994. The Coming Anarchy. *Atlantic Monthly,* February: 44–76.

Kessides, Christine. 1993. *Institutional Options for the Provision of Infrastructure.* Discussion Paper 212. Washington, DC: World Bank.

Klare, Michael. 1994/5. Awash in Armaments. *Harvard International Review* 2(4).

McNallen, Steve. 1995. South African Headhunters. *Soldiers of Fortune,* May: 62–80.

Migdal, Joel. 1988. *Strong Societies and Weak States.* Princeton, NJ: Princeton University Press.

National Diamond Mining Corporation. 1990. Kimberlite Project Negotiations with Sunshine Broulle. Unpublished Memos.

Opala, Joseph A. 1994. Ecstatic Renovation: Street Art Celebrating Sierra Leone's 1992 Revolution. *African Affairs* 93: 195–218.

Reno, William. 1995a. *Corruption and State Politics in Sierra Leone.* New York: Cambridge University Press.

——— 1995b. Reinvention of an African Patrimonial State: Charles Taylor's Liberia. *Third World Quarterly* 16(1): 109–20.

Rothchild, Donald. 1994. Restructuring State-Society Relations in Africa. In *Economic Change and Political Liberalization in Sub-Saharan Africa,* ed. Jennifer Widner. Baltimore, MD: Johns Hopkins University Press.

Shiner, Cindy. 1994. Growing Unruliness by Soldiers Sparks Coup Fear in Sierra Leone. *Washington Post,* 6 October.

Sierra Leone. 1995. Statement on the Budget. Freetown: Government Printer.

Thomas, S. 1995. La Sierra Leone est lentement asphyxié par la guerre civile. *Le Monde,* 27 June.

World Bank. 1985. *Review of Public Expenditures in Sierra Leone* (Report No 535256). Washington, DC: World Bank.

——— 1993a. *The East Asian Miracle: Economic Growth and Public Policy.* Washington, DC: World Bank.

——— 1993b. *Ghana 2000: Setting the Stage for Accelerated Growth and Poverty Reduction.* Washington, DC: World Bank.

——— 1994a. *Adjustment in Africa.* New York: Oxford University Press.

——— 1994b. *World Development Report.* Washington, DC: World Bank.

Zartman, William I. 1995. *Collapsed States.* Boulder, CO: Lynne Rienner.

3

Timber Booms, State Busts: The Political Economy of
Liberian Timber

PATRICK JOHNSTON (2004)

A combination of four issues perpetuated and worsened the decay of state institutions and transformed political corruption in Liberia during the Charles Taylor regime: the demands for political and economic liberalisation made by Western international financial institutions (IFIs); the United Nations' long-time refusal to place sanctions on the Liberian timber trade; a clandestine network of predatory foreign firms; and corrupt rent-seeking state elites. Investment from foreign timber firms in Liberia reinforced an informal, clandestine economy that thrived and took primacy after the collapse of Liberia's formal economy. Charles Taylor and his associates profited from these transactions, leaving ordinary Liberians alienated by the exigencies of collapsed political and economic institutions.

This article places the political economy of Liberian timber in the context of the theory of state failure. I explore the relationship between private investment, state failure, and war. To address this question, I focus on informal arrangements between Charles Taylor and foreign timber firms. These arrangements illustrate the connection between unregulated private investment in weak states and state failure, which, I argue, greatly increases the likelihood of internal war. Timber firms served as proxies for collapsed state agencies, including the army, cloaking Taylor with sufficient security to remain president despite widespread discontent with the regime. Taylor's private economy had serious negative effects on ordinary Liberians. Since Taylor depended on foreign investment for capital and security, not the productivity of domestic citizens and industries for these goods, he had little incentive to provide Liberians with public goods or services. The social dislocation from the state which this produced perpetuated and lengthened the duration of the country's conflict that ended in 2003. Indeed, as private investment from foreign timber firms increased, government expenditures on public goods and services decreased. The Liberian state failed to monopolise coercion throughout its territory, rendering the country subject to violence and predation. Yet this did not threaten the nature of the authority which Taylor had built, highlighting the significant difference between his notion of rule and that conventionally associated with the nation-state.

Fragile institutions and state failure

A structural explanation of the Liberian civil war can be derived from the models developed in Max Weber's theory of the state and William Reno's theory of weak 'shadow states'. This explanation shows the logic of the war, a war that has been described as 'one of the wackiest, and most ruthless, of Africa's uncivil wars' (Richburg 1997, quoted in Ellis 1999:18). A theoretical framework can be created that demonstrates how a combination of the lack of a centralised body of coercion, coupled with historically weak state institutions steeped in patronage practices, predatory foreign firms, and rent-seeking elites undermines state institutional capacity for private gain, leaving the state feeble and vulnerable to insurgency while rulers and firms remain able to benefit financially.

Preceding the civil war of the 1990s, Liberia had a history of weak and fragile political institutions. Samuel Doe, a military official in the William Tolbert regime, staged a coup in 1980 and took power as a staunch Cold War ally of the United States. Doe obtained much of his power from his ties to the West, which funded the bulk of his vast patronage network. Though he presided over a bloated bureaucracy, Doe did not build these structures according to meritocratic, hierarchical, legal-rational principles (Weber 1946:196–240). Doe's method of governance more closely resembled what Weber called 'traditional authority' (*Ibid*: 78–79). He built a state apparatus which maintained traditional practices of nepotism and patronage rather than a state with an institutional design based on technocratic expertise and rational administration.

Doe sustained this patronage-based system of rule for nearly a decade, in large measure through his alliance with the United States. Estimates report that the US poured more than US$500 million (Huband 1990:8) into Liberia between 1981 and 1985, and more thereafter. The US intended this money to be used for Doe's security, the maintenance of his political patronage networks, and for his guarantee of diplomatic solidarity with the West. These funds allowed Doe to buy domestic support and protection without building strong, durable, and adaptable state institutions to promote Liberia's long-term stability and centralised state authority.

Toward the end of the 1980s, as the Cold War came to a close, the US reduced aid to Liberia. Doe found it difficult to support the large patronage networks that he had accumulated during the previous decade, and lacking other large sources of revenue he pared down the state. He jettisoned bureaucrats and discontinued payment and bribery to others. This left Doe with few allies. At the same time, the industrial, service, and agricultural sectors of the formal economy were moribund. Angry Liberians, seeking retribution for the corruption of the regime and its failure to provide ample goods and services, along with former Doe associates affected by the cutbacks, took up arms against the state in an attempt to gain or increase access to the informal economic networks through which much of the country's commerce was beginning to move. At this level, Liberia's war was based upon significant grievances, although, as we will see, the structure of Doe's patronage-based political economy elevated other interests.

Chief among the groups seeking access to Liberia's informal economic networks was Charles Taylor's National Patriotic Front of Liberia (NPFL). Taylor's motives for warfare were a combination of greed and grievance: Taylor pursued power both for its economic privileges, but also to oust Doe, against whom Taylor carried significant grievance. Taylor had previously worked in the Doe regime as head of General Services, Liberia's main procurement agency. They fell out when Doe alleged that Taylor had embezzled US$900,000 from the General Services agency, leading Taylor to flee to America, where he was eventually imprisoned for fifteen months (Daniels 2003:25). Taylor escaped from prison, and returned to West Africa by way of Libya to start a war against Doe.

Doe's neo-patrimonial strategy faced a crisis when the United States withdrew its support: he could no longer rely on the efficacy of formal state institutions or informal patronage networks for political support. Moreover, Doe had not developed an informal clandestine economy as a means to rule to the same extent that Taylor later would do. With neither an effective means of coercion, nor an effective patronage network, insurgent factions, with his former associates as leaders, vied with each other to oust Doe. Taylor's NPFL emerged as the strongest faction, controlling most of the country except Monrovia. On 9 September 1990, Prince Johnson, a former associate of Taylor's NPFL who led the Independent Patriotic Front of Liberia (INPFL), apprehended and tortured Doe before killing him.

Yet, a West African intervention force, the Economic Monitoring Group (ECOMOG), stymied Taylor and the other warlord-led factions from gaining the Executive Mansion in Monrovia. The rebel groups retreated to the countryside, where they staged continuous attacks on Monrovia. The numerous warlord factions fought for control of strategic portions of the countryside while the interim government and the ECOMOG forces struggled to shore up order in Monrovia. Indeed, the fragile institutions that had weakened under Doe completely collapsed in his absence. This destroyed the stability which most legitimate investors sought. Most of the industries that had operated in pre-war Liberia, including the US Firestone plant, fled amid the chaos of the war.

The role of foreign firms

Not all investors shunned Liberia. As Reno (1998) has shown, Liberia attracted shady firms whose interests involved the extraction of primary commodities and/or the wartime economy of weapons trade. This international dimension exacerbated and prolonged the Liberian civil war by adding significant sources of capital and weapons for non-state rebel movements and state actors. In spite of the harmful consequences of this international trade, the prevailing Western consensus generally encouraged these commercial activities. The regulation of international trade, especially in natural resources, would have violated neoliberal principles of free trade and competition. As I show below, private investment had pernicious effects in Liberia, and proved a decisive factor in perpetuating state weakness and political instability.

In most instances, foreign firms seeking operating concessions have had to collaborate with rulers to gain them. Foreign firms have provided rulers with capital, private protection and, to varying degrees, international legitimacy. This is possible because Western policy-makers have not discriminated in their support of foreign investment. The World Bank, for example, dubbed two of the most prominent architects of the conflict timber trade, the Malaysian Samling company and the Rimbunan Hijau company, models of concession programmes and funded their exploits in timber-rich countries (Global Witness 2002a:12). These companies are known for illegal logging, dealing with insurgents and engaging in human rights abuses while Western policy-makers encourage weak state rulers to liberalise foreign investment and trade.

These circumstances create a coincidence of interests. Rulers of already weak states fear that stronger institutions will acquire their own interests if given ample opportunity. As such, strengthening institutions poses a threat to informal sources of patronage which are deeply rooted in official corruption and clandestine economies. Consequently, many weak state rulers, following the neoliberal prescription of the IFIs, reduce spending on the civil service and dramatically cut or discontinue salary payments. Under the Western model, private firms would provide services previously administered by the bureaucracy with greater efficiency and less state intervention. IFI policy-makers miscalculated, however. They presumed, it seems, that the African political elite would wish to use Western methods of consolidating power – building strong state institutions, providing necessary state services, and seeking popular legitimacy – rather than allowing institutional collapse and ruling by other means: through militarised control over commerce and primary resources. World Bank and IMF policy failed to take into consideration the notion that, without sufficient incentive to reform political and economic institutions, some corrupt rulers might willingly allow their states to crumble precisely because these rulers could prosper politically *and* economically in the shadows of state sovereignty (Reno 1995).

The synergy between foreign firms and domestic elites has been instrumental in creating state failure. Foreign firms could not successfully export minerals, oil, or other resources without first being granted operating concessions by the sovereign incumbent regime or the rebel groups that control countries' peripheral areas. In efforts to ingratiate themselves with patronage-based incumbent regimes, firms shape their behaviour to accommodate political leaders. In most instances, weak state rulers have lost domestic support and legitimacy because of their misuse of public office for private gain and because of their unwillingness to provide public infrastructure, goods, and services. To stifle political competition and dissent, then, these rulers turn to compliant foreign entrepreneurs who seek operating concessions from the regime and who are typically willing to perform political, economic, and military favours to gain them.

Unfortunately, the types of foreign firms and businessmen who collaborate with weak state rulers often do not possess the integrity assumed by Western policy-makers. A Dutch gang operating in Liberia, for example, trafficked drugs to Europe and America under the guise of legitimate business while under the personal protection of President Taylor (Kamara 1999). The end of the Cold War created a new international class of investors, often criminal, who possess large quantities of a hot commodity in weak states: small arms. The collapse of the former Eastern bloc generated a great surplus of weapons, which entrepreneurs converted into quick capital, selling them cheaply and discreetly on the international market. Many countries participate in the illicit arms trade. Investigations implicate Bulgaria, Romania, Moldova, and Slovakia, the Central Asian countries of Kazakhstan and Kyrgyzstan, and individuals from Yugoslavia, Ukraine, and Russia as central to such practices (Global Witness 2003:20). In the Liberian case, large shipments of small arms from Eastern Europe are reported to have arrived 2–3 times a month. These weapons shipments are reported to have been payments for timber concessions which had been granted by President Taylor to foreign investors (*Ibid.*:17–18). These transactions exacerbate already simmering conflicts. Foreign firms operating in weak states can act as conduits between rulers and weapons runners, transporting weapons to various locations at the demand of rulers. As a result, weak state leaders can manipulate and destabilise areas outside of their immediate control through the reach of foreign firms, as Charles Taylor did throughout much of West Africa.

Social dislocation from the state

Weak state rulers who inherit feeble institutional structures wish to find a way to remain in office without having to address the burdensome task of state-building. Since aid from IFIs has become heavily conditional, and since Cold War aid from superpowers has largely dried up, rulers have turned to foreign firms to supply the money and security to provide sufficient patronage and to field militias in order to prevent associates and rivals from making their own bids for power. This circumvents institution building. Corrupt rulers found that they could also profit personally from these arrangements. In fact, granting operating concessions to foreign firms in exchange for capital and military protection has largely severed weak state rulers' obligations to their states. In essence, as Mustapha (2002) has lamented, such countries quickly became 'states without people'. When state rulers depended on sources other than their citizens for revenues and security, rulers had less incentive to provide citizens with goods and services that would enhance their productivity. Citizens were thus left subject to the interests of predatory networks of powerful individuals and their business partners. These citizens did not enjoy privileges that would typically accompany citizenship, such as basic personal rights or a secure public order. The informal and often clandestine elite economic transactions crowded out the formal economy, including much of the agricultural and industrial sectors, leaving citizens with few avenues through which to pursue political or economic objectives. This has produced social dislocation and grievance. Since economic opportunities tend to be embedded in these informal networks, citizens must seek accommodations with them to survive. That is a strategy to which vigorous young men, who can be turned into foot soldiers, are best suited (Murphy 2003).

This structural aspect of patronage-based weak states turns the grievances and desperation of citizens into a resource for those who challenge the incumbent ruler. Rebel movements emerge out of this new social group, formed along with or headed by former regime insiders who now operate in areas not controlled by formal state power. Rebels' attempt to secure territory with abundant primary commodities that some foreign firms trade for capital and weapons reconstitutes the relationships which rulers like Doe had used to maintain his authority. Where Doe relied on internal clientelism from domestic elites, Taylor depended almost solely on foreign associates, thereby removing most ordinary Liberians from the economy and relegating them to continual poverty and violent competition for scarce resources. *The Perspective* (2001a) news magazine summed up the wider reach of this political economy particularly well: 'The empowerment of international criminals in reducing weak states to rubble for wealth is one of the effects of "globalisation" that most may have overlooked. The "Evil Empire" (Soviet Russia) may have withered. But West Africa is now battling with its abandoned children – ex-KGB officers, arms dealers prepared to do anything for money, condemning weak countries to perpetual conflicts.'

The salience of Liberian timber

The Liberian case reveals how the country's timber industry fostered and perpetuated state decay. It ensured that the state was unable to defeat rebel insurgencies and it prolonged the civil war. Timber itself is especially important and deserves consideration for several reasons. It became the largest sector of Liberia's considerable export economy during the Charles Taylor regime and evidence suggests that timber firms were crucial sources of income to sustain Taylor's predatory regime. The industry played a key role in supporting him while he was a rebel leader. Analysis of this industry also shows how private interests allowed Taylor to neglect public institutions. Foreign investment, long considered by liberals a valuable asset to developing countries, here served to hinder political, social and economic development. As the political economy of timber shows, the 'quality' of the investment, not its quantity, is more indicative of how successful it might be for a country's development prospects and stability.

Timber gave Liberian rulers extraordinary leverage in commercial and political operations, becoming the main source of money and power for Charles Taylor's warlord control of the Liberian periphery – Taylorland – after the beginning of the war in late 1989. First, compared with most forms of resource extraction, logging is relatively easy. It requires little investment for considerable returns. A few soldiers with chainsaws and trucks can generate hundreds of thousands of dollars in a relatively short time (Global Witness 2002b:8). Second, timber's saleability on the international market boomed. Third, enterprising investors and corrupt politicians were able to use timber as an ostensibly legitimate business endeavour to enhance their own political and economic status and to mask criminal activity undertaken in Liberia. Roads into Sierra Leone, for example, purportedly built for 'development' purposes, were instead used expressly as logging roads, and by the Oriental Timber Company (OTC) to move weapons into Sierra Leone for use by the Revolutionary United Front rebels. Airplanes also reportedly delivered arms covertly via a heavily guarded OTC airstrip (*Ibid.*:7–11).

This raises a question as to why the United Nations failed to sanction Liberian timber for three years after it sanctioned diamonds, which Taylor used similarly to maintain influence and fight wars in Liberia and Sierra Leone. First, timber's seemingly innocuous essence allowed it to fall under the radar of many analysts. Logging is not considered a clandestine industry and is less associated with criminal activity than more exotic fare like diamonds, drugs, and guns. Second, France and China, two members of the United Nations Security Council, depended on Liberian timber imports after the supply from other West African countries had diminished. French and Chinese diplomats had to weigh the consequences of sanctions on what they regarded as a legitimate operator in their domestic economies. However, after being placed under public scrutiny by human rights organisations, France and China reluctantly agreed to sanction Liberian timber exports in July 2003. This timing almost coincided, not surprisingly, with Taylor's exile to Nigeria after his regime came under increasing attack by the Liberians United for Reconciliation and Democracy (LURD) rebel group. Taylor could not successfully fight the rebels as timber profits fell and concern among foreign timber firms that UN sanctions were imminent threatened his primary source of revenue.

Prior to this move for timber sanctions, foreign timber firms' private militias, with standing armies of as many as 2,500 troops (Global Witness 2001:21), had harassed, extorted, raped, and forced labour on ordinary Liberians. The OTC built and maintained a military training facility behind its primary offices, where an elite force known as the 'Bush Marines' trained. Reports surfaced of gross human rights abuses against Liberians by foreign OTC employees, including public floggings and rapes of women and young girls. Other transgressions, such as separating Liberian workers from their families, destruction of private property, and widespread intimidation produced a climate of fear and paranoia in villages near logging sites (Global Witness 2003:9–10). Indeed, timber firms provided the strength to protect Taylor from dissidents, to limit citizens' access to scarce resources, and to protect timber and mineral reserves from unruly bands of Liberian strongmen, rebel groups, and angry citizens. They replaced absent military elements which the Taylor regime had jettisoned, further undermining what remained of corroding state institutions and enabling Taylor to field a more predatory armed force without concern for threats from angry Liberians.

Finally, foreign timber firms allowed Charles Taylor to use the Liberian state as a personal cash register rather than to govern in the interest of the collective. In turn, state institutions, and the collective goods and services which they should have provided, were eroded or ceased to exist, leaving instead a cast of private actors violently competing for access to Liberia's resources. Citizens were deprived of basic political and economic rights.

The political economy of Liberian timber

Presiding over a compliant parliament, President Taylor forced the Strategic Commodities Act through the Liberian Congress in late 1999. It granted him 'the sole power to execute, negotiate, and conclude all commercial contracts or agreements with any foreign or domestic investor for the exploitation of the strategic commodities of the Republic of Liberia' (Global Witness 2001:7). This policy illustrated the weakness and lack of autonomy of Liberian state institutions. No viable option existed for parliamentary members but to pass Taylor's initiative, or else fear for their personal safety. It was well known that even small-scale political opposition to Taylor would be met with harsh measures.[1] The Strategic Commodities Act further limited the ability of non-state actors and civil society groups to incorporate themselves into the formal export economy – the only viable sector of the domestic economy – without the consent of and subservience to the Taylor regime. This initiative came mostly as a formality,

---

[1]   Sam Dokie, Manna Zaykay, Nowai Flomo, Vice President Dogolea and Minister of Information Milton Teahjay all disappeared or were found dead shortly after criticising Taylor. For more, see letter from opposition party leaders Siapoe and Konah to party members illustrating human rights abuses perpetrated by the Taylor regime (see http://www.copla.org/upplppstatement.htm.). Another suspicious death was that of an American known as 'Bob Hoff', who set up a timber firm in Liberia named Interior Timber Incorporated. Hoff's timber concession included provisions for training camps for NPFL and RUF fighters. Hoff's relations with Taylor soured when Hoff excluded Taylor from a large transaction in Sinoe County. The NPFL ambushed and killed Hoff and everyone travelling with him (see Global Witness 2003:21).

since most ordinary Liberians had never held any meaningful economic clout. Taylor had controlled the extraction, distribution, and export of much of the country's resources for the past decade.

In an effort to mask the importance of timber to his regime and to thus thwart UN sanctions on timber, Taylor's regime became elusive and equivocal in its financial reports. NGO reports estimate that Liberia's timber industry was worth at least US$187 million in 2000, whereas the government reported revenues of US$6.6 or US$6.7 million (Global Witness 2001). Despite Liberia's formal GDP being significantly less than South Africa's or Nigeria's, Liberian investments in Swiss bank accounts were more than those from its wealthier African counterparts (Global Witness 2003:17).

Although the international community was reluctant to accept Taylor as Liberia's sovereign President, some of its members did still clamour to import illicit Liberian timber. Even as businessmen described the Liberian timber trade as 'organised gangsterism' (*The Independent*, 22 November 1992) diminished timber supply from Ghana and Ivory Coast increased the value of Liberian logs. This was especially the case for European and Asian markets which had historically imported large amounts of West African timber. Importers from China and France provided strategically important sources of income for Taylor. China imported roughly 46% of Liberia's exported timber in 2000, and France imported 18% (*Africa Research Bulletin* 2001). Despite criticism from human rights organisations, both countries opposed sanctions on Liberian timber until early 2003, arguing that sanctions would worsen the human cost to the lives of Liberians because of increased unemployment.

These concerns were unfounded. Foreign timber firms typically employed few Liberians. Those that did employ Liberians often "hire" them by not allowing them to cultivate their privately owned land near the logging sites, forcing them into unskilled positions under unsatisfactory working conditions. The majority of the timber firms' employees, however, are not Liberian. Aggregately, timber firms have employed only about 3,700 Liberians, or 68% of their overall employee-base (Global Witness 2001:3–4). Skilled positions tended to be awarded to outsiders. The Malaysia-based Oriental Timber Corporation, for example, hired 600 Malaysians who were brought to Liberia to fill the skilled positions. OTC executives boasted, too, about bringing Asian prostitutes to Liberia for OTC use. The OTC reportedly "changed" prostitutes every two months (*Global News Wire* 2000).

The withering away of the state?

Table 1 illustrates the dramatic decline of economic support for state institutions and services by the Taylor regime. Instead of contracting foreign firms to perform the services no longer funded by the state, Taylor used timber contracts largely for personal enrichment and allowed the state apparatus to collapse. Toward the end of Doe's reign, in 1988, Liberia spent $475.5 million on services (electricity and water, construction, trade and hotels, transportation and communications, financial institutions, government services, and others). In 1997, the year Taylor formally became President, spending on services dipped to $44.6 million, or about 9% of the amount spent toward the end of Doe's tenure. By 1999, spending on services had increased to $82.6 million, but that was still only 17% of spending in 1988. In 1999 spending on transportation and communication services, an area in which Liberia was already severely underdeveloped, was scaled back to just 16% of what it had been in 1988. Spending on electricity and water was less than 20% of what it had been in 1988, and spending on government services was less than 25% of the 1988 amount.

Table 1: State Expenditure on Public Services

	1988	1997	1998	1999
Services (Total)	475.5	44.6 (9.4%)	58.5 (12.3%)	82.6 (17.4%)
Electricity & Water	12.4	1.2 (9.7%)	1.5 (12.1%)	2.3 (18.5%)
Construction	45.4	4.3 (9.5%)	5.6 (12.3%)	6.9 (15.2%)
Trade & Hotels	89.4	8.6 (9.6%)	11.0 (12.3%)	17.0 (19%)
Transport & Comm.	136.9	12.8 (9.3%)	16.8 (12.3%)	21.8 (15.9%)
Financial Institutions	88.8	8.3 (9.3%)	10.9 (12.3%)	13.3 (15.0%)
Government Services	50.4	4.7 (9.3%)	6.2 (12.3%)	11.2 (22.2%)
Other Services	51.9	4.9 (9.4%)	6.4 (12.3%)	10.3 (19.8%)

(Source: IMF (2003). First figure is in millions of US$. Figure in parenthesis is the percentage of the 1988 expenditure.)

One exasperated bureaucrat noted a link between the decay of the Liberian state and Charles Taylor's private timber boom: 'We don't see any benefits these logs are bringing. With all the logs that are being exported every day, civil servants have not been paid for seven months' (Teahjay 2001a). In contrast to Western expectations, the increasing flow of foreign capital into Liberia has not improved the standard of living. While Charles Taylor's personal wealth has been estimated at US$4.8 billion (*The Perspective* 2001b) and timber profits grossed at least US$187 million per year (*The Perspective* 2001c), public utilities such as running water and a dependable telephone system remain absent throughout most of Liberia (Farah 2001). One diplomat noted, 'Ports in Buchanan are near closure, railway lines are overrun with grass, giant cranes are frozen in time, and factories are rotting away' (International Crisis Group 2002:6; see also Beaumont 2001:7). The human toll was remarkable: at least 40,000 Liberians (out of approximately 3 million) were estimated to have starved to death between 1990 and 1992 (*The Independent*, 22 November 1992). The average Liberian makes US$188 per year (US State Department 2003) and unemployment rates have remained high, ranging from 75 to 80% between 1992 and 2002, perhaps as many as 80% live on less than US$1 a day, and Liberian literacy rates remain among the lowest in the world, at

Table 2: Sectoral Origin of GDP at 1992 Constant Prices, 1988 and 1997–2001 (in millions of US$)

	1988	1997	1998	1999	2000	2001
Forestry	60.4	37.6	63.9	76.1	129.8	130.7
Timber (logs)	36.8	4.9	15.5	23.8	66.3	66.7
Wood	23.7	32.7	48.4	52.3	63.6	64.0

(Source: IMF estimates. International Monetary Fund Statistical Appendix on Liberia.)

around 38%. In 2001, there were only twenty-four physicians in Liberia (*The Perspective* 2001d).

Liberia continues to have a high dependence upon its export economy of primary commodities (see Table 2). Political and economic control over society is exercised through control of the informal, and often clandestine, economic markets for export of Liberia's primary commodities. He who controls trade controls politics.

Taylor's private network: informal, clandestine and criminal?

Reno's theory of the shadow state (1995;1998) argues that corrupt post-Cold War rulers have transformed their political networks from large domestic patronage machines often run through state institutions to smaller ones composed of shadowy foreign firms, mercenaries, child soldiers, and a few loyal local strongmen. This allows rulers to remain in power and personally profit without the constraints posed by strong legal-rational bureaucratic institutions and strong civil societies.

This is what occurred in Liberia. The timber-industry businessmen and associates with whom Taylor surrounded himself were not those enterprising, legitimate investors whom the West envisaged as integral to economic recovery. On the contrary. The interplay among unsavoury foreign firms, unscrupulous investors, enterprising local strongmen, and Taylor cronies resembled a mafia whose economic predation and violent tactics allowed Taylor to remain President of Liberia with hardly any centralised state military or police – without the Weberian requisite of a legitimate monopoly of violence within a given territory. These 'new' Liberian investors included, among others, gunrunners, commanders of corporate paramilitaries, and drug traffickers. The reason for the criminal element in Taylor's foreign economic network was simple: given the violence and disorder associated with his manner of rule, it would have been difficult for large, reputable corporations to engage in large-scale enterprise with Taylor. Shareholders, security commissions, and insurance underwriters would all have been uncomfortable attaching their fortunes and reputations to a former warlord. Taylor therefore tended to trade with small, criminal firms, many of which had ulterior motives, namely supplying weapons to various factions of the Liberian and Sierra Leonean wars. Chairmen of such firms were not risk-averse when they believed they would benefit from the opportunities that Taylor and his vast reserves of primary commodities offered.

Indeed, Charles Taylor dealt with a qualitatively different type of foreign investor from those sought by Western policy-makers. The Oriental Timber Corporation, and its main executive, Gus van Kouwenhoven, is a useful illustration of the new type of investor in 'weak states'. The OTC, a Malaysian business entity referred to locally as 'Old Taylor's Children', operated on the largest scale of any timber firm in Liberia. Van Kouwenhoven owned Monrovia's Hotel Africa. He was a long-time crony of Taylor's and of Doe's before him and was allegedly involved in a host of illicit gambling and gunrunning activities. Van Kouwenhoven's OTC was the most predatory transnational timber corporation in Liberia. It officially logged about 40% of all the acreage recorded by foreign timber firms in 1999 and housed a private militia of over 2,500 troops (Global

Witness 2001:21). One observer noted: 'Look, it's an open secret: Gus fronted Taylor up $5m for his logging concessions. They split the profits. Gus's ships take out the logs and they bring in the guns. It was the same deal with the diamonds' (Beaumont 2001:7).

Evidence has also implicated the OTC as one of the primary actors in the arming of the RUF insurgents in Sierra Leone. Logging highways into Sierra Leone paid for with OTC funds, for instance, were widely used for weapons transfer, as was a private OTC airstrip used covertly to move weapons (Teahjay 2001b).

Van Kouwenhoven has a checkered past. Known popularly as 'The Godfather of Liberia', he armed Charles Taylor's rebels during the Liberian civil war with funds obtained from timber concessions granted by the Doe regime. It is also widely known that he helped to rig the 1997 election in Taylor's favour.

Former Exotic Tropical Timber Enterprise (ETTE) owner Leonid Minin, reputedly the former head of the Ukrainian mafia, provides another classic case of the 'new investor' who operates in weak states in conjunction with corrupt rulers. Minin, an Israeli arms dealer based in Ukraine, owned ETTE from 1993 to 1999. Minin's primary endeavours, however, were criminal and clandestine, obfuscated, in part, by the subterfuge provided by his position in 'legitimate' timber commerce. His international criminal record spanned many countries, and his history of involvement in criminal activities ranged from trafficking in stolen works of art to arms trafficking and money laundering. A United Nations Expert Panel reported that Minin 'uses several aliases ... he has been refused entry into many countries, including (his native) Ukraine, and travels with many different passports.' Other British reports estimated Minin to operate under no less than thirty aliases, to be proficient in six languages, and to be earning between $250 and $300 million per year. Minin's main function for the Taylor regime was moving weapons from the Ukraine to West Africa and into Sierra Leone in his private jet, which he eventually sold to Taylor for use as the Liberian presidential jet (Pratt 2001).[2]

In addition to Minin and Van Kouwenhoven, several other foreign businessmen collaborated with Taylor to form the foundation of his corruption network. Talal El-Ndine, a Lebanese businessman, was at the fore. El-Ndine acted as 'paymaster' for Taylor in Sierra Leone, paying and supplying insurgents, and also paying those extracting diamonds from that country. Equally important, El-Ndine acted as a conduit between the Taylor regime and foreign firms, attracting foreign interest and investment through his numerous contacts. Another associate, Emmanuel Shaw, who was wanted on criminal drug trafficking charges in South Africa, also worked closely with Taylor and van Kouwenhoven (Pratt 2001). Shaw managed the air transport of commodities and weapons. In fact, Shaw owns the airport hangars which Taylor's associates used to transport illicit goods by air. US court documents also note Shaw's hand in privatising the Liberian oil industry for personal gain shortly before being relieved of his position as Finance Minister (Hanley 1997).

The politics of Liberian timber remained highly personalised. In this sense, Taylor fused patrimonialism with the new foreign networks he had built. Taylor

---

[2] Evidence in Pratt (2001), many news sources, and in the United Nations Panel of Exports Report appears to be legitimate. As *The Washington Post* reported, a source with direct knowledge of Taylor's dealings said: 'Taylor and his circle were deeply shaken by the report because someone high in his government obviously gave [the investigators] very good information. It is full of truth' (31 January 2001).

appointed his brother, Robert, for example, as the head of the Forest Development Authority (FDA). Robert Taylor had final authority over decisions made regarding timber concessions – decisions made in close consultation, presumably, with President Taylor. Corruption from Robert Taylor's FDA abounded. For example, the FDA did not hold the OTC responsible for any of the taxes that it agreed to pay when it signed a contract with the Liberian government. Nor did it hold the OTC accountable for failing to keep its promise to hire at least 4,000 Liberians by 2000, or to log a limited number of acres (Global Witness 2001:24). Moreover, President Taylor colluded to appoint his son, Charles 'Chuckie' Taylor, Jr., chairman of another foreign-owned firm, United Logging Company. Chuckie Taylor enjoyed unlimited operating capacity and an abundance of foreign capital in his business activities (*Ibid.*:13–18).

Timber cronyism, private militias and the undermining of state institutions

A general requisite for Taylor to grant operating concessions to foreign firms was their willingness and ability to provide him with a private militia. These militias enabled Taylor to maintain remarkable "stability" by avoiding being ousted within a failed state. First, private militias allowed Taylor to ignore the erosion in the bureaucratic control and discipline of soldiers in the Liberian national armed forces. Until the LURD insurgency became a real threat such forces barely existed. Taylor used a combination of foreign militias provided by his business associates and young Liberian boys to fight dissidents.

Liberian military spending fell from 31.2% of GDP in 1994 to 1.8% in 1997 – the year in which Taylor formally took power as President (SIPRI 2003). This illustrates his ambition to cut state spending to the national armed forces in preference to having privatised forces work exclusively for him. Milton Teahjay, who fled the Taylor regime after serving as Deputy Minister of Information, corroborated these allegations. 'Logging companies', he notes, 'now constitute the most powerful and politically insulated layer of our national bureaucracy. Logging companies' private armed militias have now replaced our national police apparatus in rural Liberia' (Teahjay 2001b).

Oscar and Maurice Cooper (Inland Logging Company), Cocoo Dennis (Salami Molawi Incorporated Logging Company), Mohammed Solarne (Mohammed Group of Companies) and Hussein, Nasser, and Abbas Fawas (Maryland Wood Processing Industries) all head foreign timber companies whose standing militias were used by Taylor (Global Witness 2001:8). These militias were recruited from the timber companies' home countries, ex-RUF soldiers from the ranks of what is known to be among the more predatory armed groups in recent history, and Liberian youths, many of whom were under the influence of mind-numbing drugs (Berkeley 2001:23; Chimutashu 2003). Taylor ensured prime effort and performance from his militias by not paying soldiers formal wages. Instead he allowed them to keep loot which they pillaged from villages. This use of disorder and insecurity as a means of control resulted in an especially predatory and coercive regime.

Taylor not only contributed to the destruction of state structures in Liberia, but, until his ousting, also threatened to exacerbate the instability he had already fostered in Sierra Leone. During Taylor's insurrection in 1989, he sought the support of then Sierra Leonean President Joseph Momoh to oust Doe. But Momoh instead offered his support to the ECOMOG contingent of West African peacekeepers who occupied Monrovia and kept Taylor from assuming the Liberian presidency in 1990. Moreover, during the early stages of the Liberian war, Momoh allowed anti-Taylor forces to use Sierra Leone as a strategic base. After Doe was ousted, Taylor set out for revenge against Momoh and to extend his regional influence into diamond-laden Sierra Leone. Foday Sankoh, a former associate of Taylor's, led Taylor-supported RUF troops against the Momoh regime. The Sierra Leonean army, impatient with Momoh's corruption, staged a coup and removed him in 1992, installing Captain Valentine Strasser as president who promised to crush the RUF rebels (Reno 2001:219–225).

Even after the Sierra Leonean military ousted Momoh in 1992, however, Taylor continued to support RUF forces. He knew that a sympathetic regime in Sierra Leone would ensure continued access to the country's considerable diamonds. Taylor provided the rebels with weapons obtained from Eastern European contacts in exchange for diamonds. Highways constructed for logging companies provided the infrastructure necessary to transport guns from Monrovia to Sierra Leone. Taylor also allowed RUF rebels to be trained in Liberia and he harboured RUF members who had fled capture in Sierra Leone. Instability and uncertainty remain a tension in Sierra Leone despite a tenuous peace agreement with the RUF in 2001.

Conclusion

This article has shown how Charles Taylor exploited timber concessions to foreign firms as a proxy for effective state institutions in Liberia. Instead of rebuilding the collapsed institutions he inherited, Taylor exploited trade in timber and other primary commodities. This strategy offered him enormous personal profit and sufficient security to remain in power. Taylor had an incentive to allow Liberia's formal economic and political structures to decay, thereby limiting political and economic opportunities for ordinary Liberians. Timber exploitation alone did not cause state failure. Rather, state failure occurred because of a long history of patrimonialism, patronage, and misrule that began before the civil war crippled Liberian institutions. These institutions failed to function during and after the civil war, not least because of timber exploitation. This alone is neither surprising nor unusual for a country under such circumstances. What is new is the way in which weak state rulers of countries such as the Democratic Republic of Congo, Angola, and Sierra Leone have managed state decay in the aftermath of the Cold War. Rather than viewing strong state institutions as desirable political tools of domination, authority, and security that would enhance their power, rulers have instead found state institutions threatening to their personal agendas and have sought authority through privatised, informal foreign networks composed of violent entrepreneurs. To avoid needing to build these threatening formal institutions, rulers in Liberia and other failed states used timber and other natural resources to connect with foreign firms, thereby enabling themselves to undermine their countries' formal economies and state institutions in order to eliminate potential threats to their illegitimate rule.

The presence of natural resources has been shown in statistical studies to increase the duration of civil wars but not to cause them (Ross 2004:5). This is because natural resources, coupled with increased global trade and an emphasis on deregulation of commerce, provide a currency to acquire weapons and to enrich faction leaders. That is, natural resources such as timber often fuel civil war, as happened in Liberia, even if they are not the primary cause of most wars. But, as we have seen in the case of Liberia, this is contingent upon the presence of a particular kind of local political economy and structural changes in the world economy. The importance of timber and other resources lies in their ability to offer incumbent rulers an alternative to building state structures. Exploitation of natural resources lures foreign firms that provide rulers with sufficient security to avoid being ousted while offering immense personal profits to these rulers. This has changed the dynamic of failed states' roles in internal wars. Undermining state institutions poses a risk, because rulers are vulnerable to civil insurgency due to the collapsed security apparatus. No longer are states Leviathans that can suppress civil dissent or easily defeat insurgents. Since states are weak and cannot quash threats, wars tend to become entrenched and difficult to resolve. But such arrangements can make rulers significant profits. It is a classic high-risk, high-gain investment scenario.

What, then, are the sources of conflict? In many weak states, ostensible neo-liberal reforms that appease Western prescriptions of downsized civil services, trade liberalisation, and privatisation of state industries in fact promote the decay of state institutions, weakening the state's ability to fend off dissident activity, thus increasing the likelihood of continuous conflict. Rather than these reforms producing the small, yet strong and capable legal-rational bureaucracies and efficient free markets envisioned by neoliberals, bureaucracies and the administration of services that reforms are intended to provide are jettisoned as commercial opportunities become limited to those with the capability, or the weaponry, to secure their place within the economy. I demonstrated this trend in post-Cold War Liberia, where Charles Taylor slashed Samuel Doe's large public patronage network and replaced former state clients with foreign businessmen who profited from Liberia's rich timber resources in exchange for protection by Taylor. The incorporation of private, non-state actors allowed Taylor to let public infrastructure decay, to manage potential political threats with the strength of firms' private militias, and to augment his pernicious influence in West African and, particularly, in Sierra Leonean affairs. This rendered commercial opportunities only to weak state rulers and gun-toting rebels, not to ordinary citizens for whom such liberal reforms were supposed to engender greater political freedom and economic prosperity.

References

Africa Research Bulletin. Liberia: What About Timber? 1 April 2001.

Bayart, Jean-François, Stephen Ellis and Beatrice Hibou. 1999. *The Criminalization of the State in Africa*. Bloomington: Indiana University Press.

Beaumont, Peter. 2001. Liberian Tyrant Brings Terror to West Africa. *The Guardian Weekly*, 13 July.

Berkeley, Bill. 2001. *The Graves Are Not Yet Full*. New York: Basic Books.

Brummer, Stefaans. 1997. And Yet Another Liberian Drug Link. *Mail and Guardian* (South Africa), 12 December.

———— Business Resumes in Liberia's Seaports. *Xinhua News Agency,* 5 September.

Chimutashu, Jacqueline. 2003. No to Child Soldiers. *The Herald* (Harare), 14 November.

Christian Science Monitor. 1992. Large Weapons Stockpiles Could Prolong Liberia War. 1 December.

CIA World Factbook: Liberia, 2002. Available online at http://www.cia.gov/cia/publications/fact book/geos/li.html

Daniels, Anthony. 2003. A Bad Man in Africa: The Murderous Liberian President Sees Himself as a Christlike Figure, *Sunday Telegraph* (London), 29 June.

Ellis, Stephen. 1999. *The Mask of Anarchy.* New York: New York University Press.

Farah, Douglas. 2002. Liberian Leader Again Finds Means to Hang On: Taylor Exploits Timber to Keep Power. *The Washington Post,* 4 June.

Global News Wire. 2000. Investigative Report on Oriental Timber Corporation. 20 March.

Global Witness. 2001. Taylor Made: The Pivotal Role of Liberia's Forests and Flag of Convenience in Regional Conflict. September, available online at http://www. globalwitness.org/reports/show.php/en.00021.html.

———— 2002a. The Logs of War. March, available online at http://www.global witness.org/reports/show.php/en.00011.html.

———— 2002b. Logging Off. September, available online at http://www.global witness.org/reports/show.php/en.00006.html.

———— 2003. The Usual Suspects. March, available online at http://www.global witness.org/reports/index.php?section=liberia.

Hanley, Charles J. 1997. His Main Occupation was Stealing. *Mail and Guardian* (Johannesburg), 19 December.

———— 1996. 'Loot, Limos, and Loyal Young Guns: The Strongmen Who Define an Age', *The Associated Press,* 16 December.

Huband, Mark. 2001. *The Skull Beneath the Skin: Africa After the Cold War,* Boulder, CO: Westview Press.

———— 1990. Taylor Leads Rebels on Road to Tribal Revenge. *Guardian Weekly,* 8 July.

The Independent (UK). 1992. EC's Timber Imports Fuel Liberia Civil War. 22 November.

International Crisis Group (ICG). 2002. Liberia: Unravelling. ICG Africa Briefing Paper, 19 September.

International Monetary Fund (IMF). 2003. Liberia: Selected Issues and Statistical Appendix. Available online at http://www.imf.org/external/pubs/ft/scr/2003/cr03275.pdf, 1–56.

Kamara, Tom. 1999. Liberia: The Emergence of a Criminal State. *The Perspective,* 19 October.

Murphy, William P. 2003. Military Patrimonialism and Child Soldier Clientelism in the Liberian and Sierra Leonean Civil Wars. *African Studies Review* 46(2): 61–87.

Mustapha, Abdul Raufu. 2002. States, Predation, and Violence: Reconceptualizing Political Action and Political Community in Africa. Unpublished paper presented at 10th General Assembly of CODESRIA, Kampala, Uganda, December.

The Perspective. 2001a. UN New Task: Handling of Horrors. 9 February.

———— 2001b. Taylor's Acquired Wealth & the Moment of Truth. 15 February.

———— 2001c. Global Witness Director Speaks on Timber and Sanctions. Personal Interview of Global Witness Director, Patrick Alley. 29 August.

———— 2001d. Taylor Proclaims Progress in Poverty. 12 February.

Pratt, David. 2001. Sierra Leone: Danger and Opportunity in a Regional Conflict. Report to Canada's Minister of Foreign Affairs, 27 July.

Reno, William. 2001. The Failure of Peacekeeping in Sierra Leone. *Current History.* May, 219–225.

———— 2000. Clandestine Economies, Violence and States in Africa. *Journal of International Affairs* 53(2): 433–459.

———— 1998. *Warlord Politics and African States.* Boulder, CO: Lynne Rienner.

———— 1995. *State Politics and Corruption in Sierra Leone.* Cambridge: Cambridge University Press.

Richburg, Keith B. 1997. *Out of America: A Black Man Confronts Africa.* New York: Basic Books.

Ross, Michael. 2004. What Do We Know About Natural Resources and Civil War? *Journal of Peace Research* 41(3): 337–356.

SIPRI Military Expenditure Database. 2003. Available online at http://projects. sipri.org/milex/mex_databasel.html.

Teahjay, Milton. 2001a. Uncontrolled Logging in Liberia Wreaks All-Around Havoc. Agence France Presse, 27 June.

————. 2001b. Logging Companies as Conduits for Domestic Repression. Available online at http://www.copla.org/teahjaypartl.html.

US Department of State. 2003. Background Note: Liberia. Bureau of African Affairs, October.

Van de Walle, Nicolas. 2001. *African Economies and the Politics of Permanent Crisis,* Cambridge:

Cambridge University Press.

Weber, Max. 1946. *From Max Weber: Essays in Sociology.* Eds. H .H. Gerth and C.W. Mills. New York: Oxford University Press.

4

Petro-Insurgency or Criminal Syndicate? Conflict & Violence in
the Niger Delta

MICHAEL WATTS (2007)

[I]f low income and slow growth make a country prone to civil war ... why [?]. ... low
income means poverty, and low growth means hopelessness. Young men, who are the
recruits for rebel armies, come pretty cheap ... Life is cheap and joining a rebel movement gives these young men a small chance of riches ... [People in the Niger Delta]
with a sense of grievance were no more likely to take part in violent protest than those
who were not aggrieved. So what did make people more likely to engage in political
violence? ... well, being young, being uneducated, and being without dependants ...
[There] was no relationship between social amenities that a district possessed and its
propensity to political violence. Instead the violence occurs in the districts with oil
wells. ... [A]lthough the risk of violence jumps sharply if there is at least one oil well,
if there are two oil wells in the district it starts to go down. And with twenty oil wells
it is lower still ... To my mind this looks more like a protection racket than outrage
provoked by environmental damage. In the absence of an oil well there is no scope for
extortion and so no violent protest. With an oil well the protection racket is in business.
But the more oil wells ... the greater the incentive for an oil company to pay up and buy
peace. ... [O]ver time the situation has evolved. There is now a huge amount of money
being directed by the Nigerian federal government to the Delta region and the oil
companies are desperately paying protection money ... Within the region local politicians are fighting it out for control of all this money and violent protest has become
an orchestrated part of the political rent seeking. *Grievance has evolved, over the course
of a decade, into greed* (Collier 2007:30–31, emphasis added).

Blood may be thicker than water, but oil is thicker than both (Anderson 2001:30).

Among the chattering classes of the Washington, DC beltway there has been a
deep concern, bordering on panic, over the implications of the growing presence of China on the African continent. It has been driven by an aggressive
expansion into the energy sector and by what is seen as a new 'scramble for oil'
against a backdrop of tight global oil markets, and a post-9/11 US obsession
with energy security including a dovetailing of the 'global war on terror' with
the 2001 Cheney Report's expressed concerns over an unhealthy dependence
upon Middle East oil imports. There are those – Frynas and Paulo for example
(2007) – who argue that the oil scramble does not resemble in any way the late
nineteenth-century African counterpart and that the hype over Sino-oil power
is exaggerated. Historical parallels aside, it is indisputable that a number of
important reconfigurations in the oil complex are in fact in train. Chinese oil
contracts from the three largest oil companies (Sinopec, CNOOC and CNPC with

a combined market value of $225 billion) have grown dramatically – from virtually nothing in 1995 to 70 contracts in 16 countries by 2007 covering a total acreage of over 8.2 million sq. kms – predicated upon an 'integrated independent energy and security model' (Vines et al. 2009). These are based on long-term stable agreements backed and linked to large infrastructure and aid projects sustained by China's massive reserves of accumulated liquidity now in excess of $1 trillion. It is a strategy that includes a number of other Asian NOCs (national oil companies) – most especially KNOC (Korea) and PETRONAS (Malaysia) – that reflects a reconfiguration of oil operations as alliances, constructed typically around bi- or tri-lateral arrangements lubricated by aid, capital, and expertise. The Gulf of Guinea is, moreover, a 'hot' new and dynamic supply zone – the so-called 'new Gulf states' – and has emerged as a major supplier to the seemingly insatiable US market. Its obvious geo-strategic advantages – large and accessible reserves of 'light, sweet crudes', a large liquefied natural gas sector and proximity to North American markets – have all contributed to the fact that Nigeria alone in 2007 supplies over 12% of total US crude imports. And not least, there are the twin developments of the new institutional and financial complexity of oil projects, especially deepwater offshore production and multi-train liquefied natural gas infrastructures, coupled with what the industry sees as the assertive 'petro nationalism' of African oil states and their national oil companies (the passing in 2007 of an ambitious new local content law in Nigeria is simply one case in point).

Whether or not all of this warrants the term 'scramble', the reality is that oil investment is substantial and growing. Cheney's National Energy Strategy Report highlighted the fact that the region was driven by a 'huge exploration investment' contributing over 30% of world liquid hydrocarbon production by 2010. Over the last five years when new oil field discoveries were a scarce commodity, Africa contributed one in every four barrels of new petroleum discovered outside of North America. It is the West African Gulf of Guinea, encompassing the rich on- and off-shore fields stretching from Nigeria to Angola, that is a key plank in George W. Bush's alternative to the increasingly volatile and unpredictable oil states of the Persian Gulf. Oil investment now represents over 50% of all foreign direct investment in the continent (and over 60% of all FDI in the top four FDI recipient countries), and almost 90% of all cross-border mergers and acquisition activity since 2003 has been in the mining and petroleum sector (WIR 2005:43). Between 1995 and 2001, FDI inflow amounted to $7 billion per year, but almost two-thirds of the portfolio was destined for three countries (Angola, Nigeria and South Africa) in which oil FDI accounted for 90% of all FDI inflows. The Gulf of Guinea figures centrally in this new African oil landscape and within the West African oil triangle Nigeria dominates, producing 2.4 million bpd with an ambitious programme to expand output to over 4 million bpd within the next decade.

Running across this picture of dynamic energy capitalism is a deep vein of political volatility. This is seen most dramatically in the Niger Delta which has experienced 15 years of deepening political turbulence and violence that burst open into something like a full-blown insurgency almost two years ago. To put the matter as starkly as I can: the Niger Delta is a vast oil basin of some 70,000 sq. kms and composed officially of nine states (Abia, Akwa-Ibom, Rivers, Bayelsa, Delta, Imo, Ondo and Edo), 185 local government areas and a population of roughly 28 million; it possesses a massive oil infrastructure consisting of

606 fields, 5,284 wells, 7,000 kilometres of pipelines, ten export terminals, 275 flow stations, ten gas plants, four refineries and a massive liquefied natural gas (LNG) sector. Currently the Delta is, more or less, ungovernable. The litany of indices speak for themselves: remotely detonated car bombs and highly sophisticated arms and equipment are the tools of the trade; over 300 foreign hostages have been abducted in the last 15 months and close to 1,000 Nigerian workers detained or held hostage; major and often spectacular attacks on offshore and onshore facilities are endemic and can be perpetrated at will. Unlike the 1980s or 1990s, militants are now willing and able to directly confront federal and state security forces. The vast cache of sophisticated arms are skillfully deployed in an environment of mangrove creeks running for hundreds of miles along the Bight of Benin in which the Nigerian security forces – to quote the Vice-President Goodluck Jonathan – 'cannot cope with the situation' (*Daily Trust*, 27 February 2007). Pipeline breaks due to vandalism and sabotage have almost doubled between 1999 and 2004 (from 497 to 895); product loss (in metric tons) due to pipeline ruptures has grown steadily from 179,000 to 396,000 metric tons over the same period (a figure roughly equal to four supertankers; see Amadi, Mekkonen & Henriksen 2006:25). According to UNDP (2007), there are currently 120–150 'high risk and active violent conflicts' in the three key oil producing states. While Nigeria meets its OPEC quota, up to 900,000 bpd are deferred (or shut-in) and another 100,000 bpd are stolen or 'bunkered'. Collectively this amounts to over one-third of national output. This is the cost that the oil companies must carry for their 'licence to operate' – a licence that is clearly in question.

The costs of this turmoil have been vast. Direct assaults on oil installations and infrastructure cost the Nigerian government $6.8 billion in lost revenue between 1999 and 2004, but in the last three years the figure has increased dramatically (currently the conflicts cost Nigeria $60 million per day, roughly $4.4 billion per annum in damages and lost revenue (www.strategypage.com/qnd/nigeria/20070630.aspx). In May 2007, Nigeria drew down $2.7 billion from its 'domestic excess crude' (a windfall profits account) to plug revenue shortfalls from oil deferment. In the face of descent into further violence, in mid-2006 President Obasanjo ordered the military to adopt a 'force for force' policy in the Delta in a vain effort to gain control of the creeks. In early 2007, the Nigerian navy had embarked upon its biggest sea manoeuvre in two decades deploying 13 warships, four helicopters and four boats to the Bight of Bonny to test 'operational capability'. May 2007, according to a Norwegian consulting company Bergen Risk Solutions (2007), witnessed the largest monthly tally of attacks since the appearance of a shadowy but militarily well-armed insurgent group called the Movement for the Emancipation of the Niger Delta (MEND) in late 2005.

Standing at the heart of these contested communities is the 'restive youth problem'[1] (as it is known in local parlance), a tectonic shift in inter-generational politics in the region that has occurred over the last two to three decades driven by the consequences of structural adjustment and state authoritarianism, and

---

[1]   Youth is a 'complex, fluid and permeable category which is historically and socially situated' (Gore and Pratten 2003:215) shaped, of course, in the Niger Delta by the political economy of oil and the cultural economy of chieftainship and customary rule – themselves shaped by long waves of accumulation extending from slavery through palm oil to the discovery of petroleum and natural gas.

given a huge boost of adrenaline by the return to civilian rule in 1999. Youth as a social category of great historical and cultural depth provides an idiom in a gerontocratic and authoritarian setting in which power, secrecy and sometimes violence can be harnessed as a sort of counter-movement, built on the ruins of failed oil development (Watts 2005). Youth organisations have multiplied and metastasised: they often refigure cultural traditional institutions like *egbesu, agaba* or mutual support clubs.[2] Since the 1980s they have directly attempted to capture organs of community power (for example Community Development Committees), but also to challenge directly gerontocratic rule; not least they have adopted an increasingly militant stance acting as the erstwhile liberators – vanguard movements in effect – for the oppressed of the region. As Gore and Pratten (2003:240) properly put it, youth represent 'shadow structures': covert and secret forms of organisation ... salient to the practices of everyday life. As a basis for access to resources and the distribution of power, these modes of collective youth action are generated at the interesting interfacing of top-down modes of governance and bottom-up responses to disorder ... expressed as counter-movements against marginalisation and coercion.'

The social field of youth violence is as complex as it is variegated, a diversity captured in the breadth of the local lexicon itself (militias, 'area boys', vigilantes, gangs, cults, secret societies) (Ukeje 2004). Many of the youth grievances – poverty, lack of employment, minimal educational opportunities – are felt widely across the region beyond a generation who would identify as militant (Ikelegbe 2006a). A far greater proportion of Deltans perceive economic neglect ('marginalisation' in local parlance) than other regions in the federation and over 50% of all respondents identify governance as the fundamental problem working against their opportunity to benefit from oil (UNDP 2005; Amadi et al 2006). According to a large survey of Niger Delta oil communities by Oyefusi, 5% of the population felt satisfied with the status quo and 36.23% revealed a 'willingness or propensity to take up arms against the state' (2007:16). Sources put the figure of trained militants at over 25,000 strong, commanding monthly salaries of over N50,000 – well above the wage that can be plausibly commanded by an educated youth in the formal sector. It is really an extraordinary train wreck. In some respects, the current crisis confirms Ken Saro-Wiwa's prescient and bleak prediction in 1990 on the 'coming war' in the Delta; 'the people must be allowed to join in the lucrative sale of oil', he said, to avoid 'the cataclysm that is building up' (ICG 2006a: 16). Small arms and light weapons are now 'endemic' in the Delta and the 'pace of acquisition and the lethality of weapons is increasing' (Ginifer and Ismail 2005:2).[3] Chief Philip Asiodu's confident claim two decades ago that the oil-producing communities 'cannot threaten the stability of the country nor affect its continued economic development' (cited in Ukeje 2001:15) now seems naive and delusional. With the emergence of the MEND

---

[2] *Egbesu* refers to a local deity within the 40 or so Ijaw clans associated with warfare but it has, as one might expect (and here a parallel with jihad is instructive), a complex set of shifting meanings (including a sense of personal or interior truth or purity); *agabas* are urban dance societies (Pratten 2006).

[3] For what it is worth, the Centre for Strategic and International Studies in Washington, DC in a briefing in April 2007 refers to a five-fold increase in Kalashnikovs in the past 30 months and the profusion of RPGs, night vision equipment and anti-aircraft missiles; the 'five best armed' militias have 10,000 combatants and 25,000 weapons. The weapons vary from AK47s to M–16s purportedly smuggled from Equatorial Guinea, Gabon and Cameroon but also acquired from Nigerian soldiers (Wellington 2007; Best and Kemedi 2005; Kemedi 2003).

in late 2005, the dynamite had exploded. MEND's spokesperson referred to a 'malignant growth' spreading violently and fast becoming 'Nigeria's Vietnam' (ICG 2006b: 29). How has it come to this? Does it all amount to, as some suggest (Collier 2007), little more than a vast criminal syndicate overlaid with a patina of social justice rhetoric?

Nigeria's perfect storm

The rise of Nigeria as a strategic player in the world of oil geopolitics has been dramatic and has occurred largely in the wake the civil war that ended in 1970. In the late 1950s petroleum products were insignificant, amounting to less than 2% of total exports. Between 1960 and 1973 oil output exploded from just over 5 million barrels to over 600 million barrels. Government oil-revenues in turn accelerated from N66 million in 1970 to over N10 billion in 1980. A multibillion dollar oil sector has, however, proven to be little more than a nightmare. To catalogue the 'achievements' of Nigerian oil development is a salutary exercise: 85% of oil revenues accrue to 1% of the population; perhaps $100 billion of $400 billion in revenues since 1970 have simply gone 'missing'. The anticorruption chief Nuhu Ribadu claimed that, in 2003, 70% of the country's oil wealth was stolen or wasted; by 2005 it was 'only' 40%. Over the period 1965–2004, the per capita income fell from $250 to $212; income distribution deteriorated markedly over the same period. Between 1970 and 2000 the number of people subsisting on less than $1 a day grew from 36% to more than 70%, from 19 million to a staggering 90 million. According to the IMF, oil 'did not seem to add to the standard of living' and 'could have contributed to a decline in the standard of living' (Sala-I-Martin and Subramanian 2003:4). Over the last decade, GDP per capita and life expectancy have, according to the World Bank, both fallen.

Petro-development offers the terrifying and catastrophic failure of secular nationalist development (ICG 2006b; UNDP 2005). It is sometimes hard to grasp the full consequences and depth of such a claim. From the vantage point of the Niger Delta – but no less from the vast slum worlds of Kano or Lagos – development oil wealth is a cruel joke. But the costs of oil are experienced not only in class terms but equally importantly geographically. These paradoxes and contradictions of oil are nowhere greater than in the oilfields of the Niger Delta. In the oil-rich states of Bayelsa and Delta there is only one doctor for every 150,000 inhabitants. Oil has wrought only poverty, state violence and a dying ecosystem (Okonta 2005). By conservative estimates there have been over 6,000 oil spills since 1970 and, according to the World Wildlife Fund report released in 2006, the Delta is one of the most polluted places on the face of the earth. The government's presence, Okonta notes, 'is only felt in the form of the machine gun and jackboots' (2005:206). The recent UNDP report on human development in the Delta was unflinching in its assessment: the 'appalling development situation' reflects the uncontestable and shameful fact that, after a half century of oil development, 'the vast resources from an international industry have barely touched pervasive local poverty' (2005:2, 1). A much publicised Commission of Nobel Laureates on Peace, Equity and Development in the Niger Delta Region concluded that the 'wealth earmarked for the region' was 'largely stolen by politicians'; the frustration and violence, they concluded, was 'rising ... and getting worse' (*Vanguard*, 2 December 2006:1). It is all too easy to be apocalyptic in tone – and to endorse a certain sort of catastrophism that afflicts so much writing about the continent – but if truth be told, Executive Chairman of the Economic and Financial Crime Commission (EFCC), Nuhu Ribadu, was right when he observed that the Niger Delta situation was 'not being taken seriously' and might 'end up like … Somalia' (*This Day*, 11 March 2007).

The heart of the Nigerian petro-state state is unearned income, and its central dynamic is the fiscal sociology of the distribution of and access to oil rents. The oil revenue distribution question – whether in a federal system like Nigeria or in an autocratic monarchy like Saudi Arabia – is an indispensable part of understanding the combustible politics of imperial oil. In Nigeria there are four key distribution mechanisms: the federal account (rents appropriated directly by the federal state); a state derivation principle (the right of each state to a proportion of the taxes that its inhabitants are assumed to have contributed to the federal exchequer); the Federation Account (or States Joint Account) which allocates revenue to the states on the basis of need, population and other criteria; and a Special Grants Account (which includes monies designated directly for the Niger Delta, for example through the allegedly corrupt designated entities such as OMPADEC (Oil Mineral Producing Areas Development Commission), abandoned in 2001, and the Niger Delta Development Commission (NDDC). Over time, the derivation revenues have fallen (and thereby revenues directly controlled by the oil-rich Niger Delta states have shriveled) and the States Joint Account has grown vastly. In short, in the post-1960 period there has been a process of radical fiscal centralism in which the oil-producing states (composed largely of ethnic minorities) have lost and the non-oil-producing ethnic majorities have gained – by fair means or foul. The process has not been linear and since 2001 there has been the beginning of an important reversal in the sense that the oil-producing states have expanded their control (in theory) over national oil income. The history, nevertheless, of post-colonial Nigeria is in a sense the history of the reconfiguration and contestation over revenue allocation.

The shifting politics of fiscal centralisation, and decentralisation, provides the ground for three important aspects of the 'new' Nigerian political economy: first, the decentralisation of corruption (associated with, in the case of the Delta, the vast increase in revenue flows associated with the increase of derivation to 13% after 1999); second, the democratisation of the means of violence (or the extent to which the state monopoly of the violent means of destruction has been undercut by the widespread deployment of arms locally by militia and other militants); and third, the rise (in part associated with changing revenue allocation) of enormous power and wealth at the level of the state governors who become not only counterweights to the federal centre but machine politicians ('Godfathers') in their own right (HRW 2007). This trio of forces frames any discussion of what is called the resource-control debate in the Delta and a political movement with a deep history dating back at least to the issues raised by the Willink Commission on the plight of the ethnic minorities in the Delta during the 1950s. It assumes great visibility as it was propelled by youth and other movements since the 1980s – and indeed captured by many governors from the oil-producing states as a means of providing political pressure on the revenue allocation process. Since Obasanjo's return to power in order to maintain a balancing act – balancing a growing Niger Delta clamour for resource control backed by an insurgency against the array of political forces rooted in the hegemony of powerful northern and southern political interests – the Federal centre has increased derivation to 13%. It drew a line in the sand in its refusal to meet the Delta's demands of 25% derivation or more – an echo of the 50% derivation of the 1960s – during the 2005 National CONFAB and in the struggle over offshore control of oil resources (which, following a Supreme Court decision, affirmed federal control over oil resources in 2002). Nonetheless, it is incontrovertible that as a consequence the oil boom since the late 1990s and the vast windfall oil profits as prices rose to $90 per barrel, has produced a vast influx of monies into the Delta through the state and local government structures. (This is despite the fact that it is perfectly clear the actual disbursement of monies and the flow of oil revenues from Abuja to the oil-producing states is marked by massive malfeasance and diversion.) Currently Rivers and Delta States, for example, receive in excess of $1 billion in federal revenues each year. Since 2004 (until the present), the four largest oil-producing states have received at least $2 billion annually such that, to take one example, in the first six months of 2006 the 23 local governments in Rivers State received more than $115 million in federal allocations (including derivation). There is a sense in which the Delta is awash in oil monies. This is in sharp contrast with, say, the 1980s and it is notwithstanding the fact that nobody believes that the full complement of statutory allocations are received in their entirety by the oil-producing states (HRW 2006).

Overlaid upon the Nigerian petro-state is a volatile mix of forces that give shape to what one can call 'the oil complex'. First, the geo-strategic interest in oil means that military (foreign, local, private and state) and other security forces are part of the local oil complex. Second, local and global civil society enters into the oil complex either through transnational advocacy groups concerned with human rights and the transparency of the entire oil sector, or through local social movements and NGOs fighting over the consequences of the oil industry and the accountability of the petro-state. Third, the transnational oil business – the majors, the independents, the indigenous operators, the national oil companies, and the vast service industry – are actively involved in the process of local development through community development, corporate social responsibility and 'stakeholder inclusion'. Fourth, the inevitable struggle over oil wealth – who controls and owns it, who has rights over it, and how the wealth is to be deployed and used – inserts a panoply of local political forces (ethnic militias, paramilitaries, separatist movements and so on) into the operations of the oil complex (the conditions in Colombia are an exemplary case). Fifth, multilateral development agencies (the IMF and the IBRD) and financial corporations like the export credit agencies appear as key 'brokers' in the construction and expansion of the energy sectors in oil-producing states (and latterly the multilaterals are pressured to become the enforcers of transparency among governments and oil companies). And not least, there is the relationship between oil and the shady world of drugs, illicit wealth (oil theft for example), mercenaries and the black economy.

It would be wrong-headed to see in the Caspian, in Colombia or in the Gulf of Guinea identical oil complexes at work – they differ obviously in their historical, cultural and political specificities. Yet they do all operate as enclaves of economic and political calculation – in essence a form of governmentality or rule – characterised by enormous turbulence and wealth creation. In short, the oil complex looks very much like an embattled zone of the most *primitive accumulation* (Harvey 2005). Empirically, the current operations of the oil complex have been radically shaped by the twin forces of post-9/11 politics, the failure of postwar US oil policy, and the tightness of global oil markets (Barnes 2005). In the face of support by neo-conservative promoters and opportunistic Washington lobbyists, strategists at the Pentagon have invented a new security threat to increase funding for the European Command's (EUCOM's) footprint in Africa (Klare and Volman 2006; Lipschutz et al. 2006). Recently, Deputy Assistant Secretary of Defense for African Affairs Teresa Whelan announced the discovery of a 'new threat paradigm' – the threat of 'ungoverned spaces' in Northwest and West Africa (http://www.jhuapl.edu/POW/rethinking/video.cfm#whelan). In practice, all four of the military services – including an Africa Clearing House on security information, supported by a Pentagon think-tank, the Africa Center for Strategic Studies housed at the National Defense University – are now involved and implicated in the new scramble for the continent. Against a backdrop of spiraling militancy across the Delta, US interests have met up with European strategic concerns in the Gulf in the establishment of the 'Gulf of Guinea Energy Security Strategy' (GGESS). By December 2005, the American Ambassador to Nigeria and the Managing Director of Nigerian National Petroleum Corporation (NNPC) agreed 'to establish four special committees to co-ordinate action against trafficking in small arms in the Niger Delta, bolster maritime and coastal security in the region, promote community development and poverty reduction, and combat money laundering and other financial crimes' (*This Day*, 9 December 2005). US military activity increased from almost no activity in 2004 to '104 ship days' in 2006 (Skorka 2007:9). The establishment of a new African command (AFRICOM) in February 2007, and the appointment of its first head William 'Kip' Ward, are the final capstone in the militarisation of American energy security policy in Africa.

Energy security is a terrifying hybrid, a perplexing 'doubleness', containing the old and the new: primitive accumulation and American militarism coupled to the 'war on terror' (Harvey 2003; RETORT 2005; Barnes 2005). Into this vortex of forces are a set of other global and imperial forces: on the one side, the presence of aggressive Chinese (and other Asian) oil companies – coupled to Asian oil service and construction companies – and the new imperial intentions of the South African energy companies on the other. Put into the mix the resurgence of Islamism in northern Nigeria and across the Sahelian belt, and the political clout of urban evangelical Christianity across the southern oil-producing conurbations and one has the makings of a perfect storm of violence and conflict.

An ungovernable Delta?

It is a measure of a certain sort of notoriety when Nigerian politics reaches the pages of *Vanity Fair*, penned no less by a prize-winning journalist and writer who, to the best of my knowledge, knows nothing of Africa or in this case the Niger Delta (Unger 2007). Sebastian Unger's account of Ijaw militants operating in the oil-rich creeks of the Niger Delta is little more than tabloid journalism, but the realities to which it speaks have been since 2006 an extraordinary combination of the theatrical and the incendiary, worthy perhaps of any tabloid's scrutiny. On 15 September 2005, Diepreye Alamieye-seigha, the Governor of Bayelsa State, a major oil-producing state in the heart of the Ijaw homeland, was arrested by the British security agencies at London airport on three counts of money laundering to the tune of £1.8 million. The Governor's arrest was designed to send a signal to unruly Governors every-where in the run-up to the 2007 elections and Obasanjo's ultimately fruit-less effort to run for a third term. Released on $1.25 million bail in early October, Alamieyeseigha dramatically escaped from house detention in central London (disguised as an old woman) and appeared rather magically in the capital of Bayelsa, Yenagoa, on 20 November to adoring crowds after, as far as we can tell, an extraordinary escape via Paris, Yaounde and finally by small boat along the creeks along the Cameroon-Nigeria border. On 9 December amidst considerable political confusion, he was seized by police in Govern-ment House after the State House of Assembly had voted 17–24 to impeach him – all under the tight security presence of the Joint Task Force and the State Security Services (SSS).

Shortly after the London arrest, on 21 September 2005, against a backdrop of deepening militancy and oil-supply disruption and undemocratic manoeu-vres by President Obasanjo to quite literally purchase the support from the senate for his third-term ambitions, Alhaji Asari-Dokubo, the charismatic and savvy leader of the Niger Delta People's Volunteer Force (NDPVF) – an insurgent militia force fighting, by its own account, for resource control and self-determi-nation in the eastern Delta – was arrested by federal forces on treason charges. Asari, a former Ijaw Youth Congress (IYC) President was arrested by police in the Rivers State's Governor's house in a sting operation and was taken to Abuja in spite of the fact that ostensibly a peace settlement, between some of the Niger Delta militants and government, had been brokered in 2004 by Obasanjo himself. Asari has been held in Abuja in SSS custody and appeared in February 2007 to stand trial amidst claims that his previous unruly behaviour in court justified the decision to hold the proceedings with him *in absentia*. In something of a circus atmosphere, Asari referred to the Judge as 'an idiot' and the 80 secu-rity agents in the courtroom were unclear as to whether and how the accused was to be removed from the courtroom.

Finally, in what proved to be a trifecta of political crises for the Ijaw commu-nity, the Central Bank reported to the Economic and Financial Crimes Commis-sion (EFCC) on 6 October 2005 that the head of Allstate Trust Bank and Ijaw capitalist, Chief Ebimiti Banigo, was guilty of corruption and had failed to meet the capitalisation requirements of $25 billion imposed by the Chairman of the Central Bank. He was subsequently arrested and the bank was, as a conse-quence, closed (amidst the loss of substantial personal savings by many depos-itors in Rivers State). All of these events – in effect the arrest and detention of three major Ijaw notables – were inevitably read as a political attack by Obasanjo's government on a region (the Niger Delta) and people (the Ijaw) that had been at loggerheads with the federal centre, a hostility marked both by the collapse of the national CONFAB in 2005 on the allocation of oil revenues (at which the Delta representatives walked out) and by the rapid descent into violence and political ungovernability across the oilfields after 2002. The stable and regularised flow of oil, as a consequence, was placed in question in an historically unprecedented way.

Out of this vortex of events – one part soap opera, one part machine politics – there emerged in late 2005, in a most dramatic fashion, a hitherto unknown group of masked insurgents (MEND) claiming to be a 'union of all relevant militant groups' (*Daily Champion*, 2 February 2006) and whose public face is a shifting, and sometimes contentious, cadre of leaders (and aliases) including Major-General Godswill Tamuno, Tom Pollo, Oyinye Alaibe, Cynthia White and the eloquent spokesperson Gbomo Jomo. Beginning with a massive attack on the Opobo pipeline in Delta State in December 2005, MEND began calling for the international community to evacuate from the Niger Delta by 12 February, or 'face violent attacks'. In a fantastically audacious series of attacks, MEND struck an oil vessel belonging to TIDEX Nigeria fifteen kilometres offshore on 11 January 2006 and four workers were kidnapped (and reportedly released for a N120 million ransom) shutting in over 100,000 bpd; on 15 January, 13 members of the Joint Task Force were killed during an attack on the Shell Benisede flow station; and in late January an AGIP platform and its riverfront Port Harcourt offices were attacked in which eight policemen were killed. On 18 January an email promised 'our operations will shift from the creeks to the cities' and from 1 February 2006 'more aggressive tactics aimed at oil company workers' (*Nigerian Tribune*, 18 January 2006). Following an earlier ultimatum and a promise to reduce Nigeria's export capacity by 30%, on 15 February MEND declared a 'state of emergency' and the launch of 'Operation Black February' to demonstrate 'its rugged guerrilla wit and dogged intelligence in hunting down every foreign foot' (*Daily Independent*, 15 February 2006). Then, in the wake of a purported peace accord in Yenagoa on 11 February, the Joint Task Force embarked upon a vicious aerial bombardment of Ijaw villages in Okerenkoko territory (ostensibly to bomb oil bunkering barges) which is the heartland of the Gbaramantu clan. In retaliation on 18 February, MEND launched the most audacious and coordinated of its attacks. Forty rebels overpowered guards and military on Willbros barge 318 (nine foreign hostages were taken) and subsequently destroyed the offshore Forcados crude loading platform, the Ekeremore-Yeye manifold and the NNPC Escravos-Lagos gas pipeline in Chanomi Creek. In a single day something like 20% of output was compromised.

The political agenda of MEND was not clear in the weeks of late December 2005 except that it self-identified as a 'guerrilla movement' whose 'decisions like its fighters are fluid'. In fact, in a press release by email – this is the modality of their politically savvy subcommandant Marcos-like exhortations and pronouncements – Jomo claimed that MEND was 'apolitical in structures ... fighters were not communists ... or revolutionaries. [They] are just very bitter men' (Bergen Risks 2007). But in spite of a welter of email denials – calling an Oporoza-based Ijaw militant group the Federated Niger Delta Ijaw Communities (FNDIC) a 'tribal assembly', claiming to have 'co-opted' the NDPVF, rejecting any connection with oil bunkering, claiming not to be 'an Ijaw militia group' (see Sahara Reporters, 2007), – there was in fact a clear political platform. In a signed statement by field commander Tamuno Godswill in early February, MEND's demands were clearly outlined:

- immediate and unconditional release of Alhaji Asari-Dokubo;
- immediate and unconditional release of Governor Alamieyeseigha;
- immediate and unconditional demilitarisation of the Niger Delta;

- immediate payment of $1.5 billion compensation from Shell approved by the Nigerian National Assembly covering four decades of environmental degradation.[4]

In an interview with Karl Maier on 21 February 2006, Jomo made it clear that MEND had 'no intention of breaking up Nigeria' but also had no intention of dealing directly with a government which 'knows nothing about rights or justice'. Resource control meant that the states would 'directly manage' oil. Other communiques reiterated that these demands were not pecuniary and 'we shall receive no money from any quarter' (*Vanguard*, 4 February 2006). Into 2006, MEND's claims that it was capable of delivering a 'crippling blow' to the oil industry were increasingly borne out. More than 15 Nigerian soldiers were killed between May and August 2006, and there were at least three kidnappings per month in the first half of 2006 (typically the hostages are all released following the payment of substantial ransoms by the government, though it is unclear whether these payments are being made to MEND).[5] In the last nine months, the escalation of attacks (44 in 2006, nineteen in the first three months of 2007) including electronically detonated car bombings, brazen attacks on government and military buildings, massive disruption of oil installations deploying sophisticated military equipment, and the audacious kidnapping of workers of virtually every nationality including Chinese and South Korean sometimes from platforms 40–60kms offshore, have confirmed the worst fears of the oil industry. In a deteriorating environment in which many oil companies have withdrawn personnel and cut back production – by mid-2006 there was 500,000–600,000 bpd deferment meeting MEND's earlier goal of a 30% shut-in. Julius Berger, the largest construction company operating in the country, announced its withdrawal from the Niger Delta and many companies began to withdraw personnel as oil workers were increasingly reluctant to be posted in the Delta (many of them were holed up in Lagos hotels). President Obasanjo bolstered the Joint Military Task Force (JMTF) in the Delta but the seeming ease with which MEND can operate – 'we navigate the creeks in pitch blackness' crowed Jomo – and overcome local security forces suggests that the MEND 'freedom fighters' control the creeks uncontested. It is quite unclear, when located on this larger canvas, what Petroleum Minister Edmund Daukoru could possibly have meant when he announced to OPEC in February 2007 in Greece that 'the worst is

---

[4]   Federal High Court sitting in Port Harcourt in February 2006 ordered SPDC to pay $1.5 billion to Ijaw Aborigines of Bayelsa State. Justice Okeke rejected a stay of execution by Shell and ordered the company to pay the Central Bank of Nigeria the full amount no later than 22 May 2006.

[5]   The companies and government have typically denied the payment of ransoms to militants but there have been reports in the press, by activists and others of payments in excess of $250,000. For example, the release of a group of Korean hostages in June 2007, mediated by Asari while still in detention (!), produced a payment of N120 million covered by the company and by Rivers State government (interview with Nigerian mediator, San Francisco, 26 June 2007). On 29 June, a ransom of $102,000 was paid for the release of the three-year-old son of a politician; the Niger Delta Militant Force Squad (NDMFS) demanded $417,000 for six kidnapped Russians. In fact, the decline in oil bunkering since 2004 has seen militias turning to kidnapping and extortion as sources of revenues as bunkering income has fallen. The ransoms are paid from the so-called state 'security' budgets which are vast and largely unaccountable; it is widely reported that government officials cream off a significant proportion (up to 50%) of paid ransoms (Briggs 2007). MEND seems to hold hostages longer than other groups (two Italian hostages were held for 99 days).

over', that 'it is a very, very temporary thing' (UPI, 28 January 2007, http://www.upi.com/Energy/analysis-nigeria-hopeful_for_oil_future).

The rise of MEND – and a number of other 'freedom fighters' who apparently stand in some sort of ambiguous and often awkward relation to MEND, such as the Martyrs Brigade and the Coalition for Military Action in the Niger Delta (COMA) – marks something of a watershed in the turbulent history of the Delta oil fields. Yet it arises on the back of a long arc of deepening violence and protest across the oilfield, especially since the late 1990s. By any estimation, the costs of the oil insurgency – MEND is its most visible and most violent culmination – are vast. A report prepared for the Nigerian National Petroleum Company (NNPC) published in 2003 entitled 'Back from the Brink' – before the latest insurgency took off – painted a very gloomy 'risk audit' for the Delta. The NNPC estimated that between 1998 and 2003, there were 400 'vandalisations' on company facilities each year (and 581 between January and September 2004); oil losses amounted to over $1 billion annually. Already by 2003 oil supply had been compromised by 750,000 bpd as a result of attacks on oil installations across the region. In April 2004, another wave of violence erupted around oil installations (at the end of April, Shell lost production of up to 370,000 bpd, largely in the western Delta), this time amid the presence of armed insurgencies. Two so-called ethnic militias led by Ateke Tom – the Niger Delta Vigilante – (NDV) and Alhaji Asari Dokubo, the Niger Delta People's Volunteer Force (NDPVF), each driven and partly funded by oil monies and actively deployed (and paid) by high ranking politicians as political thugs during elections, have transformed the political landscape of the Delta. In early 2006 MEND claimed a goal of cutting Nigerian output by 30% and they apparently succeeded. Within the first six months of 2006, there were 19 attacks on foreign oil operations and over $2.18 billion lost in oil revenues; the Department of Petroleum Resources claims this figure represents 32% of the revenue the country generated this year. The Nigerian government claims that between 1999 and 2005 oil losses amounted to $6.8 billion but in November 2006 the managing director of Shell Nigeria reported that the loss of revenues due to 'unrest and violence' was $61 million per day (a shut-in of about 800,000 bpd), amounting to a staggering $9 billion since January 2006. By the end of 2006, Minister for Petroleum Resources Edmund Daukoru claimed that the costs of the insurgency were N7.5 billion per day. Against a backdrop of escalating attacks on oil facilities and a proliferation of kidnappings (Figure 1), the Joint Revolutionary Council (apparently an umbrella group for insurgents) threatened 'black November' as an 'all out attack on oil operating companies' (*The Observer*, 5 November 2006); a similar call was made in February 2007. The elections of April 2007 – even more fraudulent than the widely condemned elections of 2003 – and the emergence of an Ijaw politician, Goodluck Jonathan, Governor of Bayelsa State, as the Vice-President elect have done nothing to dampen the ire of the militants. Between May and June 2007, 42 foreign workers were kidnapped and four pipelines detonated (http://www.alertnet.org/thenews/newsdesk/L20301606.htm, 20 May 2007).

Oil insurgency as organised crime?

There has been a raft of new books on African oil in the past year (Ghazvinian 2007; Shaxson 2007; Forest and Sousa 2006). Written for the most part by journalists (and in one case by two military men), the books are replete with colourful stories – of the devastating intersection of frontier capitalism and the worst of African kelptocracies – neatly captured by such titles as 'instant emirates', 'the Chinese are coming', 'wielding the oil weapon' in 'some of the most dangerous and dysfunctional nations on the planet'. None of this work would have been possible without 20 or so years of critical academic research and excellent investigative work by the likes of HRW, Amnesty, Global Witness and Oxfam. Whatever one thinks of the 'resource curse' literature (Auty 1999; Ross 1999) – and I think it comes close to a sort of commodity determinism – this body of work exposed the pathologies of petro-states, the complex complicities between 'Big Oil' and African 'oiligarchies', and the disastrous consequences – environmental, political and economic – of rentier political economies driven by a logic of politicised distribution of oil revenues rather than systematic accumulation, disciplined development or the construction of transparent and accountable institutions of governance. Over the decade, the 'resource curse' which, for the most part, examined the political economy of oil dependency, was taken up by economists – some concerned with the relations between resource-dependency and poor economic performance and more recently with the politics of oil – not so much at the level of corruption or fiscal mismanagement but rather sub-national conflicts and the relations between oil and civil war and rebellion. The largest and most ambitious programme emerged from the World Bank and the leadership of Paul Collier. His book *The Bottom Billion* (2007) turns resource dependency into a field theory of poverty. Oil-dependency in this analysis turns on the relation between petroleum (not so much gas) and the means by which rebellions and insurgencies are economically sustained and financed – and by extension the devastating costs for development of long and protracted conflicts (Collier et al. 2003).

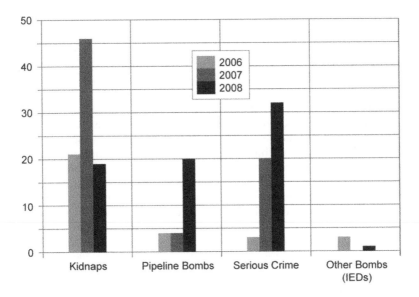

Figure 1 Oil Disruptions in the Niger Delta

This complex and variegated body of work might be dubbed the predation- or rebellion-as-organised crime theory of oil. Collier focuses on the important question of financing violence politics and offers an argument that oil provides a ground on which rebels can finance rebellions (through looting of oil resources) which are self-interested and criminal movements against the state. Collier and the economics-of-war position ('rebellion is large-scale predation of productive activities') draws upon a related and now large body of work that explores the character of oil as a source of predation by focusing on its *point* (as opposed to *diffuse*) character and its location (in relation to state power) and the ease with which it can be looted. Different political outcomes can then be deduced from specific resource couplets (Le Billon 2005): warlordism (distant/diffuse), mass rebellion (proximate/diffuse), coups (proximate/point) and secession (distant/point). Oil is characterised by the latter two (it is a point resource that varies along the axis of its location with respect to power) for which Angola and Chechnya, and Colombia and Yemen are paradigmatic cases. Relatedly, Michael Ross explores the dynamics of oil politics along two parallel axes: *lootability* (understood to be 'easily appropriated [resource] by individuals or small groups of unskilled workers' (2003: 47) and *obstructability* (that is to say the ease with which its movement or its productive networks can be interrupted or blocked). Oil (onshore and offshore) is unlootable; it is, however, readily obstructable (pipelines can be detonated, flow stations closed) onshore but not offshore. He holds open the possibility that oil (as an unlootable resource) may yield different types of outcomes (separatist in Cabinda, and non-separatist in Sudan), but believes that non-lootability yields general associations; to wit: unlootability is likely to yield separatism (control the territory, not the wealth), benefits to government (rather than the poor), reduced duration of conflicts, and enhanced army discipline.

Much could be said about Collier's work in particular: its deep cynicism ('rebellion ... is like organised crime'); its belief that motivation of conflict is unimportant (what matters is whether the organisation can sustain itself financially); its assumption that history can be reduced to rates of economic growth or the existence of prior civil conflict; its deep problems associated with the nature of the data and evidence (and sampling), and its claim that insurgent predation is 'worse' than state extortion (or exaction) and so on.[6] I simply wish to focus on its foundational claims as a way of grasping the genesis of an oil insurgency across the Niger Delta: namely, that greed is opposed to grievance, that peaceful protest stands in opposition to rebellion, that government opposes rebellion, and that rebellion equals organised crime.[7] From these assumptions Collier concluded in 2003 that the Delta resembles an 'American gangland' involving a ferocious struggle over drugs; by 2007 it was a vast protection racket run by young, unemployed and poorly educated criminals for whom life is cheap.

The first thing that needs to be said is that the very idea of an impermeable membrane separating or opposing two discrete entities – government and rebels

---

[6]   Parenthetically, this approach is related to Michael Ross' (1999) claim about another aspect of oil-politics, namely that it hinders democracy through rents (no taxation=no representation), militarisation (oil-funded securitisation), and service employment (as a way of purchasing ideological consent).

[7]   From this fact it is claimed that rebels cannot loot oil and must turn to extortion and through this extortion it is the figure of the warlord ('the rebel leader') who appears as the new predator associated with the notion of the 'end of politics' in the post-Cold War era.

– breaks down immediately. The so-called ethnic militias (the NDV and the NDPDF), for example, got their start by being supported (financially and with arms) by politicians in the oil-producing states; the decentralisation of corruption, the rise of powerful gubernatorial machine politicians, and the 'democratisation of violence' that mark post-1999 Nigeria all signal how porous is the state/rebel divide. The NDV and the NDPVF were deployed as political thugs to deliver votes and intimidate voters in the notoriously corrupt and violent 2003 elections (although they were also operative in 1999). Furthermore, a number of the arms used by the militias have been acquired from the Nigerian military (directly in relationship to electoral political thuggery and indirectly from a notoriously corrupt and undisciplined army). And last but not least, the low-level oil theft (bunkering) that is controlled by the rebels as a way of financing their struggle, is organised through a vast state-centred syndicate linking high-ranking military, politicians, the security apparatuses and the Niger Delta special military task forces, and the coast guard. The Nigerian state in its various expressions and the rebels are both oppositional *and* organically self-sustaining. The head of the Economic and Financial Crimes Commission (EFCC), Nuhu Ribadu, put the issue with great precision: the state is 'not even corruption. It is organised crime' (*The Economist*, 28 April 2007, p.56). In the same way, Collier's (and Ross's) claim that oil cannot be looted stands in sharp contrast to the existence of a vast oil theft industry. This is not the place to detail the dynamics of its structure (from low-level bunkering territories policed by differing sorts of political actors up to the syndicates – global in scope – that orchestrate a vast criminal industry). My point is that oil is looted and very effectively – at its peak in 2004/5 some 350,000 bpd were stolen perhaps inserting $4–5 billion per year into the system – and while the criminal proceeds are unevenly distributed along the commodity chain, the fact is that both rebels and states (the political classes) benefit from it. There is no question that the oil bunkering trade embraces all manner of agents motivated by all manner of desires (greed, grievance, employment, excitement) but there is no reason in principle why organised crime – but not simply extortion and sabotage as the 'obstructability' thesis claims – and grievance cannot co-exist perfectly well. Equally, there is a long history of oil theft in the Delta with no evidence to suggest that there has been, as Collier suggests, a simple shift from grievance to greed (2007:31).

Many of these Delta realities represent an empirical challenge to conceptual claims about lootability. If indeed one were to consider oil in Nigeria unlootable, it is not at all clear that it has contributed to army discipline (arguably one of the most corrupt and undisciplined in the world); it may have contributed to separatism (the Biafran war) but it is equally associated with other non-separatist politics, and it is not at all clear that it has reduced the duration of conflicts in any simple way. But the reality is that oil has been looted through theft of various sorts – organised and unorganised (hot tapping of pipelines by the poor). This structure of 'predation' has benefited a section of the military-political class, sustained all manner of insurgents (and indirectly sections of the unemployed youth), further contributed to corruption and indiscipline within the military and contributed to a vast and complex field of violence encompassing well-organised insurgents confronting the state, ethnic militias, vigilante groups resembling the mafia, anti-chieftainship conflicts, inter-ethnic struggles, and criminal activities (sometimes called 'cultism'). Needless to say the very idea (taken from Ross) that offshore oil cannot be obstructed has been shown to be spectacularly wrong: MEND has taken hostages on a platform 30 miles offshore and MEND's charismatic PR man, Gbomo Jomo, refers to MEND's abode as '200 miles offshore'.

The most striking aspect of these articulations of oil politics and civil conflict is that the agency of the oil companies – whether the national oil companies (NOCs) or the supermajors (IOCs) with whom they operate or the oil service/construction companies – has no analytical presence in the models of rebellion or civil war. At most they appear as the unfortunate corporate entities that are predated by rebels (extortion, sabotage, and kidnapping). Corporate practice and agency are conspicuously absent in any account of politics, which is astonishing because the companies themselves have acknowledged that they are a central part of the political dynamics of community conflict (most obviously in the internal reports by Shell and Chevron widely leaked in 2003 and 2004; see WAC Global Services 2003). This is not to suggest that corporations have deliberately instigated or encouraged rebellion. Rather, what passes as community development in the Delta and their related interaction with what are called 'host communities' are a central part of conflict dynamics. It is estimated that Shell spends $60 million per year on community development, yet cash payments amount to at least double that figure. In total these payments amount to perhaps $200 million per annum, perhaps 10% of the operating budget; some companies spend up to 15–17% on such activities. They represent in practice a massive infusion of cash designed to purchase consent or compliance – but in practice they help generate rebellion and community violence. One the one hand, the companies are constitutionally obliged to pay rents to local communities in which they have operations and have typically cut deals with local chiefs (many of whom operate as unaccountable fiefdoms). Community projects and 'Memoranda of Understanding' (to the extent that they exist at all) are shrouded in secrecy and ambiguity, and corporate responsibility on the ground often appears as a raft of unfinished community projects all of which have contributed to festering resentments among the youth. And the policy of 'cash payments' – used to pay for protection services from local unemployed youth to buy off local opposition and to feed vast networks of illicit payments – has had the effect of generating enormously violent conflicts among youth groups who compete to provide protection services for the company, or who attack corrupt local chiefs (that is to say, they upend the system of gerontocratic customary rule at the village level) in order to gain access to the company rents and payments that flow from oil operations in their territories (Kemedi 2003; Watts 2005).

Brief (and incomplete) history of an oil insurgency

How, then, is it possible to grasp the transformation of the Niger Delta into a space of insurgency, and why is its characterisation as a space of organised crime inadequate? I want to identify a number of key processes generated from within the heart of the oil complex. Each is an expression of a long and deeper geography of exclusion and marginalisation by which the oil-producing Delta came to suffer all of the social and environmental harms of the oil industry and yet receive in return very little of the oil revenues. At the point at which the oil revenues begin to belatedly flow (after 1999), the kleptocratic and venal system of state politics has stolen and squandered what many in the Delta felt to be their rightful heritage. It is from the geo-political contradiction of oil without and with wealth – a bequest of the oil complex – that the insurgency has drawn enormous sustenance.

What were the forces that emerged from this geo-political contradiction? The first, not surprisingly in a region of 60 or more ethnic groups and a powerful set of institutions of customary rule, was ethno-nationalism. This was central, of course, to the Ogoni movement but the banner has been taken up in the last decade or so by the Ijaw, the largest ethnic (or so-called 'oil') minorities in the Delta (the Ijaw are the fourth largest ethnic group occupying the riverine flanks of the Delta and constitute political minorities in five of the six Deltaic states). Their exclusion from the oil wealth (and the federal revenue allocation process), to say nothing of bearing the costs of oil operations across the oilfields, became central to the emergence of a new sort of youth politics. The establishment of the Ijaw Youth Council (IYC) in 1998 marked a watershed in this regard (though the mobilisation began much earlier and gained strength in the late 1980s and early 1990s), and it became the vehicle through which a new generation of youth leaders took up the struggle; many were mobilised in and around youth movements. They came to assume local positions of power, including a number who took up an explicitly militant anti-state insurgent stance, and these struggles, over tactics, played themselves out in the sometimes internecine struggles with ethnically-based youth movements like the IYC. In the wake of the hanging of Ken Saro-Wiwa, Gandhian tactics were, in some quarters, seen to have failed catastrophically.

The second force was the inability and unwillingness of the Nigerian state in its military and civilian guises to address this political mobilisation in the Delta without resorting to state-imposed violence by undisciplined military, police and security forces. In this sense the history of the Ogoni struggle was a watershed too, insofar as it bequeathed a generation of militants for whom MOSOP represented a failure of non-violent politics. The return to civilian rule in 1999 saw a further militarisation of the region in which communities were violated and experienced the undisciplined violence of state security forces. The appalling destruction of Odi (1999) and Odiama (2001) by military forces, and the violence meted out by the Joint Military Task Force based in Warri were the most dramatic instances of state intimidation. This unrelenting militarisation of the region to secure 'national oil assets' further propelled the frustrations of a generation of youth who, in the period since the 1980s, had grown in their organisational capacities.

Third, the militant groups themselves represented the intersection of two important forces. On the one hand, the rise of youth politics in which a younger generation whose economic and political prospects were stymied began to challenge both customary forms of chiefly power, and the corruption of the petro-state (whether military or civilian). These twin processes have a long history dating back at least to the famous Twelve Day Republic in which in 1966 a group of young Ijaw men led by Isaac Adaka Boro proclaimed, against a backdrop of expanding oil output, an independent Ijaw state. But the political mobilisation of the youth turned from a sort of peaceful civic nationalism increasingly toward militancy, and this in turn was driven by the violence of the Nigerian military forces but also by the politicians, especially the increasingly powerful governors, who sought to make use of the youth movements for their own electoral purposes (that is to say, political thugs to intimidate voters). Paradoxically a number of the militias often got their start by being bankrolled by the state and politicians, and indeed the NDF and NPDVF were both fuelled by machine politicians during the notoriously corrupt 1999 and 2003 elections.

Fourth, the existence and proliferation of oil theft, known locally as 'oil bunkering' (Figure 2), provided a financial mechanism through which militants could (after being abandoned by their political patrons) finance their operations and attract recruits. The organisation of the oil theft trade, which by 2004 was a multi-billion dollar industry involving high-ranking military, government officials and merchants, drew upon the local militia to organise and protect the tapping of pipelines and the movement of barges through the creeks and ultimately offshore to large tankers. This is, on its face, a case of the sort of organised crime that Collier invokes in his account of the economics of rebellion – and indeed there are explicitly criminal elements and syndicates at work in the operations of a vast bunkering business in Nigeria – yet the theft of oil provided a lubricant for a ready existing set of grievances. Rebel organisations and insurgents were, in this sense, not merely criminal gangs.

And finally, the operations of the oil companies (Omeje 2006; Zalik 2004) – in their funding of youth groups as security forces, in their willingness to use military and security forces against protesters and militants alike, and in their corrupt practices of distributing rents to local community elites – all contributed to an environment in which military activity was in effect encouraged and facilitated. A number of companies used organised (and armed) youth groups to protect their facilities (see WAC Global Services 2003). Corporate practice, and community development in particular, had the net effect of inserting millions of dollars of so-called 'cash payments' into the local economy by paying corrupt

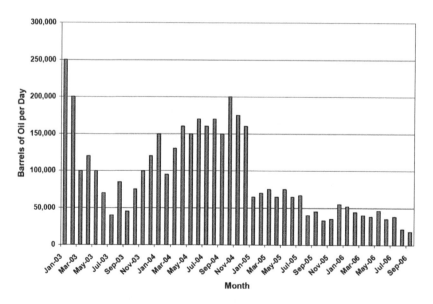

Figure 2   Oil Theft in Nigeria, 2003–2006

chiefs, violent youth groups or corrupt local officials in the hope that the oil would keep flowing. In practice, the uneven record of community development projects and the corrupt forms in which cash payments were made, produced a growing hostility (expressed in the growth of oil platform occupations, attacks on pipelines, and more recently hostage taking) to the companies. Directly and indirectly corporate practice was essential to the dynamics of local violence and the escalation of insurgent activity.

The emergence of MEND in 2005 represents the almost inevitable end-point of a process of marginalisation, alienation and political mobilisation that reached a watershed moment with the 1998 Kaiama declaration. The declaration carried more than a faint echo of Boro's 12 Day Revolution launched in 1966 in which he reminded his followers, like the IYC leadership, to 'remember too your petroleum which is being pumped out daily from your veins and then fight for your freedom' (Boro 1982:117). Boro's much vaunted 'Ijaw Republic' lasted less than two weeks, ending with his arrest by Federal troops in Oloibiri – ironically the site of the first discovery and commercial exploitation of oil in Nigeria – and his untimely death fighting for Federal forces against Biafra. Kaiama was more than the foundation stone of the IYC: it marked a massive cross-Delta (and cross-ethnic) mobilisation through mobile parliaments and an explicit recognition to diversify the tactics associated with the struggle. The question of militancy was always an object of debate within the IYC – and indeed preceded IYC, since the so-called 'first Egbesu war' in which Bayelsa youth took on security forces occurred in the late Abacha years – particularly in the face of state brutality and especially the slaughter perpetrated by Federal troops in Odi. The 'second' Egbesu war emerged from the deliberate attempts of the state – then under General Abubakar who had succeeded Abacha in 1999 – to suppress the political project expressed at Kaiama (Ibeanu and Luckham 2007). Militants in turn, as they had in the first war, occupied flow stations and provided protection for oil companies, the proceeds of which were invested in arms. While Asari Dokubo's rise to the Presidency of the IYC was much more than the victory of IYC militants – it was very much wrapped up with efforts by the Governor of Rivers to control a powerful new political force – the reality is that his ascendancy was symptomatic of a movement – he founded the NDPDF in 2003 – that saw not just occupations and seizures of oil installations as necessary but armed struggle against the state and the companies as the only response to continued state violence and corporate irresponsibility.

The rise of various militias funded as political thugs during the 2003 elections is a very complex story that by 2004 had produced a situation in which Asari's group was at war with Ateke Tom's Niger Delta Vigilante (NDV). These struggles were in part over oil bunkering territory but drew upon many disaffected youth groups in such places as Okrika, Eleme, and Nembe in a shifting set of alliances in which the borders between criminality, mafia-like vigilante groups, and politically organised insurgents were difficult to discern. The Asari and Ateke stories were very much involved with the politics and struggles in eastern Ijaw, and along the Cawthorne channel.

The emergence of MEND shifted the struggle dramatically to the western Delta – the so-called Warri axis. Here a similar set of grievances and struggles were playing out, wrapped up with the complex ethnic politics of Warri city, the failures of the companies to provide meaningful benefits to host communities, and the militancy of women most famously against Chevron in Ugborodu in

2003. As Ukiwo (2007) has shown, Ijaw marginalisation stemmed from a long history of struggle over trade during the nineteenth century in which the Itsekeri peoples emerged as a comprador class to the European trading houses (and thereby cutting off the Ijaw). The Western Ijaw built up a reputation as 'truculent' and 'pirates' and reactively resisted colonial rule until the 1920s when they were incorporated into a Western Ijaw Division cut out of the Warri Division. By the 1940s the Gbaramantu Clan – which is central to MEND's political dynamics – was involved directly in claims over land (with the Itsekeri) and by the 1970s (in the wake of the establishment of oil operations by Chevron and Shell in the mid-1960s), violent conflicts had occurred over the oil-bearing lands near Ugborodo. It was from this axis that MEND dramatically emerged in late 2005. MEND has grown from an earlier history of increasingly militant youth embracing, for example, the 'Egbesu Boys of Africa', the 'Meinbutu Boys' and others (Feibagha Ogbo, Dolphin Obo, Torudigha Ogbo) in the Warri region dating back to the early 1990s and before (Courson 2007).

MEND cannot be understood outside of the operation of the quartet of forces that I have briefly outlined, and yet at the same time is inextricably linked to local politics: struggles among and between two key Ijaw clans (Gbaramantu and Egbema) over access to oil monies, struggles with Chevron over the lack of a 'Memorandum of Understanding' for so-called 'host communities' in the clan territory, control of oil bunkering territories, and not least the complex politics of Warri city, the large oil town to the north. Here is a multi-ethnic city that has imploded since 1997 as warring ethnic groups (fuelled by machine politics) have fought for the establishment of new local government authorities as a basis for laying claim to federal oil monies (HRW 1999; 2005). Into this mix was the catalytic effect of the Nigerian special military task force ('Operation Hope') that came to quell the growing militancy across the region in which the Gbaramantu clan territory was repeatedly attacked and bombed (Courson 2007).

The appearance of MEND marked a new phase both in terms of strategic capacity but also in the franchise character of the insurgency, linking to and speaking for a number of militias and rebels. Whether it is, as Okonta (2006) suggests, not an organisation but 'an idea' is difficult to assess. Certainly the MEND militias operate with ease in and around Warri; the leadership appears, as Okonta says, articulate and politically very savvy. But MEND emerged, and is inseparable, from a number of local and regional issues – the most important of which are the longstanding antagonisms between the oil companies (especially Chevron) in the Gbaramantu and Egbema clan territories and the crisis and struggle over the creation of local government councils in Warri (itself a long festering inter-ethnic struggle) that broke open in 1997. MEND has of course been framed by a wider and pan-ethnic struggle for resource control and at the same time detonated, so to speak, by what Ijaw see as a deepening assault on their aspirations – what Oboko Bello calls 'being cut off from being a nation' – under President Obasanjo. The extraordinarily violent gunship and helicopter attacks on Okerenkoko in February 2006 and the attacks by the Joint Task Force on MEND in the wake of a truce brokered between MEND and the government in August of the same year, were consistent with a much longer history of state violence across the Warri axis. In this sense, Okonta is surely right to say that MEND is 'the violent child of the deliberate and long-running constriction of the public space in the Niger Delta ... Behind the mask of MEND is a political subject forced to pick up a KA47 to restore his rights' (2006:20).

The insurgency across the Niger Delta involves a welter of differing groups and often shadowy interests (Peterside 2007). By 2007 the reality on the ground is a dizzying and bewildering array of militant groups, militias and so-called 'cults' – the Niger Delta Militant Force Squad (NDMFS), Niger Delta Coastal Guerillas (NDCG), South-South Liberation Movement (SSLM), Movement for the Sovereign State of the Niger Delta (MSSND), the Meinbutus, the November 1895 Movement, ELIMOTU, the Arogbo Freedom Fighters, Iduwini Volunteer Force (IVF), the Niger Delta People's Salvation Front (NDPSF), the Coalition for Militant Action (COMA), the Greenlanders, Deebam, Bush Boys, KKK, Black Braziers, Icelanders and a raft of other so-called cults. At present, according to some sources, there are over 50 operating military camps in the creeks (*This Day*, 23 March 2007). With good reason MEND spokesperson Jomo could boast in March 2007 that he has 'the oil industry by the balls' (*The Economist*, 17 March 2007: 52).

This profusion is inextricably wrapped up with the intersection of generational politics, a corrupt and violent petro-state, irresponsible and shortsighted oil company practice, and the existence of a vast oil bunkering network. As Kalyvas (2001:113) suggests, viewed from the micro-level these sorts of insurgencies – an oil insurgency in this case – resemble 'welters of complex struggles' in which the notion that the rebels are criminals who operate against law-abiding states fails to capture the dynamics at work. Group interests are often 'localistic and region-specific' (*Ibid.*:112), yet, as I have tried to argue, their specificity emerges from the structured totality of the national and regional oil complex. It all makes for an enormously unstable and volatile mix of political, economic, and social forces, now located on a larger, and more intimidating, canvas of global oil instability and the 'global war on terror'.

A new dispensation?

And what of the future? The April 2007 elections were widely held to involve massive electoral fraud and ballot rigging – almost certainly worse than in the notorious 2003 electoral process. As a friend in Port Harcourt put it recently, 2003 was 'child's play' compared to 2007. Nowhere were the fraud and intimidation more pronounced than in the Delta. Nonetheless, the elections produced an Ijaw Vice-President, Goodluck Jonathan, from Bayelsa State, with strong connections to a younger generation of activists and civic groups. This is potentially a step forward. Yar'Adua, the new Nigerian President, is a machine politician from an influential Katsina political family in northern Nigeria; but he has clearly put some stock in his Delta running mate's capacity to address the insurgency. Whether the President can sell the northern powerbrokers on increased 'derivation', that is, allocating additional oil revenues to states of origin in order to appease the angry citizens of the Delta, is another matter. There are some positive signs: talk of a Niger Delta summit, the release from detention on 14 June of Asari Dokubo, and the 27 July freeing of Chief Alamieyeseigha met key demands of many of the militants. Despite their dubious political records, both are held in esteem in some quarters of the Ijaw community as freedom fighters. The possibility of a Marshall Plan for the Delta, first voiced in March 2007 by President Olusegun Obasanjo, Yar Adua's predecessor, as the 'Niger Delta Master Plan', can also be read as a measure of the centrality of the Niger Delta in current Nigerian politics. However, the sordid history of large state interventions in the Delta, with their heavy focus on force and repression, would hardly lead one to be optimistic about the consequences of pouring vast petro dollars into special development agencies. A one-month truce was declared by MEND and the Joint Revolutionary Council, a group that purportedly speaks for all militant groups, on 15 June. Within days, however, there were a number of occupations of flow stations and a spike in hostage taking. In the last two months, the Soku-Buguma pipeline alone has been attacked on 16 occasions.

That said, the presence of Goodluck at the centre of power in Abuja, together with the depth of the crisis, has pushed the new government into negotiations with the insurgents – that is to say, groups who have a political project, often embracing a panoply of local, regional and national grievances. These in turn have persuaded a number of key actors to come together under the umbrella of MEND. The Grand Commander of MEND, Tompolo, garners enormous respect and authority across the creeks and across virtually all of the militant organisations and networks. Several all-night meetings were held in July and August 2007 in the creeks. Senator David Brigidi and other representatives of the oil states' Peace and Rehabilitation Committees were present; the Vice-President himself met with a number of key actors in the Warri creeks in June. While the government has in principle agreed to the insurgents' preconditions for negotiations – including not only the release of Alamieyeseigha, but also the rebuilding of Odi and Odiama, two towns destroyed by federal forces, as well as the demilitarisation of the Delta on the part of federal forces – one has to say that the prospects for some sort of resolution remain unclear at best. In the last few weeks, we have witnessed the spectacle of the Rivers State Peace and Rehabilitation Committee doling out one million Naira to anyone who professes to be a 'cultist', a term which covers a multitude of sins but implies gang membership, and rejects the life of the 'cultism'. Gang leaders and thugs were subsequently reported in the local press as parading in the Government House chapel clutching bibles and preaching redemption. The gravity and depth of their new-found religiosity is a rather large question.

The descent of the region into its current state of violence, and pent-up political rage in the region, mean that radical changes will be required if there is to be lasting peace. Some of these, such as large-scale training programmes and mass employment schemes, major infrastructure projects, and environmental rehabilitation, will take many years, perhaps even generations. To confront resource control – not as a matter of money or percentage of revenues but as a legal and political project – will require a radical rethinking, and perhaps a restructuring, of both the constitution and institutions of governance. This effort will, of course, need to address questions like corruption, the reform of the electoral commission, and transparency within a notoriously ineffective and pathologically unaccountable system of local government, which in the oil-producing states is awash with federally allocated monies.

References

Amadi, Stella, Mekkonen Germiso and Asle Henriksen. 2006. STATOIL in Nigeria: Transparency and Local Content. NORAD: Oslo.
Anderson, Perry. 2001. Scurrying Toward Bethlehem. *New Left Review* 10: 5–31.

Auty, Richard. 1999. *Patterns of Development*. London: Hodder.

Barnes, Sandra. 2005. Global Flows: Terror, Oil, and Strategic Philanthropy. *African Studies Review* 48 (1):1–22.

Bergen Risk Solutions. 2007. Security in the Delta. Eds. Arild Nodland and Odin Hjellstad. Bergen: BRS.

Best, Shedrack and Dimieari Kemedi. 2005. Armed Groups and Conflict in Rivers and Plateau States Nigeria. In *Armed and Aimless*, eds. N. Florquin and E. Berman. Geneva: Small Arms Survey.

Boro, Isaac. 1982. *The Twelve Day Revolution*. Benin: Idodo Umeh Publishers.

Briggs, James. 2007. Guide to Armed Groups in the Niger Delta. *Terrorism Monitor* V7: 1–4.

Centre for Strategic and International Studies (CSIS). 2007. Briefing on the Niger Delta. Washington, DC: Centre for Strategic and International Studies, 14 March.

Collier, Paul. 2007. *The Bottom Billion*, Oxford: Oxford University Press.

Collier, Paul, V.L. Elliott, Håvard Hegre, Anke Hoeffler, Marta Reynal-Queral and Nicolas Sambanis. 2003. *Breaking the Conflict Trap*. Oxford: Oxford University Press.

Collier, Paul, Anke Hoeffler and Dominic Rohner. 2006. *Beyond Greed and Grievance*. Centre for the Study of African Economies, Oxford University.

Collier, Paul and Nicholas Sambanis. 2005. *Understanding Civil War*, Vol. 1. Washington, DC: World Bank.

Courson, Elias. 2007. *The Burden of Oil*. Working Paper 15. Niger Delta Economies of Violence Project. University of California, Berkeley. (http://globetrotter.berkeley.edu/ NigerDelta/).

Forest, James and Matthew Sousa. 2006. *Oil and Terrorism in the New Gulf: Framing U.S. Energy and Security Policies for the Gulf of Guinea*. Lanham, MD: Lexington Books.

Frynas, George and Manuel Paulo. 2007. A New Scramble for African Oil?: Historical, Political and Business Perspectives. *African Affairs*, 106 (423): 329–51.

Ghazvinian, John. 2007. *Untapped: The Scramble for African Oil*. New York: Harcourt.

Ginifer, Jeremy and Olawale Ismail. 2005. *Armed Violence and Poverty in Nigeria*. Working Paper, Centre for International Cooperation and Security, University of Bradford, UK.

Gore, Charles and David Pratten. 2003. The politics of plunder. *African Affairs* 102 (407): 211–240.

Harvey, David. 2005. *A Brief Introduction to Neoliberalism*, Oxford: Oxford University Press.

———— 2003. *The New Imperialism*. Oxford: Clarendon Press.

Human Rights Watch. 2007. *Criminal Politics. Violence, 'Godfathers' and Corruption in Nigeria*. New York, HRW.

———— 2006. *'They do not Own this Place': Government Discrimination Against "Non-Indigenes" in Nigeria*. New York: HRW.

———— 2005. *Rivers and Blood*. New York: HRW.

———— 1999. *The Price of Oil*. New York: HRW.

Ibeanu, Okey and Robin Luckham. 2007. Nigeria: Political Violence, Governance and Corporate Responsibility in a Petro-State. In *Oil Wars: How Wars over Oil further Destabilise Faltering Regimes*, eds. M. Kaldor, T.L. Karl and Y. Said. London: Pluto Press.

Ikelegbe, Augustine. 2006a. Beyond the Threshold of Civil Struggle. *African Study Monographs*, Centre for African Studies. Kyoto: Kyoto University 27(3): 87–122.

———— 2006b. The Economics of Conflict in Oil Rich Niger Delta Region of Nigeria. *African and Asian Studies* 5(1): 23–55.

International Crisis Group (ICG). 2006a, *Fuelling the Crisis*. International Crisis Group, Working Paper. Brussels/Dakar.

———— 2006b. *Swamps of Insurgency*. International Crisis Group, Working Paper, Brussels/Dakar.

Kalyvas, Stathis. 2001. New and Old Civil Wars: A Valid Distinction?. *World Politics* 54(1): 99–118.

Kemedi, Dimieari. 2006. Fuelling the Violence. Working Paper 10, Niger Delta Economies of Violence Project, University of California, Berkeley; http://globetrotter. berkeley.edu/NigerDelta/.

———— 2003. The Changing Predatory Styles of International Oil Companies in Nigeria. *Review of African Political Economy*. 30(95): 134–9.

Klare, Michael and Daniel Volman. 2006. The African 'Oil Rush' and US National Security. *Third World Quarterly*. 27(4): 609–28.

Le Billon, Phillippe. 2005. *Fuelling War*. Adelphi Paper 5, London: Routledge.

Lipschutz, Ronnie, Paul Lubeck and Michael Watts. 2006. Convergent Interests. Briefing Document. Washington, DC. Centre for International Policy.

Nobel Report. 2007. Commission of Nobel Laureates on Peace, Equity and Development in the Niger Delta Region of Nigeria 2007. The Elie Wiesel Foundation for Humanity, New York.

Okonta, Ike. 2005. Nigeria: Chronicle of a Dying State. *Current History*. May, 203–8.

———— 2006. *Behind the Mask*. Working Paper 11. Niger Delta Economies of Violence Project,

Berkeley: University of California (http://globetrotter.berkeley.edu/NigerDelta/).

Omeje, Kenneth. 2006. *High Stakes and Stakeholders: Oil Conflict in Nigeria.* Aldershot: Ashgate.

Oyefusi, Aderoju. 2007. *Oil and the Propensity for Armed Struggle in the Niger Delta Region of Nigeria.* Post Conflict Transition Papers No. 8 (WPS4194), Washington, DC: World Bank.

Peterside, Sofiri. 2007. *Rivers State: Explaining the Phenomena of Ethnic Militias.* Port Harcourt: Centre for Advanced Social Science.

Pratten, David. 2006. The Politics of Vigilance in Southeast Nigeria. *Development and Change* 37(4): 707–734.

RETORT. 2005. *Afflicted Powers: Capital and Spectacle in a New Age of War.* London: Verso.

Ross, Michael. 2004. How do Natural Resources Influence Civil Wars: Evidence from Thirteen Cases. *International Organization* 58(1): 35–67.

———— 2003. Oil, Drugs and Diamonds. In *The Political Economy of Armed Conflict: Beyond Greed and Grievance.* Karen Ballentine and Jack Sherman eds. Boulder, CO: Lynne Rienner.

———— 1999. Does Oil Hinder Democracy? *World Politics* 53(3): 325–361.

Sahara Reporters. 2007. Why the Niger Delta Peace Talks Fell Apart – The Kingibe Factor-Ijaw Group. 17 December.

Sala-I-Martin, Xavier and Arvind Subramanian. 2003. *Addressing the Resource Curse: An Illustration from Nigeria.* IMF Working Paper, July, Washington, DC: IMF.

Shaxson, Nicholas. 2007. *Poisoned Wells: The Dirty Politics of African Oil.* Basingstoke: Macmillan-Palgrave.

Skorka, Melissa. 2007. 21st Century US Energy Policy in Nigeria's Niger Delta. M.A. Thesis, London School of Economics, London.

Ukeje, Charles. 2004. From Aba to Ugborodu: Gender Identity and Alternative Discourse of Social Protest among Women in the Oil Delta of Nigeria. *Oxford Development Studies* 32(4): 605–617.

———— 2001. Oil Communities and Political Violence. *Terrorism and Violence* 13(4): 15–36.

Ukiwo, Ukoha. 2007. From Pirates to Militants: A Historical Perspective on Anti-state and Anti-oil Company Mobilization among the Ijaw of Warri, Western Niger Delta. *African Affairs* 106(425): 587–610.

Unger, Sebastian. 2007. Blood Oil. *Vanity Fair,* February (http://www.vanityfair.com/politics/features/2007/02/junger200702).

United Nations Development Project (UNDP). 2007. Niger Delta: Situation Assessment and Opportunities for Engagement. Port Harcourt/Abuja: UNDP.

———— 2005. *Niger Delta Human Development Report.* Abuja: UNDP.

Vines, Alex, Lillian Wong, Markus Weimer and Indira Campos. 2009. Thirst for African Oil. Chatham House. Royal Institute of African Affairs.

WAC Global Services. 2003. Peace and Security in the Niger Delta. Port Harcourt, WAC Global Services.

Watts, Michael. 2005. Righteous Oil? Human Rights, the Oil Complex and Corporate Social Responsibility. *Annual Review of Environment and Resources* 30: 373–407.

Wellington, Bestman. 2007. Weapons of War in the Niger Delta. *Terrorism Monitor* 5(10).

World Bank. 2007. *Nigeria Competitiveness and Growth.* Washington, DC: World Bank.

World Investment Report (WIR). 2005. *World Investment Report.* New York: UN.

Zalik, Anna. 2004. The Peace of the Graveyard: The Voluntary Principles on Security and Human Rights in the Niger Delta. In *Global Regulation: Managing Crisis after the Imperial Turn,* eds, Kees van der Pijl, Libby Assassi, and Duncan Wigan. Basingstoke: Palgrave.

5

Oil as the 'Curse' of Conflict in Africa: Peering through the Smoke & Mirrors

CYRIL OBI (2010)

This article is structured around three broad questions: is oil endowment really a 'curse' to Africa? To what extent can studies based on a statistical correlation between oil abundance and the onset, duration and intensity of armed conflict (Ross 2003; Collier and Hoeffler 2004; Lujala 2009; 2010) adequately capture the complex roots, forces and local and transnational ramifications of armed conflict in oil-rich African states? How is the resource curse constructed and reproduced and whose interests does it serve? These questions are impelled by the trend in some scholarly, policy and media circles which identifies oil endowment as a major factor of conflict, institutional weakness and corruption on the continent. In this essay, although 'oil' and 'resource' are used interchangeably, the emphasis is on oil as Africa's most strategic and sought after commodity in global markets.

The 'oil curse' perspective defines oil largely in terms of a central role in increasing the risk of violent conflict, poor economic growth, or acting as a disincentive for peace (Basedau and Lay 2009:758). At its core lies the notion of resource/oil abundance as underpinning the financial motives/opportunities for rebels to engage in armed conflict, or as a causal factor in (rentier) state weakness either through the propensity for corruption, misrule, authoritarianism or instability (Elbadawi and Sambanis 2000; Herbst 2000; Sachs and Warner 2001; Ross 2003; Auty 2004; Collier and Hoeffler 2004; Fearon 2005: 483–507; Rosser 2006; Le Billon 2007: 163–182; Collier 2007; Ross 2008; Lujala 2010).

More recently, some of the claims of the resource curse theorists have been challenged (Rosser 2006; Alexeev and Conrad 2009; Basedau and Lay 2009), leading them to partly move away from the initial debates over the 'greed versus grievance' causal binary. Much of the emphasis has shifted to issues related to the risk, onset, duration and intensity of armed conflict in resource-rich countries, and the exploration of the links between resource endowment and the viability or capacity of rebel groups. Of note in this regard are the works of Ross (2006), Collier and Hoeffler (2005), Collier (2007), Humphreys (2005), De Soysa and Neumayer (2007). The recent work of Lujala (2010: 15–16) examines 'empirically how the location of natural resources affects armed civil conflict', and concludes that 'oil substantially prolongs conflict when located inside the conflict zone', thereby rendering oil endowment a critical factor in the location, duration and intensity of armed conflict.

The protagonists of the resource curse thesis explore the connection between the paradox of resource abundance, conflict and poor economic growth. They

65

seek to 'explain civil war statistically, looking at a range of possible causes: social, political, geographic and economic' (Collier 2007:18). Their postulations are rooted in 'causal mechanisms linking resources and bad developmental outcomes' (Rosser 2006). Lujala (2010:15) aptly sums up the current state of knowledge by making a point of distinguishing the two main strands in resource curse thought: between resource abundance as a 'motivation and means' (incentive) for 'rebel uprisings' (armed conflict), and as a causal link to 'poor policy choices and a weak state'.

A raft of post-Cold War civil wars in resource-rich African countries such as Sierra Leone, Liberia, Côte d'Ivoire, Republic of Congo (Brazzaville), Chad and the Democratic Republic of Congo (DRC), and the insurgency in Nigeria's oil-rich Niger Delta region have provided some material and further reinforced this perspective. Such wars were specifically labelled after natural resources: as 'diamond' conflicts, 'oil', 'timber' or 'cocoa' conflicts (Smillie et al. 2000; Global Witness 2001; 2002; 2007; Alao 2007; International Crisis Group 2002). The labelling of African wars after natural resources was also given further fillip by investigative reports on the natural resource trade, corruption and conflict involving African state elites and rebel militias by international non-governmental organisations (NGOs) such as Global Witness, Human Rights Watch and the International Crisis Group (ICG). Even the Hollywood enter-tainment industry chanced upon this discourse to produce films such as 'Blood Diamond', which dwelt on the tragic role of armed rebels driven by the lust for 'conflict diamonds' in Africa's brutal wars by focusing on the Sierra Leone civil war.

The resource curse perspective has been more recently incorporated into a global development and security policy discourse to suggest that 'weak' or 'failing' resource or oil-rich states both harbour and represent a serious threat to development and security in a post-9/11 world (Morris 2006; Pham 2007; Thompson and Pearson 2007). In this context, oil-rich African states like Nigeria, Chad, Sudan and Angola have been associated in the literature or media reports with corruption, political instability and violent conflict.

The contention here is that the resource curse thesis feeds certain perspectives on the nature of the African oil-rich states built upon an internal resource conflict nexus that is subversive of development, democratic governance and national, regional and global security. Such perspectives need to be critically interrogated. Beyond such an interrogation, we need to get to the core of what is really an ideological notion of oil resource-determinism that obscures, rather than promotes, an accurate understanding of the roots and wider ramifications of violent conflict in Africa.

This article is divided into four broad parts. The introduction sets the back-ground to the resource curse thesis, while the conceptual section critically analyses the place of Africa's oil in the international political economy. It also includes a critique of the resource curse thesis as a basis for explaining violent conflict in oil-producing African states. The concluding section sums up the arguments and suggests an alternative explanatory framework for violent conflict in African petro-states.

African oil in the global political economy

Blind spots in hegemonic discussions of the oil curse in Africa include the place of Africa's oil in the global political economy, and how transnational actors and structures are deeply implicated in the corruption and armed conflicts in oil-rich states. Although Africa holds about 9% of the world's proven oil reserves, an amount that may be considered small compared to the Middle East's 62%, Africa's oil has assumed critical importance in the context of a tight global oil market in the wake of increased global demand and the shrinking number of significant oil finds to replace rapidly depleting oil fields across the world. African leading oil producers include Nigeria, Angola, Sudan, Algeria, Republic of Congo (Brazzaville), Chad, Libya, Equatorial Guinea, Gabon and Egypt.

The continent has emerged as a key factor in global energy security calculations amid growing US dependence on African oil imports,[1] and the growing concerns in the West following the recent arrival of energy-hungry Asian state oil corporations (Chinese, Indian and Korean) intent on securing a foothold in Africa's oil fields.[2] This so-called 'new' scramble for Africa's oil is impelled in part by a rapid increase in global demand by emerging industrial powers and has not only contributed to the prioritisation of the continent's prized hydro-carbon resource for global economic growth, but also included, in a post-Cold War world, its integration into a US-led paradigm of global security. However, in the context of this essay, the main focus is on the connections of transnationalised oil to capitalist accumulation on a global scale and the impoverishment of oil-producing locales in Africa.

Crude oil or petroleum is widely considered the most viable source of energy in the world. It is the energy lynchpin around which modern capitalism and consumerism as a global system revolves. Oil is a key element of global power (Obi 2009: 471). Thus, the stakes in controlling oil are very high, and constitute a core interest of the world's powers. It also means that Africa as a valued source of oil and gas supplies is central to the strategic calculations of the world's oil-dependent dominant powers.

Since oil is found more in the developing world, of which Africa is a part, its production and export has invoked historically constructed adverse political and social consequences and deleterious environmental consequences (Watts 2004; Obi 2010). It also produces and reproduces specific power relations between peoples, states and international oil companies. In this regard, African oil-owning states operate in partnership with oil multinational corporations (MNCs) that dominate the technology of oil production, alongside the global shipping powers and navies that ply and patrol the maritime oil supply routes. In this way, African oil-rich states are locked into complex and opaque trans-

---

[1] Africa presently accounts for about 12% of US oil imports and that is expected to increase to 25% by 2025, making some US strategic analysts see the continent as an 'alternative' to dependence on an oil-rich, but volatile Middle East.

[2] These Asian countries also consider Africa as being strategic to their global energy security concerns. China, currently the world's second largest oil importer, and India, that relies on an estimated 70% oil imports, are looking to Africa for more oil to fuel their rapid economic growth. Both countries have framed their quest for Africa's oil within the context of an Asian aid diplomacy that is developmentalist and non-interventionist.

national ties with global powers based largely on the joint exploitation of oil 'enclave investments' (Ferguson 2005: 378–379).

However, some analysts have argued that national/state oil corporations which own the oil reserves and control oil supplies (through resource-nationalism) are richer than the oil MNCs. While this may be true in some cases, there are four fundamental issues that oil/resource curse perspectives overlook. The first is the reality that oil MNCs largely dominate the sophisticated technology, management skills and globally integrated operations of the upstream section of the oil industry in Africa, giving them considerable leverage in dealing with individual largely 'revenue-collecting' oil-dependent states. However, oil MNCs are bound to local elites in a transnational partnership hinged upon their common interests, marked in part by a revolving-door relationship between top-level oil MNC local elites (a faction of transnational elites) and the state (Obi 2007).

The second is that the oil MNC-backed Extractive Industries Transparency Initiative (EITI) designed to improve 'governance and transparency in payments to resource-rich countries' has been critiqued for blaming failures in 'development and economic growth in mineral-exporting countries' on 'internal corruption, rather than deficient company remuneration for drilling and extracting, and sharp corporate practice which simultaneously denies and removes profits' (Bracking 2009:3–17).

Thirdly, in the period 1970 to 2008, Africa lost an estimated $854 billion to capital flight, with its 'fuel exporters' being the largest losers, underlining the connection between oil endowment and high rates of capital flight from the continent (Kar and Cartwright-Smith 2010: 10–12). This is illustrated by the case of Nigeria which between 2000 and 2008 is estimated to have 'lost capital at the rate of nearly $10 billion per year' (*Ibid.*). The foregoing assumes further significance in a context where oil MNCs made record profits (Boles 2006; Porreto 2007; 2008; Macalister 2007; 2008), and their earnings both in terms of what they make from Africa's oilfields and in terms of leveraged profits from their partnership with African states remain largely hidden behind opaque international accounting and banking practices (Adusei 2009; Bracking 2009).

Fourthly, and linked to the foregoing, is the neglect of the linkage between the burden of external debt overhang and poor economic performance of resource-endowed African states. Indeed substantial resources that could have been invested in development are lost to capital flight. As the Director of the Tax Justice Network, John Christensen, notes: 'Since the 1970s, for every dollar in external loans to Africa, roughly 60 cents left as capital flight in the same year.' Drawing upon the cases of Zambia and Angola, he notes that 'Zambia has lost US$19.8 billion in capital flight, representing 272% of the debt stock as at 2004', while 'Angola has experienced US$50 billion of capital flight representing 535% of that country's external debt' (quoted in Tax Justice Network 2008).

Kar and Cartwright-Smith (2010: 1) note that illicit flows from Africa have a lot more to do with capital flight resulting from the 'proceeds of commercial tax evasion, mainly through trade mispricing', and much less to do with the 'proceeds of bribery and theft by government officials'. This position is given much credence by the study by Ndikumana and Boyce (2008), and reports from the Tax Justice Network (2008; 2009), that emphasise how the 'aggressive tax avoidance policies of multinationals are among the darker sides of globalisation' (Tax Justice Network 2008), and also cause African resource-endowed countries to suffer the loss of massive amounts of capital.

Thus, Africa's oil remains anchored in a global political economy, consigning the continent to the position of a supplier of 'cheap' oil to the world market as well as a supplier of capital. This process of the subordination of Africa's oil production to domination by oil-MNC and transnational elites, and the demands of the global market, has meant that oil investments 'have been concentrated in secured enclaves, often with little or no benefit to the wider society' (Ferguson 2005:378). In a post-9/11 world, additional priority has been given to the security of Africa as a source of oil supply, the protection of Western oil investments and shipping, and the ability of African states to effectively police and neutralise transnational crimes, including terrorism. For this and other reasons, violent conflict in oil-rich African states is not strictly speaking the inevitable outcome of purely internal predatory or opportunistic activities. It connects a complex maze of transnational-local linkages and also includes the cumulative impact of global financial processes and policies towards Africa.

There is some evidence that in Nigeria's Niger Delta, some oil companies either made direct payments to armed groups or awarded contracts to them ostensibly to provide 'security' for oil installations (WAC Global Services 2003), thereby fuelling local conflict dynamics. Such oil multinationals have also sought to blame oil spills on acts of sabotage by oil thieves and militias while playing down the intimate relationship and complicity between the oil company and the state, in part symbolised by company payments to state security forces guarding oil installations, and bribes paid by multinationals to top state officials to secure oil contracts (Garuba 2009; Voreacos 2010).

In the case of the oil industry, corruption is not an entirely internally driven process. Oil MNCs are complicit with political and economic elites in engaging in corruption and violence, taking advantage of the character of the Nigerian petro-state and elites to reap superprofits. Commenting on the scale and scope of corruption in Nigeria, the former chairman of the country's Economic and Financial Crimes Commission (EFCC), Nuhu Ribadu, recognised his limitations (while in office) when confronted with multinationals bribing top government officials, thus: 'Most of this is happening outside Nigeria. The documents are not in Nigeria. The money is not in Nigeria. The entire transactions do take place outside' (quoted in Bergman 2009). This underscores the transnational nature of high-level corruption based on the common interest in profit and wealth by foreign MNCs and Nigerian political elites.

The transnational nature of extractive oil actors operating in oil-producing enclaves such as the Niger Delta underscores the point that the global political economy plays a defining role in power and social relations around oil and its 'curse'. Therefore the oil curse is not entirely internal to the oil-rich state, nor is the conflict or corruption limited to local and state actors; rather, it is embedded in the commodification of oil by transnational economic forces as an object of high profit and strategic value in the global market, making such actors central to the negative spin-offs from globalised oil extraction in Africa.

The oil curse thesis: a conceptual overview

An overview of the existing debate indicates that the oil curse thesis is far from being a settled issue. According to Ross (2004), 'natural resources play a key role in triggering, prolonging, and financing conflicts'. This resonates with

Billon's view with regard to the Angolan civil war, that 'abundant and secure oil rent allowed the MPLA party to wage a long and violent civil war against the National Union for the Total Independence of Angola (UNITA) since the 1970s' (2007: 39). Zeroing in on oil, Ross (2008:2) also notes, 'oil wealth often wreaks havoc on a country's economy and politics, makes it easier for insurgents to fund their rebellions, and aggravates ethnic grievances.' Exploring the resource abundance – conflict nexus, De Soysa and Neumeyer (2007:202) identify 'two distinct and prominent models explaining the link – finance for rebellion and weak states', a point similarly made by Lujala (2010:15–16). The institutional weaknesses that plague resource-rich countries are attributed to the 'rentier effect' that fuels corruption and misrule by predatory elites who privatise and personalise state power and subvert the developmental process (Herbst 2000; Fearon 2005).

As noted earlier, some of the claims of the protagonists of the resource curse thesis have been challenged. Of note in this regard is the study by Alexeev and Conrad (2009:587), in which they 'reject the claim that natural resource wealth is a curse that makes countries worse off in any significant way'. Rather, they argue, based on 'long-term growth measurements of GDP per capita levels rather than calculating growth rates over a given period of time, that oil and mineral resources enhance long-term growth, and are neutral with respect to the quality of the countries' institutions' (*Ibid.*: 586). Their regressions and conclusions 'contradict most, if not all, of the empirical literature on the resource curse' (*Ibid.*: 592), and do point to some of the methodological flaws inherent in the assumptions underpinning the resource curse thesis. They also direct attention to some of the 'blind spots' in the data sets used by resource curse protagonists, and cast some doubt on the validity of their claims.

In another vein, the neglect of the stabilising aspects of resource endowment on states by the resource curse protagonists has been critiqued. Thus, contrary to the aspect of rentier state theory which posits that resource-rich states are weak, corrupt and authoritarian and therefore susceptible to conflict, it is argued that 'governments use abundant resources to buy off opposition or suppress armed rebellion, thereby contributing to political stability and preventing armed conflict' (Basedau and Lay 2009: 758). A similar point is made by Oliveira (2007:62), who notes that resource endowment can lead to 'astonishingly successful strategies of political survival amidst decay'. Basedau and Lay draw attention to 'country specific factors' and how these can lead to different outcomes by comparing (a conflict-impacted) Nigeria with (relatively peaceful) Saudi Arabia, noting that 'countries oil-rich in per capita terms are spared from internal violence despite being highly dependent' (2009: 758, 774).

The oil curse: a critique

Lujala's recent conclusions that 'oil substantially prolongs conflict when located in the conflict zone', and access to oil plays a key role in determining the viability of rebel movements and financing conflict, merit close attention (2010: 18). While the literature on conflicts in oil-rich African countries is largely absent from the study, it is mentioned briefly that oil may be a better financing source (for rebels in the Niger Delta), through oil theft (illegal oil bunkering) (2010:

26). While Lujala makes a contribution regarding the 'lootability of oil', it is unclear if any strong connection between looted oil, Niger Delta rebels and conflict is established beyond using the abstract model to fit reality, except that, in this case, the reality is far too complex for the model. Some of the shortcomings of such an approach have been earlier empirically demonstrated by Watts (2007), who noted that any rigid demarcation between government and rebels is flawed (*Ibid.*: 651), as is the absence of the agency of oil companies operating in the Niger Delta in the 'models of rebellion or civil war'. Also a recent field study by Omotola (2010: 50) notes the 'considerable levels of support for youth militias among the people of the region', but also recognises the complications posed by violence and criminality to the struggle for resource control in the region. This further points to the problem of drawing conclusions on a rather narrow reading of a complex conflict such as that of the Niger Delta, whose roots predate the discovery of oil, and connect both 'localised global' and globalised local forces of extraction and resistance.

Another recent study challenges the view that resource endowment inevitably leads to the curse of conflict (Basedau and Lay 2009). By differentiating between the impact of resource wealth per capita, and resource dependence on the risk of civil conflict, it is posited that countries with high resource wealth per capita are able to avoid internal conflict, through distributive politics, co-optation and effective use of a sophisticated security apparatus. This point is illustrated using a high wealth per capita country – Saudi Arabia, where civil war is absent – and a low wealth per capita country – Nigeria, which faces an insurgency in the oil-rich Niger Delta region.

It is not clear to what extent these conclusions hold valid for conflicts in African petro-states, particularly since they leave out the role of historical factors, and external forces, particularly in the context of the securitisation of Africa's oil by hegemonic transnational forces. Even when the authors invoke the 'outside protection' factor to explain the role of a French garrison in securing Gabon (*Ibid.*:773), they do not go as far as to explain its connection with French political, strategic and oil interests in the country (Shaxson 2007), nor do they examine the role of oil companies investing in the oil sectors (and funding the petro-states) in Libya and Equatorial Guinea.

The resource curse thesis can be faulted on the basis of its 'prevailing evaluation methodologies on the basis of measurement errors, incorrect specification of the models and the high probability of spurious correlations' (UNRISD 2007:12). The pathologies of an oil curse therefore thrive on a determinate relationship between aspects of oil endowment and negative outcomes, a position that simplifies what is in reality a far more complex relationship that is neither inevitable nor natural. Such pathologies inform mainstream analyses of oil-endowed states such as Nigeria, Chad, Sudan, Equatorial Guinea and Angola, that on the surface reflect most of the features associated with the resource curse – corruption, conflict, instability and high levels of poverty.

Two critical points are missing in such postulations. These are the absence of the ways in which dominant global interests provide support for, and profit from, the behaviour of African petro-states. The second relates to the ways in which the 'curse' is really a political and economic construct, a product of a particular constellation of extractive transnational social forces, histories and hegemonic power relations built upon the commoditisation of oil for the global market. Oil as a commodity is not the curse, rather it is 'cursed' by the high premium placed on it by the world's most powerful and strategic actors for whom it represents a most critical fuel of globalised capital and industrial power.

It is these dominant global forces and their local partners – the ruling elites of African petro-states – that have subordinated African oil more to the interest of a globally integrated oil market, and less the demands and interests of local people and economies. While local peoples live out the harsh realities of the 'cursed oil' in the polluted oil communities of the Niger Delta, the forcibly displaced communities of Sudan or outside the fenced-off portions of oil MNC camps in Equatorial Guinea, and Angola (Ferguson 2005), the oil MNCs, transnational elites and their local partners live up the full blessings of oil wealth.

Critiquing the perspective linking oil abundance to violent conflict, Di John (2007: 977) argues that the view that 'oil states are more prone to civil conflict' as represented on the abstract modelling of the resource curse protagonists, 'does not demonstrate causality'. Such analysis is largely ahistorical, apolitical and selective in the variables and data sets that it uses in its analysis. It adds up to smoke and mirrors, as the reality of resource conflict is definitely more complex with connections that transcend the oil-rich state and its economy (Lahiri-Dutt 2006:14–17; Watts 2007).

The case of Nigeria

The conflict in Nigeria's Niger Delta[3] has also been analysed from the resource-curse perspective (Ikelegbe 2006; Collier 2007:30). Of relevance to the analysis is the focus on rebels/militias, local elites and the state motivated by the greed-driven quest to corner oil wealth/rents. Apart from this, the oil-related conflict in the Niger Delta has been analysed in the context of a 'critically weak Nigerian state' (Rice and Patrick 2008:16), considered unable to ensure security within its territory (Pham 2007). When applied to the Niger Delta, the resource curse analysis leads to the conclusion that oil 'blocks' democracy (Ross 2001; 2008), and promotes corruption and violent conflict. Such a conclusion would be rather superficial, given the nature of the political and economic elite, and the ways oil production and commoditisation spawn or deepen social contradictions, unequal power relations and inequities at two levels: state–society and local–global. In many regards, the unequal power relations and (ethnic minority) grievances in the Niger Delta were well established before oil became a significant factor in Nigeria's political economy. The emergence of oil as the fiscal basis of the state from 1970 only added a rather volatile dimension to pre-existing grievances and the quest for local autonomy in the oil-rich Niger Delta region.

The roots of violent conflict in the Niger Delta as in other oil-rich contexts in Africa do not lie in pools of oil; they lie in the inequitable (transnational, local, national and global) power relations embedded in the production of oil and the highly skewed distribution of its benefits and pernicious liabilities (Obi 2007; 2008; 2009). This was manifested in the non-response to – and later repression of – peaceful protests against the exploitation and pollution of the oil-rich region by a state–transnational oil alliance whose activities alienated the ordinary

---

[3] According to the most recent figures, as a result of the insurgency in the Niger Delta that has resulted in damage to oil infrastructure and oil production shut-ins, Nigeria has for the first time been overtaken by Angola as the continent's leading oil exporter.

people from the land and means of their livelihoods, poisoned the ecosystem, deepened pre-existing inequalities and grievances, and paved the way for the descent into violent conflict (Ukeje 2001; Okonta 2005; Ukiwo 2007; Obi 2010). They can also be explained by the high-handed response of the state to initially peaceful protests, the militarisation of the region and the complicity of oil multinationals and transnational elites benefiting from oil production (and pollution) in the region.

Some premium has been placed on the violent and criminal activities of ethnic militias and armed groups involved in oil theft, kidnapping of oil workers and extorting oil companies, thus posing threats to oil investments in the Niger Delta (Collier 2007:30–31; Ianaccone 2007). Some analysts have even gone as far as to speculate on a 'terrorist threat' possibly to attract the attention of the Western security establishment (Cesarz et al., 2003; Marquardt 2006). Such analysis and projections only tell part of the story. What is not usually explained are the fluid boundaries between resistance, militancy and criminality, and how the social conditions created both by the operations and policies of the state and oil MNCs have directly contributed to, and in some cases nurtured, the emergence of opportunistic elements manipulating the groundswell of grievances, high levels of youth unemployment and poverty to pursue different agendas. The other side of the coin is that broad brushstrokes criminalising all forms of protest in the Niger Delta region gloss over the roots of the crisis and the basis for legitimate protest, and increase the risk that such flawed analysis will lead to wrong conclusions and policies that may prove to be either short lived, or ineffective, or both.

As mentioned earlier, the WAC Global Services (2003) document has established how some oil companies through patronage/largesse to local elites and youth groups to ease entry and provide 'protection' to company interests and assets provided 'fuel' for conflict between the groups, between them and their benefactors, and within and between communities. In spite of the large sums of money devoted to oil company corporate social responsibility (CSR) budgets for the Niger Delta, these have not adequately addressed the needs of the communities, while, in some cases, they have fed into cycles of intra- and intercommunity violence (Human Rights Watch 2002; 2005; Obi 2004; Best and Kemedi 2005; Ikelegbe 2006; Kemedi 2006).

Either way, the profits go to the state, the transnational elites (including Nigerian power elites), global financial institutions and oil corporations, while the costs and real curses go to those whose lands and livelihoods are polluted or expropriated, and whose rights are trampled underfoot as they continue to live out a paradoxically impoverished existence in an oil-rich, but blighted context. What flows from the foregoing is the emergence of a transnational hegemonic class united around a common interest of the extraction of oil – and the sharing of its spoils – but having little or nothing in common with the ordinary folk in the Niger Delta, even when they share the same nationality as the Nigerian faction of the global elite.

Conclusion

From the foregoing, it is argued that the 'oil curse' is a fetish hinged upon a partial reading of the internal processes in oil-rich African countries without capturing its connections to globalised class relations and capitalist accumulation by dispossession, in which transnational elites appropriate the resources that could have gone to African workers, peasants and people in the informal sector. It seeks to divert attention from the class identities of the winners and losers from oil endowment, and the ways the (violent) oil-extractive ethos drives particular social contradictions that fuel conflict either in the form of ensuring the conditions for exploitation, resistance to dispossession, or struggles for ownership of oil (Obi 2010).

Oil endowment is not the curse, though oil is cursed by the high premium placed on it by globalised capitalism, spawning inequalities and contradictions fed by an insatiable greed for finite hydrocarbon resources by the world's industrial powers, and often at huge environmental and social costs to its victims. There are several resource-rich countries that have 'escaped' the resource curse, including Norway (Larsen 2004) and Canada. The reasons behind their 'success stories' is as much about history, as it is about politics, class relations, economic power and their control of their resources, having 'escaped' the pillage of their resources by interventionist and predatory local and transnational forces. Given this situation, the challenge is the need for a grounded understanding of the historical, socioeconomic and political conditions and structures that 'can and do mediate the relationship between resource abundance and developmental outcomes' (Brunnschweiler and Bulte 2006; UNRISD 2007:12).

Therefore, rather than an excessive focus on the ways in which abundant oil endowment provokes the 'failure' of African states: poverty, corruption and violent conflict, much more attention needs to be directed at the historical construction of grievance(s), the nature of state–society relations and the linkages between the local–national–global in what is in reality a transnationally constructed relationship, which benefits all the dominant factions embedded in globalised oil-led capitalist extraction, transfer and accumulation. Those who experience oil as a curse are mainly the majority – who are poor and whose livelihoods are alienated and threatened by the political economy of globalised capital and the depredations of a rapacious transnational elite.

Another challenge relates to the need to transcend 'resource–conflict determinism' in the search for the complex roots of, and local–global linkages to, violent conflict in Africa. An important issue to focus on is the role of the heavy external debt burden and capital flight from the continent, of which corruption is responsible for less than 10%. Given that the bulk of the capital flight from Africa has been shown to be linked to transfer pricing by multinationals, corporate sharp practices and tax evasion using transnational financial and banking processes (Tax Justice Network 2008; Bracking 2009), it is apposite to also focus attention on this source of greater loss of Africa's resources, and the mass transfer of natural wealth outside the continent by transnational elites. By analysing such processes and the impact of market-oriented economic policies aimed at deregulating Africa's economies in the 1980s and 1990s in the name of structural adjustment, the ways in which processes of financial globalisation contributed to the impoverishment of the continent can be laid bare. Beyond this, it also shows some of the limitations of ahistorical and short-term data sets that inform statistical analysis of the resource–conflict nexus.

The present conjuncture in the continent throws up a specific challenge to social scientists and humanists to radically re-engage with the oil-development discourse, and devise new vistas for the analysis of how transnational processes and actors extract and export capital from African oil-rich states, and how the contradictions from such processes and activities spawn crisis and conflict in the continent. This is a necessary step towards overcoming the limitations of perspectives that distort the picture by obscuring the role of transnational actors and processes, and paving the way for a better-informed model based on a radical political economy, which exposes the inequities, unequal power relations, inequalities and hegemonic global class relations that underpin conflict in the continent.

At the heart of an alternative model should be devising strategies for winning back the bulk of Africa's resources and capital exported from the continent rather than being directed at the development of its people. The fundamental questions posed should be: who controls the oil and whose interest(s) do they serve? For, in the service of the people through equity, social justice and sustainable development, oil can be a source of peace and 'blessings' to the majority of African people.

To tap into the blessings of oil, two issues are fundamental to a new struggle to reverse the mal-effects of an artificial oil curse: a radical transformation of the African oil state and institutions away from the current ethos that serves narrow interests, and hegemonic and transnational forces intent on fostering the integration of the continent into the global capitalist system on clearly disadvantageous terms, and the emergence of a visionary and radical leadership capable of building a new social pact with the people based on an emancipatory, transformative, environmentally sustainable and participatory developmental democracy.

References

Adusei, Aiken. 2009. Multinational Corporations: The New Colonisers of Africa. Pambazuka News, 4 June. Available from: http://www.pambazuka.org/en/category/features/56716 [Accessed 27 July 2010].

Alao, Abiodun. 2007. *Natural Resources and Conflict in Africa: The Tragedy of Endowment*. New York: Rochester Press.

Alexeev, Michael and Robert Conrad. 2009. The Elusive Curse of Oil. *The Review of Economics and Statistics* 91(3): 586–598.

Auty, Richard. 2004. Natural Resources and Civil Strife: A Two-Stage Process. *Geopolitics* 9(1): 29–49.

Basedau, Mathias and Jann Lay. 2009. Resource Curse or Rentier Peace? The Ambiguous Effects of Oil Wealth and Oil Dependence on Violent Conflict. *Journal of Peace Research* 46(6): 757–776.

Bergman, Lowell. 2009. Interview with Nuhu Ribadu: Corruption Case Exposes Scope of Bribery in Nigeria. PBS Newshour, April 24. Available from: http://www.pbs.org/newshour/bb/africa/jan-june09/nigeria_04–24.html [Accessed 29 July 2010].

Best, Shadrack and Dimieari Von Kemedi. 2005. Armed Groups and Conflict in Rivers and Plateau States, Nigeria. In *Armed and Aimless: Armed Groups, Guns and Human Security in the ECOWAS Region*, eds. Nicolas Florquin and Eric Berman. Geneva: Small Arms Survey.

Boles, Tracey. 2006. Shell and Exxon to Smash Transatlantic Profit. Timesonline. Available from: http://business.timesonline.co.uk [Accessed 29 January 2009].

Bracking, Sarah. 2009. *Hiding Conflict over Industry Returns: A Stakeholder Analysis of the Extractive Industries' Transparency Initiative*. Working Paper (BWPI) 91. Manchester: Brooks World Poverty Institute.

Brunnschweiler, Christa and Erwin Bulte. 2006. *The Resource Curse Revisited and Revised: A Tale of Paradoxes and Red Herrings*. Working Paper 06/61, December. Zurich: Centre of Economic Research, Swiss Federal Institute of Technology (CER-ETH).

Cesarz, Esther, Stephen Morrison, and Jennifer Cooke. 2003. Alienation and Militancy in Nigeria's Niger Delta. *CSIS Africa Notes*, No. 16, May. Washington, DC: Centre for Strategic and International Studies, 1–4.

Collier, Paul. 2007. *The Bottom Billion*. Oxford: Oxford University Press.

Collier, Paul and Anke Hoeffler. 2004. Greed and Grievance in Civil Wars. *Oxford Economic Papers*, 56 (4): 563–595.

—— 2005. Resource Rents, Governance and Conflict. *Journal of Conflict Resolution* 49(4): 538–562.

De Soysa, Indra and Eric Neumayer. 2007. Resource Wealth and the Risk of Civil War Onset: Results from a New Data Set of Natural Resource Rents. *Conflict Management and Peace Science* 24(3): 201–218.

Di John, Jonathan. 2007. Oil Abundance and Violent Political Conflict: A Critical Assessment. *Journal of Development Studies* 43(6): 961–986.

Elbadawi, Ibrahim and Nicholas Sambanis. 2000. *How Much War Will We See? Estimating the Incidence of Civil War in 161 Countries*. Washington, DC: World Bank.

Fearon, James. 2005. Primary Commodities Exports and Civil War. *Journal of Conflict Resolution* 49(4): 483–507.

Ferguson, James. 2005. Seeing Like an Oil Company: Space, Security, and Global Capital in Neoliberal Africa. *American Anthropologist* 107(3): 377–382.

—— 2006. *Global Shadows: Africa in a Neoliberal World Order*. Durham and London: Duke University Press.

Garuba, Dauda. 2009. Nigeria: Halliburton, Bribes and the Deceit of Zero-Tolerance for Corruption. 9 April. Revenue Watch Institute. Available from: http://www.revenuewatch.org/news/newsarticle/nigeria/nigeria-halliburton-bribes-and-deceit-zero-tolerance-corruption [Accessed 26 July 2010].

Global Witness. 2001. *Taylor-made: The Pivotal Role of Liberia's Forests in Regional Conflict*. London: Global Witness. September.

—— 2002. *All the President's Men: The Devastating Story of Oil and Banking in Angola's Privatised War*. London: Global Witness. March.

—— 2007. *Hot Chocolate: How Cocoa Fuelled the Conflict in Côte d'Ivoire*. London: Global Witness. June.

Herbst, Jeffrey. 2000. Economic Incentives, Natural Resources and Conflict in Africa. *Journal of African Economies* 9(3): 270–294.

Human Rights Watch. 2002. *Niger Delta: No Democracy Dividend*. New York: Human Rights Watch.

—— 2005. *Rivers and Blood: Guns, Oil and Power in Nigeria's Rivers State*, Briefing Paper February. New York: Human Rights Watch.

Humphreys, Macartan. 2005. Natural Resources, Conflict and Conflict Resolution. *Journal of Conflict Resolution* 49(4): 508–537.

Ianaccone, Alex. 2007. *Toward a Reform Agenda for the Niger Delta*. A Report of the Africa, Program Center for Strategic and International Studies (CSIS). Washington, DC: CSIS.

Ikelegbe, Augustine. 2006. The Economy of Conflicts in the Oil-Rich Niger Delta Region of Nigeria. *African and Asian Studies* 5(1): 23–56.

International Crisis Group. 2002. *Scramble for the Congo: Anatomy of an Ugly War*. ICG Africa Report, No. 61, December. Nairobi/Brussels: International Crisis Group.

IRIN [Humanitarian News and Analysis of UN Office for Coordination of Humanitarian Affairs] Nigeria. 2005. Conviction of Admirals Confirms Navy Role in Oil Theft. 5 January. Available from: www.irinnews.org [Accessed 25 July 2010].

Kar, Dev and Devon Cartwright-Smith. 2010. *Illicit Financial Flows from Africa: Hidden Resource for Development*. Global Financial Integrity Report, March 10. Washington, DC: Center for International Policy. Available from: http://www.gfip.org/index.php?option=com_content&task=view&id=300&Itemid=75 [Accessed 27 July 2010].

Kemedi, Dimieari, von. 2006. *Fuelling the Violence: Non-State Armed Actors (Militia, Cults, and Gangs) in the Niger Delta*. Niger Delta Economies of Violence Working Paper no. 10. Berkeley: Institute of International Studies, University of California; Washington, DC: The United States Institute for Peace; Port Harcourt: Our Niger Delta.

Lahiri-Dutt, Kuntala. 2006. 'May God Give Us Chaos, So that We can Plunder': A Critique of 'Resource Curse' and Conflict Theories. *Development* 49(3): 14–21.

Larsen, Erling. 2004. *Escaping the Resource Curse and the Dutch Disease? When and Why Norway Caught up with and Forged Ahead of its Neighbours*. Discussion Paper No. 377, May. Statistics Norway, Research Department. Oslo: Statistics Norway.

Le Billon, Philippe. 2007. Geographies of War: Perspectives on 'Resource Wars'. *Geography Compass* 2(1): 163–182.

Lujala, Paivi. 2009. Deadly Combat Over Natural Resources: Gems, Petroleum, Drugs, and the

Severity of Armed Conflict. *Journal of Conflict Resolution* 53(1): 50–71.

────── 2010. The Spoils of Nature: Armed Conflict and Rebel Access to Natural Resources. *Journal of Peace Research* 47(1): 15–28.

Macalister, Terry. 2007. Exxon and Shell see Profits Rocket. *The Guardian* (UK), 1 February.

────── 2008. Shell's Profits Branded 'Obscene'. *The Guardian* (UK), 31 January.

Marquardt, Erich. 2006. The Niger Delta Insurgency and its Threat to Energy Security. *Terrorism Monitor* IV (16): 3–6.

Morris, Daniel. 2006. The Chance to go Deep: US Energy Interests in West Africa. *American Foreign Policy Interests* 28(3): 225–238.

Ndikumana, Léonce and James Boyce. 2008. *New Estimates of Capital Flight from Sub-Saharan African Countries: Linkages with External Borrowing and Policy Options*. Working Paper Series, 116. Amherst, MA: University of Massachusetts, Political Economy Research Institute (PERI).

Obi, Cyril. 2004. *The Oil Paradox: Reflections on the Violent Dynamics of Petro-Politics and (mis)Governance in Nigeria's Niger Delta*. Africa Institute Occasional Paper No. 73. Pretoria: Africa Institute of South Africa.

────── 2007. The Struggle for Resource Control in a Petro-State: A Perspective from Nigeria. In *National Perspectives on Globalisation*, eds. Paul Bowles, Henry Veltmeyer, Scarlet Cornelissen, Noela Invernizzi and Kwong Leung Tang. New York: Palgrave Macmillan.

────── 2008. Nigeria's Foreign Policy and Transnational Security Challenges in West Africa. *Journal of Contemporary African Studies* 26(2): 183–96.

────── 2009. Structuring Transnational Spaces of Identity, Rights and Power in the Niger Delta of Nigeria. *Globalizations* 6(4): 467–481.

────── 2010. Oil Extraction, Dispossession, Resistance, and Conflict in the Niger Delta. *Canadian Journal of Development Studies* 30(1–2): 219–236.

Okonta, Ike. 2005. Nigeria: Chronicle of a Dying State. *Current History*, May: 203–208.

Oliveira, Ricardo. 2007. *Oil and Politics in the Gulf of Guinea*. London: Hurst.

Omotola, Shola. 2010. Liberation Movements and Rising Violence in the Niger Delta: The New Contentious Site of Oil and Environmental Politics. *Studies in Conflict and Terrorism* 33(1): 36–54.

Pham, Peter. 2007. Next Front? Evolving United States-African Relations in the 'War on Terror' and Beyond. *Comparative Strategy* 26(1): 39–54.

Porreto, John. 2007. Exxon Mobil Posts Record Annual Profit. 1 February. Available from: www.breitbart.com [Accessed 20 February 2009].

────── 2008. Exxon, Chevron Post Record Profits. *The Washington Post*, 2 February.

Rice, Susan and Stewart Patrick. 2008. *Index of State Weakness in the Developing World*. Washington, DC: The Brookings Institution.

Ross, Michael. 2001. Does Oil Hinder Democracy? *World Politics* 53(3): 325–361.

────── 2003. The Natural Resource Curse: How Wealth Can Make You Poor. In *Natural Resources and Violent Conflict: Options and Actions*, eds. Ian Bannon and Paul Collier. Washington D.C.: World Bank.

────── 2004. What Do We Know About Natural Resources and Civil War? *Journal of Peace Research* 41(3): 337–356.

────── 2006. A Closer Look at Oil, Diamonds, and Civil War. *Annual Review of Political Science* 9, 265–300.

────── 2008. Blood Barrels: Why Oil Fuels Conflict. *Foreign Affairs* 87(3), 2–9.

Rosser, Andrew. 2006. *The Political Economy of the Resource Curse: A Literature Survey*. Working Paper 268. Brighton: Institute of Development Studies (IDS).

Sachs, Jeffrey and Warner, Andrew. 2001. The Curse of Natural Resources. *European Economic Review* 45: 827–838.

Shaxson, Nicholas. 2007. *Poisoned Wells: The Dirty Politics of African Oil*. Basingstoke: Palgrave-Macmillan.

Smillie, Ian, Lansana Gberie, and Ralph Hazleton. 2000. *The Heart of the Matter: Sierra Leone, Diamonds and Human Security*. Ottawa: Partnership for Africa.

Tax Justice Network. 2008. Africa's Revolving Door. Equitable Taxation not Aid Will End the Looting of Africa. Tax Justice Network for Africa (TJN 4 Africa), Press Release, 10 May. Available from: http://taxjustice.blogspot.com/2008/05/tjn–4-africa-press-release.html [Accessed 27 July 2010].

────── 2009. Breaking the Curse: How Transparent Taxation and Fair Taxes can Turn Africa's Mineral Wealth into Development. 24 March. Tax Justice Network for Africa (TJN4Africa). Available from: http://taxjustice.blogspot.com/2009/03/breaking-curse-tjn4africa.html [Accessed 27 July 2010].

Thompson, Christopher and Jonathan Pearson. 2007. Pentagon Forming AFRICOM amid Threats to Oil Resources. *Alexander's Gas and Oil Connections*, 13 July.

Ukeje, Charles. 2001. Oil Communities and Political Violence: The Case of Ethnic Ijaws in Nigeria's Niger Delta. *Terrorism and Violence* 13(4): 15–36.

Ukiwo, Ukoha. 2007. From Pirates to Militants: A Historical Perspective on Anti-State and Anti-Oil Company Mobilization Among the Ijaw of Warri, Western Niger Delta. *African Affairs*, 106(425): 587–610.

UNDP Nigeria, 2006. Niger Delta Human Development Report. Abuja: UNDP.

UNRISD [United Nations Research Institute for Social Development], 2007. Report of the UNRISD International Workshop, 1–2 March. UNRISD Conference News.

Voreacos, David. 2010. Snamprogetti, ENI to pay $365 Million in Bribe Case. *Bloomberg Businessweek*, 7 July. Available from: http://www.businessweek.com/news/2010-07-07/snamprogetti-eni-topay–365-million-in-bribe-case.html [Accessed 27 July 2010].

WAC Global Services. 2003. *Peace and Security in the Niger Delta: Conflict Expert Group Baseline Report.* Working Paper for Shell Petroleum Development Company of Nigeria Ltd. December. Available from: http://www.shellnews.net/shell_wac_report_2004.pdf [Accessed 15 November 2010].

Watts, Michael. 2004. Resource Curse? Governmentality, Oil and Power in the Niger Delta, Nigeria. *Geopolitics* 9(1): 50–80.

———— 2007. Petro-Insurgency or Criminal Syndicate? Conflict and Violence in the Niger Delta. *Review of African Political Economy* 24(114): 637–660.

6

Defence Expenditures, Arms Procurement & Corruption in Sub-Saharan Africa

SUSAN WILLETT

Within neoliberal discourse, corruption, understood as the 'misuse of public power for private or political gain', has been identified as a major obstacle to development in that it reduces domestic investment, discourages foreign direct investment (FDI), inflates government expenditures and distorts public spending by shifting resources from education, health and infrastructural investment into sectors more malleable to corruption, such as the security sector.

In its 2006 *Development White Paper*, the UK Department for International Development committed itself to scrutinising public spending and procurement in the defence sector in developing countries as part of its broader anti-corruption campaign and as an extension of its work on security sector reform. The goal was to improve transparency and accountability in military budgeting and arms procurement in developing countries. In November 2007, DFID tentatively launched its Transparency in Defence Expenditures (TIDE) initiative. The stimulus for this initiative was inspired by a paper produced by the IMF economists Gupta et al. (2000), who hypothesised that corruption is highly correlated with (1) high shares of military expenditure in both GDP and overall government expenditure; and (2) high levels of military procurement spending in relation to both GDP and total government spending. Without evaluating the suitability of their methodology to the context of sub-Saharan Africa (SSA), DFID officials commissioned a series of consultancy papers from defence economic 'experts' to explore the extent of corruption in military expenditures and arms procurement in sub-Saharan Africa, using the quantitative methodologies favoured by Gupta et al.

This article attempts to show that DFID's neoliberal assumptions about the nature of corruption in arms procurement are highly biased, and that studies based on neoliberal methodologies produce a prejudicial picture of the nature of corruption in military procurement in SSA. In much of the development literature, corruption in the security sector has been treated as though it was exclusive to emerging market economies and poorer developing economies. However, there is a growing body of evidence which suggests that misgovernance and corruption in the security sector are more widespread (Kaufman 2004) than the neoliberal institutions have been willing to acknowledge. Multinational companies, including British-based companies operating outside the OECD region, have been implicated in providing lucrative bribes to government officials in developing countries, in gross violation of the OECD Anti-Bribery Convention. A number of high-profile arms procurement corruption cases in SSA highlight the role that multinational companies have played in arms corruption on the continent, strongly suggesting that corruption in arms procurement is far more complex and more common than DFID is willing to acknowledge.

Furthermore, for corruption in arms procurement to thrive, there have to be financial institutions willing to launder the ill-gotten gains of graft. This implies that a web of transnational corruption exists that links transnational arms companies to corrupt foreign officials and global financial institutions. Given this global pipeline of corruption, a focus that seeks solely to demonise political and military elites in the developing countries can only provide a very partial picture of what is actually going on in the world of corrupt arms transactions. Such partiality leaves donors open to accusations of hypocrisy and discrimination, thus undermining the supposed solidity and consistency of their good governance, anti-corruption and security sector reform programmes.

The challenge of measuring military expenditures and corruption in SSA

The IMF Working Paper produced by Gupta et al. (2000) relies on the elegant algorithms of econometric analysis that seek observable patterns in quantitative data in order to reveal significant statistical correlations. The models are built upon probabilistic assumptions, e.g. when x occurs, y will follow. Gupta et al. hypothesised that corruption is correlated with high shares of military expenditure in both GDP and overall government expenditure, as well as with high levels of military procurement spending in relation to both GDP and total government spending. To be able to test this hypothesis in the sub-Saharan African context, reliable statistical data on military expenditures and arms procurement in SSA needed to exist, but as Hartley (2007) revealed, statistics on defence expenditure and arms procurement in the region are weak and, in some cases, non-existent. Datasets on military expenditures in SSA, while being available from a number of sources including the Stockholm International Peace Research Institute (SIPRI), the Congressional Research Service (CRS) and the United Nations Office of Disarmament Affairs (UNODA), are often incomplete, rarely correspond with each other and, as the collators of the data admit, are often unreliable, as transparency and accountability in military budgeting in SSA are notoriously poor.

Currently, the most reliable and consistent time series data on military expenditures in SSA are supplied by SIPRI, whose data suggest that formal military expenditures and arms procurement levels in SSA are well below the international average. In 2006, total military expenditure for sub-Saharan Africa amounted to just under US$9 billion, or some 0.8% of global military spending (SIPRI, 2007). The average military burden – military expenditure measured as a percentage of GDP – for the 30 SSA countries for which SIPRI had data in 2005 was only 1.5%, less than half the average military burden during the height of the Cold War, when SSA military expenditure averaged between 4–5% of GDP. This implies that military expenditure in the region is relatively low. However, reference to regional averages masks the wide variation in country-level military expenditures across the continent. For example, between 1998 and 2004, Gambia averaged a very low rate of military expenditure at 0.6% of GDP, while Eritrea, engaged in a border war with Ethiopia, expended an average of 30% of GDP during this same period. Moreover, there is a marked disparity in absolute levels of military spending. South Africa, for example, spent only 1.5% of its GDP on defence in 2005, but with a budget of US$3.6 billion accounted for over one-third of total military expenditure in sub-Saharan Africa. Compare South Africa with Mali, with a budget of only US$33.6 million, but which spent 2.3% of GDP on the military and the scale of disparity becomes apparent. This lack of correspondence draws attention to the wide differences on the continent, and cautions against making over-hasty assumptions about cross-country comparisons or correlations between high military expenditures and other variables.

Above all, there is a problem with the reliability of existing country-specific data on military expenditures. Omitoogun and Hutchful (2006:2) conducted a series of case studies on military budgets in SSA and noted that 'data on military expenditure ... were very weak and needed improvement'. Most of their sample countries 'have been known to engage in collusion to hide the cost of military activities from the general public and donors of economic assistance ... who make aid conditional on low military budgets' (*Ibid*.: 242). By way of illustration, it would be expected that African states involved in conflict, or having recently emerged from conflict, would record higher levels of military expenditure as a proportion of GDP than those countries not at war. While this assumption certainly holds for the majority of conflict states, as Table 1 illustrates, certain conflict-bound states, including Chad, DRC, Ethiopia, Nigeria, Sierra Leone and Sudan, record official levels of military expenditure well below 2% of GDP. If we change tack and examine the Corruption Perception Index ranking for SSA states that is produced by Transparency International (Table 2), it is apparent that these same states have a very poor record on corruption, all being listed as among the most corrupt states in the world.

The military burdens of those SSA countries listed by Transparency International (TI) as the least corrupt are recorded in Table 3. Despite lower levels of corruption than most SSA states, Botswana, Namibia and Lesotho have relatively high military burdens.

Table 1: Military Burden (ME/GDP) of SSA Countries in Conflict 1998–2005

Country	1998	1999	2000	2001	2002	2003	2004	2005
Angola	(5.2)	(9.9)	(2.21)	(1.4)	(1.8)	(2.2)	(4.0)	(5.7)
Burundi	6.6	6.3	6.0	8.0	7.2	7.3	6.6	6.
CAR					14.8	16.7	15.6	15.4
Chad	1.2	1.7	1.9	1.8	1.7	1.5	1.1	1.0
Congo Republic	–	–	–	1.4	1.7	1.9	1.7	1.4
DRC	1.2	1.7	1.9	1.8	1.7	1.5	1.1	1.0
Djibouti	4.4	4.2	4.0	3.9	4.2	–	–	–
Eritrea	35.3	37.4	36.3	24.7	23.7	24.1	–	–
Ethiopia	6.7	10.7	9.6	5.0	3.9	2.9	2.8	2.6
Nigeria	0.9	1.4	0.8	1.3	1.9	1.1	1.8	0.8
Rwanda	4.4	4.2	3.4	3.3	2.9	2.5	2.3	2.9
Sierra Leone	–	–	4.1	2.4	1.7	1.8	1.2	1.0
Sudan	2.4	4.1	4.8	2.9	3.2	2.3	–	–

Note: there are no available figures for Somalia or Côte d'Ivoire, and the figures for Angola should be seen in the context of highly uncertain economic statistics, due to the impact of war on the Angolan economy.
(Source: SIPRI Military Expenditure Database 2007)

Table 2: Corruption Perception Index for Sub-Saharan Africa

Country	Global Ranking in Corruption	Country	Global Ranking in Corruption
Botswana	31	Guyana	123
South Africa	43	Mauritania	123
Cape Verde	49	Niger	123
Mauritius	53	Zambia	123
Namibia	57	Burundi	131
Seychelles	57	Cameroon	138
Ghana	69	Ethiopia	138
Senegal	71	Gambia	143
Gabon	84	Togo	143
Lesotho	84	Guinea-Bissau	147
Swaziland	84	Nigeria	147
Madagascar	94	Congo Republic	150
Tanzania	94	Cote d'Ivoire	150
Burkina Faso	105	Kenya	150
Djibouti	105	Liberia	150
Eritrea	111	Sierra Leone	150
Mozambique	111	Zimbabwe	150
Rwanda	111	CAR	162
Uganda	111	DRC	168
Benin	118	Equatorial Guinea	168
Malawi	118	Chad	172
Mali	118	Sudan	172
São Tomé and Principe	118	Somalia	179
Comoros	123		

(Source: Transparency International Corruption Perceptions Index (CPI) 2007
Available from: http://www.transparency.org/policy_research/surveys_indices/cpi)

Table 3: Least Corrupt Countries in SSA and Military Expenditure Levels (US$ 2005)

Country	Military Expenditure (US$ millions)	Average Military Expenditure/GDP 1998–2005	CPI Score Rank 2005	CPI Global
Botswana	313.0	3.5	5.4	31
South Africa	3568.0	1.4	5.1	43
Mauritius	12.3	0.2	4.0	53
Namibia	187.0	2.9	4.5	57
Ghana	80.0	0.75	3.7	69
Senegal	124.1	1.4	3.6	71
Gabon	110.0	1.8	3.3	84
Lesotho	33.6	2.9	3.3	84
Swaziland	(48.8)	1.7	3.3	84
Madagascar	54.0	1.2	3.2	94
Tanzania	135.0	1.5	3.2	94
Burkina Faso	76.2	1.3	2.9	105

Note: Military expenditure figures for Gabon are for the years 2000–2005.
(Source: SIPRI Military Expenditure Database 2007 and Transparency International's Corruption Perception Index 2007)

Indeed, they appear to have spent a higher proportion of their GDP on defence than conflict-prone states such as the DRC, Chad, Congo and Nigeria listed in Table 1. How can this phenomenon be explained? The fact that less corrupt countries have a higher military burden may be attributable to the fact that the governments of these countries are committed to greater transparency and accountability in their military budgets than the afore-mentioned fragile states. If this is indeed the case, the whole notion of using the military burden as a benchmark to judge the 'excessiveness' of military expenditures is called into question, as is the supposed correlation between military expenditures and corruption.

Data on the share of defence spending in government expenditure are even less readily available. World Military Expenditures and Arms Transfers (WMEAT), produced by the US Department of State, provides the only reliable source of time series data on the defence share of government expenditures in SSA. However, collection of these data ended in 2002, and the latest available set are for the year 2000. The WMEAT data reveal some dramatic differences between SSA nations, as Table 4 shows. For 1999, the median share was some 8%, with the highest shares in Eritrea (51.1%) and Sudan (46.8%), and the lowest shares for Cape Verde (2.2%) and Mauritius (0.9%).

The weakness and unreliability of existing data on military expenditure in SSA suggest that the quantitative approach adopted by DFID, and Gupta et al. have limited utility in the SSA context. If the Gupta hypothesis of the relationship between military expenditures and corruption is accepted, it would have to

Table 4: Defence Share of Government Spending (%), 1990–1999

Country	1990	1999	Country	1990	1999
Angola	39.8	41.1	Kenya	9.8	7.1
Benin	(19.4)	8.3	Lesotho	17.1	6.5
Botswana	10.8	9.8	Liberia	NA	8.3
Burkina Faso	17.5	5.9	Madagascar	6.9	7.4
Burundi	12.7	26.7	Malawi	4.8	2.2
Cameroon	8.1	10.6	Mali	(8.6)	8.7
Cape Verde	(2.8)	2.2	Mauritania	12.3	18.9
CAR	(6.6)	15.4	Mauritius	1.5	0.9
Chad	16.5	12.7	Mozambique	NA	9.1
DRC	(16.1)	NA	Namibia	5.9	7.2
Republic of Congo	11.1	8.4	Niger	(8.4)	6.4
Djibouti	20.1	12.7	Nigeria	7.6	8.1
Equatorial Guinea	NA	16.5	Rwanda	19.8	22.7
Eritrea	(34.6)	(51.1)	Senegal	(6.3)	8.2
Ethiopia	39.8	29.1	Sierra Leone	20.8	13.5
Gabon	13.7	7.3	Somalia	NA	NA
Gambia	5.1	5.4	South Africa	12.6	5.0
Ghana	3.4	3.1	Sudan	(61.5)	46.8
Guinea	5.0	7.4	Swaziland	6.6	4.6
Guinea Bissau	(4.0)	6.1	Tanzania	8.7	10.1
Côte d'Ivoire	(3.9)	3.4	Togo	14.0	9.4
			Uganda	25.9	13.9

Note: NA 1/4 not available: figures in brackets are for nearest year to 1990 (e.g. 1989 or 1991).
(Source: WMEAT (2002))

be assumed, on the basis of existing statistical data, that corruption in military affairs in SSA was on the decline. However, the qualitative studies commissioned by SIPRI on the military budget process in selected SSA countries suggest that this is far from the case (Omitoogun 2003; Omitoogun and Hutchful 2006). These studies strongly suggest that corruption in the security sector is increasing, and that this trend appears to be proportional to the amount of military expenditure which has gone 'off budget'.

Donors and defence budgets in SSA

During the 1990s, multilateral and bilateral donors attempted to control 'excessive' levels of military expenditure in aid-dependent countries, using a 'benchmark' of 2% of GDP. According to Omitoogun and Hutchful (2006), this had the unintended consequence of increasing secrecy surrounding military budgets in many SSA countries. One of the reasons for this was that donors had failed to take into account the legitimate security needs of recipient countries. The net effect was that an increasing amount of military spending was pushed 'off budget', thus reducing the reliability of military data upon which donor judgments are based.

The case of Uganda is illustrative of the inability of the state to provide basic security under donor terms of conditionality, which forced it to fund military campaigns with off-budget sources of income. In the 1990s, Museveni's Government, facing the costly task of attempting to contain the Lord's Resistance Army (LRA), was unable to realistically bring its military budget to below 2% of GDP, given the manpower, logistical and arms expenditure needs required to conduct a campaign on its northern border. At the time, President Museveni's Government was dependent for more than 60% of its expenditures on international aid, and was thus under considerable donor pressure to rein in military spending. In 1998–99 Museveni exceeded the 2% benchmark. The donors, led by the IFIs, suspended aid to Uganda, and only resumed lending when the government returned military expenditure to the 2% 'acceptable level'. Faced with these intractable demands Museveni implemented several creative accounting techniques to enable him to allocate sufficient resources to his military campaign, while allowing him to keep official military expenditures below the 2% benchmark. Resources earmarked for other government departments were diverted to the Ministry of Defence. In 2001 Museveni openly asked the donors to lift the 2% ceiling, and requested permission to spend twice what the government had officially allocated to the military in 2000. In effect, the request was merely an attempt to gain permission to officially spend what was already being allocated to the military. Reluctantly, and in the face of international pressure to find some kind of solution to the human rights violations perpetuated by the LRA, the donors agreed. Since then, there has been a steady rise in official military expenditures. Under sustained military pressure from the Uganda People's Defence Force (UPDF), the LRA has to all intents and purposes been defeated. Peace negotiations are under way at the time of writing.

Where budgets have been kept within donor-defined levels of acceptability, military forces have suffered from chronic under-funding, which is reflected in low pay and allowances, inadequate training, poor living and working conditions, a lack of medical services and an absence of basic equipment (Henke and

Rupiya 2001; Omitoogun 2003). In certain circumstances, this state of affairs has proved destabilising on two counts:

- resources are insufficient to sustain effective military capabilities, which limits the capacity of the state to provide basic security; and
- low pay and poor working conditions can lead to severe grievances and even mutiny amongst military personnel which, in extreme cases, can result in full-scale military coups, as in the case of Côte d'Ivoire in 2002.

The experience of Uganda, and to a lesser extent Côte d'Ivoire, forced a realisation among donors that their policy on excessive military expenditures had considerable shortcomings. Donors began to reformulate their policies towards military expenditures in early 2000. The new policy approach, largely formulated by DFID, placed emphasis on the 'process' or 'good governance' approach to military budgeting. New weight was given to applying sound financial management principles to the military sector (Ball and Fayemi 2004). On paper these reforms sound very plausible; however, as Omitoogun and Hutchful (2006) have noted, a number of serious structural obstacles need to be overcome before sound financial management principles can be applied to the military sector in most SSA countries.

First, there is a general lack of qualified accountants. The systematic downsizing of the civil service, and reductions in public sector pay under the terms of IMF-imposed structural adjustment programmes during the 1980s and 1990s, resulted in a widespread exodus of skilled professionals from public sector employment across Africa, which meant there was an acute shortage of personnel able to audit and reconcile accounts. The outcome has been that, all too often, unqualified personnel perform budget preparation and the reconciliation of accounts. Unless efforts are made to recruit and pay accountants a decent salary, sound financial management of government accounts, including defence budgets, will remain unattainable.

Second, there is a need to introduce integrated defence planning systems. The majority of African states lack the capacity and skills to design and implement defence planning procedures and military budgeting processes. As a consequence, military budgeting is extremely ad hoc and inefficient, often rendering security forces bereft of even the most basic of equipment, such as uniforms and boots, let alone any military equipment.

Finally, the necessary legal and institutional mechanisms that ensure and enforce accountability tend to be weak in almost all SSA countries. Oversight of the military budget is plagued by weak control by the ministry of defence, a lack of coherent defence policy, weak parliamentary control and limited involvement of civil society.

Even where institutional arrangements for accountability and public scrutiny exist, they are often bypassed under the rubric of national security (Adekanye 1999; Omitoogun and Hutchful 2006). The general absence of transparency and accountability mechanisms in the defence budgetary process allows for the systematic manipulation of military data by corrupt officials. The manipulation of military accounts, and the secrecy that surrounds this, have arisen to hide graft and the mismanagement of resources from public scrutiny, but also to deceive donors about the true cost of military activities.

'Off-budget' military funding and corruption

As already noted, a significant proportion of arms procurement transactions in SSA occur 'off budget'. The secret and shadowy nature of 'off-budget' funding creates ample opportunity for malfeasance. A variety of highly innovative off-budget mechanisms that enable the funding of procurement and other military 'excesses' have evolved in Africa.

- *Asset transfers*: The redistribution of existing assets to the benefit of the armed forces that may involve the reallocation of resources from other budgetary headings or state revenues. Examples include the Ugandan Government's initial allocation of resources to the police budget, later redirected to the military, to augment the costs of the campaign against the LRA in the North of Uganda (Omitoogun 2003). During the border war between Eritrea and Ethiopia (1998–2000), Ethiopia diverted the proceeds of the privatisation of state companies to fund its war effort, in particular the US$300 million purchase of Sukhoi Su–27s from the Russians (*Africa Confidential* 1999).
- *Natural resource predation*: The pillage of natural resources such as diamonds, copper, coltan, oil and timber, and the use of revenues for arms procurement and the personal gain of warlords and generals alike, is well documented in the DRC, Liberia, Sierra Leone and Angola (Renton et al. 2007; Global Witness various; UN Security Council 2003). In Nigeria, the notoriously corrupt cash-call system that operated in the state-owned oil industry is thought to have funded Nigeria's role in the ECOMOG operations in Liberia and Sierra Leone between 1990 and 1999. The figures for these 'peace' operations did not appear in Nigeria's defence accounts, but are thought to have cost an estimated US$12 billion (Adekanye 1999). In Angola, it has been estimated that as much as US$1 billion a year of state oil revenues have been siphoned off into shell companies for use in a tangled web of corruption and backroom arms deals (Global Witness 2004). In the DRC, a total of US$80 million was appropriated from the state-owned diamond mining company (MIBA), of which US$20 million is thought to have been used to buy weapons from Ukrainian and Czech arms suppliers (*Africa Confidential* 2004).
- *Taxes and levies*: Soldiers and rebel groups often augment their wages and raise money for weapons through the imposition of informal taxes and levies, and other illegal activities. Warlords in Somalia organised 'tax zones' to raise resources to prosecute their clan wars. In Burundi, soldiers augment their wages by imposing taxes on farmers' crops and levies on border trade (Nimubona and Sebudadi 2007). Soldiers employ road blocks all over Africa to extract payments to embellish their paltry wages.
- *Shadow trade*: In the Niger Delta, officers in the Joint Task Force are reportedly involved in the criminal gangs that are engaged in the illegal bunkering of oil (*Africa Confidential* 2007). Some 30,000–100,000 barrels of oil are stolen each day; the revenue from oil is thought to buy arms for the militias (*Africa Confidential* 2006). West Africa has become a major exporter of cocaine. It is not produced in the region, but the networks linking Colombian and Venezuelan drug barons with their West African business partners, which include senior military officers and government officials, have established

complex and lucrative transshipment operations along the West African seaboard. The President and senior military officers in Guinea-Bissau are thought to be at the centre of the cocaine trade in West Africa (*Africa Confidential* 2007).

- *The diversion of humanitarian assistance and aid*: Humanitarian relief for the victims of armed conflict in SSA opened up opportunities for new income streams for both the military and rebel groups. In Liberia, the widespread diversion of relief supplies and assets was believed to have significantly assisted those involved in the fighting (Atkinson and Leader 2000; Savage et al. 2007). In southern Sudan, the fraudulent 'redeeming' or buying-back of slaves, a campaign that raised millions of dollars in charity in the US and other developed countries, enabled the Sudan People's Liberation Army to use the diverted funds to buy arms and ammunition (Harker 2000). Ethiopia is thought to have diverted humanitarian aid to procure weapons in the build-up to its border war with Eritrea (Cooper and Kyzer 2003).
- *External military assistance*: After years of ignoring Africa, the US has dramatically increased military assistance to the region. The total amount of US military sales to, and financing and training expenditures for, eight African countries considered strategic partners in the 'war on terror' has increased from about US$40 million over the five-year period 1997–2001, to over US$130 million between 2002–2006 (LeMelle 2008). Under the Trans-Saharan Counter-Terrorism Initiative (TSCTI), the Pentagon supplied US$500 million to increase border security and counter-terrorism capacities in Mali, Chad, Niger and Mauritania. The African Contingency Operations Training and Assistance programme (ACOTA) has provided small arms and training for peacekeeping operations to Benin, Botswana, Côte d'Ivoire, Ethiopia, Gabon, Ghana, Kenya, Malawi, Mozambique, Nigeria, Senegal, South Africa, Uganda and Zambia. Another source of external support is derived from neighbouring African states. They may supply arms or other forms of military assistance to rebel groups, or state forces, involved in conflict. For example, in the civil war in the Republic of Congo 1993–2002, Angola and Chad provided military assistance to President Sassou-Nguesso. In the DRC, Laurent Kabila received military assistance in the form of arms, training and supplies from neighbouring states, including Zimbabwe, Angola, Namibia and, in the early days of the war, Rwanda and Uganda.
- *Diaspora contributions*: Funds raised from diasporas are another means of augmenting 'off-budgetary' resources. Eritrea was reported to have raised US$400 million for its war effort in the form of donations from the Eritrean diaspora (*The Economist* 1999). These funds are thought to have been used to purchase MiG–29s from the Ukrainians.
- *Peacekeeping*: Volunteering soldiers for UN or African Union peacekeeping operations (PKOs) is another means of generating extra funds. Ethiopia, Ghana, Nigeria, Kenya, Mozambique, Namibia, Senegal, South Africa, Uganda and Zimbabwe are among those countries that have volunteered for PKOs. Rarely do UN payments for these forces appear in annual military budgets. The failure to declare payments offers opportunities for malfeasance. In certain cases, corrupt military officers have banked soldiers' pay (Hutchful 2003). During Nigeria's involvement in ECOMOG missions in West Africa, generals benefited from revenues written off as expenses (Adebayo 2002). Millions of dollars were diverted into private bank accounts as part of this ruse.

- *Prolonged conflict*: Many conflicts in Africa are purposely prolonged by the military and rebel groups, because the conditions of instability enable warlords and generals to rob their nations of resources and funds. Plundered resources provide the income with which militias and the armed forces are able to purchase arms so that they can continue to prosecute war. The diversity and opacity of these resources makes it almost impossible to monitor off-budgetary procurement trends. Subsequently, little is known about the nature of the arms being procured, how much is being spent, the scale of bribes and kickbacks involved, or where and how the ill-gotten gains from corrupt practices in this form of procurement are laundered.

Arms procurement and opportunities for corruption

Even in the context of 'best practice' in defence procurement, i.e. with proper systems of public accountability and transparency in decision-making and auditing, the large and technically complex nature of defence contracts makes it hard for civilian authorities to fully comprehend and assess whether or not a contract is necessary, appropriate or indeed 'value for money'. Challenging equipment specifications is a highly technical process and one that requires a combination of strategic, engineering and accounting expertise. In South Africa, where most of these skills exist and parliamentary oversight mechanisms and auditing procedures have acquired a considerable degree of sophistication, the size and complexity of the recent 'Strategic Procurement Package' created an ideal environment for corruption to flourish.

In the 1995 Defence White Paper, the South African Ministry of Defence highlighted the need to re-equip the South Africa National Defence Force (SANDF) to meet the national security needs of the new democracy. This resulted in the Strategic Arms Procurement Package, which was signed off in December 1999, costing the South African taxpayer US$4.8 billion. The South African Government claimed that the package would pay for itself in the long run, through counter-trade and offset agreements. There was a huge public outcry about this allocation of scarce public expenditure resources at a time when the Reconstruction and Development Programme, designed to lift poor black people out of poverty, had been abandoned.

Controversy associated with the 'Arms Deal', as it has become known, spread, as irregularities in the tendering process and general lack of transparency came to light. Several high-level investigations have been conducted into accusations of corruption involving bribe-takers – African Defence Systems (ADS) and senior figures within the ANC, including former Defence Minister Joe Modise, Tony Yengeni, ANC Chief Whip and former chairman of the Parliamentary Defence Committee, and brothers Shamin and Shabir Sheik, who have links to senior ANC officials. Bribe-payers, notably BAE Systems, the European Aeronautic Defence and Space Company (EADS) and Thales/Thompson, have also been implicated. Despite substantial evidence of widespread corruption in the deal, the major players have not been prosecuted to date, and the various phases of the US$4 billion arms deal continue unabated.

The sheer size of the 'Arms Deal', the South African Department of Defence's ill-preparedness to manage the simultaneous acquisitions, SANDF's questionable ability to absorb the state-of-the-art equipment, the choice of expensive, offensive weapon platforms such as the new Gripen JAS 39 fighter aircraft, at a time when the southern African regional security environment has achieved relative stability, all point to a government agenda quite divorced from its stated objective of re-equipping the country's navy and air force.

Given the resource constraints of most African buyers, including South Africa, a number of non-currency methods of payment for arms procurement have evolved, including counter-trade and offsets. Trading prospects are enhanced, both for suppliers and recipients, as trade is facilitated through a cashless, mutual exchange of needs.

Offsets are industrial or commercial compensation practices required as a condition of purchase of defence articles and/or services. They include co-production arrangements, licensed production, sub-contractor production and overseas investment or technology transfer. As offset arrangements tend to favour countries that have attained a degree of industrialisation, few arms deals involving sub-Saharan countries involve offset agreements. South Africa is an exception to this rule.

Offset agreements are outlawed in all other forms of government procurement by Article XVI of the WTO plurilateral Agreement on Government Procurement, but are often the decider in defence deals because of their anticipated economic benefits. However, as Dunne (2006:43) has shown in the South African case, offset deals often have questionable economic benefits. The prices of the new weapons systems appear to have been inflated by the offset arrangement. Hidden costs include unanticipated capital expenditure on imported equipment, which has had a detrimental effect on the balance of payments; an increase in state expenditure on R&D in order to realise technology transfers; and the downward revision of anticipated job creation. Overall, the economic benefits to the South African economy remain unclear and there may even be considerable opportunity costs in the long run. Finally, in the non-competitive and non-transparent arrangements that surrounded South Africa's offset arrangements, the potential for corruption was extensive.

Counter-trade is far more common in arms transactions in SSA. This type of transaction takes various forms, including barter and counter-purchase arrangements. Barter refers to the direct exchange of goods-for-goods where no cash is involved. Although barter is as old as trade itself, contemporary barter deals are more common than is often realised. State-to-state transactions between African governments often involve barter. For example, Zimbabwe Defence Industries supplied the DRC armed forces with light weapons in exchange for mineral concessions. Angola was also thought to benefit from mineral concessions extended by President Laurent Kabila in exchange for military assistance. Counter-purchase, on the other hand, is a form of exchange that commits the arms seller to purchase a compensatory amount of commodities. In the context of developing countries this normally involves primary commodities. The arms contractors can either market these counter-purchased goods themselves or employ a specialist commodity broker to do the job for them. On the whole, defence firms try to avoid counter-purchases because they inevitably incur extra transaction costs.

Offsets and counter-trade are notoriously difficult to monitor and audit, because the deals are complex, multi-layered, take a long time to negotiate and are subject to fluctuating currency rates and/or commodity prices. This ambivalence provides ample opportunity to inflate deals with bogus expense claims, 'bonuses', 'incentives' and commissions.

The bribe-makers

The main focus of DFID's concern with corruption in military expenditures and arms procurement is on the demand side of corruption dynamics, namely, on the corrupt role of political and military elites in SSA. But for bribe-takers to exist there have to be bribe-makers. Transparency International (2007) has noted that the arms market is one of the most corrupt sectors in the world. Despite accounting for less than 1% of total world trade, the arms trade accounts for around 50% of all corrupt transactions, according to a report issued by the US Government (US Department of Commerce 2000:11). A 2006 survey revealed that approximately one-third of all defence companies claimed that they had lost defence contracts because competitors had offered bribes to secure sales (Control Risks 2006).

The payment of large 'commissions' by arms companies to individual officials in defence procurement deals can provide an incentive for the recipient to increase the technical specification of the weapons and even to persuade governments of the need to purchase entire systems, often entirely unnecessarily. The helicopter scandal in Uganda is a case in point. In 1998 the Ugandan Government purchased four second-hand Mi–24 helicopters from the Republic of Belarus at an inflated price of US$12.3 million (Ochieng 1998). The helicopters were not airworthy. Reportedly, Museveni's brother, Major General Salim Saleh, received a US$800,000 'incentive' to seal the deal. In 1998, the South African Government's last-minute decision to switch from the Italian Aermacchi MB–339 trainer aircraft, the preferred option of the South African Air Force, to the more expensive BAE Systems-built Hawk 100 trainer, is thought to have occurred as a result of substantial sweeteners offered by BAE Systems to the late Joe Modise, then Minister of Defence, and his aide Fana Hlongwane (Roeber 2004:61; Groenink 2007).

The sums involved in bribes are often life-changing for the individuals involved. Payments come in a number of forms, and are made through a variety of channels such as the brown envelope or the Swiss bank account, and take the form of luxury commodities such as cars, villas, private jets and access to private clubs. The scale of 'commissions' and bribes is unknown, and varies from sale to sale. A conservative estimate made by TI UK has put it at 10% of a contract's value (TI UK 2002). However, findings by the UK Special Fraud Office inquiry into the 2006 Tanzania arms scandal found that commissions of 29% were paid, and suggest that bribes may be significantly higher than TI's estimates (Leigh 2006; McGreal 2007). Estimating the total cost of corruption in the arms trade is fraught with challenges, but extrapolating from World Bank figures on global rates of corruption, Transparency International's defence team has conservatively estimated that corruption within the global defence sector averages around US$20 billion per annum (TI UK 2002).

The firms and the government officials who facilitate arms sales often refer to bribes as 'commissions' or 'incentives'. European arms manufacturers in stiff competition with each other, and with US defence giants, like to think that their commissions and 'incentive packages' create a 'level playing field' in a highly competitive defence market. Before the OECD Anti-Bribery Convention was introduced in 1997, these incentives were seen as legitimate practice in defence sales, notably when the payments were made abroad. Since the introduction of the OECD Convention, it is illegal for corporations from OECD countries to offer bribes to foreign officials; however, evidence from recent investigations into arms scandals suggests that the paying of bribes to secure arms sales continues to be widely practised outside the OECD region.

The Bribery Payers Index 2006 (BPI) produced by Transparency International found that Northern companies tend to offer more bribes in Africa than in any other region of the world (TI 2006:8). Of this trend, TI has observed that:

> It would seem that many foreign companies do not resort to bribery while operating in the 'developed' world, where institutions are strong and there is a significant threat of legal retribution for illegal activities. However, in less developed countries (many of which are characterised by poor governance and ineffective legal systems for dealing with corruption), it appears that many companies continue to engage in corrupt practices. The result is that the countries least equipped to deal with corruption are hardest hit, as their anti-corruption initiatives are undermined. (TI 2006:10)

A number of factors have contributed to the rise in corruption in the arms trade sector during the last decade. On the supply side, the end of the Cold War simultaneously dampened demand for weapons systems and increased competition between arms suppliers. Arms manufacturers responded by aggressively marketing their wares, often resorting to bribes to secure deals (Gupta et al. 2000). On the demand side, opportunities for rent-seeking increased with the growing opacity of military procurement and with a reduction in the number of suppliers due to increasing levels of consolidation and concentration in the global defence industry.

The arms industry is 'hard-wired' for corruption, mainly because of both the special treatment it receives from governments and the secrecy that sanctions every aspect of its transactions. Arms companies from the rich West bribe the political and military elites of poor countries to purchase weapons they cannot afford, and often do not need. These sales are justified on the basis of the national economic, employment and security interests of rich Western states, but there is a high cost to such deals, which contributes to the burden of national debt in poor countries, diverts scarce national resources from social spending, and often contributes to the undermining of the security of nations through the purchase of expensive and inappropriate equipment.

The role of the International Financial Institutions

Every single corrupt arms deal involves a financial pipeline that enables bribery to take place. It is not just the corrupt African elites, or the arms companies and their agents, that are prepared to pay bribes and mask their shadowy deals. There are other less visible players – including banks, offshore shell companies, accountants and lawyers – which facilitate the funding of arms deals and help to launder ill-gotten gains.

In laundering money, large amounts of cash are usually spread among many different accounts – such as in free-trade zones, financial offshore centres, and tax havens – where they are converted into financial instruments such as money orders, bonds, investments in trusts or charities, or into shell companies. The money is then transferred to other locations, sometimes in the form of payments for bogus 'goods and services' issued by holding companies owned by lawyers or accountants on behalf of unnamed beneficiaries. The funds are then wired back to their originators as part of the earnings of a legitimate business. It is a relatively simple process that leaves either no paper trail, or one that is so complicated that it is difficult to trace. Because the objective of money laundering is to return the illegal funds in a legal form to the individual who generated them, launderers prefer to move funds through stable financial systems – hence the central role of banks in the money laundering process.

A few examples reveal how global and widespread the money laundering of illegal arms receipts is. In 2006, *Africa Confidential* reported that Kenyan banks had been involved in the laundering of the ill-gotten gains of Nigeria's military and political elites in the late 1990s (*Africa Confidential* 2006). Extensive investigations into the 'Angolagate' scandal, involving illicit arms transfers to Angola worth US$790 billion orchestrated by key members of the French political elite, have revealed that a number of Portuguese banks were involved in transferring illegal commissions. In total, some 70 transfers took place, totalling US$54 billion. Fifty of these transfers, to a total value of US$21 million, were deposited in Portuguese banks. The largest transfers were to the state-run Caixa Geral de Depositos (CGD) and the Banco Comercial Português (BCP), the country's two largest banks. The Nacional de Crédito, Nacional Ultramarino, Comercio e Industria, Totta and Açores, Pinto and Sotto Mayor banks, and the Portuguese branches of Spain's Banco Bilbao and Britain's Barclays, are also on the list of institutions contained in the indictment (Inter Press Service 27 January 2009).

Until relatively recently, the bribes or incentives involved in arms deals were not considered illegal, and banks readily complied with their clients' need to launder their ill-gotten gains. Since 9/11, anti-money-laundering legislation and practice have been tightened up. More than 150 countries promised to cooperate with the US in its fight against the financing of terrorism, 81 of which (including the Bahamas, Argentina, Kuwait, Indonesia, Pakistan, Switzerland and the EU) actually froze the assets of suspicious individuals, suspect charities and dubious firms, or passed new anti-money-laundering laws and stricter regulations (the Philippines, the UK, Germany). Nevertheless, 19 'black holes', or poorly regulated financial services and offshore banking facilities, still persist in Russia, Indonesia and Israel, to name the most prominent.

Money launderers are resilient. They adapt fast to changing circumstances. Alternative banking systems are being established beyond the bounds of the West's financial regulation and jurisdiction. Defunct banks in territories with corrupt politicians, lax regulation and porous tax regimes are being purchased. The cash-hungry countries of Montenegro, Serbia, Macedonia, Ukraine, Belarus and Albania are proving willing participants.

Hypocrisy and discrimination

In December 2006, in response to political pressure from the highest levels in the British Government, the Director of the Serious Fraud Office announced his decision to terminate the investigation into accusations of BAE corruption in the al-Yamamah deal. By failing to conduct full investigations into arms trade scandals, the British Government exposed itself to accusations of hypocrisy and discrimination. It was a major setback in the campaign to control corruption in the transnational arms industry.

In July 2007, Jacob Zuma, himself implicated in corrupt arms dealing in South Africa, accused the British Government of double standards, and posed a pertinent question to the Newsnight investigator Peter Marshall: 'Why should the rulers [of the West] be allowed to pick and choose on matters that relate to the application of law?' (Newsnight 28 July 2007). Whatever his own culpability, Jacob Zuma has a point. DFID and other donors are hardly in a position to impose yet more levels of pernicious conditionality on development aid when their own governments are implicated in diverting scarce resources towards expensive and corrupt arms deals and in repressing enquiries into corruption. This state of affairs not only makes a mockery of DFID's good-governance and anti-corruption programmes, but also undermines its security sector reform agenda, which is a critical component of its post-conflict work.

If the British Government hoped that UK involvement in arms scandals could be covered up and would quietly disappear, it has had a nasty shock, as the US Department of Justice has decided to prosecute BAE Systems for its prominent role in corruption in the global arms trade. The US appears to be the only country currently willing to impose the ethical and legal principles governing the arms trade and embodied within international law. Cynics may argue that it is motivated by its own national interests in preserving the dominance of US arms companies within the international arms market. While there may be some truth to this accusation, if the US Department of Justice can help to regulate the ruthless and corrupt transnational arms industry, whatever its motivation, this may open up opportunities for challenging corruption in the military sector in SSA.

Conclusion

DFID's cautious attempt to tackle corruption in arms procurement through its TIDE programme has been put on the back burner. Not only did the neoliberal methodologies employed to analyse the problem prove inadequate to the task in the SSA context, but it became increasingly apparent to DFID officials that British companies and, by implication, the British Government which had sanctioned and supported British defence companies' sales abroad, were heavily implicated in arms procurement scandals. Given DFID's past record of attempting to control excessive military expenditures, and its more recent attempts to improve transparency and accountability in defence budgeting, it appears to be hopelessly out of touch with the reality of Africa's military and security environment. It should therefore come as little surprise that its endeavour to design an anti-corruption policy for arms procurement and expenditures in SSA has failed to take off.

Corruption in the arms trade is a phenomenon that can only be controlled when it is identified as a 'global governance' problem, one in which the rule of law and, in particular, anti-corruption legislation, has to apply to all parties engaged in corruption. These actors include Western politicians who promote arms sales, civil servants who oversee the licensing of arms exports, export credit guarantee services, arms company salesmen and executives, 'independent agents', political and military elites in recipient countries and the offshore banks which launder the ill-gotten gains. Only then can the global pipeline of covert deals, bribery, kickbacks, money laundering and secrecy be overturned, and ethical and legal principles upheld.

As a first step in regaining moral authority, Western governments need to adhere to, and actively enforce, the 1997 OECD Anti-Bribery Convention. This requires the provision of adequate resources to empower the OECD Anti-Corruption Committee to effectively investigate and prosecute those arms companies engaged in corruption in the developing world. A second step should be to impose conditions on export licences to ensure that companies comply with anti-corruption legislation and practice. Scrutiny of individual arms export licences should also be undertaken by government committees, to ensure both greater transparency in the licensing process, and increased company compliance with anti-corruption legislation. To complement these measures, arms companies should be made to adopt internal auditing systems capable of detecting corruption and the payment of bribes. Finally, government support for the domestic arms industry through the supply of export credit guarantees should be conditional upon anti-corruption compliance. Once the West has put its own house in order, it will be in a stronger position to start tackling the complex and challenging nature of security sector corruption in the developing world. To lead by the example of 'best practice' is a first and necessary step in the challenging task of dismantling the transnational web of corruption in arms procurement and the arms trade.

References

Adebayo, Adekeye. 2002. *Building Peace in West Africa: Liberia, Sierra Leone and Guinea-Bissau.* Boulder, CO: Lynne Rienner.

Adekanye, Bayo J. 1999. *The Retired Military as Emergent Power Factor in Nigeria.* Ibadan: Heinemann Educational Books.

Africa Confidential. 1999. Ceasefire under Threat. 40(22), 5 November.

———— 2004. Post-War Clean Up. 45(21), 22 October.

———— 2005. Nigeria: The Net Widens. 46(15), 22 July.

———— 2006. Breaking the Arms Embargo. 47(23), 17 November.

———— 2007. Nigeria: A Tale of Two Cities. 48(18), 7 September.

Atkinson, Philippa and Nicholas Leader. 2000. *The Joint Policy Operations and the Principles and Protocols of Humanitarian Operations in Liberia.* HPG Report No. 3. London: Overseas Development Institute, Humanitarian Policy Group.

Ball, Nicole and Kayode Fayemi. 2004. *Security Sector Governance in Africa: A Handbook.* Lagos: Centre for Democracy and Development.

Control Risks. 2006. International Business Attitudes to Corruption Survey 2006, Simmons and Simmons. Available from: www.controlrisks.com/pdf/corruption_survey_2006_V3.pdf

Cooper, Tom and Jonathan Kyzer. 2003. II Ethiopian Eritrean War, 1998–2000. Air Combat Information Group. 2 September. Available from: www.acig.org/artman/publish/article_189.shtml

Dunne, Paul. 2006. The Making of Arms in South Africa. *The Economics of Peace and Security Journal* 1(1): 39–48.

The Economist. 1999. Carnage on the Plain. 17–23 April.

Global Witness. 2002. *All the President's Men.* Washington, DC: Global Witness, March.

———— 2004. *Rich Man, Poor Man: Development Diamonds and Poverty Diamonds.* Washington, DC: Global Witness, October.

———— 2005a. *Extracting Transparency.* Washington, DC: Global Witness, September.

———— 2005b. *The Riddle of the Sphinx: Where has Congo's Oil Money Gone?* Washington, DC: Global Witness, December.

———— 2005c. *Timber, Taylor, Soldier, Spy.* Washington, DC: Global Witness, June.

———— 2007. *Oil Revenue Transparency: A Strategic Component of US Energy Security and Anti-corruption Policy*, Washington, DC: Global Witness, March.

Groenink, Evelyn. 2007. Arms Deal: Who Got R1bn in Pay-offs? *Mail & Guardian Online*. Available from: www.mg.co.za/article/2007-01-12-armsdeal-who-got-r1bn-in-pay-offs

Gupta, Sanjeev, Luis de Mello and Raju Sharon. 2000. *Corruption and Military Spending*. IMF Working Paper No. 00/23, Washington, DC: International Monetary Fund.

Harker, John. 2000. The Harker Report: Human Security in Sudan: The Report of a Canadian Assessment Mission. Prepared for the Ministry of Foreign Affairs, Ottawa, February.

Hartley, Keith. 2007. Military Expenditure Data for SSA Nations: Report for DFID. York, Canada: Centre for Defence Economics, University of York.

Henke, Daniel and Martin Rupiya. 2001. Funding Defence: Challenges of Buying Military Capability in sub-Saharan Africa. Strategic Studies Institute (SSI) monograph. Available at: http://www.strategicstudiesinstitute.army.mil/pubs/display.cfm?pubID1/4198

Hutchful, Eboe. 2003. Ghana. In *Military Expenditure Data in Africa: A survey of Cameroon, Ethiopia, Ghana, Kenya, Nigeria and Uganda*, ed. Wuyi Omitoogun. Oxford: Oxford University Press.

Inter Press Service. 2009. Portugal 'Angolagate' Tribes in Local Banks. Lisbon 27 January. Available at: http://www.humanrights-geveva_info?portugal-angolagate-bribes-in,3676

Kaufman, Daniel. 2004. Corruption, Governance and Security: Challenges for the Rich Countries and the World. Available at: http://ssrn.com/abstract1/4605801

Leigh, David. 2006. Fraud Office Inquiry into BAE Tanzanian Deal. *The Guardian*, 13 November. Available from: http://www.guardian.co.uk/politics/2006/nov/13/armstrade.foreignpolicy

LeMelle, Gerald. 2008. *African Policy Outlook 2008*. Washington, DC: Foreign Policy in Focus, 7 February.

McGreal, Chris. 2007. Arms Deal Investigation Probe BAE Payment to South African. *The Guardian*, 6 January. Available from: http://www.guardian.co.uk/world/2007/jan/06/bae.armstrade

Newsnight. 2007. David Marshall interview with Jacob Zuma. London: British Broadcasting Corporation, July.

Nimubona, Julien and Christophe Sebudadi. 2007. Le Phénomène de la Corruption au Burundi: Révolte Silencieuse et Résignation. Bujumbura: International Alert, March. Available from: http://www.eurac-network.org/web/uploads/documents/20070504_9136.doc

Ochieng, Levi. 1998. Military Copters Condemned by S. African Firm. *The East African*, 3 September.

Omitoogun, Wuyi. 2003. *Military Expenditure Data in Africa: A Survey of Cameroon, Ethiopia, Ghana, Kenya, Nigeria and Uganda*. Oxford: Oxford University Press.

Omitoogun, Wuyi and Eboe Hutchful. 2006. *Budgeting for the Military Sector in Africa: The Process and Mechanisms of Control*. Oxford: Oxford University Press.

Renton, David, David Seddon and Leo Zeilig. 2007. *The Congo: Plunder and Resistance*. London: Zed Books.

Roeber, Joe. 2004. The Politics of Corruption in the Arms Trade: South Africa's Arms Trade Scandal and the Elf Affair. In Transparency International, *Global Corruption Report 2004: Political Corruption*. London: Pluto Press.

Savage, Kevin, Mulbah Jackollie, Maxim Kumeh and Edwin Dorbor. 2007. Corruption Perceptions and Risks in Humanitarian Assistance: A Liberia Case Study. Humanitarian Policy Group Background Paper. London: Overseas Development Institute, April.

SIPRI Military Expenditure Database. Available from: http://www.sipri.org/contents/milap/milex/mex_database1.html

Transparency International. 2006. Bribery Payers Index 2006 Analysis Report. Available from: www.transparency.org/policy_research/surveys_indices/bpi/bpi_2006

Transparency International. 2007. *Addressing Corruption and Building Integrity in Defence Establishments*. Working Paper No. 2, London: Transparency International.

Transparency International UK. 2002. *Corruption in the Official Arms Trade*. Policy Research Paper 001. London: Transparency International UK.

UN Security Council. 2003. Panel of Experts on the Illegal Exploitation of Natural Resources and other Forms of Wealth of the DRC, 5/2003/027. 23 October, New York: United Nations.

US Department of Commerce. 2000. *The National Export Strategy Trade Promotion Coordinating Committee Report*. Washington, DC: US Department of Commerce, March.

WMEAT. 2002. *World Military Expenditures and Arms Transfers 1999–2000*. Washington, DC: US Department of State.

Section Two:
Global Security Governance

7

Somalia: 'They Created a Desert and Called it Peace(building)'

KEN MENKHAUS (2009)

Explanations of Somalia's extraordinary 20-year crisis – featuring civil war, state collapse, failed peace talks, violent lawlessness and warlordism, internal displacement and refugee flows, chronic food insecurity, piracy, regional proxy wars and Islamic extremism – have tended to fall in one of two camps. One assigns blame primarily to internal factors perpetuating the country's crisis; the other emphasises the role of external drivers. Both have ample evidence on which to draw. Accurate analysis of the Somali crisis must account for both internal and external conflict drivers and the mutually reinforcing dynamics that have developed between them.

A case can also be made that the relative salience of these conflict drivers has changed over time. In the early years of the Somali disaster, internal factors – warlordism, clannism, poor leadership, economic constraints and others – were decisive in perpetuating the civil war and undermining external peacebuilding efforts. External policies in the 1990s at times made things worse – by failing to provide timely diplomatic mediation when it was most needed in 1991, and intervening clumsily in the UN Operation in Somalia in 1993-94 – but were not a root cause of the crisis. However, in recent years external actors have come to play an increasingly central role in perpetuating or exacerbating the Somali crisis. In some instances, external actors have intentionally set out to cultivate divisions and lawlessness in Somalia, or to use the country to play out proxy wars against regional rivals. In other cases, external interventions have been well intentioned but ill-advised, falling victim to the law of unintended consequences and in the process making things worse.

Things are certainly worse in Somalia. The two-year period of 2007-08 was a calamity of enormous proportions for the country, arguably as bad as the disastrous civil war and famine of 1991-92. A fierce insurgency and counter-insurgency pitting Ethiopian occupying forces against armed resistance led by the radical Islamist group *al-Shabab* devastated the country and polarised politics in Somalia still further. Somalia staggered into the year 2009 as the world's worst humanitarian crisis, with 1.3 million internally displaced persons and 3.5 million people in need of emergency aid. Some positive developments in early 2009 offered hope – Ethiopian forces withdrew, and a power-sharing accord between the weak Transitional Federal Government (TFG) and moderate elements of the opposition led to a new, more broad-based government. But in its first months in power the new TFG showed little capacity to extend its authority, and several radical Islamist insurgency groups, one with links to *al-Qaeda*, gained control over most of southern Somalia and pushed into parts of the capital Mogadishu.

This is the exact opposite of what the US and its allies sought to promote when they supported the December 2006 Ethiopian military intervention in Somalia to oust the Islamic Courts Union (ICU) in Mogadishu. Most Somalis are bewildered by external policies that have laid waste their already desperately poor country while simultaneously promising to support peacebuilding efforts there.

This article documents the humanitarian, political and security dimensions of the current Somali crisis and assesses the policies of one set of external actors – the loose coalition of Western governments and the UN which have sought to support the TFG, moderate Islamism, African peacekeeping and power-sharing in Somalia. It advances the thesis that Western and UN actors treated Somalia in 2007 and 2008 as a post-conflict setting when in fact it remained in a state of open and heavy armed conflict. In some cases, Western and UN polices inadvertently helped to inflame armed conflict and insecurity there. As a result, there was no peace for peacekeepers to keep, no state to which state-building projects could contribute, and increasingly little humanitarian space in which aid agencies could reach over 3 million Somalis in need of emergency relief. The gap between Somali realities on the ground and the set of assumptions on which aid and diplomatic policies toward Somalia have been constructed is wide and deep.

The path to catastrophe

The current crisis in Somalia is the culmination of a series of developments since 2004, when national reconciliation talks produced an agreement on a Transitional Federal Government, or TFG.[1] The TFG, led by President Abdullahi Yusuf, was intended to be a government of national unity, tasked with administering a five-year political transition. But the TFG was viewed by many Somalis, especially some clans in and around the capital Mogadishu, as a narrow coalition dominated by the clans of the President and his Prime Minister, Mohamed Ghedi (ICG 2004: 1). It was also derided by its critics as being a puppet of neighbouring Ethiopia. Yusuf's deep animosity toward any and all forms of political Islam alarmed the increasingly powerful network of Islamists operating schools, hospitals, businesses and local sharia courts in Mogadishu. By early 2005, serious splits emerged within the TFG between what became known as the 'Mogadishu Group' and Yusuf's supporters. Facing deep opposition in Mogadishu, the TFG was unable to establish itself in the capital, taking up residence instead in two small provincial towns. Weak and dysfunctional, the TFG appeared destined to become yet another stillborn government in Somalia, which has not had an operational central government since 1990 (Menkhaus 2007).

However, the coalition of clans, militia leaders, civic groups and Islamists which formed the Mogadishu Group were themselves divided, and war

---

[1]   A more detailed account of recent events in Somalia since 2004 can be found in Menkhaus (2007).

erupted between two wings of the group in early 2006.[2] This war was precipitated by a US-backed effort to create an alliance of clan militia leaders to capture a small number of foreign *al-Qaeda* operatives believed to be enjoying safe haven in Mogadishu as guests of the hardline Somalia Islamists, especially the jihadi militia known as *al-Shabab*. The Alliance for the Restoration of Peace and Counter-Terrorism, or ARPCT, as the US-backed group was called, clashed with local Islamists in a war that originally began over real estate and business disputes between two rival businessmen (Barnes and Hassan 2007:4). Within months the Alliance was decisively defeated, paving the way for the rise of the Islamic Courts Union, or ICU, which for seven months in 2006 came to control and govern all of Mogadishu and most of south-central Somalia.

The ICU was a broad umbrella group of Islamists, and for a brief period was poised to end Somalia's 16 years of state collapse. The ICU quickly delivered impressive levels of street security and law and order to Mogadishu and south-central Somalia. It reopened the seaport and international airport and began providing basic government services (*Ibid.*: 4). In the process, the ICU won widespread support from war-weary Somalis, even those who did not embrace the idea of Islamic rule. To its credit, the US government made a good-faith effort to support negotiations between the ICU and the TFG, with the aim of creating a power-sharing government.[3]

But then things went wrong. A complex power struggle emerged within the ICU, pitting against each other Hawiye clan interests, Islamic moderates, hardline but cautious Islamists, and confrontational jihadists in the *al-Shabab* militia (ICG 2007:5–9). The hardliners began pushing the ICU into increasingly bellicose and radical positions that alarmed neighbouring Ethiopia and the United States. The ICU declared jihad on Ethiopia, hosted two armed insurgencies opposed to the Ethiopian government, made irredentist claims on Ethiopian territory, and enjoyed extensive support from Ethiopia's enemy, Eritrea, which was eager to use the ICU to wage a proxy war against Ethiopia. In short, the hardliners in the ICU did everything they could to provoke a war with Ethiopia, and in late December 2006 they got their wish (Prendergast 2008). For its part, the United States understandably grew increasingly frustrated with the ICU's dismissive non-cooperation regarding foreign *al-Qaeda* operatives in Mogadishu, and as a result became more receptive to, and supportive of, an Ethiopian military solution.[4]

Ethiopia's US-backed military offensive against the ICU was a rout. The ICU militias took heavy losses in the first engagements, and when they fell back to

[2] Due to space limitations, the complex details of clan politics in shaping support for and opposition to the TFG are not provided here. For our purposes it is enough to note that clannism is one of a number of important elements contributing to the political divisions in Somalia today. For more details, see ICG (2004; 2007), Barnes and Hassan (2007) and Menkhaus (2007).

[3] It was never clear that any of the main players in the Somali saga – hardliners in the TFG (including the President and Prime Minister), Ethiopia and hardliners in the ICU – would have been willing to see these power-sharing negotiations succeed, but at the time it was the best hope to bring peace to Somalia.

[4] The precise position of the US Government vis-à-vis the Ethiopian military offensive and occupation of southern Somalia remains the subject of debate, with conflicting accounts even within the US Government. These debates centre around whether and to what extent the US acquiesced, gave tacit support for, gave a 'green light' to, or actively requested Ethiopian military action against the ICU. What is indisputable is that, once the Ethiopian offensive was immanent, the US Government actively provided it with support.

Mogadishu angry clan and business leaders forced the ICU to disband and return weapons and militiamen to the clans (Barnes and Hassan 2007). While core ICU supporters fled toward the Kenyan border, the Ethiopian military marched into Mogadishu unopposed. Within days the TFG relocated to the capital to govern over a shocked and sullen population. It was a scenario no one had foreseen, and set the stage for the current catastrophe.

Enmity between Ethiopian highlanders and Somalis is deep, rooted in centuries of conflict. The Ethiopian government, its allies and its enemies all understood that a prolonged Ethiopian military occupation of the Somali capital would be resented by Somalis and was certain to trigger armed resistance. The proposed solution was rapid deployment of an African Union peacekeeping force to replace the Ethiopians. But African leaders, not unlike their European and North American counterparts, were reluctant to commit troops into such a dangerous environment, and after long delays were only able to muster a force of 2,000.[5] So the Ethiopian forces stayed, joined in their efforts by TFG security forces which Ethiopia trained.

Within weeks, a complex insurgency – composed of a regrouped *al-Shabab*, ex-ICU sharia court militias, clan militias and other armed groups – began a campaign of armed resistance. Attacks on the TFG and the Ethiopian military occurred each day, involving mortars, roadside bombs, ambushes and even suicide bombings. The Ethiopian and TFG response was extremely heavy-handed, involving attacks on whole neighbourhoods, indiscriminate violence targeting civilians and widespread arrest and detention. TFG security forces were especially predatory toward civilians, engaging in looting, assault and rape. The insurgency and counter-insurgency produced a massive wave of displacement in 2007: 700,000 of Mogadishu's population of 1.3 million were forced to flee from their homes.

This disastrous level of violence and destruction had other costs as well. The already fragile economy of south-central Somalia collapsed; the TFG was unable to establish even a token civil service or advance the political transition; Ethiopia took heavy losses and, as predicted, became trapped in a quagmire in Mogadishu; and thousands of Somalis became radicalised by their treatment at the hands of the TFG and Ethiopian forces, and, despite deep misgivings about the insurgents' indiscriminate use of violence, became either active or passive supporters of the increasingly violent *al-Shabab* and other armed groups.

By late 2007, open splits occurred in both the opposition and the TFG. These splits had the potential to be negative – leading to uncontrolled splintering of Somali political actors – or positive – providing a new opportunity for the creation of a centrist coalition in Somalia and marginalising hardliners on both sides. In the opposition, exiled ICU leaders established an umbrella group with non-Islamist Somalis, called the Alliance for the Re-Liberation of Somalia, or ARS. This alliance prompted the *al-Shabab* to publicly break with the 'apostate' ARS. In the TFG, the corrupt and deeply divisive Prime Minister Ghedi was finally forced to resign, and a new Prime Minister, Hassan Hussein Nur 'Adde', came to lead a promising moderate wing of the TFG. He formed a new cabinet that included many technocrats from the Somali diaspora, and reached out to the opposition, pledging himself to unconditional peace talks. His efforts were viewed with deep hostility by the hardliners in the Yusuf camp.

---

[5]   AMISOM forces levels eventually reached 3,000 by late 2008.

The international community, led by UN Special Representative for the Secretary-General Ould Abdullah, sought to forge a centrist coalition of TFG and opposition figures. In June 2008, a UN-brokered peace accord was reached in Djibouti between moderate elements in the TFG and moderate leaders in the ARS, the latter led by Sheikh Sharif Sheikh Ahmed and Sharif Hassan (known locally as the 'two Sharifs'). The Djibouti Agreement was finally signed on 18 August and in November a follow-up agreement was reached. The Djibouti agreement and the follow-up accord called for a cessation of hostilities, a joint security force, deployment of a UN peacekeeping force, withdrawal of Ethiopian forces, a two-year extension of the TFG mandate, and an additional 275 Parliamentary seats created for the opposition, so that the parliament would constitute a unity government.

Supporters of the agreement saw it as a major breakthrough and called for strong international support for implementation of the agreement. In mid-2008 their initial hope was that any agreement that facilitated the withdrawal of Ethiopian forces would open the door for an end to the insurgency. They pointed to the fact that most of the war-weary Somali public wanted to see the agreement implemented as well. By late 2008 the logic in support of the accord had changed. With Ethiopia threatening to pull out unilaterally by the end of the year, and with *al-Shabab* consolidating control over most of southern Somalia, proponents of the accord argued that the moderate coalition formed by the agreement was the only hope to stave off a take-over of the capital by *al-Shabab*. Critics of the deal argued that the moderates on both sides exercised little control over the armed groups engaged in fighting, that UN peacekeepers would take too long to effectively deploy and would only energise *al-Shabab*, and that the accord ran the risk of further fragmenting both the ARS and the TFG in ways that could marginalise the very moderates the international community was trying to support.

By early 2009, Somalia appeared to have weathered the worst of its crisis. Ethiopian forces withdrew as promised, while the Djibouti agreement produced a new, more broad-based government featuring moderate Islamist leadership of Sheikh Sharif, leader of the old ICU. *Al-Shabab* was in short order deprived of its main nemeses, and faced growing resistance from clan militias that were allied with the new TFG and which had no interest in seeing a radical jihadist group with *al-Qaeda* links take power. *Al-Shabab* was unable to exploit the so-called strategic vacuum created by the Ethiopian withdrawal. But, as argued below, hopes that 2009 would witness the expansion of the TFG's authority and the marginalisation of radical insurgents in Somalia did not materialise in the first half of the year.

Humanitarian catastrophe

The humanitarian nightmare in Somalia is the result of a lethal cocktail of factors. The large-scale displacement caused by the fighting in Mogadishu is the most important driver. The displaced have fled mainly into the interior of the country, where they lack access to food, clean water, basic health care, livelihoods and support networks. Internally displaced persons, or IDPs, are among the most vulnerable populations in any humanitarian emergency. With 700,000 people out of a population of perhaps 6 million in south-central Somalia forced to flee their homes, the enormity of the emergency is obvious.[6]

Second, food prices have skyrocketed, eroding the ability of both IDPs and other households to feed themselves. Food prices have gone up due to a global spike in the cost of grains and fuel; chronic insecurity and crime, which has badly disrupted the flow of commercial food into the country; and an epidemic of counterfeiting of the Somali shilling by politicians and businesspeople, which has created hyperinflation and has robbed poorer Somalis of purchasing power. Mother Nature is not cooperating either: a severe drought is gripping much of central Somalia, increasing displacement, killing off much of the livestock, and reducing harvests in farming areas.

Third, humanitarian agencies in Somalia are facing daunting obstacles to delivery of food aid. There is now very little 'humanitarian space' in which aid can safely be delivered to populations in need.[7] Until recently, the TFG and its uncontrolled security forces were mainly responsible for most obstacles to delivery of food aid. TFG hardliners viewed the movement of food aid to IDPs as support to an enemy population – terrorists and terrorist sympathisers in their view – and sought to impede the flow of aid convoys through a combination of bureaucratic and security impediments. They also harassed and detained staff of local and international nongovernmental organisations, or NGOs and UN agencies, accusing them of supporting the insurgency. Uncontrolled and predatory TFG security forces, together with opportunistic criminal gangs, erected over 400 militia roadblocks (each of which demanded as much as US$500 per truck to pass) and kidnapped local aid workers for ransom.

However, since May 2008 an additional threat to humanitarian actors is jihadist cells in Mogadishu linked to the *al-Shabab*. They are engaged in a campaign of threats and alleged assassinations against any and all Somalis working for Western aid agencies or collaborating with the UN and Western NGOs. Not all *al-Shabab* members embrace this policy – indeed, some *al-Shabab* cells provide protection for aid convoys while nearby *al-Shabab* groups actively target aid workers – but jihadist cells in southern Somalia are now increasingly fragmented.

To summarise, Somali aid workers and other civic leaders have faced a terrifying combination of threats from hardline elements in the TFG, criminal gangs and *al-Shabab* cells. This has infused political violence with a high level of unpredictability and randomness in Mogadishu that has eroded the ability of astute Somali aid workers, businesspeople and civic figures to make calculated risks in their movements and work. When threats and attacks occur, aid workers are never sure whether they were targeted by the TFG or the *al-Shabab*. 'We used to know where the threat was and how to deal with it', said one. 'Now we have no

---

[6]   The total population of Somalia is unknown and the subject of debate. The most common estimate is 8 to 9 million for the entire country, including the population of secessionist Somaliland in the northwest.

[7]   As of late 2008, there has been a sharp debate between various UN and NGO humanitarian aid agencies, donors and diplomats over whether adequate humanitarian space exists to permit effective food relief operations in the country. Some argue that the extraordinary number of assassinations of local and international aid workers has resulted in an almost complete evacuation of aid workers across the country, leaving aid agencies with no means of monitoring food shipment distribution. Others argue that, despite the difficulties posed by the security crisis, some aid agencies have successfully relied on local partners to move food aid to the 3 million Somalis in need. For recent discussions, see UN OCHA (2009) and BBC 2008.

idea who is shooting us.' Attacks initially believed to be the handiwork of an *al-Shabab* cell are latterly suspected of being ordered by one of the TFG hard-liners; in the swirl of rumours and accusations, uncertainty reigns.

However, the one thing that is certain is the casualty rates among aid workers, which currently earn Somalia a ranking as the most dangerous place in the world for humanitarian workers. In the period from 1 July 2007 to 30 June 2008, 20 aid workers were killed in Somalia – nearly a third of the 65 human-itarian casualties worldwide during that period, and two more humanitarian deaths than occurred in Afghanistan, which is widely considered the most dangerous place for aid workers.[8]

These attacks have put thousands of Somali professionals, aid workers, moderate Islamic clerics, businesspeople and civil society leaders at immediate risk, and have prompted a flight of aid workers and civil society figures to the relative safety of Nairobi or Hargeisa, the capital of the self-declared independent republic of Somaliland. The July 2008 assassination of the top national officer for the UN Development Programme in Somalia was especially jarring, prompting relocation of most UN local staff and suspension of UNDP activities. But the most devastating attack was the 29 October 2008 synchronised suicide bombing attacks by *al-Shabab* which struck five targets in Somaliland and Punt-land, which left over 20 Somalis dead, including several UN staff members who were killed when one car bomb completely destroyed the UNDP compound in Hargeisa (CNN 2008). Both local and international aid agencies are now either not able to conduct operations at all or are operating at extremely limited capacity. This severe restriction on humanitarian access is occurring at precisely the point when local coping mechanisms are breaking down and when 3.2 million Somalis are at immediate risk. The country is on the cusp of a human-itarian disaster at a time when aid agencies are severely stretched in their ability to respond and admit that Somalia is an 'accountability free-zone' in terms of their ability to monitor shipments of food aid.[9]

A critical dimension of this reduction of humanitarian space is the role that Western foreign policies have inadvertently played in creating it. *Al-Shabab* threats aimed at aid workers are in direct response to the US designation of *al-Shabab* as a terrorist organisation in March 2008, and the May 2008 US missile strike on a safe house in central Somalia that killed the *al-Shabab*'s leader, Aden Hashi Ayro. Prior to those policies, *al-Shabab* was directing its attacks against the TFG and the Ethiopian military. After the missile attack on Ayro, the group declared its intent to widen the war to any and all Western targets inside and outside the country, including Somalis working in any way with the West. Threats and violence by hardliners in the TFG against civil society figures and aid workers also can be traced back to Western policies, inasmuch as the TFG police force, which is implicated in attacks on and abuse of Somali civilians, has been provided with training and even salaries by Western donors.

The new TFG government has promised to work to improve security and access for aid agencies but currently lacks the ability to deliver on that promise. Aid agencies which have pragmatically worked with *al-Shabab* groups to deliver

---

[8] Ten additional aid workers were killed in Somalia between July and October 2008, raising the total to 30 deaths for the year. The UN reports that between January and the end of October 2008, there were 152 security incidents involving humanitarian aid workers. See UN OCHA (2009: 6).

[9] Interview by the author, Nairobi, November 2008.

food aid into areas controlled by that group have come under fire from UN and donor state diplomats upset that *al-Shabab* may be using its control over the distribution of food relief to shore up its power base, and to profit from possible diversion of food aid. For their part, humanitarian aid organisations have resented efforts to politicise their work by diplomats instructing them on who they may and may not work through on the ground.

Political paralysis

The assassination campaign by TFG hardliners and fragments of the *al-Shabab* movement is the latest attack on Somalia's once vibrant civil society and has the potential to develop into a violent purge of all professionals and civic figures. Somali civic figures are in shock at this latest threat, and are either fleeing the capital or keeping a very low profile. This is an enormous setback for hopes to consolidate peace in the country, as civil society leaders are essential supporters of the centrist coalition of the new TFG. The group of people most needed to support peace and co-existence are being silenced or driven out, clearing the playing field for extremists.

The Djibouti agreement and the new TFG coalition produced a sense of cautious optimism among Somalis. However, any initiative openly designed to marginalise hardliners and build a centrist coalition faces immediate dangers, and Sheikh Sharif's TFG is no exception. Open rejection of the Djibouti agreement by the *al-Shabab* leadership and hardline elements within the ARS itself highlighted the fact that the former ARS leadership has no control over a principal source of the insurgency.[10]

Internal fragmentation of *al-Shabab* and other Islamist insurgencies makes the challenge of implementation even greater, since any understanding reached with *al-Shabab* leaders may or may not influence the behaviour of individual cells. Indeed, growing evidence suggests that at least some militias now calling themselves *al-Shabab* are just sub-clan militias 'rehatting' themselves for reasons of political expediency; some have no discernible Islamist ideological agenda, and do not answer to *al-Shabab* leadership. 'The militia who call themselves *al-Shabab* are just the same Haber Gedir gunmen who have occupied us for years', observed a Somali resident from the Jubba Valley. 'They just put a turban on their heads and gave themselves the new name, but their treatment of us is the same'.[11]

While implementation of the Djibouti agreement has been the current preoccupation of the diplomatic corps, other political problems loom large. The first is the TFG's virtual collapse as a government. The TFG has never been functional, despite the best efforts of the international community to pretend otherwise. After almost four years of existence, the TFG still has almost no capacity to govern and almost no functional civil service. Cabinet ministers have no ministries to oversee, and no budget. Armed groups fighting against *al-Shabab* are doing so as allies of the TFG in negotiated arrangements with the government, not under its command and control. No progress has been made

---

[10] The ARS is now divided between the moderate wing, led by the two Sharifs and known as 'ARS-Djibouti', and the ARS-Asmara wing headed by Hassan Dahir Aweys. Aweys rejects the Djibouti accord.

[11] Correspondence with the author, July 2008.

on key transitional tasks. The TFG has lost control over most of the countryside and the capital.

Military advances by *al-Shabab* and *Hisbul Islamiyya*, a rejectionist militia headed by ex-ICU leader Hassan Dahir Aweys, have pushed the TFG into a few neighbourhoods of the capital. This has not been so much a reflection of the strength of *al-Shabab* and *Hisbul Islamiyya* as it has been a function of the utter lack of capacity of the TFG to sustain a fighting force. The possibility that the TFG could be defeated entirely is real, and a recipe for trouble. *Al-Shabab*'s links to *al-Qaeda* are likely to prompt Ethiopia to move its military back into Somalia. *Al-Shabab* has every reason to draw Ethiopia back into Somalia, as that would allow it to once again cast its role as that of a Somali resistance movement to Ethiopian imperialism, rather than being viewed by Somalis as a tool of *al-Qaeda* and Eritrea, the latter of which is using Somali Islamist groups in a proxy war against Ethiopia.

Even in the event of an insurgent victory over the TFG, fighting is unlikely to end. Instead, most Somali observers expect *al-Shabab* and *Hisbul Islamiyya* to fight one another. Whatever the outcome, two significant interpretations of the current battle are emerging from Somali political discussions. The first is the observation that the current battle is a war of Islamists. All three of the main protagonists in the battles in 2009 – the TFG, *al-Shabab* and *Hisbul Islamiyya* – identify themselves as Islamists. This is a remarkable shift in the Somali political landscape, underscoring the ascendance of political Islam in Somalia and yet exposing the fact that Islamism has failed to serve as the unifying force so many Somalia have hoped that it would. Second, the battles of 2009 are increasingly being described by Somalis in the country as a war within the Somali diaspora. Many of the leaders of the TFG and insurgents are diaspora members, reflecting the diasporisation of the Somali political and economic elite over the past decade. 'Unhyphenated Somalis' stuck in the country with no foreign passports are increasingly angry that they serve as the principal victims of a war over which their hyphenated cousins from the diaspora maintain control.

Counter-terrorism blowback

Far from rendering Somalia a less dangerous terrorist threat, the effect of the 2007–08 Ethiopian occupation was to make Somalia a much more dangerous place for the US, the West and Ethiopia itself. Somalis were radicalised by the extraordinary level of violence, displacement and humanitarian need. They blame the Ethiopian occupation and the uncontrolled TFG security forces for the catastrophe. But the blame does not stop there. Most Somalis are convinced that the Ethiopian occupation was authorised and directed by the United States. Although this is a misinterpretation of the complex and often turbulent rela-tionship between Addis Ababa and Washington – two allies with distinct agendas and preferences in the Horn of Africa – it has been an article of faith in the Somali community. The Somalis are not entirely wrong. In 2007 and 2008, the US did provide intelligence to the Ethiopians; was a major source of development and military assistance to Ethiopia; shielded Ethiopia from criti-cism of its occupation in the UN Security Council; collaborated with the Ethiopians and the TFG in multiple cases of rendition of Somalis suspected of terrorist involvement; and engaged in gunship and missile attacks on suspected terrorist targets inside Somalia since the Ethiopian occupation. These and other policies gave Somalis the clear impression that the United States had orchestrated the Ethiopian occupation and is therefore responsible for its impact.

Moreover, the West has also been held responsible for the abuses committed by the TFG security forces under Abdullahi Yusuf's presidency until late 2008. This, too, is a partial misreading; Western donors and aid agencies had little or no control over the actions of these armed groups and were frequently furious with them over their mistreatment of civilians and disruption of relief aid. But the fact remains that the TFG police were in 2007 trained by, and received salaries from, the UN Development Program, through which Western donor states channelled their 'rule of law' assistance to the TFG. For Somalis whose businesses were looted and whose family members were raped or killed by uncontrolled TFG security forces, the West is partly culpable for their suffering.

As a result, anti-Americanism and anti-Western sentiment in Somalia have been very high, posing the risk that more Somalis could become either passive or active supporters of *al-Shabab*. Events since early 2009 have partially reversed this animosity toward the West and the US, thanks to the withdrawal of Ethiopian forces, Western support for the new TFG, and Somali hopes for a policy shift in the Obama administration. Even so, Western and UN policies in Somalia face high levels of suspicion and mistrust among many Somalis.

Conclusion

For years, observers of the Horn of Africa opined that the Somalia crisis could not get any worse. Yet it has, and dramatically so. The country today faces a level of humanitarian, social, security and political disaster on a scale that would have shocked policy-makers of 2006 had they had a glimpse into the future. The evidence speaks for itself. Policies pursued by Ethiopia, the United States and Western donors in the past three years have produced outcomes that advance no one's interests, save perhaps a growing number of extreme jihadist cells in the country.

Throughout the crisis of 2007 and 2008, the international community's insistence on treating Somalia as a 'post-conflict' setting, with aid programmes for rule of law, security sector reform and key transitional tasks, appeared increasingly out of touch with grim realities on the ground, and eventually reached the point of willful blindness. Political pressures from key donor states or aid agencies to downplay the humanitarian crisis, stay silent on TFG human rights abuses, and maintain aid programmes in spite of gross levels of abuse and insecurity to help maintain the legitimacy of the TFG, were critical in driving this dysfunctional policy approach.

Somalia has long faced severe internal challenges to peacebuilding and state-building. In recent years it has had to shoulder the additional burden of external policies which have actually helped to make things worse, not better. Finding innovative and constructive policies to confront Somalia's intractable crises will not be easy, but it will be impossible if not based on a more accurate and clear-eyed assessment of the situation on the ground.

References

Barnes, Cedric and Harun Hassan. 2007. *The Rise and Fall of Mogadishu's Islamic Courts*. Africa Programme Briefing Paper, April. London: Chatham House.

BBC News. 2008. Somalia nearing a 'Total Famine'. 4 December. Available from: http://news.bbc.co.uk/2/hi/africa/7764937.stm

CNN. 2008. *Al Qaeda* Blamed for Somali Bombing Wave. 29 October. Available from: http://www.cnn.com/2008/WORLD/africa/10/29/somalia.blast/index.html

International Crisis Group. 2004. Somalia: Continuation of War by other Means? Africa Report 88, 21 December. Brussels/Nairobi: ICG.

———— 2007. Somalia: The Tough Part is Ahead. Africa Briefing Paper 45, 26 January. Nairobi/Brussels: ICG.

Menkhaus, Ken. 2007. The Crisis in Somalia: A Tragedy in Five Acts. *African Affairs*, 106(424): 357–390.

Prendergast, John. 2008. *15 Years after Black Hawk Down: Somalia's Chance?* Enough Strategy Paper No.18, April. Washington, DC.

United Nations, Office for the Coordination of Humanitarian Affairs. 2009. Somalia Consolidated Appeal 2008, 1 December. Nairobi: OCHA.

8

The Burundi Peace Negotiations: An African Experience
of Peace-Making

PATRICIA DALEY (2007)

In August 2005, the former rebel leader, Pierre Nkurunziza, was installed as
the President of a newly-elected Hutu majority government in the central
African state of Burundi. This marked the culmination of almost nine years of
a formal peace process that followed a trajectory of peace negotiations, peace
and ceasefire agreements, a transitional government and democratic elections
(*Irinnews.org*, 2002a; b; Reyntjens 2005). Yet, it is an uneasy peace as ceasefire
agreements were not reached with all warring factions and low-intensity
violence and a culture of impunity pervade Burundi society.

Since independence from Belgian colonial rule in 1962, Burundi has been
highly unstable, with six governments between 1962 and 1966, the abolition
of the monarchy (1966), four successful coups d'état (1965, 1976, 1987 and
1994), and the assassination of its first democratically-elected President,
Melchoir Ndadaye, in October 1993. Like their neighbours in Rwanda, the
people of Burundi have been subjected to episodes of genocidal violence; an estimated 200,000 people were killed in 1972 and a further 20,000 in August
1988, and since Ndadaye's assassination in 1993, warfare waged by the military and government-backed militias against rebel groups and their supporters
has killed some 200,000 people and forced over 350,000 into exile (ICG 1998;
Arusha Peace and Reconciliation Agreement for Burundi 2000).

The Burundi peace negotiations originated essentially from a regional thrust
for peace and have been represented as a successful attempt by Africans at
regional peace-making (Bentley and Southall 2005; Mpangala and Mwansasu.
2004). Peace negotiations started in 1996 and culminated in the signing of the
Arusha Peace and Reconciliation Agreement in August 2000. Rebuffed by the
rebels and signed reluctantly by the political parties, it became a peace agreement without a cessation of hostilities. Fighting continued even after the 2005
elections, as it took a further year before a ceasefire agreement was signed with
the last remaining rebel faction.

Scholars have long challenged the appropriateness of the Western-derived
peace imposed on Africa, and more recently, have criticised the promotion of a
'liberal peace', structured by hegemonic neoliberal political economic practices
(Mafeje 1995; Hansen 1987; Richards 2005; Willett 2005). Using the Burundi
peace negotiations as an example, this article examines the prevailing concept
of peace that informs contemporary conflict resolution in Africa, especially the
ways in which it has been structured by neoliberalism and the relationship
between peacemaking and protracted wars. Also of importance is the way
different interest groups (local, regional and international) shape the outcome

and, in essence, define the peace appropriate to Africa, such that accords can be signed whilst fighting continues; in effect normalising extreme forms of violence.

This article draws on research conducted since 1998 with Burundi politicians in Belgium, Tanzania and Burundi, and with members of the facilitation team from the Mwalimu Nyerere Foundation. Archival data from the Arusha negotiations were gathered at the Foundation and from newspapers, news websites and reports of international NGOs.

The article argues for peace negotiations to be seen not primarily as attempts to end warfare and promote social justice, but as arenas of political struggles beyond that envisaged between the belligerents, due to the prevalence of a multitude of supporting actors seeking to promote vested interests. The resulting peace agreement is not necessarily consensual or reflective of a compromise for the sake of peace; it marks, essentially, a temporary stalemate between the manoeuvrings of international, regional and local actors. The Burundi peace process represents struggles between different competing visions of peace; the neoliberal one supported by Western donors, and that of regional actors, seeking to establish a new mode of politics on the continent. Unable to incorporate the perspectives of civil society and without international political clout and financial resources, regional actors conceded to the imposition of a 'liberal peace', which, while promoting ethnic equity through power-sharing among the elites and democratic elections, leaves the extant social system intact and is not conditional on the cessation of direct violence.

The peace problematic in Africa

War and peace are complex terms. Their meanings depend largely on how we conceptualise violence. War refers to the use of violence to settle political differences, in effect, the struggle for state power. Galtung (1969) distinguishes between 'direct violence' (fighting) and 'structural violence' (indirect forms of violence stemming from exposure to conditions of poverty and powerlessness). He argues that 'negative' and 'positive' peace result from the ending of direct and structural violence respectively, even though the latter is difficult to achieve, being reliant on efforts to end social injustice. Useful as it may be in articulating the brutality of poverty, this dichotomy has become less so in our quest to make sense of the persistence of direct violence after peace agreements have been signed and democratic elections have been held to resolve political differences. 'Negative peace' seems far from being achieved in many post-conflict countries in Africa. Recently, scholars of African warfare have questioned this dichotomy of war and peace. Richards (2005:4–5), for example, asks us to see war and peace as existing along a continuum, defining war as a 'long-term struggle organised for political ends'. Thus, he contends we can understand why 'peace can often be more violent and "dangerous" than war'. However, history has shown that states can achieve 'negative peace' and can go some way to address social injustice. Why not contemporary Africa? Steans (1998:106–7) refers us to classic realist thought in which 'hegemonic states dominate international institutions and by doing so "manage" international security', thus ensuring that war and peace have different meanings in hegemonic and weak states.

During the Cold War, proxy wars fought on the continent of Africa helped to maintain the peace in Europe and North America. In post-colonial Africa, 'peaceful' states could include dictatorial, militaristic or one-party regimes. Indeed, the formula for a peaceful society in Africa seems to involve the tolerance of higher levels of direct and structural violence. The end of the Cold War and the rise of economic liberalism produced new explanations for warfare and new frameworks for peace. Conflict resolution models tend to employ the popular discourse that represents African wars as essentially primordial, often arising from age-old innate and irrational enmities and, even when the interpretations attempt to avoid ethnic reductionism, they draw on two prevailing academic discourses. The first links ethnicity with notions of greed or grievance harboured by conflicting parties (Berdal and Malone 2000). And the second represents war in the post-Cold war period as 'new', non-ideological and fuelled by the avariciousness of tribal 'warlords', aiming to capture state resources for private gain (Kaldor 2001). 'New wars' are presented as being of greater complexity and in need of multifaceted solutions. Such approaches interpret war and peace as confined within the boundaries of the nation-state, thus failing to consider the ways in which global geo-politics and market-based economic systems influence regional and local politics and exacerbate the conditions for war. Post-Cold War transformations in conflict resolution under neoliberalism are well-documented (Duffield 2001; Clapham 1998; Richards 2005; Tull and Mehler 2005). These include an increased role for non-state actors in the negotiation process, a proliferation of mediators, and power-sharing instead of winner-takes-all elections.

Power-sharing means dividing the institutions of governance between political parties and rebel movements, in the context of a new constitution and democratic elections. Theoretically, it is appealing as the lack of equity among groups is seen as a significant factor in African conflicts and it also reflects the sidelining of state sovereignty inherent under neoliberalism (Bangura 1994; Clapham 1998; Tull and Mehler 2005). Power-sharing can satisfy greed and grievance while still retaining 'democratic principles and procedures', making it 'compatible with democracy while diminishing its most destabilising side effects' (Spears 2000:105). Indeed, many political parties, especially the weaker ones, prefer to gain constitutionally protected political advantage through negotiations before committing themselves to the electorate (Bangura 1994). Tull and Mehler (2005) note that power-sharing agreements, by enabling rebel leaders to gain state power, can lead to the reproduction of 'insurgent violence', as rebellion becomes the means to gain political leverage and international acceptance, thus making access to political power difficult for those who champion non-violence. Power-sharing can legitimise and normalise violence as part of the political discourse. Theoretically, multipartyism and democratic elections should lead to greater representation and accountability, but experience suggests that, in the context of neoliberalism, they are easily manipulated by the elite, and can lead to xenophobia and sectarian violence.

The proliferation of non-state organisations and consultants as mediators has turned peace into a veritable industry. In addition to the UN, the African Union and Western governments, numerous international, regional and local NGOs have been active in formulating and promoting peace initiatives. The nature of the peace problematic is such that the motivations of individual actors beg investigation, especially since the proliferation of mediators seems to protract warfare rather than lead to swift resolutions. As Clapham (1998:209) notes, with respect to the Rwandan war of the 1990s, 'mediators are not merely bystanders ... but participants, whose involvement weakens or strengthens the position of different internal parties, and may ... strengthen the position of those domestic factions which are most adamantly opposed to the negotiated settlement'.

Despite the inflated assumptions about the commitment of the belligerents to the peace process, explanations for the failure of peace agreements focus either on the lack of political will on the part of the signatories or claim that the 'spoilers' see war as more profitable than peace, rather than a peace process that privileges aggression and denies agency to those most affected by warfare. Peacemaking, in spite of the incorporation of a host of actors – the political elite, warring factions and external mediators – excludes the people, who are represented as victims of rapacious elites and warlords, and whose well-being is assigned to international humanitarian and development agencies.

The goal of the 'liberal peace' is to enforce rapid modernisation of African societies. This is to be accomplished by 'transform[ing] the dysfunctional and war-affected societies that it encounters on its borders into cooperative, representative and, especially, stable entities', and involves 'reconstructing social networks, strengthening civil and representative institutions, promoting the rule of law, and security sector reform in the context of a functioning market economy' (Duffield 2001:11). Ultimately, the 'liberal peace' necessitates the entrenchment of neoliberal political economic practices, which, hitherto, have undermined state sovereignty, focusing as they do on non-state actors; the market for economic development and personal liberation; civil society and/or external ('non-territorial') actors for humanitarian and welfare intervention, and multipartyism for diffusing political tensions and mediating competition.

Richards (2005) contends that 'liberal peace' takes wars out of their social contexts, and argues that instead of conflict resolution, one should focus on conflict transformation which would re-socialise war and re-direct 'the social energies deployed in war to problem-solving ventures on a co-operative basis' (Richards 2005:18). Radical as it may seem, Richards' project is based on advocating a more participatory vision of peace which could fit well with neoliberal conceptualisation of civil society. The importance of collective responsibility for long-term peace is indisputable. Peace must rest with the return of agency to the people affected. But the shortcomings of Richards' analysis lie with his focus on peace as resting primarily within the capacities of local communities.

The 'liberal peace' envisages a process of 'creative destruction' commonly known as post-war reconstruction, which has become a major policy arena for development agencies, multinational corporations, non-governmental organisations (NGOs) and private military contractors; two key policy areas are demobilisation and reconciliation. However, without the space for alternative and progressive conceptualisations of peace, demilitarisation and reconstruction often result in a shift in the nature of direct violence, from military combat to low-intensity violence (human rights violations, including sexual violence) on a generalised scale (Amnesty International 2004). Consequently, post-war reconstruction has had limited success in Africa because it tends to reinforce the social system within which violence and inequalities are embedded (Mafeje 1995; Spears 2002; Tull and Mehler 2005). Rather than, as Duffield (2001:11) claims, 'liberal peace reflect[ing] a radical development agenda of social transformation', it constitutes, instead, a form of 'negative peace' that normalises extreme violence.

In sum, the liberalisation of peace-making has resulted in the proliferation of mediators, the inclusion of non-state actors, the sharing of power between belligerents, the privileging of violence as a mechanism for political inclusion, and what amounts to the de-politicisation of warfare (Clapham 1998; Tull and Mehler 2005; Richards 2005). Thus, the dominant conflict resolution model, in spite of its liberalisation, upholds a non-transformative concept of peace.

The situation in Burundi epitomises the inconclusiveness of neoliberal peace-making. A detailed examination of the Burundi peace negotiations and subsequent events (1996–2005) enables us to identify, more specifically, the inherent limitations in neoliberal conflict resolution. This is achieved by constructing a narrative of the peace process that examines the impetus for peace, the key issues that stalled the talks and the contributions of a multiplicity of actors: regional states, mediators, especially the leadership (Julius Nyerere and Nelson Mandela), the protagonists (Burundi government, political parties, rebel movements, and their negotiating positions) and Western donors, multilateral organisations, peace consultants, international NGOs and civil society organisations, especially women in light of UN Security Council Resolution 1325. The actualities of peace-making are investigated through a focus on the key issues debated and the tenets of the peace accord. Implementation of the accord, post-Arusha, reveals the temporality as well as the contradictory outcomes of the 'liberal peace' that, whilst appearing to open the political space for marginalised ethnic elites and women, for example, eschews genuine public participation and institutionalises violence as the mode of political contestation.

The Burundi peace process: a regional thrust for peace

The Burundi peace negotiations, spearheaded by Tanzania, arose from a regional initiative by neighbouring states concerned about the protracted nature of the conflict and its destabilising impact on the region. This initiative was given impetus through the actions of the US-based Carter Center which sponsored the first two preliminary meetings on Burundi and the region. It took four years from the beginning of the talks (April, 1996) before the peace agreement was reached (August, 2000) – aspects of which are still being implemented by the democratically-elected government that took office in August 2005.

Warfare in Burundi is commonly represented by the media and by the international community as an age-old ethnic conflict between the majority Hutu and minority Tutsi ethnic groups – the latter having dominated the state, almost uninterrupted, since independence from Belgian colonialism in 1962. Alternative explanations, while recognising that violence manifests itself largely along ethnic lines, focus either on the prevalence of ethnic inequalities in a *rentier* and neo-patrimonial state or on the failure of the postcolonial state to transcend discriminatory colonial practices based on racial and social hierarchies (Ngaruko and Nkurunziza 2000; Daley 2006). The first two perspectives provide the underlying discourse of the peace negotiations and provided the foundations for the neoliberal governance and economic reforms outlined in the peace agreement. However, the process of negotiations and the implementation of reforms reflect the tensions between neoliberalism and ethnic-based ideologies, and attempts to chart a new mode of politics in the region. These tensions highlight the competing perspectives on peace arising from the contradictions inherent in neoliberalism, as it simultaneously opens and narrows the political space.

The anti-state critique at the foundation of neoliberalism manifests itself in the promotion of a multiplicity of actors in peace-making. In the case of the Burundi peace negotiations, states retained key roles in the procedures. Financial support for the talks came from international donors (the UN, EU, US, Canada etc.), regional states (Uganda, Tanzania, Kenya, Zaire [DRC] and later South Africa) acted as overseers, supporting the mediatory roles of Julius Nyerere (April 1996-October 1999) and Nelson Mandela (1999–2000).[1] Regional states sought to define the nature of the peace process and to exert influence on the agreement. After regional summits in June and July 1996, they issued communiqués advocating a negotiated settlement to the crisis in Burundi and national reconciliation. They called for an arms embargo and the denial of visas to those opposed to peace. The Tutsi officers' coup of 25 July 1996 that returned Pierre Buyoya, a former Tutsi President and coup-leader, to power was condemned and regional states called for the immediate restoration of the National Assembly and the lifting of the ban on political parties.

There were two mechanisms that regional states sought to use to exert influence over the peace process. The first was the proposal for the establishment of a regional peace-keeping force, which, although requested by the interim Burundian (Hutu) President, Sylvestre Ntibantunganya, and his Tutsi Prime Minister, Antoine Nduwayo, met with considerable opposition from the military and the Tutsi-dominated parties (*Daily News*, 19 January 1996; Bunting et al. 1999). Protests by members of the Tutsi political class and their supporters threw the country into the chaos that culminated in the July 1996 *coup d'état*.

Opposition to the regional peace-keeping force, especially one which involved troops from neighbouring states, arose partly from intermittent proposals by a variety of actors for the incorporation of Burundi into a neighbouring state (Tanzania) in order to provide a geographic solution to the problem of ethnicity. It was mainly for this reason that many Burundians, Hutus and Tutsis, as well as external observers, questioned the motivations behind the involvement of the Tanzanian state in the peace negotiations and accused it of bias. In fact, Nyerere, who was close to the first elected leader of Burundi, Prince Louis Rwagasore (the Prince was part of the decolonisation movement), was opposed to coups, and was sympathetic to the plight of the Burundian Hutu refugees who sought asylum in Tanzania in large numbers after the 1972 genocide, and after 1993. Given the narrow political base of the military leadership of Burundi under Buyoya, any attempt to foster peace and negotiations was interpreted as support for the rebels. The convergence of neoliberal peace and neoliberal democracy undermined elements in Tanzanian society who used xenophobic attacks on the refugees to bolster their political ambitions.

The second mechanism by which regional states sought to exert pressure on the Burundi regime was regional sanctions. The economic embargo that was in place from October 1996 to January 1999 was not effective, in the sense that it was difficult to seal road, rail and air links to land-locked Burundi. Consequently, there were widespread violations and profiteering by regional elites (*The East African*, 11 March 1998). Furthermore, the lack of support from Western

---

[1] The Organisation of African Unity (OAU) gave its approval with declarations at two summit meetings in November 1995 and March 1996. International support was given in UN Security Council Resolutions 1049 (5 March 1996) and 1072 (30 August 1996).

governments meant that goods and weapons continued to be transported via daily flights to and from Belgium, France and other EU countries. Despite their ineffectiveness, opposition to the sanctions was such that regional states were forced to ease them twice to enable the importation of essential goods, including fuel, medicine, foodstuffs, and educational and agricultural goods.

The Burundi military regime launched an international campaign against the sanctions, arguing that it was the poorest of the poor who suffered most from sanctions. The government's 'diplomacy', which was, according to Bunting et al. (1999: not numbered), 'dynamic, aggressive and effective', had the support of the international community. The World Bank, the UN, Western countries and international NGOs, such as the International Crisis Group and Action Aid, were very critical of the regional initiative (*Irinnew.org*, 1998; ICG 1998; Mthembu-Salter 1998). The French ambassador to Tanzania, Jacques Migozzi, was reported to have said 'The blockade does not resemble those placed against Iraq and Libya. This was decided by heads of state in the region. They lack global status' (Baraka and Mfinange 1998). France's objection to the embargo seemed to rest on the fact that it was a purely African initiative, but also sanctions undermined neoliberal free market ideology and affected French and Belgian businesses.

International donors sought to punish the peace-makers by withdrawing their financial support. The European Union, for example, called for an audit of monies spent on the talks and reduced its financial support for Tanzania. Nyerere criticised the neoliberal approach to peace, when he argues: 'We have to balance the significance of their financial contribution, the power of the governments and multilateral organisations they represent and the amount of damage the pursuit of their own parochial interests can cause to the process. This should be measured against the need for the funding, diplomatic relations with the countries and the institutions they represent and the overall peace process' (Burundi Peace Negotiations 1998:14–15).

The financial shortfall was filled by regional governments and the OAU. Almost in retaliation against regional stubbornness, several Western countries increased 'humanitarian' aid to Burundi. In sum, sanctions marked an important step in the move by African states to find regional solutions to their problems and, in spite of near universal external opposition, they worked, in that they eventually brought the Burundi government to the negotiating table.

However, it was the influence of South Africa, through its mediator, Nelson Mandela, that forced the peace agreement. After Nyerere's death, the Burundi government, along with international peace advisers and the US, supported a South African mediation headed by Mandela (*Irinnews.org*, 1999). An African mediator, with limited knowledge of Burundi politics, was also preferable to the military wing of Burundi's political elite, which argued that a South African mediation would correct 'a number of weaknesses observed in the methodology and management' (*Ibid.*).

Coming from a regional superpower, Mandela was considered to have brought 'a lot of clout' to the negotiations, as South Africa 'had the military capacity to support any agreement' (Interview with member of facilitation team, 2005). One manifestation of the clout that Mandela brought was that numerous presidents, including the then US President Clinton, went to the signing. However, the limited regional knowledge of the South African Ministry of Foreign Affairs enabled the Burundi military elite to turn the negotiations to their advantage.

The South Africans made concessions to the Buyoya regime without consideration of their full consequences.

The actors in the drama of liberal peace

The peace industry in Africa has set up an array of donors and peace consultants. Those with vested interests in the region, such as the former colonial power, Belgium, and francophone countries – France, Switzerland and Canada – and major donors such as the US, the European Union and the UK sent special envoys or supplied facilitators to play leading roles on committees. Non-governmental organisations, such as the London-based International Alert, Washington-based Search for a Common Ground, Rome-based *Comunità di Sant'Egidio*, and South Africa's ACCORD, became active participants in the peace process.

While the Western media criticised the regional states, these same media directed little criticism to the activities of Western observers – as representatives of donor countries and multilateral blocs – who attempted to steer the negotiations to suit their interests. According to the reports by the Tanzanian Facilitation Team, the special envoys from outside the region 'displayed a tendency to want to dominate and control the process', holding alternative 'secret' peace talks concurrently in Europe (Burundi Peace Negotiations 1998). These were meant to undermine the Tanzanian initiative, but their impacts were greater in Burundi, where they led to an intensification of the violence, as those members of the political elite who were not invited to the talks felt marginalised and were worried about exclusion from any peace pact. These alternative talks also conveyed international legitimacy on the Burundi regime and the President's refusal to accept regional mediation. As well as institutions, individual international 'consultants' also tried to influence the peace process; some provided advice to the belligerents and colluded in attempts to shift the talks away from Tanzania's control.

Political parties, ethnicity and governance reform

In line with neoliberal governance reforms, all political parties were invited to the negotiating table – those that fought the 1993 elections and those formed after the elections. Giving them equality of status led to a proliferation of parties and may well have contributed to factionalism within the rebel movements. Many parties lacked a recognised constituency and had not tested their legitimacy with the disenfranchised Burundi population. A similar situation existed in the Rwandan peace talks of the early 1990s where, according to Clapham (1998:205), any protagonist 'who could muster evident support ... had to be admitted... on terms of broad equality with existing regimes' and was given a status 'that only very inadequately reflected their popular support or military strength'.

In all, there were 84 delegates from the Burundi political parties, the government and the National Assembly. The key political parties to the negotiations were *Front Pour la Démocratie au Burundi* (FRODEBU), which won the democratic elections of June 1993, whose President was assassinated, and whose dominance of a temporary coalition was overthrown by the July 1996 coup; *Union Pour le Progrès National* (UPRONA), the ruling party, aligned to the coup leaders; and *Conseil National Pour le Défense de la Démocratie* (CNDD), a breakaway party from FRODEBU. Representatives of the military participated as part of UPRONA or the government delegation and as consultants to one of the committees. Those rebels, PALIPEHUTU-FNL (*Parti Pour la Libération Du Peuple Hutu/Forces National de Libération*) and CNDD-FDD (*Conseil National Pour le Défense de la Démocratie/Forces pour le Défense de la Démocratie*), who continued to fight, were not recognised by Nyerere, who refused to acknowledge leaders who 'gained power by force' (*Africa Confidential*, 1999). They were, however, invited by Mandela to join the negotiations.

Ethnic ideology was a determining factor in the alignment of the political parties at the negotiations. They organised themselves into two broad interest groups: Group of 7, comprising Hutu-dominated parties, and Group of 10, made up of Tutsi-dominated parties with the addition of the Government of Burundi and the National Assembly. By enabling participants to articulate a common position on key issues, these groupings may have increased the effectiveness of the debates; nevertheless, they reinforced ethnicity as the basis of political discourse and obscured the fact that not all parties were ethnically exclusive in their membership.

The degree of ethnic allegiance varied from the integrated FRODEBU and UPRONA to the Tutsi extremist and ironically named *Parti Socialiste et Pan-Africaniste* (INKINZO) and the purely Hutu *Parti Pour la Libération Du Peuple Hutu* (PALIPEHUTU). Individual parties articulated moderate to extremist ethnic ideologies. And within the broad groupings, there were considerable internal divisions. Disagreements over approach created leadership crises and breakaway movements. The partnership of the Government of Burundi, National Assembly and UPRONA (G3) were often at variance with the rest of the G10. These differences among the Tutsis often reflect divisions among the political, military and entrepreneurial elites from the province of Bururi and between the Bururi elite and those from Muramyva and other regions. Amongst the Hutus divisions were manifested mainly over the issue of whether to negotiate with the Buyoya government and the power-sharing arrangements, leading to the creation of internal and external wings of the various Hutu-dominated political parties. Radical Hutus were often critical of those with allegiance to UPRONA, and some rebel movements sought negotiations not with political parties but with the military – considered to be the real power in the regime.

In the discussions at the peace negotiations, there was widespread agreement that the cause of warfare was not ethnicity. Protocol, Article 4 states; 'the parties recognise that the conflict is fundamentally political, with extremely important ethnic dimensions; It stems from a struggle by the political class to accede to and/or remain in power' (Arusha Peace and Reconciliation Agreement for Burundi 2000:16).

Yet, the realm of politics was confined to political parties that were perceived as being defined largely by ethnicity. This may be because, apart from those expressing extreme ethnic ideologies, there were very small differences between the parties. Few had a conceptualisation of democracy that extended beyond the demand for equality between Hutus and Tutsis. Democracy simply amounted to equal guaranteed access to state institutions and ethnic quotas in the judiciary and army. Participating in the negotiations and signing the agreement secured parties a stake in government, which they would not necessarily have achieved through democratic elections.

Civil society representation

Current neoliberal governance reforms argue for the promotion of civil society actors. In peace-making, the proliferation of non-state actors implies a greater role for civil society participation. In practice, however, peace-making continues to deny representation and thus political agency to local civil society groups campaigning for peace. At Arusha, two reasons were put forward against their participation. First, a majority among the Burundian negotiators were reluctant to have civil society groups as independent members. They cited the rules of procedure agreed in 1998, that any new group would need unanimous support in order to be admitted. This, apparently, was to prevent the Burundi military class bringing in carefully selected civil society representatives. The second reason was that Burundi's civil society organisations, many dominated by Tutsis, were not sufficiently independent from the state and representative of 'all groups'. The peace accord notes, 'the notion of civil society [in Burundi] is in fact a new one and is not well understood by the population, just as civil society itself does not understand its own mission' (Arusha Peace and Reconciliation Agreement for Burundi, Report of Committee IV, Reconstruction and Development:125, Para 2.5.6.1). This seems a coded reference to the lack of ethnic inclusiveness in many civil society organisations, and the inevitable dominance of these organisations by the educated Tutsi elite. In the end, civil society representatives were requested to participate as part of the delegation of the political parties they were affiliated to. However, their exclusion as independent participants reinforced the idea that peace-making is solely the prerogative of political parties and rebel movements, not the collective responsibility of the people.

The role of Burundi women in intervening in the peace process has been lauded by numerous academics and NGOs (Burke et al. 2001). However, a detailed examination of their involvement proves instructive. *Women for Peace*, a Burundi organisation, was established in 1993, well before the peace negotiations began (*Ibid.*). However, the women's campaign only gained momentum when it was co-ordinated under an umbrella organisation, CAFOB (*Collectif des Associations et ONGs Féminines du Burundi*), and attracted international support, although its effectiveness depended on its co-operation with women's organisations in the region. In 1998, a delegation of women from Uganda, Rwanda and Tanzania visited Buyoya, Museveni and Nyerere, seeking explanations for the exclusion of women's organisations from the talks; this intervention led to concessions by the parties. Three women were appointed to the negotiations by the government and three by FRODEBU. Representatives of women's organisations were allowed to attend as observers in October and December 1998 (Arusha III), but their status and credentials were questioned; namely, were they representing women or existing political parties. Reportedly, the women's viewpoints did not differ from these of other party delegates and some were wives of colonels. The inclusion of women, even as tokens, was beneficial, in that, as a group, women are probably the most victimised in war time and patriarchal practices might be difficult to defend in their presence.

The Burundi women's movement also benefited from a new policy framework, supported by Security Council Resolution 1325 (2000), which stresses the importance of women's 'equal participation and full involvement in all efforts for the maintenance and promotion of peace and security' (para. 5). With the support of UNIFEM and the Mwalimu Nyerere Foundation, an All-Party Burundi Women's Peace Conference was held in Arusha from 17 to 20 July 2000, just over a month before the signing of the peace agreement. The fifty Burundi women who participated came from all social groups, including the diaspora and refugee camps. The conference drew up proposals to engender the draft peace agreement outlining how specific gender-related clauses could be incorporated (Burke et al. 2001). Virtually all of these gender-specific changes were later accepted by the parties to the agreement because, according to one member of the Facilitation Team, 'at that stage they did not matter'.

The negotiations: schedules and outcomes

The details of the negotiations have been set out to show that peace is an industry in the West and that the consultants, international NGOs and peace industry experts sought to manipulate the process for their own purposes. Experts on Burundi are familiar with these processes, but these details are repeated here in order to drive home the point that Western peace concepts failed to validate the lives of Africans. In 1996, the US created the Africa Crisis Response Initiative in order to stop genocide in Burundi, but it was the same government of the US that supported the military coup of Buyoya when he came to power in July 1996. Buyoya, who had just returned from an internship in the US, had been given money to establish a 'peace foundation'.

The first All Party Peace Talks (Arusha I) took place on 21 June 1998; all parties except those fighting attended, including the special envoys from the EU, US, Canada, OAU, Switzerland, *Communita di Sant'Egidio* (a Rome-based Catholic NGO) and the UN. The multinational team reflected the interests of the international community and, as such, the talks were structured 'within the broad contextual framework of the international community' (Butiku 2004). Five broad areas of concern were identified: the nature of the conflict, democracy and good governance, peace and security, reconstruction and development and guarantees of implementation of the agreement, and five committees were established to negotiate the issues and reach an agreement on each of them.

At the second All Party Peace Talks on 20 July 1998 (Arusha II), each committee drew up its agenda and worked independently of the others with regular consultations with the Facilitation Team (Bunting et al. 1999). Competing interests dogged the selection of committee chairs and vice-chairs; Western donors, international NGOs and the Burundi government sought to influence the appointments. The Facilitation Team was concerned that some committee chairs and vice-chairs, who originated from outside the continent, did not fully support the peace process and were obstructive, often failing to perform their duties (Burundi Peace Negotiations 1998).

Four more peace talks and numerous intercessional consultations took place before a draft agreement was submitted to all parties in March 2000. In April, Mandela issued a statement saying that the draft agreement would not be changed. However, external pressure forced him to make changes, after which, according to one observer, 'the draft agreement started to unravel' (Interview, member of Facilitation Team, 2001).

The first change was to Protocol I following a request from Louis Michel, the Belgian Prime Minister and Minister of Foreign Affairs, who, on a visit to Arusha in July 2000, asked Mandela for two paragraphs implicating the Belgian colonial state in the murder of the democratically-elected Prime Minister, Prince Louis Rwagasore, in 1961, to be removed.[2] The circumstances surrounding the death of Rwagasore were one of the few points on which all the Burundi parties were agreed. Mandela went against the wishes of the Burundians and proceeded to remove the paragraphs, unilaterally, with the justification that Burundi would need aid from Belgium. This action may have undermined the legitimacy of the agreement and led to parties not keeping their commitments. After this, various groups were able to put pressure on the facilitator for changes to the draft document.

In its criticisms, the Burundi government said the draft agreement was not practical – it was 'replete with confusion, ambiguity and double standards' (*Irinnews.org*, 2000). For the government and the Tutsi elite, reform of Tutsi-dominated state institutions, such as the military and the *gendarmerie*, was the most contentious. Retaining the status quo was seen by many Tutsis as the guarantor of their security. Hutus, on the other hand, saw their repression as being linked to the mono-ethnic security services and demanded the 'restructuring and retraining of the army' (FRODEBU, 6th plenary, 19 October 1998). The armed Hutu groups, excluded initially from the talks, made themselves significant players in less than one year. From June 1999 to January 2000 they became a force to be reckoned with if peace was to be achieved. In late 1999, CNDD-FDD conducted a scorched earth policy in the southern and eastern Burundi provinces of Bururi, Makamba and Ruyigi. Human Rights Watch (2000) reports that FDD insurgents not only killed or kidnapped civilians, but looted and burnt houses, schools, health centres, communal offices, in Kinyinya, Gisuru and Nyabitare. In response, the government intensified its repressive tactics using the military and the *gendarmerie*, while Tutsi militias attacked civilians, as a means of expressing their dissatisfaction with the negotiations.

The Burundi regime sought to by-pass the Arusha committees by negotiating directly with Mandela in South Africa. Buyoya proceeded to manipulate the process to obtain a result that disproportionately favoured the Tutsis and secured the continuation of his presidency during the first interim period of the transitional government, when key issues relating to the ceasefire negotiations and governance would be decided (*Irinnews.org*, 2000; ICG 2000).

In June 2000, Mandela held closed door talks with the rebels and representatives of the Burundi government in South Africa. While the rebels sought to renegotiate the whole agreement, the Burundi military elite made a deal with the South Africans regarding the ethnic balance in the transitional government and the army. What became known as 'the Pretoria compromise' was supposed to ensure the security of the Tutsi. Buyoya emerged with assurances that Tutsis would constitute 50% of the Senate, 60% of the government and political parties with 5% or more of the vote would gain a place in government. Tutsis would also make up 50% of the army. The government may have hoped to

---

[2] See Republic of Burundi, Interim Strategic Framework for Accelerating Economic Growth and Reducing Poverty, November 2003, Burundi (Endnotes).

exclude Hutu rebels, because as soon as the agreement was reached, the military started to recruit Hutus into the lower ranks.

The Arusha Peace and Reconciliation Agreement for Burundi was signed on 28 August 2000 amidst disagreements. The pressure to reach an agreement was so intense that articles relating to the establishment of the Senate and the composition of the armed forces were added to the draft agreement on the eve of signing, after last-minute concessions were made by FRODEBU, without the approval of the other G7 parties. Agreement was not reached on several issues: leadership of the Transitional Government, arrangements for a ceasefire, the composition of the armed forces and the treatment of political prisoners.

A scaled-down version of the agreement was signed by Buyoya and by the G7 (Hutu parties). The G10 (Tutsi parties) claimed they signed 'under extreme international pressure and with reservations'. The rebel movements, CNDD-FDD and PALIPEHUTU-FNL, refused to sign. Consequently, it was a peace agreement without a ceasefire.

The main tenets of the peace agreement focused on the establishment of a three-year transitional government; with the transitional period divided into two 18-month intervals headed alternatively by a Tutsi and a Hutu; legislative power was to be exercised by a National Assembly of at least 100 members and a Senate comprising two delegates from each province (one Tutsi, one Hutu). During the transitional period a new constitution was to be produced and approved by the Senate and National Assembly, and an independent electoral commission established to organise elections. Refugees were to be repatriated and reintegrated into their former communities and the monitoring and guaranteeing of the process would be the job of an Implementation Monitoring Committee (IMC), supported by the presence of an international peace-keeping force.

Arguably, the peace agreement followed a standard formula aimed at instituting a system for power-sharing between political parties (rebel movements would register as parties) and ensuring the presence of ethnic and gender plurality within the political structures. Power-sharing is aimed at rectifying ethnic inequalities without the displacement of those already in power, since the proposed size and membership of the National Assembly and the Senate allowed for the incorporation of past presidents and representative of most factions. Furthermore, the stipulation of the electoral commission that parties must be multi-ethnic forced the main political parties to recruit members from other ethnic groups. Ethnic competition is not anathema to neoliberalism, which promotes group and individual rights in the context of the free market.

Post-Arusha developments

The incompleteness of the Peace Agreement in 2000 (which was witnessed by so many luminaries) resulted in its slow implementation. It took a year before the Transitional Government was constituted and five years from the signing of the Agreement before a democratically elected government was *in situ*. In between there were two attempted coups – in April and July 2001. Some elements of the Burundi ruling class with an ethnic base used their political resources to delay implementation. Once the political leaders understood the machinations of Western donors, they sought to rearrange their politics to suit.

Faced with numerous petitions for and against candidates for leadership, the regional states decided that Buyoya should be Transitional President for the first eighteen-month period with Dometien Ndayizeye (G7 and FRODEBU) as Vice-President (Chhatbar 2001). They threatened further sanctions if Buyoya failed to abide by the conditions; even so, he later sought to change the clause in the Constitution that prevented him from running as President. The transitional government sworn in on 1 November 2001 had 26 Cabinet posts, of which 14 went to Hutus; Tutsis retained the key ministries of defence, foreign affairs and finance. Four women party members were made ministers.

In the Introduction, a distinction was made between the instant peace accord of neoliberal peace and the long-drawn-out concept of African peace. The contradiction between these views became manifest in the establishment of the regional peacekeeping force. By this time the AU had taken a firmer position against genocide in Africa. Despite considerable Tutsi opposition to the force, AMIB (African Union Mission to Burundi) started on 18 October 2001 and was made up initially of 701 South African troops. Following UN Security Council Resolution 1554, AMIB was converted to ONUB (United Nations Mission in Burundi) in June 2004 and increased to 5,650, incorporating troops from Ghana, Nigeria and Senegal, all countries external to the region. ONUB's presence helped to maintain a semblance of stability during the implementation of the accord, but did not stop the fighting and human rights violations by all sides.

Ceasefire negotiations between the Transitional Government and the Hutu rebel movements proceeded, with the Facilitation Team headed initially by the then deputy President of South Africa. The commitment of African leaders meant that what was a long and tortuous process ended with binding agreements. The lengthy process was due to a) the intervention of too many mediators (holding meetings in Rome, Libreville, South Africa and Dar es Salaam); b) factionalism in the rebel movements (CNDD-FDD had split into two factions headed by Jean-Bosco Ndayikengurukiye and Pierre Nkurunziza, as did PALIPEHUTU-FNL headed by Alain Mugabarabona and Agathon Rwasa); and c) the intensification of the war – both the government and rebels used the post-accord period to rearm. Even FRODEBU, as late as November 2002, was reported to have established a rebel group, Ramico-Pax (Tindwa 2002).

The smallest factions of the two rebel movements (Ndayikengurukiye's CNDD-FDD and Mugabarabona's PALIPEHUTU-FNL) were the first to reach a ceasefire agreement with the government on 7 October 2002. A year later, on 16 November 2003, Nkurunziza's CNDD-FDD and the government agreed to the *Pretoria Protocol on Political, Defence and Security Power Sharing in Burundi*, which gave CNDD-FDD 40% of the integrated general staff and the officer corps in the army. In the new army, Burundi National Defence Force, military command posts would be shared 50/50 on an ethnic basis. CNDD-FDD also signed a ceasefire agreement on 3 December 2002 in which it would become a party and be allocated two ministerial posts. Nkurunziza was made Minister for Good Governance. The largest branch of PALIPEHUTU-FNL, headed by Agathon Rwasa, joined the ceasefire talks in April 2005 after regional Heads of State declared the FNL to be a 'terrorist organisation'. FNL increasingly relied on terror tactics against civilians to strengthen its negotiating position. For example, in August 2004, FNL massacred 152 Congolese refugees at Gatumba camp for no discernible reasons (HRW 2004).

After a turbulent drafting phase, on 28 February 2005 a referendum on the new Constitution showed overwhelming support from 91.2% of voters.

UPRONA's central committee and three other Tutsi parties had urged a 'no' vote and refused to sign a code of good conduct during the elections.

Thirty-four political parties fought the communal and parliamentary elections that were finally held from June to August 2005. CNDD-FDD was confirmed winner of the municipal communal (senatorial) polls held on 3 June; of the 3,225 seats, CNDD-FDD won 1,781, followed by FRODEBU with 822, UPRONA came third with 260 seats and Movement for the Rehabilitation of Citizens (MRC) gained 88 seats (*Irinnews.org*, 2005). This pattern was repeated in the elections for the National Assembly, held on 4 July 2005: CNDD-FDD gained 58.55% of the votes, FRODEBU 21.69, UPRONA 10%, CNDD 4% and MRC 2%. At the end of August 2005, Pierre Nkurunziza, as the head of the largest elected party, was chosen as President by the National Assembly and Senate. Tutsis were co-opted onto the National Assembly and the Senate in order to reflect the 60/40 ethnic quota of the Peace Agreement and the Constitution. Reyntjens (2005:130) points to the 'unconstitutional' composition of the Cabinet, having representation from parties that did not gain 5% or more of the vote: MSP-Inkinzo and PARENA have one seat each, and two ministers are without party affiliations. Both UPRONA and FRODEBU are under-represented and CNDD-FDD has proportionately more seats than it holds in the National Assembly. Women obtained 35% of the Cabinet seats, achieving greater representation than envisaged in the peace agreement, and than acquired in the local elections, where they gained 5.4% of the communal presidency and 33.3% of the vice-presidency (ONUB 2006b).

CNDD-FDD's victory was no surprise for those in the region, or for external observers. The party's growing popularity after February 2005 meant that Nkurunziza was invited to visit several Western countries. As soon as the Arusha agreement was signed, CNDD-FDD presented itself as the legitimate opposition to UPRONA, wooing, challenging and even kidnapping FRODEBU members of the government. It is difficult to know how CNDD-FDD garnered popular support; reports that voters were intimidated, especially in the areas it controlled, are balanced by those that point to admiration for its long struggle (Ligue ITEKA 2005). Many voters may have opted for the party that was more likely to bring an end to the warfare. However, violence, ranging from massacres, summary executions, scorched-earth policy, to bombing and rape, was used by all factions to articulate political differences and to influence the accord.

As noted, a neoliberal interpretation of the Burundi conflict explains the multiplicity of political parties as a reflection of competing entrepreneurial cliques, among both the military and political elite (Nkurunziza and Ngaruko 2002). Burundi's heavily aid-dependent and indebted economy has been liberalised since 1988. The impact of the war meant that structural adjustment was suspended between 1993 and 2004. A 'greed and grievance' argument supports intense competition among ethnic elites who, primarily, rely on the state for accumulation in the context of a limited resource base and diminishing rents. Ngaruko and Nkurunziza (2000:384–385) claim that 'state predation by power holders who share its rents has led to rebellions by those excluded, triggering, in turn, repression by the army, whose primary role has appeared to be the defence of the system of predation'. While this is a plausible explanation, their argument that neoliberal economic reforms would reduce elite hold on state resources is not proven in Burundi, where the assassination of the democratically elected President was considered by some to have been linked to his attempts at reforming the activities of companies operating in the free trade zone.

Furthermore, although current economic liberalisation programmes may claim to have an anti-poverty focus, the economic recovery strategies proposed in the peace accord have led to greater hardship at a time when people are attempting to rebuild household and community institutions.[3] The privatisation of the state marketing boards and the cutbacks in state expenditure have had negative implications for employment and the provision of social welfare policies, without displacing the power of ethnic elites. In 2002, at a time of acute demand in health and other social services, the government introduced policies of cost-recovery in the health centres. Consequently, people have been detained in hospitals because of non-payment of hospital fees. HRW (2006) reports that 1,076 people were detained in 2005, of whom 621 were held in the principal hospital. Since 2000, public sector workers, such as medical staff, teachers and the judiciary, have taken strike action for increased wage rates and the payment of overdue salaries (*Irinnews.org*, 2005).

The Disarmament, Demobilisation and Reintegration (DDR) programme, which started in December 2004, was administered by the World Bank as part of its Central African Multi-Country Demobilisation and Disarmament Program (MDRP) and implemented by NGOs with the assistance of the National Ceasefire Commission. At an estimated cost of US $84.4 million, the DDR programme aimed to demobilise the estimated 70,000 ex-combatants by giving them direct monetary payments. Such payments varied according to rank, ranging from US$500 for ordinary ranks to $3,000 for the generals. The prospects of demobilisation with remuneration provided by the international community encouraged many young Burundian men to join the rebel movements and the army during the implementation of the peace agreement (HRW 2003). However, DDR was not a smooth process. Former rebels were reluctant to move into cantonments, and demobilisation payments were not always forthcoming, causing protests from combatants and state-sponsored armed groups (*Irinnews.org*, 2005d). By September 2005, only 16,634 were demobilised and the new army was to be limited to between 28,000 and 29,000. Many combatants were demobilised without being disarmed.

The issue of impunity was on the agenda when it affected the ability of politicians to return and participate in the elections. Buyoya was reluctant to set up the provisions allowing for the return of political exiles to participate as members of the transitional government, despite the request from the IMC (*Irinnews.org*, 2001). A temporary immunity law was eventually passed covering 'crimes with a political aim committed after 1 July 1962 to the date of promulgation (27 August 2003)', amidst considerable opposition from human rights groups, Tutsi opposition parties and extremist organisations (*Irinnews.org*, 2003).

With regard to the Truth and Reconciliation Commission (Protocol I: 6), the political leaders were keen to protect themselves from any future criminal charges. On 1 September 2004, the National Assembly passed a law allowing the UN to set up a non-Judicial Truth Commission, with a substantial international component and the creation of a special chamber within the Burundi justice system to tackle crimes against humanity (*Irinnews.org*, 2005b). It is

---

[3] ICG, 2000: 4, fn.10. See Draft Arusha Peace and Reconciliation Agreement for Burundi, 17 July 2000, Chapter 2, Article 2, Paras. 6 & 7.

unlikely that these bodies will receive meaningful support from the government, political parties or regional leaders. As one key participant claimed: 'truth and reconciliation is no longer considered to be necessary ... realizing that wrong things were done in past, but the future does not involve exclusion' (Interview with member of Facilitation Team, 2005). This viewpoint is in sharp contrast to that presented in post-election reports by human rights organisations citing the continuation of summary execution and torture by Burundian soldiers, intelligence agents and FNL rebels; and rape, thefts and murders by criminal elements, especially ex-paramilitary armed gangs (HRW 2005; Ligue ITEKA 2005).

Conclusion

A close examination of the procedures, actors and their positions during the Burundi peace negotiations reveals neoliberal peace-making as a contested terrain, in which long-term cessation of hostilities may not be top of the agenda. Thus, the commitment of many of the actors to the ending of direct violence appears questionable. The victory of CNDD-FDD reinforces the notion that the political kingdom can be won through violence. On the part of the belligerents, fighting intensified during and especially after the peace agreement. The Buyoya government used violence against civilians and, with the help of international actors, attempted to control the negotiations until the outcome was beneficial to the Tutsis and to the President. CNDD-FDD, the stronger of the rebel movements, gained the upper hand by perpetrating warfare in order to attain an agreement that benefited it. FRODEBU was perceived to have made too many compromises and lost credibility.

Many parties signed the agreement out of political and economic opportunism nurtured by external actors. Power-sharing arrangements seemed to legitimise opportunistic behaviour. The immediate financial gains were from donor funds allocated to the various post-conflict reconstruction programmes. While peace negotiations may provide an ideal opportunity for tackling social injustice, in the case of Burundi inequalities were interpreted as the problem of access by ethnic elites to state institutions, which could be resolved largely through power-sharing, despite the awareness of some participants of the endemic structural conditions that reproduce inequalities and violence.

Although it was right not to treat women as an essentialist category, the absence of a gendered understanding of the state and of the nature of violence has contributed to the proliferation of sexual violence even in areas considered peaceful and 'safe' (ONUB 2006a; Ligue ITEKA 2005). Moreover, the narrow reading of war as fighting between the state and rebel movements has meant that Hutu and Tutsi militias, criminal gangs and others who use the state of war to perpetuate violence have been able to continue to wreak havoc in many communities.

Finally, the regional initiative marked a significant and progressive step to the ending of genocidal violence and the abuse of human rights in Africa, yet it did not have the full backing of international forces for peace. From the perspective of the region, two lessons can be learnt from the Burundi peace negotiations. First, that the potential exists for a major commitment by regional leaders to bring an end to protracted conflicts in Africa, especially those that are genocidal and can have regionally destabilising effects. Second, that with collective leadership, African leaders have the capacity to promote a new mode of politics, one that says no to coups and the overthrow of democratic regimes, and that this capacity can be mobilised and supported largely by African professionals. However, the asymmetrical power relations between Western donors and NGOs and regional and local actors, and their multiple and often competing interests, resulted in the Arusha Agreement reflecting not just the minimal conditions for peace, but one which institutionalises violence as part of the political discourse. Creating such spaces of peace requires a radical transformation of the state, much more than that envisioned in contemporary approaches to power-sharing and reconstruction programmes. It is not sufficient just to ensure that peace remains on the agenda of regional and international organisations, a perspective on peace must be articulated, one which is long-term in its outlook, opposed to all forms of violence, is inclusive and gives agency to a multiple-voiced political community.

References

AfricaNews online. 1997. Burundi: Foes Open Dialogue in Paris. 6 October.

Africa Confidential. 1999. Losing a Peacemaker. 21–22 October, 40(21): 2.

Amnesty International. 2004. *Burundi: Rape – The Hidden Human Rights Abuse*, AFR 16/006/2004.

Arusha Peace and Reconciliation Agreement for Burundi. 2000. 28 August, Arusha, Tanzania.

Bangura, Yusuf. 1994. *The Search for Identity: Ethnicity, Religion and Political Violence.* Geneva: UNRISD.

Baraka, Elias and Bahir Mfinange. 1998. France Unrepentant over Economic Help to Burundi. *The Express.* Dar es Salaam, 4 May.

BBC News. 2000. Mandela Slams Burundi's 'Failed' Leaders. 16 January.

Bentley, Kristina A. and Roger Southall. 2005. *An African Peace Process: Mandela, South Africa and Burundi.* Cape Town: HSRC Press, Nelson Mandela Foundation and Human Science Research Council.

Berdal, Mats and David Malone. 2000. *Greed and Grievance: Economic Agendas in Civil Wars.* Boulder, CO and London: Lynne Rienner.

Bunting, Ikaweba, Bismarck Mwansasu and Walter Bagoya. 1999. *Overview of the Burundi Peace Process.* Dar es Salaam: Report of the Mwalimu Nyerere Foundation.

Burke, Enid de Silva, Jennifer Klot and Ikaweba Bunting. 2001. *Engendering Peace: Reflections on the Burundi Peace Process.* Nairobi: UNIFEM (United Nations Development Fund for Women).

Burundi Peace Negotiations. 1998. Report of the First Session of the Burundi Peace Negotiations. Arusha, 15–21 June.

Butiku, Joseph, W. 2004. Facilitation of the Burundi Peace Negotiations. In *Beyond Conflict in Burundi*, eds. Gaudens Mpangala and Bismarck U. Mwansasu. Dar es Salaam: The Mwalimu Nyerere Foundation.

Chhatbur, Sukhdev. 2001. Mandela proposes that Buyoya leads the first phase of Interim Govt. Internews (Arusha), *AllAfrica.com*, 11 July.

Clapham, Christopher. 1998. Rwanda: The Perils of Peacemaking. *Journal of Peace Research* 35(2): 193–210.

Daily News. 1996. UNHCR Chief wants Aid Workers in Burundi Protected. 19 January.

Daley, Patricia. 2006. Ethnicity and Political Violence in Africa: The Challenge to the Burundi State. *Political Geography* 25(6): 657–679.

Duffield, Mark. 2001. *Global Governance and the New Wars: The Merging of Development and Security.* London: Zed Books Ltd.

Front Pour la Démocratie au Burundi (FRODEBU), 'Presentation at 6th Plenary on 19 October', *Report of the third Session of the Burundi Peace Negotiations, Arushi, Tanzania October 12–22, 1998.*

Galtung, Johan. 1969. Violence, Peace and Peace Research. *Journal of Peace Research* 6(3): 167–191.

Hansen, Emmanuel. 1987. *African Perspectives on Peace and Development.* London: The United Nations University and Zed Books Ltd.

Human Rights Watch (HRW). 2006. Une Santé Chèrement Payée: La Détention des Patients sans Resources dans les Hôpitaux Burundais. 18(8)(A).

—— 2005. Burundi: Missteps at a Crucial Moment. 4 November.

—— 2004. Burundi: The Gatumba Massacre: War Crimes and Political Agendas. Human Rights Watch Briefing paper, September.

—— 2003. Everyday Victims: Civilians in the Burundian War.

—— 2000. Burundi: Neglecting Justice in Making Peace. 12(2)(A) April, *http://www.hrw.org/reports/2000/burundi/*.

International Crisis Group (ICG). 2000. Burundi: Neither War Nor Peace. *Africa Report*. No. 25, Nairobi/Brussels: ICG. 1 December.

—— 1998. Burundi Under Siege: Lift the Sanctions: Relaunch the Peace Process. 28 April.

Irinnews.org. 2005a. Burundi: Outpatients Suffer as Nurses Begin Strike to demand Better Terms. 7 March.

—— 2005b. Annan Recommends Dual Inquiries on Genocide. 29 March.

—— 2005c. BURUNDI: CNDD-FDD Confirmed Winner of Communal Polls. 16–24 June.

—— 2005d. BURUNDI: Para-military Youth in Protest over Demobilisation Payments. 24 June.

—— 2003. Burundi: Approval of Temporary Immunity Law Sparks Heated Debate. 3 September.

—— 2002a. Burundi: 2 Factions Sign Ceasefire Agreement, Others Given 30 Days to Comply. 8 October.

—— 2002b. Burundi: Government, Main Rebels Sign Ceasefire Deal. 6 December.

—— 2001. IMC Meeting Calls for Repeal of Law. 7 June.

—— 2000. Focus on Signing the Peace Accord. 4 August.

—— 1999. Burundi: Government suggests South African Mediation. 19 October.

—— 1998. BURUNDI: Sanctions a 'Blunt Instrument'– UNDP. 16 December.

Kaldor, Mary. 2001. *New and Old Wars: Organized Violence in a Global Era*. Cambridge: Polity Press.

Ligue ITEKA. 2005. 'Déclaration de la Ligue ITEKA: Violence Certaines Localités du Burundi I', http://www.ligue-iteka.africa-web.org.

Mafeje, Archie. 1995. Demographic and Ethnic Variations: A Source of Instability in Modern African States. Paper presented at conference on Academic Freedom and Conflict Resolution in the Countries of the Great Lakes, Arusha, Tanzania, 4–7 September.

Mpangala, Gaudens and Bismarck U. Mwansasu. 2004. *Beyond Conflict in Burundi*. Dar es Salaam: The Mwalimu Nyerere Foundation.

Mthembu-Salter, Gregory. 1998. *A Policy Past its 'Sell-by' Date: An Assessment of Sanctions against Burundi*. London: Action Aid, December.

Ngaruko, Floribert and Janvier D. Nkurunziza. 2000. An Economic Interpretation of Conflict in Burundi. *Journal of African Economies* 9(3): 370–409.

Nkurunziza, Janvier D. and Floribert Ngaruko. 2002. Explaining Growth in Burundi: 1960–2000. Draft paper. Oxford: Centre for the Study of African Economies, Oxford University.

Organization of African Unity (OAU). 2000. International Panel of Eminent Personalities to Investigate the 1994 Genocide in Rwanda and the Surrounding Events. Special Report, OAU, 7 July.

Reyntjens, Filip. 2005. Briefing: Burundi: A Peaceful Transition After a Decade of War? *African Affairs*, 105(418): 117–135.

Richards, Paul. 2005. New War: An Ethnographic Approach. In *No Peace No War: An Anthropology of Contemporary Armed Conflicts*, ed. Paul Richards. Oxford: James Currey; Athens, OH: Ohio University Press.

Spears, Ian. 2000. Understanding Inclusive Peace Agreements in Africa: The Problems of Sharing Power. *Third World Quarterly*, 21(1): 105–118.

—— 2002. Africa: The Limits of Power-Sharing. *Journal of Democracy* 13(3): 123–136.

Steans, Jill. 1998. *Gender and International Relations: An Introduction*. New Brunswick, NJ: Rutgers University Press.

The East African. Nairobi. 1998. Business as usual in Burundi. 11 March.

Tindwa, Peter. 2002. Burundi's FRODEBU Forms Military Wing. *The Tanzanian Guardian*, 3 June.

Tull, Dennis M. and Andreas Mehler. 2005. The Hidden Cost of Power-Sharing: Reproducing Insurgent Violence in Africa. *African Affairs* 104(416): 375–398.

United Nations Operation in Burundi (ONUB). 2006a. Monthly Report of Human Rights Violations and Breaches of Common Rights. Burundi: ONUB

—— 2006b. Position des Femmes élues aux Communales. Gender Unit, June, Bujumbura: ONUB.

Willett, Susan. 2005. New Barbarians at the Gate: Losing the Liberal Peace in Africa. *Review of African Political Economy* 106: 569–599.

9

Blair's Africa: The Politics of Securitisation & Fear

RITA ABRAHAMSEN (2005)

At the Labour Party Conference that followed shortly after the *al-Qaeda* attacks of September 11, 2001, UK Prime Minister Tony Blair delivered what is widely perceived as one of the most important – and also most powerful – speeches of his political career. With the televised images of the collapsing Twin Towers still etched on people's minds, the speech expressed the Prime Minister's hope that 'out of the shadows of ... evil should emerge lasting good' and outlined his vision of a new, reordered world founded on justice and 'the equal worth of all' (Blair 2001).

Central to the construction of this new world order was Blair's renewed promise to help Africa. 'The state of Africa,' he declared, 'is a scar on the conscience of the world.' In his characteristic, almost-messianic style, Blair assured his audience that the scar could be healed 'if the world as a community focused on it.' This would entail a much more interventionist role for Britain and what he called the 'international community', and Blair portrayed the new world order as one where the United Kingdom was always ready to defend human rights and democracy in Africa. Thus, he told his audience, 'if Rwanda happened again today as it did in 1993, when a million people were slaughtered in cold blood, we would have a moral duty to act there also.'

This speech, and in particular his description of the continent as a 'scar on the world's consciousness,' is emblematic of Blair's compassionate and intensely moral discourse on Africa. In the wake of September 11, Britain's Africa policy appears at first glance to diverge from the US approach. Whereas US policies toward Africa have moved increasingly toward a more aggressive and militarised approach, justified as part of the 'war on terrorism' and aimed at securing access to strategic resources and military bases, British policies continue to attract attention for their explicitly humanitarian, moral agenda, as seen for example in the launch of Blair's Commission for Africa (see Abramovici 2004; Ellis 2004; Keenan 2004; Lyman and Morrison 2004).

This article argues that while Britain's actions on the African continent are less visibly militarised than US policies, New Labour's approach to Africa has changed in subtle yet important ways following the events of September 11. The centrality of Africa in Blair's speech to the Labour Party Conference following September 11 is indicative of these changes. The continent had comparatively few direct links to the *al-Qaeda* networks, and it is not immediately clear why the Prime Minister would choose to devote so much attention to Africa at a time when on his own admission many Britons were 'anxious, even a little frightened'.

My suggestion is that the Prime Minister's attention to Africa is part of an ongoing 'securitisation' of the continent, evident not only in the British government's discourse but also more broadly in, for example, US policies and in academic debates. Through this securitisation, dealings and interactions with Africa are gradually shifting from the category of 'development/humanitarianism' to a category of 'risk/fear/security,' so that today Africa is increasingly mentioned in the context of the 'war on terrorism' and the dangers it poses to Britain and the international community. Given Blair's global profile, these issues go beyond UK foreign policy and raise important questions relating to Africa's place within structures of power and global governance.

The argument proceeds in three stages. First, I outline the key points of securitisation theory as developed by the Copenhagen School of IR theory. While this theoretical framework is useful, I argue that it also requires some modifications in order to fully capture the significance and nuances of New Labour's policy toward Africa. The second part of the article illustrates the progressive representation of Africa and underdevelopment as dangerous and as a potential risk to the West.[1] Viewing securitisation as a specific speech act, I analyse the manner in which the continent and its underdevelopment have come to be treated increasingly as a security issue in various government policy statements. At the center of this process is the link between New Labour's much discussed 'ethical dimension' to foreign policy and the events of September 11. The former entailed from the outset a presentation of poverty as a potential risk in an increasingly globalised world, and post-September 11 this discourse acquired a much more explicit security dimension.

Finally, arguing that securitisation is not merely a symbolic or linguistic act, the article discusses the politics and potential implications of framing Africa as a security issue. I conclude that the securitisation of Africa may have helped mobilise support for the 'war on terrorism,' but that it has very little to offer in terms of solving the continent's development problems. By contrast, securitisation is more likely to have damaging implications for Africa and its peoples.

Securitisation theory

Since the end of the Cold War, the agenda of security studies has been both 'broadened' and 'deepened' to include new sectors and referent objects. Economic, societal, political, and environmental risks have been added to the conventional preoccupation with military threats, while individuals, groups, communities, and even ecological systems have been conceptualised as referent objects alongside the state (see Barnett 2000; Krause and Williams 1997; Smith 1999).

The theory of securitisation as developed by the Copenhagen School is best understood in this context of a broader security agenda,[2] but it differs from many accounts in its more nominalist approach to security. Unlike most 'critical' or 'human' security studies, the Copenhagen School does not regard security as an unquestionable good, as something to be maximised and realised as widely

---

[1]   In other words, this article does not seek to evaluate New Labour's policy in sub-Saharan Africa. For such an evaluation, see Abrahamsen and Williams 2009.

[2]   The Copenhagen School refers to the research project developed principally by Barry Buzan and Ole Wæver at the Conflict and Peace Research Institute (COPRI), Copenhagen, since the mid-1980s. For critical evaluations, see Huysmans 1998a; McSweeney 1996; Williams 1998; 2003.

as possible by states, groups, and individuals (Wæver 1995:57); instead, security is seen to bring its own dangers. Politically and normatively, therefore, the crucial question is no longer 'more or less security?' but whether or not an issue should be treated as a security issue (see Huysmans 1998b).

In securitisation theory, security is not an objective condition but the outcome of a specific social process. Drawing on the understanding of speech acts developed by John Austin and John Searle, the Copenhagen School examines security practices as specific forms of social construction and securitisation as a particular kind of social accomplishment. The social construction of security issues (who or what is being secured, and from what) is analysed by examining the 'securitising speech acts' through which threats become represented and recognised. These speech acts are not a straightforward description of an already existing security situation: they bring it into being *as* a security situation by successfully representing it as such. In the words of Ole Wæver:

> What then is security? With the help of language theory, we can regard 'security' as a speech act. In this usage, security is not of interest as a sign that refers to something more real; the utterance *itself* is the act. By saying it, something is done (as in betting, giving a promise, naming a ship). By uttering 'security' a state representative moves a particular development into a specific area, and thereby claims a special right to use whatever means are necessary to block it (1995:55).

By regarding the utterance itself as the primary reality, the approach of the Copenhagen School allows in principle for an almost indefinite expansion of the security agenda. In practice, however, it is not the case that anything and everything can be securitised or that any 'securitising actor' can attempt to securitise any issue and referent object (Williams 2003). Different actors have very different capacities to make effective claims about threats and to present them in forms that will be recognised and accepted as convincing by the relevant audiences. In short, not all claims are socially effective, and not all actors are in equally powerful positions to make them. Similarly, while empirical contexts provide crucial resources and referents for actors attempting to securitise an issue, they cannot ultimately determine what are accepted as security issues or threats (Buzan et al. 1997). Rather than wholly open and expandable then, the securitising speech act is deeply sedimented and structured, rhetorically, culturally as well as institutionally (Williams 2003).

The Copenhagen School further limits the security agenda by insisting that security is not synonymous with 'everything that is politically good or desirable,' but argues instead that the concept has to be reserved for a much more specific usage (Buzan et al. 1997:2–5, 203–212; Wæver 1995: 47). Securitisation, according to the Copenhagen School, is the specific speech act of framing an issue as an 'existential threat' that calls for extraordinary measures beyond the routines and norms of everyday politics. In the words of Buzan et al.:

> The distinguishing feature of securitisation is a specific rhetorical structure.... That quality is the staging of existential issues in politics to lift them above politics. In security discourse, an issue is dramatized and presented as an issue of supreme priority; thus by labeling it as security an agent claims a need for and a right to treat it by extraordinary means (1997:26).

Securitisation, in this conceptualiation, is not simply about the avoidance of harm; instead, its defining feature is the ability to place an issue above the normal rules of liberal democratic politics, and hence justify emergency action to do whatever is necessary to remedy the situation. As the following exploration will show, New Labour is increasingly presenting African issues within a narrative of security. Increased globalisation, the prevalence of conflict on the African continent, and the attacks of September 11 provide the key empirical context for these claims, yet it is the *speech act*, not the objective condition, that makes Africa and its underdevelopment a security issue.

That said, the African case raises a number of difficult issues for securitisation theory. From a strict Copenhagen School perspective, Africa cannot be regarded as successfully securitised. While 'securitisation' is increasingly evident, policies toward the continent are still subjected to the normal rules of the liberal democratic political game, and the continent, while frequently presented in terms of threat, has not merited emergency action. As a number of critics have argued in different contexts, this points toward a weakness in the approach of the Copenhagen School (Bigo 2000a; 2000b).

The insistence on defining security as 'existential threat' and the sharp distinction between normal, everyday politics and 'emergency action' mean that many of the processes and modalities whereby issues come to be feared and experienced as potentially dangerous cannot be adequately captured within this perspective. In most cases, this is a very gradual process and only very rarely does an issue move directly from normalcy to emergency. Rather than emergency action, most security politics is concerned with the much more mundane management of risk, and security issues can be seen to move on a continuum from normalcy to worrisome/troublesome to risk and to existential threat – and conversely, from threat to risk and back to normalcy. The process of securitisation is thus better understood as gradual and incremental, and importantly an issue can be placed on the security continuum without necessarily ever reaching the category of existential threat.

It is this *process* of securitisation that can be seen in key elements of New Labour's policies toward Africa. In the case of Africa, the normalcy end of the security spectrum approaches the continent largely in terms of development/humanitarianism, whereas the other extreme places it in the context of the 'war on terrorism'. In the first instance, Africa's problems are perceived mainly in terms of economic underdevelopment, political mismanagement, and resulting human suffering. In the latter, these same problems become a threat to British national security and 'our way of life'. By moving issues along such a continuum, political actors can achieve a degree of flexibility with regard to what kind of action should be taken toward a particular problem, country, or issue. Securitisation is not therefore merely a symbolic or linguistic act but has clear practical and political implications for how to deal with particular issues, in this case with Africa and its underdevelopment. Accordingly, to ignore Africa's securitisation simply on the grounds that it is not an 'existential threat' would be to miss significant changes in Britain's international (and domestic) policies and also to overlook important possibilities for political critique and engagement.

According to Wæver, 'something is a security problem when the elites declare it to be so' (1995:54). In other words, securitisation is a political choice, a decision to conceptualise an issue in a particular way. Clearly there can be numerous different reasons and motivations for placing an issue within a narrative of security, one being to give an issue a new sense of importance and urgency. As Buzan has pointed out in the context of environmental security, invoking the concept of national security 'has an enormous power as an instrument of social and political mobilisation' (Buzan 1992:13).

Viewed positively, therefore, the process of securitising Africa and underdevelopment could be a potent weapon against the marginalisation of the continent and a way of justifying increased development assistance to a disgruntled British electorate that is preoccupied with hospital queues and late commuter trains.[3] Importantly, development assistance has increased significantly during Labour's time in office, and bilateral aid to sub-Saharan Africa stands at £528 million in 2001/2002, and is set to increase to £1 billion by 2005/2006 (Amos 2002a).[4] Securitisation might thus be seen as a tactical move in order to defend a continuation of this assistance in the face of competing claims from various domestic constituencies and the increasing financial demands of the ongoing 'war on terrorism'. On the other hand, British development assistance still stands at only 0.35% of GDP, a long way off the 0.7% target set by the United Nations.

Yet while a tactic of securitisation may facilitate a limited increase in development assistance to Africa, there are numerous reasons to question the desirability of approaching the continent's problems in security terms. Most security discourses are underpinned by an 'us against them' distinction and a logic of threat. As Jef Huysmans has argued, securitisation is a form of politics that identifies a community on the basis of expectations of hostility and functions as a technique of government that integrates a society politically by reference to a credible risk or threat (1998b:577). For this reason, securitisation tends to encourage policy responses formulated along the axis of 'threat-vulnerability-defence,' where the imperative concern is to provide a distance – or even to eliminate – the perceived threat (Wæver 1995:64).

Importantly, though, such policies are not to be understood exclusively in terms of existential threats or external enemies but also relate to more mundane, everyday practices of managing and containing risks. The military analogy at the base of so many security narratives is one reason to question the desirability of securitisation. It also informs the Copenhagen School's insistence that security is not necessarily a positive phenomenon to be maximised. By approaching security as a speech act, or social construct, the question becomes not so much who or what threatens or who is to be secured as whether or not an issue should be treated as a security issue. The normative question, in the words of Huysmans, is not 'more or less security,' but 'to securitise or not to securitise?' (1998b:572). In relation to Africa and its underdevelopment, it may well be that securitisation is both politically undesirable and woefully inadequate in terms of relieving the continent's social and economic troubles.

Globalisation and the fear of underdevelopment

Britain's traditional relationship with its former colonies in Africa is best described as one of willful neglect, with policy-makers regarding the continent

---

[3]   This might be one reason why development NGOs sometimes speak the language of securitisation.

[4]   Unless otherwise stated, all speeches are from the Foreign and Commonwealth Office Web site, fco.gov.uk.

as a 'source of trouble rather than of opportunity' (Clapham 1996:88). After their election victory in May 1997, however, New Labour promised not only a radical change in domestic policy but also a new approach to foreign policy. Britain was to become a 'force for good in the world,' 'the champion of the oppressed,' as the then Foreign Secretary, Robin Cook, put it (Cook 1997a; 1997b).

Willful neglect, it seemed, had come to an end, as Labour's 'ethical dimension' to foreign policy entailed an explicit pledge to give the African continent 'a new priority on the international agenda' (1999). Time and time again the government expressed its commitment to Africa, and when re-elected for the second term, Blair vowed to devote more attention to the continent, while the Foreign Secretary argued in *The Independent* that 'Africa matters'. 'We cannot,' he wrote, 'be content with a world in which four continents are going forwards and one is going backwards' (Straw 2002a; see also Amos 2002b).

Such general statements on Africa's importance in international affairs contain the beginning of its securitisation, and as a tentative genealogy of the process of securitisation, I focus on two interrelated aspects of Labour's policy discourse. First, the emphasis throughout the government's foreign policy pronouncements on interdependence and globalisation; and second, and more specific to Africa, the interpretation of poverty and underdevelopment as dangerous.

Interdependence and globalisation are key tropes in New Labour's 'third way' foreign-policy discourse. Elected on a commitment to the principles of social justice – to health, education, and equality – New Labour announced that these values were also to form the basis of the government's international endeavours. In an increasingly globalised and interdependent world, the argument went, the separation of domestic and foreign policy no longer made sense. Instead, both had to be informed by the same principles and the same values, implying very strongly that the government's moral obligations did not stop at the 'water's edge' (Cook 1997b).

Accordingly, policy papers and speeches repeatedly refer to the 'growing interdependence and interconnectedness of the modern world' (DFID 2000:15; Blair 1997; Cook 1997b). Distant events, it is argued, can have a direct and immediate impact on the daily lives of Britons, in the same way as decisions and actions taken by the people and government of Britain can affect the choices and possibilities of other states and societies. Global warming, deforestation, polluted and overfished oceans, the spread of AIDS... these are only some examples of challenges that show no respect for national frontiers and that are often invoked by the government to illustrate the progressive irrelevance of distance and boundaries (DFID 2000).

The desire to 'make globalisation work for the poor,' as expressed in Labour's second White Paper on development, is underpinned by this image of a shrinking world. An active promoter of globalisation (especially in the form of free trade), the government believes that globalisation 'creates unprecedented new opportunities for sustainable development and poverty reduction,' if only it is 'wisely managed' (*Ibid.*:13, 15). If it is not wisely managed, the multitude of dangers that show no respect for boundaries might affect Britain. Hence, globalisation must be made to work for the developing world, not only because of altruism but also because of British self-interest.

The rhetoric here is clearly neoliberal and utilitarian, albeit with a 'leftist' or 'solidaristic' gloss. In New Labour's vision, moral duty abroad is easily reconciled with 'hard-nosed' self-interest, as a wealthy and prosperous Africa is seen to benefit not only Africans but also Britons. In the words of Robin Cook, the global economy is not a zero-sum game; instead, '[i]f we are all prosperous, we all win. If there is widespread poverty, we all lose' (Cook 1998). In a shrinking world, what is good for the poor is also good for Britain, and New Labour's foreign policy discourse thus fuses altruism and self-interest. As Clare Short, the former Development Secretary, put it, 'if we don't make faster progress in reducing poverty, the consequences in growing population, environmental degradation, war and disease will damage the prospect of the next generation *wherever they live*' (Short 1999, italics added).

As this last statement indicates, the concern with interdependence and 'making globalisation work for the poor' is closely connected to a second important aspect of New Labour's policy discourse; namely, a perception and representation of underdevelopment and poverty as dangerous. This, of course, is nothing new. The association of poverty with danger can be traced back at least to the eighteenth century, when rapid industrial improvements made the existence of widespread poverty appear as a threat to the wealth and 'civilised' way of life of the upper sections of the population. The 'dangerous classes' therefore needed to be controlled through domestic welfare arrangements (Gordon 1991; Proccacci 1991).

Jeremy Bentham, for example, argued for the provision of relief for the indigent poor in order to prevent dangers to the security of the state, life, and property. Importantly, Bentham insisted that this relief be provided in such a manner as to be consistent with the liberal economy and not impede individuals' willingness to enter the market place (Bentham 1950). Today, international development aid can be regarded as a potent way of containing 'the dangerous classes' abroad. President Harry Truman, in a speech frequently credited with marking the dawn of the 'development era,' argued for development assistance because '[t]heir poverty is... a threat both to them and to the more prosperous areas' (Truman 1949). Needless to say, as with Bentham's relief for the indigent, development assistance has since its inception been provided in a manner that is consistent with the liberal economy or in a manner that seeks to produce the forms of liberty that are conducive to participation in the free economy.

Fear of poverty and the 'dangerous classes' can thus be regarded as an intrinsic part of international development aid, and since the end of the Cold War this apprehension has found renewed expression and is articulated primarily in the association of underdevelopment with conflict. As Mark Duffield has observed, the view that underdevelopment causes conflict has become a main site of consensus among aid donors. Indeed, Duffield perceptively argues that development has reinvented itself as 'a structural form of conflict prevention,' so that, despite a history of failure, development has been repackaged as a valuable and indispensable tool in the armory of liberal peace (2001:121). By the same token, in the post-Cold War era, security establishments also began embracing the broadening of the security agenda to include non-military aspects, as a means of maintaining their own relevance in a changed international environment (Wæver 1995:62). The result has been an increasing merger of the development and security agendas, to the extent that the two are at times almost indistinguishable, particularly in relation to Africa.

In New Labour's policy documents, this merger of development and security is clearly evident, and the link between poverty and conflict has been made in numerous contexts. Cook, for example, when outlining Britain's approach to conflict prevention in a speech to the UN General Assembly, identified the fight against poverty and the promotion of sustainable development as a key priority. Similarly, the link between poverty and conflict was explicitly made in the Foreign and Commonwealth Office's first annual report on human rights in 1999 (Cook 1999; FCO 1999). The framework document – *The Causes of Conflict in Sub-Saharan Africa*, jointly produced by the Department of International Development (DFID), the Foreign and Commonwealth Office (FCO), and the Ministry of Defence – also devotes considerable attention to poverty and under-development (DFID 2001).[5] As 'a result of economic decline,' the document states, 'governments find themselves unable to fulfil promises of more jobs, better wages and improved public services. Important sections of the popula-tion – particularly young men – become disillusioned, marginalised and frus-trated' (*Ibid.*: 14). Inequality between groups is accordingly regarded as one of the root causes of conflict, and a comprehensive framework for conflict preven-tion hence means that development programmes should prioritise 'poverty reduction and the reduction of group inequalities' (*Ibid.*:21).

Taken together, the emphasis on globalisation as interconnectedness and the view of underdevelopment as the main cause of conflict contain the building blocks of New Labour's securitisation of Africa. While representing globalisation as an opportunity for greater prosperity for all, the government stresses that it simultaneously brings risks. If the world is becoming 'smaller' and more interconnected, other people's conflicts can spill over and affect Britain and jeopardise international stability. In short, if underdevelopment causes conflict and we live in an interconnected and shrinking world, we cannot rest secure that such conflict will be easily contained within national boundaries. As the White Paper on globalisation puts it, 'There can be no secure future for any of us – *wherever we live* – unless we promote greater social justice' (DFID 2000:14). As speech acts, such pronouncements move Africa and underdevelopment away from the categories of 'development/humani-tarianism' and along a continuum of 'risk/threat.' Africa, despite the frequent references to moral obligations and mutual benefits, is increasingly placed within a logic of fear, and although development aid remains the key policy response its justification has shifted perceptibly away from 'helping' Africa toward 'defending' Britain against its dangers of underdevelopment. While far from an 'existential threat,' the shift toward 'defending' is clearly evident in a statement by the UK Foreign Secretary, Jack Straw: 'We make these efforts [in Africa] not just because the people of Britain have a conscience... But we care about Africa because it is no longer possible to neglect the world's problems without running the risk of eventually suffering the consequences' (Straw 2002a). The events of September 11, 2001 moved Africa further along this continuum of 'risk/threat'.

---

[5]   The joint production of the document is in itself evidence of the greater policy coherence between development and more 'political' departments associated with the post–Cold War merger of secu-rity and development. See Macrae and Leader 2000.

Post-September 11: 'Terror thrives in Africa's rich ruins'

The further securitisation of Africa does not follow automatically from the terrorist attacks on the United States.[6] The *al-Qaeda* cells responsible for the attacks had no more (and probably fewer) links to countries in sub-Saharan Africa than to London, Hamburg, or Florida. Nevertheless, 9/11 quickly came to provide a direct reference for the securitisation of Africa since the attacks were widely interpreted to demonstrate beyond dispute that conflict and unrest in one part of the world could spill over and destroy the lives of thousands on the other side of the globe. 'Interconnectedness' really had become dangerous. As Blair put it in his speech to the Labour Party conference, 'we are realising how fragile are our frontiers in the face of the world's new challenges. Today conflicts rarely stay within national boundaries' (Blair 2001); or in the words of the UK Foreign Secretary, 'It is no longer necessary to prove a direct link between a troubled faraway country and the order of our own societies... Six months ago, no American could have proved a link between the chaos of Afghanistan and the safety of the thousands working in the World Trade Centre.' Now, the changed Manhattan skyline is a constant reminder that 'disorder abroad can threaten security at home' (Straw 2002a). In the same way as Afghanistan's turmoil is seen to have brought devastation to the United States, so Africa's perceived disorder is believed to threaten the West. Thus, while for Straw a shattered window of the British ambassador's home in Kinshasa becomes not 'an immediate threat to British security,' 'neither can we take the view that conflicts such as the war in Congo [are] none of our business.' It has to be 'our business' because of globalisation and interdependence. According to Straw, this is the 'lesson of September 11' and 'we cannot ignore the world and hope that it will go away' (*Ibid.*).

The securitisation of Africa is further helped by the association of underdevelopment with conflict and the discourses on the 'failed state' that have gained such prominence in political studies and international relations in recent years (see Helman and Ratner 1993; Jackson 2000 especially Chapter 11; Kaplan 1994; Rotberg 2004; Zartman 1995). Indeed, both the British and the US governments have drawn a direct link between 'weak' or 'failed states' and the attacks of September 11. Significantly, just as the anniversary of the terrorist attacks was approaching, Foreign Secretary Straw devoted an entire speech to the topic of 'failed and failing states' (Straw 2002b). The dreadful events of September 11, he argued, give us a vision of one possible future: 'A future in which unspeakable acts of evil are committed against us, coordinated from failed states in distant parts of the world.' The speech refers specifically to Somalia, Liberia, and the Democratic Republic of Congo (DRC), invoking the Hobbesian image of a 'state of nature,' without order, where 'continual fear and danger of violent death' render life 'solitary, poor, nasty, brutish and short' (*Ibid.*).

In common with academic writings on the 'failed state,' the Foreign Secretary represents Africa (and other poor areas of the globe) as 'zones of chaos,'

---

[6] I use the terms *terrorism* and *terrorist* when referring to the type of violence that targets a sample of non-combatant, non-office-bearing individuals of a political community so as to terrorise the remainder of that community. Such violence is primarily symbolic, rather than strategic, the death of the victims being a message to a third party.

prone to barbarism, anarchy, and arbitrary violence (see Kaplan 1994; Helman and Ratner 1993; and Cooper 2002a). The problem, according to New Labour, is that these 'zones of chaos' cannot be isolated from the 'zones of peace' but are instead connected through numerous licit and illicit networks of finance, trade, and services. The 'failed states' of Africa (e.g., the DRC, Liberia, Sudan, and Somalia) are perceived as lucrative, murky spaces, or 'black holes' in an otherwise ordered world, where criminal organisations and terrorist networks obtain money, weapons, diamonds, and oil outside the conventional trading, banking, and financial systems. In the catching terms of the headline writers, 'Terror Thrives in the Rich Ruins of Africa.' Speculations abound about the links between these 'black holes' and terrorism; for example, the funding of Hizbollah has been traced to the Congolese diamond trade, whereas Sierra Leonean diamonds are said to be a source of income for *al-Qaeda* (see Farah 2002; Peninou 2001; Global Witness 2003).

'Failed states,' then, are seen as a 'free trade zone for the underworld,' and following September 11 they are not simply dysfunctional states damaging to the local population and a cause of local/regional conflict; first and foremost they are *dangerous* states threatening the stability of 'the zone of peace'. In the words of Robert Cooper, a senior British diplomat who has been influential in shaping Blair's foreign policy agenda, 'failed states' (or 'premodern states,' in Cooper's vocabulary) may provide a base from which 'non-state actors, notably drug, crime, or terrorist syndicates,' may launch 'attacks on the more orderly parts of the world' (Cooper 2002a; see also 2002b; 2003).[7] The point is made even more forcefully by Foreign Secretary Straw, who links 'failed states' directly to British social problems and national security: '[A]s well as bringing mass murder to the heart of Manhattan, state failure has brought terror and misery to large swathes of the African continent, as it did in the Balkans in the early 1990s. And at home it has brought drugs, violence and crime to Britain's streets.' Accordingly, 'we need to remind ourselves that turning a blind eye to the breakdown of order in any part of the world, however distant, invites direct threats to *our national security and well-being*' (Straw 2002b).

In a more recent speech, Chris Mullin, the Foreign Office Minister for Africa, argues that there are 'sound practical reasons why we cannot afford to ignore the state of Africa. The most immediate of these is terrorism.' According to Mullin, the 'fact that in parts of Africa such as Somalia entire societies have imploded makes them a ready breeding ground for terrorism.' The 'failed state' of Somalia and other 'weak states' on the continent are seen by Mullin to 'present terrorists with space in which to plan and export attacks. These are not anomalous incidents but symptoms of a problem in Africa which poses a serious, direct and continuing security threat to us...'(Mullin 2004).

Similar concerns are clearly evident, but expressed in more compassionate and careful terms, in Blair's speech to the 2001 Labour Party Conference, where the potential benefits and risks of globalisation form a central theme. The threat is not simply *al-Qaeda* or terrorism but is much more broadly conceived. 'Today,' according to Blair,

> the threat is chaos, because for people with work to do, family life to balance, mortgages to pay, careers to further, pensions to provide, the yearning is for order and stability and

---

[7]   Tony Blair provides the foreword for Cooper's more extended treatment of these ideas in *Reordering the World* (2002b).

if it doesn't exist elsewhere, it is unlikely to exist here. I have long believed this interdependence defines the new world we live in (Blair 2001).

The quotation is worth dwelling on. For Blair, 'chaos' is represented by those who do not go to work, who don't have mortgages to pay or careers to further. These people exist 'elsewhere' and they have the capacity to destroy the order and stability of 'here'. This is the seldom-noticed corollary to New Labour's vision of interdependence: the capacity of 'elsewhere' to impact on 'here'. While 'elsewhere' is not defined, the speech soon turns to the former Yugoslavia and to Rwanda, Sierra Leone, the DRC, Zimbabwe, and, more broadly, 'the state of Africa'. Clearly this is where 'chaos' lurks, and where order and stability need to be imposed through the reasoned intervention of the 'world community,' lest its disorder travels through the increasingly interconnected world to the 'zones of peace'. As a result, the question of how to deal with the 'elsewhere' in order to secure the 'here' occupies an increasingly central role in the government's policy toward Africa.

The politics of securitisation

Securitisation is not merely a question of representation, or a symbolic act, but has clear political implications (Huysmans 1998b). Identifying something as a security issue is not an innocent practice: it changes the legitimate modes of engagement with a particular problem. Framed as a development/humanitarian issue, Africa encourages compassion and particular policy responses formulated and implemented primarily by the Department for International Development. Approached as a security issue, by contrast, Africa may encourage fear and unease, and this may in turn potentially facilitate policy responses of a more militarised and illiberal nature, shifting the institutional responsibility toward the FCO and perhaps also the Ministry of Defence.

It is in the Prime Minister's invocation of the 'elsewhere' that we begin to glimpse the politics and the potential implications of New Labour's securitisation of Africa. Like most security discourses, the government's securitisation of the continent is founded on expectations and fear of harm or hostility, and the threatened community itself becomes unproblematic, a taken-for-granted unit whose common values and shared identity need no elaboration or justification in the face of external animosity (*Ibid.*; Wæver 1995; see also Walker 1993; Campbell 1998).

Viewed in this light, securitisation can be seen as a powerful political strategy that shapes and maintains the unity of a political community. In the case of New Labour's securitisation of Africa, this logic is clearly evident. Blair's speech to the Labour Party Conference in 2001 is littered with references to 'community,' which he insists is the 'governing idea of modern social democracy'. The 'world community' or the 'international community' is not defined, but it seems to include states that believe 'that we are a community of people' and that respect justice, reason, and tolerance. The problem with 'failed states' is that they are part of global networks, linked to the 'zone of peace' through a multiplicity of licit and illicit relationships, but at the same time they are not part of the Prime Minister's 'international/world community' in that they do not subscribe to the values he regards as universal (justice, reason, and tolerance).

Thus, while Labour's policy discourse on Africa stops short of identifying a specific enemy (as in, say, a country), there is a clear elaboration of a sense of threat arising from chaos, instability, and underdevelopment. The effect is twofold.

First, the fear that Africa's underdevelopment may harm or give rise to hostile actions toward the 'international community' helps define and reinforce the unity of that community and also to mobilise political and public support for the 'war on terrorism'. The timing of both Blair's speech to the party conference and Straw's address on 'failed and failing states' is important in this regard. The former was delivered barely three weeks after the terrorist attacks on the Twin Towers, just as the attacks on the Taliban's bases in Afghanistan were about to start. The latter speech was delivered shortly before the anniversary of September 11 and, importantly, during the build-up to the war on Iraq. Iraq figures prominently in the speech, with the Foreign Secretary justifying the impending war and action on 'failed states' in Africa as part of the same 'war on terrorism'. At a time of intense debate and fierce opposition to the government's policies, the securitisation of Africa can thus be seen as part of a political strategy to unify public and party support behind the government. In this sense, the securitisation of Africa is part of wider political struggles and closely linked to other security narratives in a complex and ongoing process.[8] Drawing Africa into these security debates can nevertheless be seen to help legitimise the government's 'war on terrorism,' even giving it a 'humanitarian face' by linking it to the eradication of poverty and underdevelopment.

Second, the securitisation of Africa (and other poverty-stricken parts of the globe) is part of a delineation of who belongs to Blair's 'international community' and who doesn't, or, in Nietzschean terms, who is inside and outside the gates. This same 'international community' and its shared values are then in turn held up to the securitised 'outside' as the exemplar of what they have to become in order to get past the gatekeeper (see Williams 2001). In this way, securitisation helps define exactly which developments and phenomena are to be opposed and if possible eradicated. Seen from this perspective, securitisation becomes a profoundly political act determining not only the boundaries of political communities but also how to deal with those on the outside.

Rather schematically, it could be argued that the policies that follow from securitisation are formulated to win over, contain, or destroy the external enemy or threat. In the case of 'failed' and 'underdeveloped' states, a strategy of containment is on its own rendered largely ineffective by Labour's understanding of the world as increasingly interconnected and borderless. Because the 'zones of chaos' cannot successfully be sectioned off from the 'zones of peace,' strategies to win over the enemy predominate and operate alongside strategies of containment. At the same time, the possibility of destruction is never ruled out. Conquest and conversion, as William Connolly has remarked in a different context, remain the two authorised responses to otherness (1991: 43).

The Blair government's main answer to the problem of how to deal with those who do not subscribe to the values of the 'international community' is conver-

---

[8]   As Didier Bigo (2002b) has argued, securitisations are also frequently part of political struggles between political and professional agents in specific arenas, the former intent to mobilise public support, the latter to maintain their professional legitimacy. This is probably also the case in relation to Africa's securitisation in recent years.

sion, or strategies of assimilation and incorporation: the dangerous areas must be included (or won over) in order to be controlled and managed. Hence, for Blair, 'the starving, the wretched, the dispossessed, the ignorant, those living in want and squalor from the desert of northern Africa to the slums of Gaza, to the mountain ranges of Afghanistan: they too are our cause.' And the cause is 'to bring those same values of democracy and freedom to people around the world' (Blair 2001).

This fairly aggressive liberal universalism cannot be understood without reference to security and the ambivalent relationship between freedom and security in liberal societies (see Dean 1999). While liberalism seeks to free the individual from the clutches of the state, it is also concerned to ensure that people will exercise that freedom according to appropriate standards of civility and reason. In other words, in order to act freely, the subject must first be shaped, guided, and molded into one capable of exercising that freedom in a responsible manner. Thus, what makes it possible for the free inhabitants of modern liberal societies to be governed via state mechanisms that appear to rest on their consent is the fact that the vast majority of those people have already been trained in the dispositions and values of responsible autonomy (Hindess 1996). Security, in other words, is best achieved through creating and expanding the conditions where people can enjoy the right kind of rights and liberties. At the level of international relations, development assistance can be regarded as a government practice seeking to shape and regulate the behaviour and conduct of freedom in recipient states and societies (see Foucault 1991).

Through detailed interventions to reduce poverty, increase literacy, promote free trade, create representative institutions and practices, and build capacity and institutions, development aid can be seen as a technique of government whereby Africa comes to conform to the liberal values of the 'international community,' such as free markets and democracy. Development interventions also create a framework within which the West can introduce itself 'as an intimate, regular presence' in African states and in the life of their populations (Defert 1991:232; see Ferguson 1994). Development, in other words, serves to guide states and their populations toward the responsible conduct of their freedom, so that 'we' can continue to enjoy our freedom and way of life.[9]

At the same time, it is important to remember that liberalism always contains the possibility of illiberal interventions in the lives of those who do not conform to the accepted standards of civility or possess the attributes required to join the liberal community. In John Stuart Mill's formulation, for example, liberty applied only to human beings 'in the maturity of their faculties,' and hence he regarded authoritarian government of the colonies as perfectly consistent with liberal values (Mill 1976). Liberalism's principled belief in equality can thus be seen to function simultaneously as a dividing practice, so that those who do not make use of the opportunities available for improvement toward civility or the 'maturity of their faculties' can legitimately be excluded and treated outside conventional liberal rules of engagement. Today, states that refuse to reform according to the rules and norms of the 'international community' face at best abandonment and the withdrawal of development assistance, at worst illiberal interventions to enforce compliance and ensure the survival of the international community. In Cooper's fairly blunt terminology, this means that '[a]mongst

---

[9] This is Cooper's 'new liberal—and voluntary—imperialism,' a world where 'the efficient and well governed export stability and liberty' to welcoming poor and 'failed' states (Cooper 2002b).

ourselves, we keep the law but when we are operating in the jungle, we must also use the laws of the jungle' (Cooper 2002a).

The war on Iraq can be seen to demonstrate the willingness of the British government to engage in illiberal acts to defend the liberal values of the 'international community,' but it is important to note that the process of securitisation does not automatically dictate such spectacular responses. As argued above, the process of securitisation is gradual and incremental, and an issue can move along a continuum of risk/fear without ever reaching the stage of 'existential threat' where it merits 'emergency action' (as with Iraq). Instead, most security politics is concerned with the more mundane everyday management and containment of risk, and the securitisation of Africa is thus entirely compatible with the feeble response to the brutal and prolonged conflict in the DRC or the Sudan. Rather than spectacular emergency politics or military action, securitisation is more likely to give rise to policies of containment or policing.

This is clearly evident in proposals for how to deal with the 'failed state'. Regarding such states as the potential breeding grounds of terrorism, the Foreign Secretary suggests a division of labour whereby Western countries take responsibility for different parts of the poor world. 'This could mean,' Straw argues, 'the EU, NATO or the OSCE taking the lead in dealing with problems around the margins of Europe; the French or ourselves (perhaps jointly) in parts of Africa; and countries like Canada or the US under the OAS in the Americas' (Straw 2002b). In effect, Western countries are assigned policing duties across the globe in order to contain or 'quarantine' disorder, and the reasoning and justification is not all that different from Mill's endorsement of illiberal rule of the 'uncivilised' nations. And while a lot less spectacular than any emergency or military action, by invoking the concept of 'national security' such illiberal actions can be more easily justified. Through securitisation, the government reserves, in a sense, the right to 'use the law of the jungle' should it at any stage deem this necessary.

Importantly, there are signs that relations between Africa and the West are becoming increasingly militarised in the aftermath of September 11. Most notably, the Horn of Africa has become a major military hub for Task Force 150, a naval unit jointly operated by the United States, Britain, France, Spain, and Germany, while the US Pan Sahel Initiative has dedicated $100 million to 'anti-terrorist' activities in the Saharan states of Mauritania, Mali, Chad, and Niger (US Department of Defense 2003; Ellis 2004; Keenan 2004; see also the Introduction to this Reader). More than 1,300 US military personnel are stationed in the Horn, patrolling the coast of East Africa, while the number of US military troops in the Sahel is thought to be approximately 1,000 (*Ibid.*).

While less visibly militarised, there are similar changes in Britain's engagement with the continent. In May 2003, Britain launched its counter-terrorism programme, which is designed to develop the 'counter-terrorism and security capacity of weaker nations so as to best support them in protecting our shared interests'. The programme has been allocated £20 million in its first three years of operation, and the main areas of operation are Africa, the Middle East, and Asia.[10] Another aspect of this development is the increasing emphasis on security sector reform, whereby development resources are used to train and equip police and soldiers. In Sierra Leone, for example, DFID co-operates with the

---

[10] Information from www.fco.gov/globalissues.

Ministry of Defence and the FCO in a substantial effort to reform the state's security apparatuses, including a wholesale restructuring of the country's intelligence services. This is not to say that any of these activities are in and of themselves wrong, but to demonstrate the extent to which interactions with Africa are increasingly conducted in an explicit security context linked to the 'war on terrorism'.

Conclusion

Blair's Africa may be a 'scar on the conscience of the world,' but it is simultaneously a dangerous place that can impinge on 'our national security and well-being' and that 'poses a serious, direct and continuing security threat to us' (Blair 2001; Straw 2002b; Mullin 2004). New Labour's policy discourse has placed the African continent firmly within a logic of fear and linked its underdevelopment to a threat of terrorism. While it cannot be argued that the continent and its development problems have been securitised in the strict sense outlined by the Copenhagen School, it is clear that Africa has moved increasingly from a category of 'development/humanitarianism' toward one of potential risk, threat, and danger. The continent is by no means always and uniformly placed in a security context, but it is ever more frequently drawn into 'security' debates where aspects of Africa's underdevelopment are regarded as representing a threat to the West, as possibly facilitating terrorism, and so on.

   This is not to deny any relationship between Africa and terrorism; nor is it to argue that 'failed states' cannot pose a threat to Britain or harbour criminal individuals and groups intent to harm and kill representatives of what Blair calls the 'international community'. Terrorist networks may well obtain resources, launder money, and operate from bases in states with weak security apparatuses and porous borders, as evidence, for example by the *al-Qaeda* attacks in Kenya in December 2002 and in August 1998. Similarly, 'failed states' clearly have destructive impacts on their own societies, and my argument is not intended as a defence of predatory, vicious, or neglectful rule. My point is that securitisation is not the answer to these problems, and that as a speech act the securitisation of Africa is likely to do more harm than good.

   The process of securitisation does not necessarily or immediately give rise to radically different policies toward Africa and underdevelopment, nor is it likely to lift the continent above the normal rules of the liberal political game so as to require emergency action. Instead, securitisation is entirely compatible with the continent's continued marginalisation in international affairs; but nevertheless it has important political and ethical implications. By conceptualising and representing Africa within a framework of risk/threat, the relationship to the continent is changed in subtle, yet significant ways. By approaching Africa as a security concern, rather than as a developmental or humanitarian challenge, policy becomes guided by the desire to ensure more and better security for 'us'. While better security for Britain is presented as simultaneously providing a better life for people in Africa, the securitisation of the continent leads to policy responses informed by a desire to safeguard the 'here' against the 'elsewhere'.

   This has potentially damaging consequences. Africa is given a negative image, wrapped up in a politics of fear that may contribute toward suspicion and hostility toward Africa's peoples. In this way, securitisation may contribute to deteriorating race relations in Britain and help justify strict immigration controls and asylum laws, as well as the erosion of civil liberties in the face of perceived terrorist threats.[11] Mullin's recent remark that it is 'not widely realised that there are more Muslims south of the Sahara than in the Middle East,' but that fortunately 'most of them... are moderates,' testifies to the ease with which securitisation can be used to cast suspicion on large groups of innocent people (Mullin 2004).

At the same time, securitisation serves to draw attention away from the West's contribution to the problems of underdevelopment and 'state failure.' Despite the attention to globalisation and interconnectedness in New Labour's discourse, underdevelopment, chaos, and state failure become the expression of 'otherness,' rather than an outcome and reflection of certain deficiencies and shortcoming in contemporary international relations between the North and the South. The way in which decades of development policies advocating economic liberalisation and state curtailment have contributed to the weakening of the capacities and integrity of these states is overlooked, and the West remains, in the vocabulary of the Foreign Secretary, the 'doctor' able to both 'prevent' and 'cure' state failure (Straw 2002b; Chossudovsky 1999; Reno this volume; Abrahamsen 2001). Policies informed by this logic may perpetuate the underlying causes of 'state failure,' rather than contribute to their solution.

New Labour's aggressive liberal internationalism and attention to the 'wretched of the earth' cannot be reduced to the personal moral dedication of the Prime Minister, despite the prevalence of such interpretations in the media (see Young 2001; McGuire 2001). Rather, the 'ethical dimension' to foreign policy is intrinsically linked to a concern with security. The securitisation of Africa is in turn intimately linked to other security narratives in a complex and ongoing process, and in the aftermath of September 11 this securitisation can be seen as part of a strategy for mobilising support for the 'war on terrorism'. It has, however, very little to offer in terms of solving Africa's development problems, and may even exacerbate these by placing the African continent and its peoples on a continuum of fear and thereby facilitate relations and policies underpinned by a desire to safeguard the 'international community,' if necessary by recourse to illiberal means.

This analysis of New Labour's Africa policies also poses some important questions for the understanding of security and securitisation in liberal societies. While the securitisation framework approaches security in fairly realist terms, making survival (existential threat) and exceptional politics the determining feature, this article has argued that securitisation is better understood as a gradual, more incremental process that can include more liberal strategies of incorporation and management of threats. Security is a pervasive technology in liberal societies precisely in the sense of the continuous production of governable subjects. In this sense, the social realm is never fully desecuritised. This does not, however, mean that liberal security governance is produced only through the continual production of enemies and existential threats, as has sometimes been suggested, and it is vital that a distinction between a more realist securiti-

---

[11] Note the recent drop in asylum applications in the United Kingdom, where in 2003, compared with 2002, there was a 41% decline in new applications (excluding dependants), reflecting similar developments in other industrialised countries. BBC News, August 24, 2004. For critical comments, see Human Right Watch (2003). On the erosion of civil liberties, see Tony Bunyan (2002).

sation perspective and a liberal governmental approach to security is not over-drawn, since in practice the two are often interconnected. The crucial point, both in terms of both practical analysis and normative judgment, is to recognise the different forms or logics of security that are at work, their transformations, tensions, and interactions, as well as their political consequences. The case of New Labour's policy toward Africa provides an excellent case in point, and the co-existence of different forms of security logic is clearly seen in, for example, the United Kingdom's security sector reform programme in Sierra Leone, where it is often very difficult to discern where the DFID ends and the Ministry of Defence begins.

Development has always been motivated, at least in part, by fear and has aimed to pacify danger through shaping and modifying behaviour in accor-dance with accepted norms of modernity and civilisation. What is new in New Labour's securitisation of Africa and underdevelopment is not therefore the fear of the poor or 'dangerous classes,' as such, but rather the explicit links drawn between Africa, international security, and terrorism. As proponents of 'human security' have sometimes argued, making an issue a 'security' issue can give it a useful political priority, and there may indeed be some benefits arising from framing the continent as an explicit part of the 'security' agenda. At the same time, the governmental technologies of development can hardly be considered an unqualified boon to the continent, to put it mildly, and the movement of the continent toward a threat categorisation has serious downsides. The securiti-sation of Africa thus involves a multiplicity of forms and technologies of secu-rity governance, and an understanding of these processes and dynamics is crucial to thinking about the continent's future.

References

Abrahamsen, Rita. 2001. Development Policy and the Democratic Peace in Sub-Saharan Africa. *Conflict, Security and Development* 1(3): 79–103.

Abrahamsen, Rita and Paul Williams. 2001. Ethics and Foreign Policy: The Antinomies of New Labour's 'Third Way' in Sub-Saharan Africa. *Political Studies* 49(2): 249–264.

Abramovici, Pierre. 2004. Precious Resources in Need of Protection: United States: The New Scramble for Africa. *Le Monde Diplomatique.* July 22.

Amos, Baroness. 2002a. New Partnership for Africa's Development: The Challenges and Opportu-nities. Speech by the Parliamentary Undersecretary for Foreign and Commonwealth Affairs to the South Africa Business Association. London. January 28.

——— 2002b. British Policy Towards Africa: Championing a New Partnership from the North. Speech at Wilton Park. September 3.

Barnett, Jon. 2000. *The Meaning of Environmental Security.* London: Zed Books.

Bentham, Jeremy. 1950 [1894]. *The Theory of Legislation.* London: Routledge.

Bigo, Didier. 2000a. The Möbius Ribbon. In *Identities, Orders, Borders,* eds. Mathias Albert, David Jacobson, and Yosef Lapid. Minneapolis, MN: University of Minnesota Press

——— 2000b. When Two Become One: Internal and External Securitisations in Europe. In *Inter-national Relations Theory and the Politics of European Integration: Power, Security, and Community,* eds. Morten Kelstrup and Michael C. Williams. London: Routledge.

Blair, Tony. 1997. The Principles of Modern British Foreign Policy. Speech at Lord Mayor's Banquet London. November 10.

——— 2001. Speech to the Labour Party Conference. Reprinted in *The Guardian* October 2. http://www.guardian.co.uk/politics/2001/oct/02/labourconference.labour6

Bunyan, Tony. 2002. The War on Freedom and Democracy. Statewatch Analysis 13. Available at: http://www.statewatch.org/news/2002/sep/04freedom.htm

Buzan, Barry. 1992. Environment as a Security Issue. In *Geopolitical Perspectives on Environmental Security,* ed. Paul Painchaud. Quebec: Cahier du GERPE, Laval University.

Buzan, Barry, Ole Wæver and Jaap de Wilde. 1997. *Security: A New Framework for Analysis*. Boulder, CO: Lynne Rienner.

Campbell, David. 1998. *Writing Security: United States Foreign Policy and the Politics of Identity*. Minneapolis, MN: Minnesota University Press.

Chossudovsky, Michel. 1999. Human Security and Economic Genocide in Rwanda. In *Globalisation, Human Security, and the African Experience*, eds. Caroline Thomas and Peter Wilkin. Boulder, CO: Lynne Rienner.

Clapham, Christopher. 1996. *Africa and the International System*. Cambridge: Cambridge University Press.

Connolly, William. 1991. *Identity/Difference: Democratic Negotiation of Political Paradox*. Ithaca, NY: Cornell University Press.

Cook, Robin. 1997a. British Foreign Policy. Speech launching the Foreign Office Mission Statement. London. May 12.

———— 1997b. Britain's New Approach to the World. Speech to Labour Party Conference. Brighton. October 2.

———— 1998. Promoting Peace and Prosperity in Africa. Speech to UN Security Council. New York. September 24.

———— 1999. Conflict Prevention in the Modern World. Speech, UN General Assembly, 54th session. New York. September 21.

Cooper, Robert. 2002a. The New Liberal Imperialism. Observer Worldview Extra. April 7. Available at: http://www.guardian.co.uk/world/2002/apr/07/1

———— 2002b. *Reordering the World: The Long Term Implications of September 11*. London: Foreign Policy Centre.

———— 2003. *The Breaking of Nations: Order and Chaos in the Twenty-First Century*. London: Atlantic Books.

Dean, Mitchell. 1999. *Governmentality: Power and Rule in Modern Society*. London: Sage.

Defert, Daniel. 1991. 'Popular Life' and Insurance Technology. In *The Foucault Effect*, eds. Graham Burchell, Colin Gordon, and Peter Miller. Chicago, IL: University of Chicago Press.

Department of International Development (DFID). 2000. *Eliminating World Poverty: Making Globalisation Work for the Poor*. White Paper on International Development. London: DFID.

DFID (with FCO and Ministry of Defence). 2001. *The Causes of Conflict in Sub-Saharan Africa: Framework Document*. London: DFID.

Duffield, Mark. 2001. *Global Governance and the New Wars*. London: Zed Books.

Ellis, Stephen. 2004. Briefing: The Pan-Sahel Initiative. *African Affairs* 103(412): 459–464.

Farah, Doug. 2002. Terror Thrives in the Rich Ruins of Africa. *Washington Post*, reprinted in *Sunday Independent* (Cape Town). January 6.

Ferguson, James. 1994. *The Anti-Politics Machine* (Minneapolis, MN: Minnesota University Press.

Foreign and Commonwealth Office. 1999. *Human Rights: Annual Report, 1999*. London: FCO.

Foucault, Michel. 1991. Governmentality. In *The Foucault Effect*, eds. Graham Burchell, Colin Gordon, and Peter Miller. Chicago, IL: University of Chicago Press.

Global Witness. 2003. For a Few Dollar$ More: How al-Qaeda Moved into the Diamond Trade. April 17. Available at: http://www.globalwitness.org/library/few-dollar-more-how-al-qaeda-moved-diamond-trade

Gordon, Colin. 1991. Governmental Rationality: An Introduction. In *The Foucault Effect*, eds. Graham Burchell, Colin Gordon, and Peter Miller. Chicago: University of Chicago Press.

Helman, Gerald B. and Steven R. Ratner. 1993. Saving Failed States. *Foreign Policy* 89: 3–20.

Hindess, Barry. 1996. *Discourses on Power: From Hobbes to Foucault*. London: Basil Blackwell.

Human Rights Watch (HRW). 2003. An Unjust 'Vision' for Europe's Refugees. June 17. Available at: http://www.hrw.org/reports/2003/06/17/unjust-vision-europe-s-refugees

Huysmans, Jef. 1998a. Revisiting Copenhagen, or about the Creative Development of a Security Studies Agenda in Europe. *European Journal of International Relations* 4(4): 488–506.

———— 1998b. The Question of the Limit: Desecuritization and the Aesthetics of Horror in Political Realism. *Millennium* 27(3): 569–589.

Jackson, Robert. 2000. *The Global Covenant*. Oxford: Oxford University Press.

Kaplan, Robert D. 1994. The Coming Anarchy: How Scarcity, Crime, Overpopulation, and Disease Are Rapidly Destroying the Social Fabric of Our Planet. *Atlantic Monthly*. February: 44–76.

Keenan, Jeremy. 2004. Americans and 'Bad People' in the Sahara-Sahel. *Review of African Political Economy* 31(99): 130–139.

Krause, Keith and Michael C. Williams. 1997. *Critical Security Studies: Concepts and Cases*. Minneapolis, MN: University of Minnesota Press.

Lloyd, Tony. 1999. Speech to the Africa Day Conference. Lancaster House, London. May 26.

Lyman, Princeton M. and J. Stephen Morrison. 2004. The Terrorist Threat in Africa. *Foreign Affairs* 83(1): 74–86.

Macrae, Joanna and Nicholas Leader. 2000. *Shifting Sands: The Search for Coherence between Political and Humanitarian Responses to Complex Emergencies.* Humanitarian Policy Group, Report 8. London: Overseas Development Institute.

McGuire, Stryker. 2001. Onward, Christian Soldier. *Newsweek,* December 3.

McSweeney, Bill. 1996. Identity and Security: Buzan and the Copenhagen School. *Review of International Studies* 22(1): 81–93.

Mill, John Stuart. 1976 [1859]. Considerations on Representative Government. In Mill, *Utilitarianism: On Liberty and Considerations on Prerepresentative Government,* ed. H. B. Acton. London: Dent.

Mullin, Chris. 2004. Our Role Is to Help Africa Help Itself. Speech to Council on Foreign Relations. New York. February 4.

Peninou, Jean-Louis. 2001. Horn of Africa: Al-Qaida Regroups? *Le Monde Diplomatique,* December.

Proccacci, Giovanna. 1991. Social Economy and the Government of Poverty. In *The Foucault Effect,* eds. Graham Burchell, Colin Gordon, and Peter Miller. Chicago: University of Chicago Press.

Reno, William. Ironies of Post-Cold War Structural Adjustment in Sierra Leone. *Review of African Political Economy* 23(67): 7–18.

Rotberg, Robert I. 2004. *When States Fail: Causes and Consequences.* Princeton, NJ: Princeton University Press.

Short, Clare. 1999. Speech to the Labour Party Conference. Bournemouth. September 30.

Smith, Steve. 1999. The Increasing Insecurity of Security Studies. *Contemporary Security Policy* 20(3): 72–101.

Straw, Jack. 2002a. Africa Matters. *Independent on Sunday.* London. February 3.

Straw, Jack. 2002b. Failed and Failing States. Speech to the European Research Institute. Birmingham. September 6.

Truman, Harry. 1949. Inaugural Speech. *Public Papers of the President.* Washington, DC: US Government Printing Office.

US Department of Defense. 2003. Joint Task Force Horn of Africa Briefing. News Transcript. January 10. Available at: www.defenselink.mil/news.

US Department of State. 2002. *The Security Strategy of the United States of America.* Washington, D.C.: The White House.

Wæver, Ole. 1995. Securitization and Desecuritization. In *On Security,* ed. Ronnie Lipschutz. New York: Columbia University Press.

Walker, Rob, B. J. 1993. *Inside/Outside: International Relations as Political Theory.* Cambridge: Cambridge University Press.

Williams, Michael C. 1998. Modernity, Identity, and Security: A Comment on the Copenhagen Controversy. *Review of International Studies* 24(3): 435–39.

―――― 2001. The Discipline of the Democratic Peace: Kant, Liberalism, and the Social Construction of Security Communities. *European Journal of International Relations* 7(4): 525–553.

―――― 2003. Words, Images, Enemies: Securitization and International Politics. *International Studies Quarterly* 47(4): 511–531.

Young, Hugo. 2001. Simple but Heartfelt Vision of Promises and Dreams. *The Guardian,* October 3.

Zartman, William I. 1995. *Collapsed States: The Disintegration and Restoration of Legitimate Authority.* Boulder, CO: Lynne Rienner.

10

Abductions, Kidnappings & Killings in the Sahel & the Sahara

FRANKLIN CHARLES GRAHAM IV (2011)

It is understandable that since 2001 the media and Western policy-makers have focused on the capture of tourists, aid workers and foreign dignitaries in the Sahel and Sahara. Yet, kidnappings and hostage-takings make for head-lines that obscure the more fundamental, endemic issues of pervasive, persistent poverty and the United Nations' millennium goals and development. Their headlines and official reports depict terrorists as profiting from the region's 'ungoverned spaces' and 'invisible desert borders'. This is, after all, a region that is 'sparsely populated and [with] loosely patrolled borders' (Glickman 2003:167; Brulliard 2009; CSIS 2010:3). The most recent inci-dents include the kidnapping of seven people affiliated with the energy company, Areva, in northern Niger on 16 September 2010 (*Toronto Star* 2010). Such incidents highlight the exponential rise in kidnappings in the Maghreb and Sahelian states since 2001 (Alexander 2010). Experts believe that the most recent rise in kidnappings took shape in 2003 with the abduction of thirty-two foreigners, mostly German. El Para, a former member from *Groupe Salafiste pour la Prédication et le Combat*, and 50 followers abducted this large group of tourists in the Algerian Sahara. They succeeded in procuring a ransom of €5 million before releasing the hostages. Upon the release, the band of kidnappers was pursued by African and Western special forces through the northern regions of Mali, Niger, and Chad. In the end most of the kidnappers, El Para excluded, surrendered to local Toubou people who in turn sold them to Chadian authorities working in collaboration with US special forces (*Africa Confidential* 2006; *Sahara Focus* 2009a). Thus, the scene was set for the current preoccupation with kidnapping and hostage-taking, rather than the long-term, underlying realities that foster such behaviours.

Most kidnappings are smaller in scale and end without incident. The taking of two United Nations envoys in Niger in December of 2008, Robert Fowler and Louis Guay, concluded when *al-Qaeda in the Islamic Maghreb* (AQIM) released them (in addition to three other hostages) for a ransom the Swiss government paid (Thorne 2009). In November of 2009, Pierre Camatte, a botanist conducting research on traditional cures for malaria around Ménaka, Mali, was abducted (*Sahara Focus* 2009b; Thorne 2009). He was released three months later when France negotiated a prisoner release in Mali of three suspects wanted for seditious acts in Algeria and Mauritania (Gearon 2010). There are exam-ples of other hostage-takings, however, that have ended in disaster. Edwin Dyer, an English chef on vacation in Mali during January 2009, was executed by AQIM four months later (Keenan 2009). Michel Germaneau, a French aid worker with previous ties to the Algerian petrol industry, was allegedly killed in retaliation for a failed rescue attempt by a joint Mauritanian-French military operation in northern Mali during July 2010 (Barchfield 2010). Christopher Leggett, an American aid worker suspected by AQIM of proselytising, was killed during an attempted kidnapping in July 2009 at Nouakchott, Mauritania (Mohamed 2009; Thurston 2010). From Mauritania to Chad, foreigners have become targets for ideological, political or economic gain. Given the success rate, abductions are likely to continue and the media will remain focused on them, and not the issues of poverty, famine, and the political marginalising of inhabitants in the Sahara and remote parts of the Sahel.

To combat attacks on Western interests, the United States and European powers implemented the Global War on Terror (GWOT), a set of programmes designed to assist Maghreb and Sahel governments to fight terrorism and govern remote areas in the Sahara and Sahel effectively (Antil 2006; Berschinski 2007). These programmes, however, have the consequence of locking down space – in other words, diminishing local people's capacity to pursue their livelihoods. The region's activities, pastoralism, commerce and tourism, have increased in risk, depreciated in profits or dropped off altogether. Poverty and political marginalisation are nothing new (Jackson and Rosberg 1986; Moreira and Bayraktar 2008), yet the GWOT has placed the region's inhabitants in a state of further impoverishment and greater alienation from governments whose representatives live considerable distances away.

AQIM takes responsibility for abducting foreigners, and the media are quick to highlight such claims. The facts on the ground are quite different. Criminal gangs and people seeking quick profit as a temporary alternative to their persistent poverty have been the real actors in most kidnappings and hostage-takings. Based on qualitative interviews and observations conducted in southern Algeria, northern Niger, northern Mali, eastern Mauritania and southern Morocco between 2006 and 2008, it is shown that terrorists have an uneasy form of collaboration with such criminal gangs and individual actors. Outsiders, for their part, tend to misinterpret these various actors as all being terrorists. This misinterpretation is based on three false conceptions. In the first instance (as is argued below) the myth of the Sahara and Sahel as 'ungoverned' and 'lawless' is perpetuated. Western powers justify military involvement in the area precisely because they view the region as a no-man's-land. On paper GWOT programmes are designed to improve law enforcement of Sahelian and Saharan governments (Roberts 2003; Antil 2006; Berschinski 2007; Jourde 2007). In practice the policing inadvertently curtails major livelihood practices of local communities. The second major misconception is that Islam currently unites a diverse assemblage of distinct cultural and ethnic peoples into one pan-Islamic whole (see below). The United States and Western Europe foreign policy experts – perhaps out of expediency – hold fast to an overarching paradigm that Muslim society as a whole is monolithic, violent, a threat to Western interests, and rapidly spreading (Glickman 2003; CSIS 2010; Filiu 2010).

Also, AQIM portrays a simplified picture of GWOT allies as neo-colonials, even though such a ploy has little success with recruitment. AQIM's success with local populations is limited and largely confined to cash exchanges for foreign hostages. The Sahara and Sahel have their share of rebels. Insurgent ideologies are largely designed to resist deteriorating socio-economic conditions, the imposition of central authority, the status quo of little to no political representation, and the exploitation of local resources by foreign companies and *rentier* states (Bonte 2001; Demante 2005; Zoubir and Benabdallah-Gambier 2005; Obi 2008; Cristiani and Fabiani 2010). They are not designed as a war against Western powers. Such insurgent interests have little affinity to the aims of terrorists, while at the same time promoting poor-to-antagonistic relations with GWOT allies. Finally, in a concluding section of this paper, the misconceptions generated through the day-to-day interactions between foreigners and Africans are examined. The seemingly endless showcases of material wealth, medical supplies, and food aid create an image in kidnappers' minds (as well as most Africans') of the West as endowed with limitless capital, an image constantly reinforced by outside assistance and foreigners' lifestyles in Africa (Samoff 2004; Miles 2008). Given these three factors, the act of abducting foreigners, as a means to easy money, can be understood. The kidnapper/hostage-taker has long witnessed outsiders (both terrorists and GWOT agents) as a threat to their political, social and economic order. If the GWOT proponents are serious about ending violence in the Sahara and Sahel an overhaul of the policies is needed, beginning with reductions in military and economic coercion and a plan for addressing the region's chronic problems.

Governed spaces: The Sahel and Sahara

Many desert countries rank the lowest in population density. Mauritania and Libya, for instance, contain large swaths of the Sahara desert, and as such are in the top ten least densely populated countries in the world. The Sahara also occupies large swaths of Algeria, Mali, Niger and Chad. Even its borderlands settlements are scattered and infrequent. Within the Sahel proper, Claude Raynaut et al. (1997), in their macro-scale study of Sahelian populations, observed that there are more animals than people in the northern Sahel. Thus experts are accurate to characterise both the Sahara and the sub-region of the northern Sahel as regions that are 'vast' and 'sparsely populated'. Beyond this demographic dimension, however, fact quickly shifts to interpretation.

For the Sahara and its fringes there is no effective central authority. Historically, the Sahara and northern Sahel are home to Arab, Tuareg and Toubou people who primarily engage in pastoralism (Bonte 1998; Demangeot and Bernus 2001), in addition to other socio-economic activities for survival (Bernus 1981; Retaillé 1993 and 1998). These groups also provided a mixed lot of caravan traders, warriors, and bandits who conducted a lucrative trans-Saharan trade until the late nineteenth century (Conte 1991; Triaud 1993). Maritime trade slowly eroded the trans-Saharan routes but not before pastoral groups installed slaves, captives and artisans in Saharan oases and Sahelian villages that served as ports of call and centres of agricultural production (Brusberg 1985; Zeltner 1989; Gremont 2010). Such demographic complexity grew apace with European intrusions in the late nineteenth and early twentieth centuries. Further disruptions were the result of the imposition of arbitrary colonial administrative boundaries and customs, the promotion of private property and agriculture, and the shrinking of the pastoral commons. Nomadic groups, such as Fulani cattle herders, who once inhabited agricultural zones, migrated north, further constricting the pastoral commons (Claudot-Hawad 1993; Park 1993). Colonial administrations went about converting desert oases into military posts and provincial towns. Large numbers of Wolof, Halpulaar,

Bambara, Songhaï, Djerma, Hausa, and Sara attached to the European administration moved with their families to the colonial enclaves carved into the Sahara and northern Sahel.

In spite of these many changes wrought by colonial jurisdiction, control of the Sahara was feeble at best. The colonial enclaves were understaffed. Planning was miniscule and development underfunded. The collection of taxes and customs duties was lax, difficult to enforce, and occasionally wrought with graft (Bernus et al. 1993). Although the new settlements, a growing population rate, and arbitrary borders reduced pastoral commons, the pastoralists nonetheless gained a new opportunity from the opening up of competitive European markets to the north and south of them. There were expanded opportunities to engage in clandestine trade in cattle, sheep, cloth, and comestible goods, particularly in the anglophone colonies (Raynaud 1948). Even as the African independence movements replaced their colonial superiors in the 1950s and 1960s, promising an end to this illicit trade (Bernus 1981), such idealism proved hollow in practice. The new African regimes had inherited a weak state structure and even weaker economies (Gammer 2000; Hastings 2009). Locally, officials contributed indirectly to the continuance of smuggling through their acceptance of bribes or directly through the brokerage and transport of goods. African states' lacklustre performance in paying their employees, and the unforeseen consequences of trade liberalisation from World Bank programmes in the 1980s and 1990s, assured their continuance (Meagher 2003; Samoff 2004).

Fundamentally, revenues from animals and comestible goods are far too small to provide the money and materials needed to support twenty-first-century terrorism. However, practices put in place the structures that allow the flow of contraband that does. Even before decolonisation, officials admitted their inability to control smuggling (Arditi 2003; Thompson 2009). After independence, when rebellions, civil wars and insurgencies created new demands, insurgents took an active hand in the illicit trade, both as the suppliers and buyers of weapons, ammunition, vehicles and other supplies (Pierre and Quandt 1995; Lecocq and Schrijver 2007; Guichaoua 2009). Today the commodities found in these markets include cigarettes, narcotics, and illegal immigrants shipped northwards (Brachet 2005; Walther 2009). Moving south are gasoline and electronics from Europe and North Africa (Author Interviews October 2006 and December 2007; Collyer 2007). Arabs monopolise the trade (Gutelius 2007), though it is common to find Tuaregs and Toubous employed as drivers, navigators, and security for these operations. This is especially the case after drought and civil war destroyed flocks, and since tourism's decline since the 1990s (Interviews October 2006; Walther and Retaillé 2010). Additionally, civil servants in practice facilitate the movement of goods. The Niger government recognises the benefit of transporting illegal aliens. It generates badly needed revenue and authorities do little to curtail the practice beyond the posting of billboards that are meant to discourage such migrations (Brachet 2005; Walther 2009; Thurston 2010). As for the smuggling of goods, it is more than a market for arms to terrorists; it is also a part of people's livelihoods.

In the Sahara and remote parts of the Sahel, both trade and authority are decentralised and highly competitive. Rivalries and intrigues do at times lead to violence. What is difficult for Western policy-makers and the media to differentiate are incidents that are acts of terrorism versus ones which are not. For example, when four French tourists were killed in Mauritania during Christmas

2007, the experts and media attributed the shootings to AQIM (Petrou 2009; Thorne 2009). Mauritanians, however, held a different view. They saw similarities between the incident and previous robberies involving foreigners. In their judgment, the French tourists were simply victims of a robbery that went wrong (Interviews February 2008). Another example, the abduction of Robert Fowler and Louis Quay, highlights the complexity in distinguishing a desperate act from terrorism. There was delay of three months between the capture of these two United Nations envoys and the ransom paid to AQIM for their release, along with that of three other hostages (Thorne 2009). The question arises: Why such a delay? One explanation is that AQIM did not actually kidnap the envoys. It is as reasonable to posit that a group familiar with their mission kidnapped the envoys and then sold them to AQIM, or transferred them to another group in contact with AQIM for a quick return (Keenan 2009; Sahara Focus 2009a). Since Nouakchott, Bamako, Niamey and Ndjamena have weak holds on their respective peripheries, it is fairly easy for hostage-takings and other forms of violence to occur without terrorism being the motivation of the perpetrators.

In such murky circumstances, there is every possibility for such incidents involving foreigners to occur without terrorism as the motivation. Nonetheless, the Western powers are quick to assume that any violence directed at Western interests is a terrorist act and thus invoke the two-edged sword of the GWOT: the use of hard power (both military and economic) and selected humanitarian programmes that purport to help end terrorism (Sheehan 2005; Huysmans et al. 2006; Mitchell 2010). Explicit examples of this strategy are in Afghanistan and Iraq. In other parts of Central Asia and Africa, covert operations are conducted in the name of the GWOT (Hafez 2008; Hastings 2009; Kurečić 2010; Sørbø 2010). For the Sahara and Sahel, there is a pattern of military build-up, masked with charity, to deflate pre-existing tensions between local populations and their national governments. The restricting of space (of the commons) as part of the strategy only serves to generate more conflict between interest groups. Add to this state of tensions the decline in legal commerce far from international borders and GWOT's attempts to clamp down on smuggling and other forms of illegal trade. Licensed merchants in the interior towns of Agadez, Niger and Kiffa, Mauritania complain of drops in sales and deliveries with increased regulations on transport or the threat of hijackings in route (Interviews December 2007 and February 2008). Pastoralists experience infringements on movements. Both terrorist and soldier patrols block routes, confiscate property and in extreme cases shoot animals, people, or both (Interviews October 2007). Pronouncements from GWOT officials and the negative press coverage regarding the threat of terrorism serve to further stifle tourism (Walther and Retaillé 2010). Taxi drivers who would normally earn a living driving tourists to heritage sites find themselves competing with others to transport illegal immigrants to state borders (Interviews October 2007 and February 2008). Humanitarian assistance, such as vaccinations, the construction of wells, and the donation of motor pumps fails to compensate the affected local populations for the damage caused by the presence of both terrorists and soldiers. With each cycle of increased tensions, initiated by governmental actions to implement GWOT tactics, the tension level only increases instability and alienation among the affected inhabitants of the Sahara and Sahel.

The GWOT also undermines regional long-term security by training and supporting, both financially and materially, militaries utilised by the national political elite to suppress political dissent. There are a number of examples of this practice. The Niger government, for example, initially blamed the *Mouvement des Nigériens pour la Justice* (MNJ), a politico-military organisation fighting for greater autonomy in northern Niger, for the Fowler-Guay abduction (BBC News Africa 2008; Graham IV 2010). Morocco persists in labelling the Polisario, Western Sahara's independence movement, as a gang of criminals, smugglers and cohorts with terrorist organisations (Ousman 2004; Zoubir and Benabdallah-Gambier 2005). Even Amadou Toumani Touré, the President of Mali, whom most view as more tolerant of the Tuareg than other Sahelian politicians, scrapped diplomacy for force in dealing with Ibrahim Bahanga's insurgency at Tin Zaouâtene in 2008, with GWOT assistance (*Sahara Focus* 2009a). If these groups, and others like them, have ties to terrorists it is out of expediency more than choice. They share the same battlegrounds, after all, and have the same adversaries (i.e. national governments). Their goals, however, differ from those of jihadis. Ultimately, the suppression of dissent, or even the voluntary disbandment of these groups without resolution, provides the foundation for violence to resurface. Collectively or individually, dissent fosters closer alliances with extremists. Hard power does achieve one thing, an atmosphere of uncertainty and intermittent violence, pushing ideologues who are not terrorists closer to extremes.

Co-equating Islam with terrorism

The perception of a pan-Islamic movement pitted against the West has deeper roots than the current war on terror. Colonial administrations in the late 1800s and early 1900s, much like contemporary independent governments, had their own cadres of experts. Such experts consistently interpreted and conflated tensions by lumping together diverse groups that in fact had little or no ties with each other. It is worth noting, however, that when colonial administration was weak, Western weaponry and military action became the primary tactical advantages against Africans. Some Muslim societies organised and resisted the approaching 'infidels'. The Toucouleur and Sokoto empires and the Mahdist movement in Sudan, though short-lived, were large enough in scale to alarm the most confident of colonial regimes. Such organised resistance to European encroachments was the exception. Most annexations of territories and peoples occurred without incident (Kolapo 2007). Even in the Sahara, where Arab, Tuareg and Toubou groups are commonly perceived as xenophobic and warlike, organised resistance to European colonialist rule was isolated, small in scale, and contained by military forces (Le Rouvreur 1962; Bernus et al. 1993; Triaud 1996).

Isolated attacks did occur over time, but rarely in the name of Muslim versus Christian. Caravans, colonial agents and small-scale military patrols were attacked for various reasons, including material gain, animosities over colonial practices, competition over resources, or personal grievances (Chapelle 1957; Frémeaux 1993). Acts of banditry had long been acceptable practice in pastoral societies. Before European colonial domination, the competition within and between pastoral groups to meet immediate needs and expand control of land and resources was accepted practice (Claudot-Hawad 1993; Gremont 2010). During the colonial period, the targets, not the goals, of attacks changed. The targets were no longer exclusively families, clans or confederations. Centralised authority became another adversary. Nevertheless, the response by colonial officials was, for the most part, limited. The colonial bureaus paid greater attention to the policing and development of agricultural zones, not pastoral ones (Frémeaux 1993; Triaud 1993). On site, local populations did little to help in the apprehension of suspects, either out of ignorance or, in certain cases, through non-compliance. Custom also played a part, as it was, and is, common for pastoralists to aid individuals whether they are victims or perpetrators (Bernus 1981). In Toubou society, for instance, it is acceptable for families to aid bandits and murderers (Zeltner 1989). Incidents involving the disappearance or death of colonial officials in the Tibesti Region of Chad were common until the 1950s (Chapelle 1957; Le Rouvreur 1962; Beltrami and Proto 2005). It stood to reason that pastoralists, regardless of their individual clan or familial affiliations, would sooner help other pastoralists than the colonials.

In terms of collective threats, European powers in the Sahara (French, English and Italian) recognised one by the early 1900s, a movement whose ideology traced back to the Mahdist uprising in the Sudan (Thompson 2009). The *Sanusiyya*, a sub-group of Salafists, preached a pan-Islamic doctrine and advocated the use of violence against foreigners. This tactic bears some resemblance to AQIM's current methods. Organised in Cyrenaica with support in Fezzan to the west, this movement attacked colonial outposts far removed from Tripoli, Cairo and Fort Lamy prior to and during the First World War (Triaud 1996). French officials erroneously linked the violence in the eastern Sahara with that of the Tuareg revolts in north-eastern Mali and northern Niger that occurred during the same period (Clozel 1916; Simon 1919). Hindsight after the War revealed that the Tuareg rebels had no affiliation with the insurgency to the east. Their grievance was with the dramatic socio-economic changes that took place in the short tenure of French administration (Bernus 1981). Despite differing ideologies and conditions among the varied Saharan peoples, the response to dissent and resistance by every European colonial power was military force and occupation. French and Italian forces killed the *Sanusiyya* leadership and disbanded its followers. Such resistance persisted in the Italian territory until 1931 (Rainero 1980). Liquidating the movement did not extinguish the message, however. *Sanusiyya* resistance again flared up during the intrigues of the Second World War, with the Allies managing to play upon divisions to suppress those sympathetic to the Axis powers (Thompson 2009).

With decolonisation, naturally, changes came in the administering of the Sahara and Sahel, but what did not change was lack of state integration. With the exception of Mauritania, Arabs, Tuaregs and Toubous living far from Bamako, Niamey and Ndjamena had little sense of national identity. Furthermore, the established inequalities between them and national elites that existed before decolonisation continued. The disaffected, especially the young, sought alternatives to post-colonial systems that catered to the educated, urban elites from the south. Droughts, the destruction of flocks and the disbanding of family members during times of famine in the 1970s and 1980s brought many young men from the Sahel to Algeria and Libya. There, they gained work opportunities and in some cases exposure to radical politics (Boucek 2004; Zoubir and Benabdallah-Gambier 2005; Boubekeur 2008). For a short time Qaddafi in Libya supported extremists, as part of his anti-Western campaign. Through state backing, trained 'jihadis' were sent to conflicts in Lebanon and Afghanistan in the 1980s. By the 1990s, however, Qaddafi changed his policies both at home and abroad. Estranged Libyans returning from abroad organised the Libyan Islamic Fighting Group to replace what they perceived as a false Islamic theocracy (Boucek 2004; Pargeter 2005). For their part, Arab and Tuareg combatants, those from Mali and Niger particularly, returned to participate in 1990s rebellions (Gutelius 2007; Lecocq and Schrijver, 2007). Algeria also faced the threat posed by radicalism shifting to violence. By the 1990s Algiers could not prevent civil war. The long-term one-party rule of the *Front de Libération Nationale* (FLN) was notorious for corruption, mismanagement and human rights' violations (Pierre and Quandt 1995). Guerrilla warfare in the countryside was common and terrorist attacks occurred in the major cities.

In all of these conflicts, violence directly affected the security of foreigners living and working in the Sahara and Sahel. The Polisario, fighting for the independence of the Western Sahara, killed French and Africans in a night raid at the mining town of Zouérat in 1977 (Bonte 2001). Rebels abducted bystanders, both foreign and domestic, in the 1990s Malian and Nigérien rebellions to obtain political leverage, material gain, or money (Grégoire 1999; Demante 2005). They also carjacked NGO vehicles, dropping off the workers 50 km out of town and selling the vehicles for cash or exchanging them for needed weapons and supplies at markets hundreds of kilometres away (Interviews January 2008). Militants in the Algerian civil war did not discriminate between Algerian and foreigner (Pierre and Quandt 1995). During the Nigérien rebellion of 2007 – 2009, the MNJ abducted Chinese workers, later releasing them unharmed (Guichaoua 2009). These actions were not a pan-Islamic front against foreigners. The goals within this varied landscape of actors typically involve the need for both development and political representation. Conversely, the co-optation, dispersion, and/or repression of these various actors create a vacuum for extremist elements to fill. As they champion the call for holy war against 'despotic' African regimes, AQIM seeks to fill this vacuum (Antil 2006; Berschinski 2007).

The growth of radicalism is for some a nuisance and for a few an opportunity. As mentioned above, the deployment of national forces and sorties by AQIM greatly reduce commerce, animal husbandry and tourism. Despite these dislocations and disruptions, most in the Sahara and Sahel avoid both terrorists and military patrols (Interviews October 2007 and February 2008; Brulliard 2009). For those in contact with Salafi clerics, whose financing comes from Wahhabi donors, there are options. First, not all Salafis preach violence. Most are *Salafiyya Ilmiyya* or Da'wa Salafis who practise non-violence and abstention from politics. Beyond their doctrinal concerns, they offer immediate assistance of food and cash to the needy (Ousman 2004; Gutelius 2007; Boubekeur 2008). Migrating Africans passing through Saharan posts (those who are delayed en route) frequently need money since bribes and expenses quickly deplete their purses and wallets (Brachet 2005; Collyer 2007). Some seek Salafi charity to return home or continue on to North Africa or Europe (Interviews May and October 2007). Jihadi Salafism differs from the *Ilmiyya* branch by advocating violence and the potential for greater material rewards to those who join their ranks. Those recruited are likely to be shipped off to other battlefronts in the Afghanistan and Iraq wars. Significant numbers of North Africans fight, or have fought, on the side of the Taliban forces and Iraqi insurgency (Boubekeur 2008; Alexander 2010). By contrast, the commitment of Western aid in the region is irregular, in part due to poor logistics and lack of security (Zoubir and Benab-dallah-Gambier 2005; Solé-Arqués 2009).

In Mali, Niger and Chad, the representation of Arab, Tuareg and Toubou groups in the military and police materialised after the 1990s (Lecocq and Schrijver, 2007), but most serve in the more populous parts of these countries, not in their local communities. This effort at national integration serves the state (Moreira and Bayraktar 2008; Ilkjaer and Boureima 2010), but fails to address the problems that occur between local communities and state services in the north (Interviews October 2006 and January 2008). These circumstances are glossed over by many proponents of the GWOT because terrorism is understood more in terms of cultural conflict between Western powers and Muslims. Socio-economic disparities that push individuals and whole groups to the margins are not given priority, even if they are recognised as factors that lead to alienation and resistance.

The lines between agency, insurgent, and terrorist are not always clearly defined. The chronic, endemic problems affecting minorities – especially those of corruption, poverty, and state repression – overlap and blur into the West's preoccupation with the conflict identified with (often ill-defined) terrorist organisations. Some call the Sahara and Sahel 'breeding grounds of terrorism' (Bruguière 2010; Filiu 2010). The continued military involvement in the area may help to ensure that this characterisation becomes irrefutable. At present, however, most of the population have no desire to join jihadis and related causes. The deaths of Christopher Leggett and Michel Germaneau were unfortunate, but were more likely mishaps than the executive orders of the AQIM leadership (Petrou 2009). Edwin Dyer's execution was also tragic, yet merited greater press coverage for AQIM. In claiming to have murdered all three men, the terror group raises the ante in future hostage-takings. AQIM also hopes to increase recruitment of fervent individuals who adopt the mythology of an anti-Western pan-Islamism (Ousman 2004). Given the current socio-economic climate of the Sahara and Sahel, however, it is more likely that profiteers and out-of-work insurgents will initiate further foreigner abductions and the selling of them to AQIM or AQIM contacts. These people are not terrorists *per se*, as their primary motivation is taking advantage of a lucrative opportunity. This activity has remarkable similarities with the Somali pirates and the Ogoni activists in the Niger Delta (Obi 2008; Hastings 2009), insofar as a political or ideological motive is not at the heart of the action.

Foreigner – African encounters

> The richest businessman in any of these countries [Mali, Mauritania, Morocco or Senegal] could move to Europe and there, he would take orders from the poorest European (Interview February 2008).

Africans and Europeans interacted with each other for millennia, but inequalities between the two only deepened during colonial rule. The technologies, lifestyles, colonial practices, and infrastructures Europeans brought to their colonies increased disparities between foreigner and African (Kapoor 2008). In the Sahara and its fringes Africans watched warily as Europeans arrived with motorised transport, advanced weaponry, and troops from far-off lands. Even the benign introduction of animal vaccinations and cement wells (to name but a few innovations) served to maintain order and justify foreign dominion (Rainero 1980; Bernus 1981; Thompson 2009). Upon independence the coloniser left and was replaced with other foreign actors. Under the various banners of national development, humanitarian assistance, adventure, and in the past 10 years, the promise to remove the threat of terrorism, these actors perpetuate the established foreign domination over local populations. Multinational corporations (MNCs) introduce heavy machines, materials, and pollution in the desert, as well as increased demands on what little water is available. All this is for one purpose, the extraction of oil, natural gas, uranium, iron ore, and the search for other mineral resources (Bonte 2001; Chamaret et al. 2007; Guichaoua 2009). In their impressive 4 × 4 vehicles, international non-government organisations (INGOs) occasionally visit to distribute medicines, food, and other implements for development projects (Sørbø et al. 1998; Sørbø 2010). Foreign military advisors enter the region embedded with national forces. Together they arrive in helicopters and armoured personnel carriers equipped with advanced weaponry and supported by unmanned drones and GeoEye satellite imagery (*Sahara Focus* 2009a). One unanticipated consequence of such practices, without the participation of local Africans, is to undermine the security of foreigners and place them at risk of violence, whether instigated by criminals, local insurgents or terrorists.

Local populations have no stake or role in the presence of foreign firms or national forces posted in the Sahara. They are at best a disproportionate minority of short-term labourers and low-ranking civil servants. During the colonial era, Africans were employed in private firms and the administration, but with the exception of a few individuals, indigenous jobs were limited to clerks, foot soldiers and colonial works labour (Kolapo 2007). Recruitment was for the most part limited to Africans residing in the South. Decolonisation broke the 'thatched roof' ceiling in the civil service but not the barrier between the African elite and marginalised groups. In fact, African independence parties expanded the public sector not to create jobs for a multi-ethnic society but to absorb newer generations of their urbanised constituents (Jackson and Rosberg 1986; Sørbø et al. 1998). Within MNCs and NGOs, foreigners retained the key-level positions into the 1980s (Gammer 2000; Bonte 2001). Change has come in the last two decades, however. The companies and NGOs made the transition from hiring only foreigners for engineering and upper-level administration, to the training and hiring of Africans (Wermus 1995; Dillard 2003; Chamaret et al. 2007). While profiled for its positive qualities in creating local stakeholders and leadership roles in Africa, little attention was paid to the demographics of who precisely entered these highly sought-after positions. Currently, high-status positions are filled, almost exclusively, by ethnic groups that monopolised political, economic, and educational advantages since colonial times. This practice of exclusion extends to the Sahara and Sahel for Arab, Tuareg and Toubou peoples. As such, they have no choice but to identify with their neighbours: the smugglers, drug traffickers, criminals, kidnappers and terrorists that the current GWOT is determined to suppress.

The 'Africanisation' policy MNCs and NGOs apply in their management creates or exacerbates existing ethnic divisions. The socio-economic disparities that flow from such practices are counterproductive to both regional stability and state integration. An example is the seven Areva employees abducted in northern Niger in September 2010. None were native to the area. Five are French, one Togolese, and the other Malagasy (*Toronto Star* 2010). Even among those Nigériens employed by Areva and its affiliates, locals, with the exception of temporary manual labourers, are not included (Interviews October 2006). In northern Niger, local Tuareg, Arab and Fulani communities have no attachment to AQIM, but neither do they have any affiliation with the laws a Zarma-Hausa ruling elite in Niamey imposes on them. Nor do they have any real stake in the MNCs extracting uranium from their commons (Guichaoua 2009). Thus, for a few, kidnapping is more than an economic act of necessity. It is an act of defiance, one that extremists seek to interpret as a campaign to regain direct control over land and resources. Since pastoral commons have already been drastically reduced, tourism has declined, and waged work opportunities have dwindled since the recession in 2008, the criminals and ideologues mingling with the local people offer more than national and international agents who are passing strangers in the region.

For training and surveillance purposes, African governments deploy soldiers in the Sahara and remote parts of the Sahel. Their presence is, above all, to disrupt, detain, and disband terrorists and insurgents, anyone or any group identified as 'enemies of the state'. They, in addition to the foreign advisors that accompany them, are but temporary visitors. The armed forces of Mali, Niger, Chad and Algeria are made up of soldiers not from the desert. They come from the more humid Sahel and the Mediterranean. They have little or no stake in the welfare of this region, unlike the pastoralists, merchants, and holy men (both reformist and radical) who live here. The hard-power tactics these militaries practise, backed by the military assets of the United States, France, and the United Kingdom are double-edged. On one hand, if history repeats itself, GWOT allies are likely to suppress AQIM and other extremists much like colonial regimes liquidated the *Sanusiyya*. In doing this, jihadism may resurface with each new generation, particularly if their success includes the deaths of innocent bystanders. So too will the unresolved insurgent movements in Algeria, Libya, Mali, Niger and Chad, since the level of integration into their respective state-level systems is poor for Saharan populations (Claudot-Hawad 1993; Boubekeur 2008; Solé-Arqués 2009). With the exception of the joint Mauritanian-French raid in northern Mali during July 2010, the Western powers have largely kept secret their direct involvements in the covert training, equipping, and funding of African militaries and satellite surveillance of the region (Jourde 2007; Alexander 2010; Bruguière 2010). Even so, this masks nothing. The local people are aware of Western involvement in their localities and the AQIM is quick to label these manoeuvres as a new imperialism in their broadcasts (Interviews October 2007; Jourde 2007; Keenan 2009).

This trend of involvement is exacerbated by the infrastructure, material supports, and volume of goods brought in by MNCs, NGOs and militaries. Vehicles, laptops, solar panels, cell phones, weapons, in addition to food and medicines, become commodities that thieves, smugglers, and ideologues vie for (Obi 2008; Guichaoua 2009; Solé-Arqués 2009). The GWOT material assistance upgrades African nations' militaries considerably but also creates opportunities for bribing officials and the stealing or raiding of warehouses for supplies (Berschinski 2007; Jourde 2007). Food and medical aid appear benign enough. Still, in the hands of terrorists they are tools to encourage, persuade, or extort compliance from an abstinent population (Ousman 2004; Boubekeur 2008).

The same is true when political regimes control such assets (Benini 1993; Claudot-Hawad 1993). The levels of humanitarian and military assistance flowing into the region are not only inducements for corruption and theft; such availability also reinforces the economic incentive to kidnap foreigners. Many Africans perceive no end to the wealth that MNCs, NGOs and Western powers possess (Interviews February 2008). A company that raises the capital needed to extract minerals from the desert or a government that donates thousands of tonnes of food aid or medical supplies has the ability to raise millions of euros to free their nationals from a terrorist group. And, as such, this widens the potential for the abduction of foreigners by either unscrupulous individuals or groups in order to profit from the presence of such alien elements in their commons.

Finally, the very lifestyle that foreigners bring with them to Africa is alien to Africans. It is also idealised by many Africans (Andreotti 2007; Kapoor 2004; 2008). For those who exalt Western lifestyles, the luxurious hotels in the capital, the gated houses with servants, the supermarkets stocked with imported, processed foods, even the trivial act of drinking bottled water, are all mistakenly perceived as easily obtainable. Even tourist packages that depict African journeys as local experiences still cater to Western comfort and tastes (Donaldson and Tyner 1999; Forbes 2005; Odularu 2008). Compared to living in huts, tents or shantytowns, working in sectors of the economy that net little advancement and having to draw water from wells or dilapidated tap systems, large numbers of Africans strive for foreign tastes. African elites mimic Western behaviours that they once enjoyed at universities in France, England, the United States, and Russia. Those who crave such lifestyle opportunities have little choice but to remain impoverished or they may turn to migration, informal trade, and/or crime (Andreasson 2005; Brachet 2005; Interviews October 2006 and 2007). In terms of abduction as a means to such ends, an individual or group must devote much time and effort to planning and execution of the act. Abduction is, however, neither new nor exclusive to the taking of foreign nationals (Amnesty International 2007; Bengali 2008). Abduction is an old and tested stratagem. Ransoming foreign nationals brings with it the potential of large returns (Bengali 2008; Cristiani and Fabiani 2010). It is, therefore, nothing extraordinary to expect that the exclusionary practices of foreigners and elites within Africa, with their displays of material wealth, produce conditions for incidents of kidnapping and robbery that are not limited to terrorists. Both criminal elements and opportunists disaffected by such levels of disparity are also players. It is an old story cloaked by the fear of a 'global jihad'.

Conclusion

The Sahara and its fringes are governed by a complex growing number of actors who have witnessed foreign agents, both non-African and African, destabilising their political order and socio-economic activities for over a century. Colonial regimes, national elites, MNCs and NGOs changed the pastoral commons by reducing the territory greatly through the seizure of land by eminent domain and settlement. The influxes of people from colonial times to the present clandestine migrations have further complicated the demography. Arab, Tuareg and Toubou see themselves as the proper stewards of the Sahara and northern Sahel, though their numbers, poverty and political marginalisation exclude them from political participation. The emergence of extremism is not because these territories are vast and Arab, although the Tuareg and Toubou are Muslim. Instead, jihadists have found a social environment where local populations have antagonistic relations with their respective governments. Life in the Sahara was difficult before El Para and his followers abducted tourists in Algeria. AQIM's growth and GWOT's build-up, however, have escalated the insecurity and violence. Most local people cope with these difficulties through their herds, trade, and philanthropy within their communities or through outside assistance. The terrorist and counterterrorist activity in the region, however, jeopardises the security of pastoralists and their animals, reduces licensed commerce in specific areas, increases rivalry in smuggling operations, and leads to international NGOs withdrawing their personnel and assistance. The negative press generated from the violence ruins what little tourism still exists and provides weak states with the needed military assistance to suppress political rivals. Clandestine trade continues but the current benefits may not be universally distributed and are likely to diminish, given the commitment of GWOT backers to suppress it.

Criminals, ideologues and other people pushed by poverty or political motivation are the culprits abducting foreigners and attacking Western targets in the Sahara and Sahel. The question that remains is whether these actors believe their cause is Muslim versus Westerner or if personal experience, economic difficulties, antagonisms over central authority, or grievances regarding foreigners profiting from natural resource extraction motivates their actions. Despite what these various groups think of AQIM, the terrorist organisation has a purpose for them. To put it in crude terms, AQIM is a 'clearing house'. By selling their prisoner to AQIM they reduce their risk of capture and earn quick money. AQIM can demand top ransoms thanks to both the Western media who link all violence occurring in the region to AQIM and the support of Wahabi donors and *Al-Qaeda* (Berschinski 2007; Gutelius 2007). Even if AQIM does not have a foreigner or group of foreigners detained, the hostage(s) will, in all likelihood, filter into their camp. AQIM bears the greater risk, but then this helped it grow from an unknown in 2003 to an organisation capable of extorting millions of euros from national governments.

Despite the proliferation of violence, however, Western powers and their counterparts in Algiers, Nouakchott, Bamako, Niamey, and Ndjamena have not lost local populations to violent extremists. Most Saharans and Sahelians shun violence. At the same time, local populations in the Sahara and its fringes do not acquiesce in their governments and outside actors exploiting their commons and constricting their socio-economic networks without participation and/or some form of compensation paid to them. Because of this, many Arabs, Tuareg and Toubou are non-aligned in the war on terror. The situation where Toubou groups sold El Para's group to Chadian authorities is a good example of this. Had the tables been turned, the Toubou (if the risk was minimal and benefits worth it) might have sold captured authorities to the terrorists. Expectations run high among policy-makers that local people will collaborate with GWOT allies, given Western humanitarian efforts, but this is far from reality. Westerners and their recent enemies are both seen as opportunities in rare situations, and as nuisances and threats in most others. To maintain a status quo of backing up military and economic coercion through covert means against *al-Qaeda* in the Islamic Maghreb may succeed in stamping them out, but the long-term foreign presence will only be interpreted by zealots as a new neocolonialism and will become a recruitment tool to indoctrinate newer generations who believe such rhetoric in the Sahara and Sahel, or in other regions. The failure of state integration and the lack of local participation with MNCs and NGOs that work in the Sahara and northern Sahel have become manifest in an environment where abductions and killings are lucrative, profitable and now in default of other declining activities, a tenuous livelihood strategy for a minority of local actors.

References

Africa Confidential, 2006. Drowning Season. 4 (2).

Alexander, Yonah. 2010. Maghreb and Sahel Terrorism: Addressing the Rising Threat from al-Qaeda and other Terrorists in North and West/Central Africa. International Center for Terrorism Studies. Arlington, VA: Potomac Institute for Policy Studies.

Amnesty International. 2007. Civilians in Peril in the Wild North. Audio interview (AI Index: AFR 19/003/2007). Available from: http://www.amnesty.org/en/library/info/AFR19/003/2007 [Accessed 15 November 2011].

Andreasson, Stefan. 2005. Orientalism and African Development Studies. *Third World Quarterly* 26(6): 971–986.

Andreotti, Vanessa. 2007. An Ethical Engagement with the Other. *Critical Literacy: Theories and Practices* 1(1): 69–79.

Antil, Alain. 2006. L'Afrique et la "Guerre Contre la Terreur". *Politique Etrangère* 3: 583–591.

Arditi, Claude. 2003. Le Tchad et le Monde Arabe: Essai d'Analyse des Relations Commerciales de la Période Précoloniale à Aujourd'hui. *Afrique Contemporaine* 207(3): 185–198.

Barchfield, Jenny. 2010. France's Sarkozy calls Niger kidnappings worrying. *The Guardian*. September. Available from: http://www.guardian.co.uk/world/feedarticle/9277924

BBC News Africa. 2008. Tuareg Rebels Deny UN Kidnapping. BBC News Africa, 16 December. Available from: http://news.bbc.co.uk/2/hi/africa/7784641.stm.

Beltrami, Vanni and Harry Proto. 2005. The Tubus of Central-Eastern Sahara. *Africa: Rivista Trimestrale di Studie Documentazoine dell'Instituto per l'Africa e l'Oriente*. 60(2): 221–258.

Bengali, Shashank. 2008. Kidnappers Extract Huge Ransoms in Forgotten part of Africa. McClatchy, 30 July. Available from: http://www.mcclatchydc.com/2008/07/30/45958/kidnappers-extract-hugeransoms/html.

Benini, Aldo A. 1993. Simulation of the Effectiveness of Protection and Assistance for Victims of Armed Conflict (Sepavac): An Example from Mali, West Africa. *Journal of Contingencies and Crisis Management* 1(4): 215–228.

Bernus, Edmond. 1981. *Touaregs Nigériens: Unité Culturelle et Diversité Régionale d'un Peuple Pasteur*. Paris: Editions l'Harmattan.

Bernus, Edmond, Pierre Boilley, Jean Clauzel, and Jean-Louis Triaud. 1993. *Nomades et Commandants: Administration et Sociétés Nomades dans l'Ancienne AOF*. Paris: Karthala.

Berschinski, Robert G. 2007. *AFRICOM's Dilemma: The 'Global War on Terrorism', 'Capacity Building', Humanitarianism, and the Future of US Security Policy in Africa*. Strategic Studies Institute Paper. Carlisle, PA: US Army War College.

Bonte, Pierre. 1998. Fortunes Commerciales à Shingîti (Adrar mauritanien) au Dix-Neuvième Siècle. *Journal of African History* 39(1): 1–13.

————— 2001. *La Montagne de Fer. La SNIM (Mauritanie): Une Entreprise Minière Saharienne à l'heure de la Mondialisation*. Paris: Karthala.

Boubekeur, Amel. 2008. *Salafism and Radical Politics in Postconflict Algeria*. Carnegie Papers 11. Washington, DC: Carnegie Endowment for International Peace.

Boucek, Christopher. 2004. Libya's Return to the Fold? *Strategic Insights* 3(3): 1–9.

Brachet, J., 2005. Constructions of Territoriality in the Sahara: The Transformation of Spaces in Transit. *Stichproben: Vienna Journal of African Studies* 8: 237–253.

Bruguière, Jean-Louis. 2010. America's Maginot Line Defense Against Terror. *New Perspectives Quarterly* 27(2): 44–47.

Brulliard, Karin. 2009. Radical Islam meets a Buffer in West Africa. *Washington Post*, 12 December.

Brusberg, Frederick. 1985. Production and Exchange in the Saharan Air. *Current Anthropology* 26(3): 394–395.

Chamaret, Aurelie, Martin O'Conner, and Gille Récoché. 2007. Top-down/Bottom-up Approach for Developing Sustainable Development Indicators for Mining: Application to the Arlit Uranium Mines (Niger). *International Journal of Sustainable Development* 10(1/2): 161–174.

Chapelle, Jean. 1957. *Nomades Noirs du Sahara: Les Toubous.* Paris: Plon.

Claudot-Hawad, Hélène. 1993. *Les Touaregs: Portraits en Fragments.* Aix-en-Provence: Édisud.

Clozel, Lieutenant, 1916. Dépêche Télégraphique Chiffrée, n. 1038, adressée à Colonies, Paris. Documentation Française, *Notes et Documents* 0518 (17), 7 Juin.

Collyer, Michael. 2007. In-between Places: Trans-Saharan Transit Migrants in Morocco and the Fragmented Journey to Europe. *Antipode* 39 (4): 668–690.

Conte, Edouard. 1991. Herders, Hunters and Smiths: Mobile Populations in the History of Kanem. In *Herders, Warriors and Traders: Pastoralism in Africa*, eds. John G. Galaty and Pierre Bonte. Boulder, CO: Westview Press.

Cristiani, Dario and Riccardo Fabiani. 2010. AQIM Funds Terrorist Operations with Thriving Sahel-based Kidnapping Industry. *Terrorism Monitor* 8(4): 6–8.

CSIS (Center for Strategic and International Studies). 2010. The Dynamics of North African Terrorism, Conference Report. Washington, DC: CSIS Middle East Program. Available from: http://csis.org/files/attachments/ 100216_NorthAfricaConferenceReport.pdf [Accessed 15November 2011].

Demangeot, Jean and Edmond Bernus. 2001. *Les Milieux Désertiques.* Paris: Armand Colin.

Demante, Marie-Jo. 2005. Crise, Développement Local et Décentralisation dans la Région de Gao. *Afrique Contemporaine* 215(3): 195–217.

Dillard, Mary E. 2003. Examination Standards, Educational Assessments, and Globalizing Elites: The Case of the West African Examinations Council. *Journal of the West African Examinations Council* 88 (4): 413–428.

Donaldson, Daniel P. and James Tyner. 1999. Marketing a 'Sense of Place': Representations of Africa in Ecotour Websites. *Geographical Bulletin* 41(2): 103–112.

Filiu, Jean-Pierre. 2010. *Could al-Qaeda Turn African in the Sahel?* Carnegie Papers 112. Washington, DC: Carnegie Endowment for International Peace.

Forbes. 2005. Open Desert. *Forbes* 176: 100–106.

Frémeaux, Jacques. 1993. La Mise en Place d'une Administration aux Marges Sahariennes de l'OAF (1891–1930), In *Nomades et Commandants: Administration et Sociétés Nomades dans l'Ancienne AOF*, eds. Edmond Bernus, Pierre Boilley, Jean Clauzel, and Jean-Louis Triaud. Paris: Karthala.

Gammer, Moshe. 2000. Post-Soviet Central Asia and Post-Colonial Francophone Africa: Some Associations. *Middle Eastern Studies* 36(2): 124–149.

Gearon, Eamonn. 2010. Maghreb Mayhem. *The Middle East*, 1 April. 25–27.

Glickman, Harvey. 2003. Africa in the War on Terrorism. *Journal of Asian and African Studies* 38(2–3): 162–174.

Graham IV, Franklin Charles. 2010. What the Niger Coup d'Etat Means to the World. *Review of African Political Economy* 37(126): 521–526.

Grégoire, Emmanuel. 1999. *Touaregs du Niger – Le Destin d'un Mythe.* Paris: Karthala.

Gremont, Charles. 2010. *Les Touaregs Iwellenmedan (1647–1896): Un Ensemble Politique de la Boucle Niger.* Paris: Karthala.

Guichaoua, Yvan. 2009. *Circumstantial Alliances and Loose Loyalties in Rebellion Making: The Case of the Tuareg Insurgency in Northern Niger.* MICROCON Research Working Paper 20. Brighton: MICROCON.

Gutelius, David. 2007. Islam in Northern Mali and the War on Terror. *Journal of Contemporary African Studies* 25(1): 59–76.

Hafez, Mohammed M. 2008. Radicalization in the Persian Gulf: Assessing the Potential of Islamist Militancy in Saudi Arabia and Yemen. *Dynamics of Asymmetric Conflict* 1(1): 6–24.

Hastings, Justin V. 2009. Geographies of State Failure and Sophistication in Maritime Piracy Hijackings. *Political Geography*, 28(4): 213–223.

Huysmans, Jef, Andrew Dobson, and Raia Prokhovnik. 2006. *The Politics of Protection: Sites of Insecurity and Political Agency.* New York: Routledge.

Ilkjaer, Lisbet and Sourghia Soumana Boureima. 2010. A Model for Developing Performance Indicators in Niger. *International Journal of Police Science and Management* 12(2): 195–205.

Jackson, Robert H. and Carl G. Rosberg. 1986. Sovereignty and Underdevelopment: Juridical Statehood in the African Crisis. *The Journal of Modern African Studies* 24(1): 1–31.

Jourde, Cedric. 2007. Constructing Representations of the "Global war on Terror" in the Islamic Republic of Mauritania. *Journal of Contemporary African Studies* 25(1): 77–100.

Kapoor, Ilan. 2004. Hyper-Self-Reflexive Development? Spivak on Representing the Third World 'Other'. *Third World Quarterly* 25(4): 627–647.

———— 2008. *The Postcolonial Politics of Development.* New York: Routledge.

Keenan, Jeremy. 2009. Al-Qaeda Terrorism in the Sahara? Edwin Dyer's Murder and the Role of Intelligence Agencies. *Anthropology Today* 25(4): 14–18.

Kolapo, Femi J. 2007. *African Agency and European Colonialism: Latitudes of Negotiations and Containment.* Lanham, MD: University Press of America.

Kurečić, Petar. 2010. The New Great Game: Rivalry of Geostrategies and Geoeconomies in Central Asia. *Hrvatski Geografski Glasnik* 72(1): 21–48.

Lecocq, Baz and Paul Schrijver. 2007. The War on Terror in a Haze of Dust: Potholes and Pitfalls on the Saharan Front. *Journal of Contemporary African Studies* 25(1): 141–166.

Le Rouvreur, Albert. 1962. *Sahéliens et Sahariens du Tchad.* Paris: Berger-Levrault.

Meagher, Kate. 2003. A Back Door to Globalisation? Structural Adjustment, Globalisation and Transborder Trade in West Africa. *Review of African Political Economy* 30(95): 57–75.

Miles, William F.S. 2008. The Rabbi's Well: A Case Study in Micropolitics of Foreign Aid in Muslim West Africa. *African Studies Review* 51(1): 41–57.

Mitchell, Katharyne. 2010. Ungoverned Space: Global Security and the Geopolitics of Broken Windows. *Political Geography* 29(5): 289–297.

Mohamed, Ahmed. 2009. Christopher Leggett Death: Al Qaida said it Killed American in Mauritania for Proselytizing. *Huffington Post,* 25 June.

Moreira, Emmaneul P. and Nihal Bayraktar. 2008. Foreign Aid, Growth and Poverty: A Policy Framework for Niger. *Journal of Policy Making* 30: 523–539.

Obi, Cyril. 2008. Enter the Dragon? Chinese Oil Companies and Resistance in the Niger Delta. *Review of African Political Economy* 35(117): 417–434.

Odularu, Gbadebo. 2008. Does Tourism Contribute to Economic Performance in West Africa? *Anatolia: An International Journal of Tourism and Hospitality* 19(2): 340–367.

Ousman, Abdelkérim. 2004. The Potential of Islamist Terrorism in Sub-Saharan Africa. *International Journal of Politics, Culture and Society* 18(1): 65–105.

Pargeter, Alison. 2005. Libya: From Rogue-State to Partner. *Journal of Middle Eastern Politics* 1(2): 5–9.

Park, Thomas Kerlin. 1993. *Risk and Tenure in Arid Lands: The Political Ecology of Development in the Senegal River Basin.* Tucson, AR: University of Arizona Press.

Petrou, Michael. 2009. Al-Qaeda in North Africa. *Maclean's* 122(17): 26–28.

Pierre, Andrew J. and William B. Quandt. 1995. Algeria's War on Itself. *Foreign Policy* 99 : 131–148.

Rainero, Romain. 1980. La Capture, l'Exécution d'Omar el-Mukhtar et la Fin de la Guérilla Libyenne. *Cahiers de Tunisie* 28 (111/112) : 59–73.

Raynaud, Jean. 1948. Rapport d'Enquête Administrative Relative à Certain Trafic de Bovidés/Trafic des Tissus. Documentation Française, *Notes et Documents* 2188.

Raynaut, Claude, Emmanuel Grégoire, Pierre Janin, Jean Koechlin, and Philippe Lavigne Delville. 1997. *Societies and Nature in the Sahel.* London: Routledge.

Retaillé, Denis. 1993. Afrique: Le Besoin de Parler Autrement qu'en Surface. *Espaces Temps* : 51–62.

———— 1998. L'Espace Nomade. *Revue de Géographie de Lyon,* 73(1) : 71–82.

Roberts, Hugh. 2003. *North African Islamism in the Blinding Light of 9–11.* Crisis States Programme. London: Development Studies Institute.

Sahara Focus. 2009a. Western Security Compromised in Saharan Hostage Taking. *Sahara Focus.* 5(2). Available from: http://www.menasborders.com/newsroom/Western%20Security%20com/promised%20by%20Algeria%20and%20AQIM%20in%20Saharan%20hostage%20taking.pdf [Accessed 13 November 2011].

———— 2009b. Frenchman Taken Hostage. *Sahara Focus.* 5(4). Available from: http://www.menas.co.uk/pubsamples/SF0904.pdf [Accessed 13 November 2011].

Samoff, Joel. 2004. From Funding Projects to Supporting Sectors? Observation on the Aid Relationship in Burkina Faso. *International Journal of Educational Development* 24(4): 397–427.

Sheehan, Michael. 2005. *International Security: An Analytical Survey.* Boulder, CO: Lynne Rienner Publishers.

Simon, Henri. 1919. Le Ministère des Colonies, Adressée à Monsieur le Gouverneur Général de l'Afrique Occidentale Française. Paris, no. 42. Documentation Française, *Notes et Documents* 0518 (20), 28 Février.

Solé-Arqués, Ricardo. 2009. Chad: Internal Power Struggles and Regional Humanitarian Crisis. In *Humanitarian Response Index, 2008.* New York: Palgrave.

Sørbø, Gunnar M. 2010. Local Violence and International Intervention in the Sudan. *Review of African Political Economy* 37(124): 173–186.

Sørbø, Gunnar M. et al. 1998. *Norwegian Assistance to Countries in Conflict.* Evaluation Report 11.98.

Oslo: Royal Ministry of Foreign Affairs.

Thompson, Todd M., 2009. Covert Operations, British Views of Islam and Anglo-Sanusi Relations in North Africa, 1940–45. *The Journal of Imperial and Commonwealth History* 37(2): 293–323.

Thorne, John. 2009. Kidnapping Westerners is a Lucrative Business in the Sahel. *The National*. 20 December. Available from: http://www.thenational.ae/news/worldwide/africa/kidnapping-westerners-is-a-lucrative-business-in-the-sahel?pageCount=2.

Thurston, Alex. 2010. Counterterrorism and Democracy Promotion in the Sahel Under Presidents George W. Bush and Barack Obama from September 11, 2001, the Nigerien coup of February 2010. *Concerned African Scholars* 85: 50–62.

Toronto Star. 2010. Al Qaeda Kidnapping Hikes Fear Factor. *Toronto Star*. 24 September. Available from: http://www.pressdisplay.com/pressdisplay/viewer.aspx.

Triaud, Jean-Louis. 1993. Un Mauvais Départ: 1920, l'Aïr en Ruines. In *Nomades et Commandants: Administration et Sociétés Nomades dans l'Ancienne AOF*, eds. Edmond Bernus, Pierre Boilley, Jean Clauzel, and Jean-Louis Triaud. Paris: Karthala.

Triaud, Jean-Louis. 1996. Les 'Trous de Mémoire' dans l'Histoire Africaine le Sanusiyya au Tchad: Le Cas du Ouaddaï. *Revue Française d'Histoire d'Outre-Mer* 83(2) : 5–23.

Walther, Olivier. 2009. A Mobile Idea of Space. Traders, Patrons and the Cross-Border Economy in Sahelian Africa. *Journal of Borderland Studies* 24(1): 34–46.

Walther, Olivier and Denis Retaillé. 2010. *Sahara or Sahel? The Fuzzy Geography of Terrorism in West Africa*. CEPS/INSTEAD Working Paper No. 2010–35. Luxembourg: CEPS/INSTEAD.

Wermus, Daniel. 1995. Re-Colonisation or Partnership? *Entwicklung Développement* 45: 20–22.

Zeltner, Jean-Claude. 1989. Tripolitaine et Pays Toubou au XIXe siècle. *Islam et les Sociétés au Sud du Sahara* 3: 90–105.

Zoubir, Yahia H. and Karima Benabdallah-Gambier. 2005. The United States and the North African Imbroglio: Balancing Interests in Algeria, Morocco, and the Western Sahara. *Mediterranean Politics* 10(2): 181–202.

Section Three:
Cultures of Conflict & Insecurity

11

The Political Economy of Sacrifice: *Kinois* & the State

THEODORE TREFON (2002)

Since the early 1980s, 'collapse', 'oppression', 'illusion', 'bankruptcy', 'corruption' and 'criminalisation' have become unavoidable terms when referring to the Zaire of Mobutu and, subsequently, the Congo of Kabila *père* and *fils* (Turner 1981; Callaghy 1984; Young 1984; Young and Turner 1985; Braeckman 1992; Leslie 1993; Weiss 1995; Bustin 1999a; McNulty 1999; Lemarchand 2001). These works focus on the 'failure' of sub-Saharan Africa's largest state, attributing it to deep-rooted historical processes, Cold War politics, aggressive industrial capitalism and personality cult. This state crisis terminology is representative of a continent-wide examination of the (in)appropriateness, and future survivability, of the Weberian nation-state model for the African post-colony.[1]

In contrast to what has become a tradition of condemning the inability – or unwillingness – of the Congo/Zaire authorities to 'manage the country' according to Western perceptions of how states should function, this article argues that state-society relations in Kinshasa are not always as poorly organised as outside observers tend to believe; there is order in the disorder. Function and dysfunction overlap. This applies to all social and political levels, ranging from neighbourhood, professional or ethnic associations and networks to the level where political decisions are made. The *Kinois* (which is what the residents of Kinshasa call themselves) have entered into a new phase of post-colonialism. Selectively rejecting the legacy of Belgian colonialism, they combine global approaches to local problems while blending 'traditional' belief systems and behaviours with their own unique forms of 'modernity'. They are not a generation behind their counterparts in cities in neighbouring countries. In many respects they are a generation ahead, especially when it comes to adapting to adversity by developing strategies to deal with daily survival issues.[2] Paradoxically, 32 years of dictatorship and crisis – and subsequently an unfinished transition period largely dominated by war, pillage and rebellion – have helped them invent new political, economic, cultural and social realities.

The *Kinois* have proven themselves remarkably clever at mobilisation for economic survival thanks to trade, community, religious and kinship networks.

---

[1] There are also a number of important works on this subject: Widner 1995, Zartman 1995, Allen 1999, Chabal and Daloz, 1999, Dunn, 2001.

[2] Some of the terms used to describe these strategies are 'adaptative ' (Tshilemalema 1986) 'survival' (Nzongola 1986) 'coping' (Newbury 1986) and 'resilience' (De Boeck 1996).

They have even succeeded in exporting their well-structured 'informal' activities beyond their borders to elsewhere in Africa and Europe (MacGaffey and Bazenguissa-Ganga 1999; 2000). Moreover, despite monumental political and economic constraints, they keep up the struggle to improve their quality of life. Authorities have also learned to adapt. This is witnessed in the way that they have accommodated themselves to the priorities of the international community. Donors and non-governmental organisations are increasingly 'acting on behalf of the state' in many areas of public life. To do so, however, they need to rely on qualified Congolese working in state institutions. This counters the argument that the Congo state does not exist – a point developed below.

In marked opposition to their inventiveness for physical, social and cultural survival, the *Kinois* have proven themselves abysmally inapt with respect to transforming political discourse and political desires into political mobilisation. While economic survival was tolerated under the Mobutu dictatorship, political mobilisation was not. Moreover, mobilisation aimed at inducing political change is perceived as a long-term commitment transcending the demands of daily combat. It would require ever more sacrifice, but provides no guarantees of success. This attitude helps explain the failure of the Inter-Congolese Dialogue and implementation of the Lusaka Accords.[3]

Kinshasa, to paraphrase Thomas Turner, seems to be 'permanently on the verge of insurrection' (Turner 1981). Insurrection, however, has not yet fully taken place. The people of Kinshasa have, nonetheless, taken to the streets on numerous occasions during the years of Mobutu's version of 'democratic transition' and subsequently during the presidency of Laurent Désiré Kabila. Notable examples include the lootings of 1991 and 1993 (Devisch 1995a), the Christian March of 1992, days of generalised strikes known as *journées de villes mortes*, the welcome of the *Alliance des Forces Démocratiques de Libération* in May 1997 and the subsequent 'rebel' and Tutsi hunt during the invasion of August and September 1998 (Yoka 1999:119–125). Although some of these demonstrations were indeed violent, the relative non-violent behaviour of the *Kinois* in these situations is paradoxical. It can perhaps be explained by the fact that the Congolese have the bloodbaths of the post-independence rebellions and the two Shaba wars in their collective memory and are not ready to risk that degree of bloodletting again (de Villers and Omasombo 2004).

Research space

Most political scientists study the post-colonial state by looking at large geographical spaces or political entities ranging from the African continent as a whole, to geographical regions (such as West Africa or Southern Africa), and sometimes linguistic spaces (such as French-speaking or Lusophone Africa) or sometimes individual countries. Attempting to understand political dynamics and social evolution by looking at a specific urban population, although a valuable analytical tool, is an uncommon approach in political science. Urban anthropologists, notably with respect to 'the modern Western city', have made some progress in doing so, although Ulf Hannerz's (1980:79) plea more than twenty years ago 'to seek further illumination in the political economy of

---

[3]   For background on the Inter-Congolese Dialogue see the International Crisis Group's report at http://www.intl-crisis-group.org/projects/ showreport.cfm? reportid=488

urbanism' has not been sufficiently heeded. In the case of Kinshasa, studying urban dynamics is important for three main reasons.

First, even though Mobutu was fond of repeating that *'Kinshasa n'est pas le Zaïre'*, the evolution of the city is intimately linked to the political economy of the country as a whole. Revenues generated by the copper mines of Shaba or the diamond fields of Kasai were controlled by a Kinshasa-based political elite. The capital's predominance in terms of infrastructure, administration, employment, investment, services and image is overwhelming (de Maximy 1984; Pain 1979; Gondola 1997). Mobutu made some attempts to transfer the seat of power from Kinshasa to Gbadolite, his native 'mini-Versailles-in-the-jungle', but was unsuccessful. The political will of the dictator was unable to match the uncontrollable dynamics of the megapole's expansion.

Second, like Jeffery Herbst (2000), we can consider that the degree of political control in Africa decreases in relation to the distance from the capital city. Herbst attributes this to low population densities (in the pre-colonial period), enabling people to migrate in order to avoid political oppression. Bierschenk and Olivier de Sardan (1997) explain in a study of rural Central African Republic that 'the state stops 12 kilometres from the capital'. Land tenure practices in the Kinshasa hinterland support this hypothesis because traditional authority – *le droit coutumier* – is just as important to local populations as modern law with respect to access, usufruct and ownership of real estate *(cadastre)*. In the Zaire of Mobutu, huge parts of the country were beyond the effective reach of any form of state authority – a situation which has been exacerbated today due to war and rebellion. This reality is encapsulated in the title of Roland Pourtier's (1997) article *'Du Zaïre au Congo: un territoire en quête d'Etat'* ('From Zaire to Congo: a territory in search of a state'). The state – and of course foreign occupying forces – manifest themselves primarily in areas where rent-generating activities are possible.

A third factor is simply a demographic one. An estimated one out of ten Congolese live in Kinshasa. With its approximately 6 million inhabitants (DDK 1998), it is the second largest city in sub-Saharan Africa (after Lagos). It is also the second largest French-speaking' city in the world (even though only a small percentage of *Kinois* speak French correctly). It is more populous than 25 out of 56 African countries – a contrast admittedly exaggerated by the very small African island countries (United Nations 2001).[4]

The 'creation' of Kinshasa goes back to the early 1880s. During the Leopoldian period, Leopoldville was a cluster of small villages. In the colonial period, the European city, surrounded by black townships, was organised to serve the needs of the Belgian 'civilising mission'. The spatial segregation of black and white districts was as strictly controlled as was migration from village to town. The early post-colonial period was characterised by very rapid demographic growth – peaking at 9.4% in 1970 (Bruneau 1995:105). The growth rate has subsequently halved to approximately 4% (UN 1997:159). Like most other African cities, Kinshasa's current morphology derives from colonial planning. There is the former *ville blanche*[5] which is the commercial and administrative district (where

---

[4]   Like all statistics from Congo, demographic figures need to be considered with considerable reserve. The last population census was carried out in 1984, so figures are based on extrapolations that do not necessarily take into account major demographic influences like AIDS, war casualties or migration of people fleeing war and crisis in the Kivus.

[5]   Gombe, Limete, Ngaliema and Binza.

white expatriates still reside – and as a kind of historical revenge, many expatriates working in the diplomatic corps or NGO community are obliged to live there for perceived security reasons); there are the planned townships or *cités planifiés*[6] (these are settlements which were occupied in the immediate post-independence 'first-come first-served' frenzy for land); and third, the 'anarchic extensions' in the southern[7] and eastern zones of the periphery which are interesting examples of urbanisation without urban planning.

Oppression, crisis and sacrifice

The crisis that hit Kinshasa and the *Kinois* in the early 1980s, transforming what was once *kin la belle* into *kin la poubelle* (Kinshasa the beautiful, Kinshasa the dump) cannot be dissociated from deep-rooted historical processes. A key component of such processes was patrimonialism. The Congo Free State mapped out in Berlin in 1885 was King Leopold's personal property. The Belgian monarch exploited it ruthlessly and with impunity (Willame 1972; Emerson 1979; Hochschild 1998).

A second factor was Belgian paternalism. The Belgian colonial system was based on the triumvirate of church, administration and large corporations and justified itself in terms of its 'civilising mission'. It concentrated on the relative material well-being of the population and basic primary education. The obvious limits of this mission were the complete absence of political responsibilities. No elite leadership had been trained. All important decisions emanated from Brussels. Even the European settler community in Congo enjoyed no political rights. Paternalism did not start breaking down until the early 1950s. A. A. J. van Bilsen's 1956 30-year plan for 'emancipation' was considered by the Belgian colonial authorities as being completely unrealistic (Slade 1960; Young 1965). Amongst the first Belgian intellectuals to openly speak about 'emancipation', van Bilsen was viewed in Belgium and by Europeans in the Congo as a revolutionary dreamer.

Third, the abysmal lack of political preparation led to one of the African continent's most brutal post-colonial transitions. The major political events were the mutiny of the *Force Publique* only a few days after independence; secessionist attempts, notably in Katanga, but in Southern Kasai as well; the failed UN intervention; the Kasavubu-Lumumba rivalry and the subsequent assassination of Lumumba (De Witte 2001); the West's desire to maintain control over the Congo's mineral wealth (Bezy et al. 1981:83–111) and to contain perceived Soviet expansion (Legum 1961; Vanderlinden 1985). These factors led to the *coup d'état* of 25 November 1965 that was to mark the beginning of a 32-year-long dictatorship (Chomé 1974).

A fourth factor can be summarised as the Mobutist predatory state. The Congo-Zaire post-colony abdicated from its role as provider of basic social and administrative services, rapidly transforming itself into a social predator (Schatzberg 1991). Mobutu, like King Leopold, exploited the Congo and its resources as if they were his personal property. Because of Cold War politics and Western capitalist interests, Zaire received nearly unconditional support – particularly from

---

[6] Barumbu, Kinshasa, Kintambo, Linwala, Kasa-Vubu, Ngiri-Ngiri, Bandalungwa, Kalamu, Lemba, Matete and Ndjili:

[7] Ngaliema, Selembao, Mont Ngafula, Kisenso.

Washington, Brussels and Paris. Until the fall of the Berlin wall, the West backed a regime characterised by violence, nepotism, personality cult of the 'supreme leader' and a host of other human rights abuses (Braeckman 1992; Wrong 2001). Liberation movements in Angola and Mozambique were manipulated by Mobutu who also played upon the 'me or chaos' syndrome (Stockwell 1978; Bustin 1999b). While the utility of Zaire-as-buffer zone was somewhat of a myth, the mineral wealth of Shaba/Katanga was, and remains, very real, despite the near collapse of GECAMINES. The West was also very interested in recycling its petro-dollars. This led to the financing of a number of mega projects such as the Inga Dam and the Inga-Shaba high-tension line (Willame 1986). To attract Western investments and to diversify his international support, Mobutu played one backer against the other. The Congolese people are still suffering to meet debt repayment schedules elaborated in the form of structural adjustment programmes related to these mega projects.

These processes, combined with the shrinking of state resources due to mismanagement and corruption, are the root causes of sacrifice in Kinshasa today. When anthropologists refer to 'sacrifice', they usually do so in the context of ritual and religion, emphasising the word's literal meaning: 'to make sacred' (De Heusch 1985: 1–17). The use of the term in this article is much more prosaic: it pertains to the hard Kinshasa reality of 'doing without'. People do without food; they do without fuelwood; they do without primary health services; they do without safe drinking water. They also do without political participation, security, leisure or the ability to organise their time as they would like. Parents are not only forced to decide which child will be able to go to school in a given year, they also have to decide who shall eat one day and who shall eat the next. In Lingala,[8] the noun used to express sacrifice – *tokokufa* – literally means 'we are dying'.

When we look at public health statistics, Kinshasa should be a vast dying ground. Those that have not died of AIDS, should be dead from starvation. Those that have not died of hunger should be dead from either water-borne diseases, or simply exhaustion, because, due to transportation problems, people are forced to walk very long distances. These are the daily sacrifices that the *Kinois* are forced to make. The vast majority of households in Kinshasa (comprising approximately seven individuals) dispose of less than $50 per month – just about enough to cover the food bill. Many families have less. Ritual sacrifice encounters the sacrifice of poverty when parents accuse their children of being witches in order to change the course of their 'bad luck' (De Boeck 2004).

The Kinshasa 'bargain'

The popular political philosophy of the *Kinois* is largely dictated by addressing immediate and basic needs. In order to do so, they have invented *la coop*, a diminutive of the French word 'coopération'. When a *Kinois* says *na kei kobeta coop*, it means 'I'm going to strike a deal', or 'I'm going to work'. *Na kei kobeta coop* is on the lips of millions of *Kinois* every morning, even though it has been many years since the idea of work has meant a secure, salaried job in the formal

---

8   Lingala is one of the four vehicular languages spoken in Congo. Lingala slang is the most commonly used language in Kinshasa.

economy. For the vast majority of the *Kinois*, 'work' is any small job, activity or opportunity that provides enough francs to buy food or pay for a collective taxi fare. Work entails 'breaking stones', *kobeta libanga:* the notorious forced labour imposed on the people of what was then the Congo Free State during the late Leopoldian period to build the Kinshasa-Matadi rail line. Today, *kobeta libanga* means being fearless, daring to take any risk, doing the physically impossible and the morally unimaginable. It implies trickery, 'wheeling and dealing', acting as a go-between or bargaining. In English the word 'bargain' best captures the practice and spirit of *la coop.*[9]

The Kinshasa bargain is an agreement between two or more parties that provides a return. It can be solicited by a 'beneficiary' or imposed on a 'victim'. Anyone who is in need of either a good or service, or who needs to resolve a problem is invariably the 'client' of a go-between. This applies to dealing with a civil servant in order to obtain an administrative document, buying a bag of cooking charcoal or manioc or 'simply' hailing a taxi. Given the overwhelming precariousness of life in Kinshasa, people have been forced to depend on, i.e. 'bargain' with, others. All the *Kinois* are subject to this system that takes place in all sectors of daily life cutting across the entire social spectrum. Those that try to evade this form of solidarity are quickly brought to order, usually by trickery but sometimes by force. Like in formal economies where 'tax evasion' is sanctioned, evasion of paying a 'solidarity tax' is also sanctioned. This is a kind of urban variant of the 'levelling process' that regulates relations between individuals and their clans in traditional acephalous societies.

'Bargaining' Kinshasa-style entails disregarding moral values such as honesty, respect or altruism. The emerging (a)morality in Kinshasa dictates that it is better to 'sell your soul to the devil' than to be scrupulous. Cunning is required to meet immediate needs. Durkheim's theory of anomy appropriately describes this situation (Durkheim 1991). Anomy is a situation whereby moral, cultural and legal norms are abandoned or transformed, creating a social crisis. An imbalance exists between the desire to attain social values such as success, prestige, or power, and the objective means available to people to attain these values. This generates the sentiment that socially unacceptable behaviours such as fraud, violence or corruption are necessary to meet vital needs. As a response to the anomy that characterises the Congo on the state level, new forms of social organisation such as the Kinshasa 'bargain' emerge on the level of relations between individuals.

The process of acculturation brought on by colonialism and contact with Western values, particularly in urban areas, is one way of accounting for the disappearance of 'traditional' forms of solidarity. Economic crisis and poverty are other determinants contributing to this attitudinal and behavioural shift. Another explanation relates to the mid-1970s Mobutist doctrine of 'return to authenticity'. This MPR *(Mouvement Populaire de la Revolution)* creation had the effect of undermining individual initiative because the MPR claimed to be responsible for all Zairians 'from cradle to grave'. This was a bizarre and perverse adaptation of the paternalistic policies practised during the colonial period. Some of Mobutu's aphorisms proclaimed at popular rallies during the apogee of his power reveal how the 'supreme leader' perceived civic morality. This perception is epitomised by his famous declaration *yiba, kasi mingi te* (steal, but don't steal too much). Another landmark political speech, one that foreshadowed

---

[9]   Parts of this section are based on Nzeza (2004).

massive nationalisation of large and small foreign-owned companies, officially launched the 'fend for yourselves' fashion *(débrouillez-vous)* that has never lost its currency in Kinshasa.

This political context helps explain the relative (but not exclusive) dishonesty of *la débrouille* phenomenon that has already been written on extensively by mainly Western political scientists: Jackson (2001; 2002), economists – Marysse and De Herdt (1996), De Herdt and Marysse (1999) and anthropologists such as De Boeck (1996) and MacGaffey (1986). It is not uncommon to hear a thief caught 'red-handed' say: 'if I don't steal, what am I going to eat?'. The need to procure food for oneself or the family is frequently the explanation given to account for the multiple forms of *la débrouille*. The means – corruption, theft, extortion, collusion, embezzlement, fraud, counterfeiting and prostitution – justify the ends: survival!

The collective social values and practices characteristic of rural life in Congo have given way to the demands and contradictions of a market economy in which the individual is central. Attitudes and behaviours have evolved due to the degree of crisis and specifically the difficulties in finding cash-earning employment. Always looking for new ways to cope, poverty is psychologically transformed into 'despair solidarity'. While the *Kinois* are able and willing to extend psychological support, financial and material constraints limit this solidarity to a pragmatic system of exchange. People help each other primarily if they can expect something in return. Debt, whether it be in the form of a loan, a service rendered or a favour, is expected to be redeemed at some point.

The nearly universal recourse to faith in the face of the despair and suffering caused by poverty is prevalent in Kinshasa. One of Kinshasa's most famous Christian singers, Eva Mbikayi, sings in a popular song: *naboyi souffrance* (I deny suffering). Suffering takes the form of hunger, poor health, and physical debilitation, just as it takes the form of psychological stress resulting from the complexities of survival 'here and now' and uncertainty about the future. The psychological constructions elaborated to 'deny' this suffering are indicative of the remarkable capacity of the *Kinois* to not 'give up the fight' for survival. Whether or not the *Kinois* deny or accept suffering is difficult to ascertain. The relevant point is that they act to reduce these forms of suffering. These psychological constructions and actions even help to achieve well-being, which is an often overlooked or underestimated dimension of contemporary social dynamics in Kinshasa. Adherence to the ever-increasing number of revelation churches presided over by all sorts of pastors, preachers, and prophets is one dimension of this quest for well-being. The Jesus of the Belgian missionaries was replaced by the doctrine of Mobutism. When Mobutism failed, hope in Jesus took on new meaning. The fact that churches may be filled on Sunday morning does not, however, mean that the *Kinois* believe that God alone can help them mitigate their survival problems. Religious soul-searching must not be confused with material problem-solving: hence the perpetual need to 'bargain'. The overlapping of religious sentiment and pragmatic survival preoccupations is captured by Eva Mbikayi who sings in characteristically Kinshasa style: *Eloko na sengi yo longola mosika na ngai pauvrete. Ngai na lingi lisusu mobola te ngo Jesus, ngo papa, bateya ngai prosperity. Nkolo sunga mpo nazua awa na seya mozinga* (help me chase poverty away. I don't want to be poor any more, Jesus, my father. You told me about prosperity. Let me have it here and now!).

Invention in the vital service sectors

The implications of dictatorship and the stalemate of the two Kabila regimes have resulted in a severe crisis in the vital sectors which most urban populations tend to take for granted. Paradoxically, however, the relative (but not total) abdication of the state from these sectors has resulted in a process of 'indigenisation'. This refers to the ways in which the *Kinois* have entered into a 'post' post-colonial phase by using their own – opposed to imported – resources, networks and ideas to adapt to adversity. The process has contributed to the 'unwhitening' of the post-colonial political economy and social system. Public health is increasingly co-managed by the World Health Organisation – along with competent Congolese staff. At the same time, however, there is a marked shift away from Western-style health care toward a syncretic form of healing based on faith systems and traditional pharmacopea. The education system which was basically free until the 1980s is now 'privatiscd'. Parents struggle to pay for school fees even though the image of the university diploma is increasingly tarnished. Few parents can afford to send all their children to school at the same time. Most families are forced to sacrifice the education of some of their children, other families alternate years. This explains why many finish secondary school when they are already in their late 20s. Few, however, do finish school: in the past few years, approximately 120,000 high school diplomas were granted per year.[10] In a country of approximately 55 million people, half of whom are under the age of 15, the number is shockingly low. The two examples developed below – food security and water procurement – are intended to demonstrate the mechanisms of invention in the face of political and economic constraints.

Food Security and the 'Rurbanisation' Process
Power, prestige and status in Kinshasa increasingly derive from the ability to eat or the ability to distribute food, or money for food, to others. Up until the 1980s, approximately 15% of the national budget was devoted to the agricultural sector. Today that figure is less than 2%, an insignificant sum when compared to the total official state budget.[11] Hunger and malnutrition has become a very serious problem. Approximately 50% of the *Kinois* eat only one meal per day. 25% eat only one meal every two days (Ministère de la Santé Publique, 1999:47). Food expenditures represent between 50% and 70% of household budgets (Marysse and De Herdt 1996). Belgian families, for reasons of comparison, devote 16% of their budgets to food. Although it is difficult to establish whether or not Mobutu deliberately kept his people hungry as a political tool, the situation convincingly reflects Sylvie Brunei's analysis of hunger and politics: 'The people who control food supplies are the people with the power. Keeping certain segments of the population in a chronic state of hunger is a way of manipulating them because the effort devoted to daily survival hampers their capacity to organise themselves and fight for political change' (Brunei 2002:72, author's translation).

[10] Figures provided by the Rectorat, University of Kinshasa.
[11] The national budget this year is $330 million, which is less than half of that of the city of Douala (Cameroun)! In 1996 it was $300 million (Délégation, 1998: 9).

Despite the war which has cut the city off from its former supply areas in the provinces of Equateur and Orientale and despite the decay of the road infrastructure, a famine situation has never developed. Food security is not much worse today than in 1997 because important supply changes and innovations have taken place.[12] Most importantly Bandundu has replaced other food supply sources and now provides between 80 and 90% of agricultural produce for Kinshasa. River transport along the Kwilu has replaced road transport because of the poor quality of the roads and the inadequate number of lorries and pick-up trucks. It is now estimated that at least 150–200 locally made wooden boats ply the Congo river from Kinshasa to Bandundu and Kasai. River transport of food owes its expansion to commissioning agents *(des agents commissionaires)* who bulk goods to be sent to a particular destination; group travellers together and arrange for their transportation; and facilitate communications because they have cell phones. This is very useful in sending and receiving money in lieu of the banking sector. The work of these agents is based on trust, ethnicity and social capital. It can be viewed as a people-based response to a failing state and formal private sector involvement.

Other innovations include what can be termed 'rurbanisation'. This is the phenomenon of practising rural subsistence activities in an urban-style landscape (Trefon 2000a; 2000b). The explosion of urban and peri-urban agriculture is a notable example. Any casual observer can see that manioc is planted all over the city. Although this is a significant contribution to household food supplies, people complain that eating *pondu*-manioc leaves – without the salt or oil they have to buy – is not very appetising. Similarly, animal husbandry has also expanded considerably. Aside from the goats which can be seen grazing along the Boulevard du 30 Juin (the Champs Elysées of Kinshasa), the increasing number of shops in Kinshasa which sell animal feed is a reliable indicator of small-scale breeding for family consumption and sale. Above, reference was made to the dense movement of people from the *cités* towards the former *ville blanche* every morning. But there is also a massive movement of people from these *cités* towards the outskirts of Ndjile, Masina or Kimwenza. A common sight in the morning is the outward movement of men and women with hoes and machetes – in the evening they return with agricultural produce and fuelwood. It is significant that men participate in activities that were until only recently strictly gendered and carried out by women.

The 'rurbanisation' of Kinshasa can also be viewed in terms of a linguistic paradox. In Lingala, the word 'city' does not exist. The word *mboka* signifies village and *mboka ya mundele* which translates as the 'white man's village' is used to refer to the city. The popular language still opposes what was formerly the European city with the African *cité*. People still say, 'I'm going to town' when they go to the centre of Kinshasa (to work, take care of administrative or banking problems or to shop) and 'I'm going to the *cité*' when returning home.

Another form of innovation in the food security sector is the way the Congolese authorities negotiate with – and manipulate – the international donor community into acting on their behalf. This is a strong counter-argument to those who claim that the Congo state does not exist. In practice, the efforts of bilateral and multilateral donors and the thriving NGO sector, depend considerably on people working in state administrations. Authorities do not have funds

---

[12] For a detailed study on innovation in the food security sector in Kinshasa see Tollens (2004).

to carry out projects. They are, however, involved in their implementation. Political appointees obviously changed after 1997 but a surprising number of technical and administrative staff have held onto their positions. Bureaucracies are surprisingly stable despite the fact that salaries are often unpaid or paid only after long waits.

Last but not least, important changes in cropping patterns have taken place over the last decade, notably in Bandundu and Bas-Congo. There is a notable increase in the production of cowpeas which have become an important source of vegetable protein. There is also more and more millet found in the dry savannahs of southern Bandundu. In the inland valleys of Bas-Congo, such as around Mawunzi, and in the Kwilu region of Bandundu, rice production has increased. There has also been a sizeable increase in the production of maize in Bandundu, which is shipped to Kinshasa and to Kasai provinces. The maize produced now in Bandundu makes up for the loss of maize supplies from Equator province.

Water

The water sector in Kinshasa, like food procurement, is characterised by sacrifice and innovation. Approximately one-third, or approximately 2 million *Kinois*, do not have access to the public distribution network. Throughout the city, 25% of families have to walk more than one kilometre per day to fetch water (Ministère de la Santé Publique 1999: 55). In the district of Kisenso for example (which can be considered as either a newly urbanised district or a semi-rural one), people have to walk two and a half hours per day for water (Oxfam/Great Britain 2001:31). They have drastically reduced their consumption of water because of its cost in terms of money, time and fatigue. Tap water, when available, is reserved for drinking, washing food and then for cooking. Rain, river or well water is used for personal hygiene, laundry and washing the house. Water is always recycled: it is never wasted.

To compensate for the water board's[13] limited service, the *Kinois* have adapted various types of supply strategies. People dig wells and collect rainwater in whatever kinds of containers are available – even using discarded plastic motor oil bottles as canteens. They also go to rivers where water is free, or to the *parcelle*[14] of a family member. Another option is buying water from individuals who are connected to the distribution network. Getting the water home is the next ordeal. Depending on the volume of water and the distance home, different techniques are adopted. It can be carried in pails on the head (by women, girls and boys), rolled in wheelbarrows (by older boys), put in barrels and rolled along the ground (by men), or transported by car or taxi (by men or women).

Early in the morning, women and children gather their pails and start queuing at springs or public taps for what they call 'water duty' *(likelemba ya mayi)*. Families sometimes rotate this water duty: one morning one mother will be responsible for the chore, the next day it will be someone else's job. In contrast to this pragmatic solidarity, long waits can also seriously strain relations: high population densities in the poorer neighbourhoods create huge crowds at places where water can be found. People argue and fight over whose turn it is next.

The quality of water from all of these sources is poor and it is consequently recommended to boil it for 30 minutes in order to eliminate bacteria. Boiling

---

[13] Regideso *(Régi des Eaux)* is the Congolese water board.
[14] A *parcelle* is a house lot. In Kinshasa, however, it is not uncommon to have many households sharing space and resources on a single lot.

water, however, raises another serious dilemma because practically all families in Kinshasa use charcoal as the primary source of cooking fuel. But access to charcoal is just as difficult as it is to water. Women thus have to make difficult strategic choices of how to use their limited sources of charcoal and consequently prefer using it to cook food as opposed to boiling water. Despite the prevalence of water-borne intestinal diseases, boiling water is not perceived as being a priority. Bacterial contamination also develops when water is stored in containers that are not regularly cleaned. While basic hygiene dictates that these containers be sterilised, few households do so. People do not want to use their precious water to wash a container. The same attitude applies to carbon filters. These filters should be scrubbed and washed regularly and the carbon element needs to be replaced periodically. If not, serious diseases such as typhoid fever, cholera, hepatitis A, or diarrhoea can result. In this context, it is not surprising that 30% of all registered medical visits in Kinshasa in 2000 were water-related (Oxfam/Great Britain 2001:31). Despite public health efforts carried out mainly by international humanitarian groups, people remain largely unaware of the relationship between unsuitable drinking water and disease.

The state's management of this theoretically public service is indisputably insufficient. Yet, the state performs the double role of, one, providing some service and, two, collaboration with the international community in the latter's involvement in infrastructure maintenance, development and investment. Unable to deal directly with water processing and distribution, authorities, as mentioned above concerning food security, have negotiated with the international community to act on their behalf. The Congo state has delegated a part of its responsibilities to international, bilateral and non-governmental organisations that have both the financial means and the technical savoir-faire to bolster the deficient water board.

The most important international actors are the International Committee of the Red Cross, the European Union, OXFAM/Great Britain, and OXFAM/Quebec. Congolese ministry authorities dealing with inter-sectoral problems of energy, planning, reconstruction, public health, public works, urbanisation and habitat all collaborate with these international agencies. As outside assistance tends to be based on short- to mid-term agendas (influenced by political decisions and availability of funding), the international community remains dependent to a large extent on Congolese ministerial authorities and water board staff. Despite their precarious economic position, these people are elements of relative stability in their sector. Thus, while the state may well be weak or corrupt, circumventing it is not an efficacious option for donors or NGOs. The case is clear for the water sector but the same argument can be made for other development sectors as well.[15]

Being *Kinois*

Despite all the city's problems, *Kinois* still consider their city to be the capital of pleasure-seeking potential: *ambiance*. This potential helps people evolve in a world beyond that of despair and sacrifice. The sentiment of *ambiance* has completely erased the colonial perception equating Leopoldville with a 'city of temptation' *(un lieu de perdition)*. When the capital was still called Leopoldville,

[15] For more information on the crisis and innovation in the water sector, see Maractho and Trefon (2004).

residents did not have a meaningful name for themselves. The term *Leopoldvillois* did not have much currency and never commanded much respect. *Evolué*, the term bestowed upon 'civilised' blacks until independence was a coveted social promotion – but one reserved for a small minority.[16] *Evolués* were also cynically called *mindele-ndombe* which also translates from Lingala as 'white blacks'. *Lipopois* ('Lipopo' was the Congolese transformation of Leopoldville) was a name that had some resonance in the *independence cha-cha* euphoria, but, again, was never adopted to a significant degree. Most people, at least up until 1971 when Mobutu 'zairianised' city names, put their ethnic or regional affiliation first. *Citoyen* was another label bestowed on members of the new Mobutu version of the nation-state, also with a limited (and short-lived) degree of self- or collective respect.

Being *Kinois*, however, is another matter entirely. Referring to oneself as a *Kinois* is a sign of prestige. In contrast to a generation ago, today people clearly put forward their belonging to the human tribe known as *Kinois*. They are, however, simultaneously or alternatively, Kongo,[17] Pende, Yaka or Ngbandi when, for reasons of social, political or economic opportunism, it is convenient for them to shift from one identity to another. Kinshasa is an 'ethnic mosaic'. All of the country's approximately 300 ethnic groups are represented in the capital.

The overlapping and multiplication of identities has helped *Kinois* counteract the negative effects of political oppression and economic constraints because it broadens their solidarity networks. Under Mobutu, knowing Lingala and belonging to the Ngbandi ethnic group facilitated access to sinecure public service jobs and political power through the MPR. When Laurent Kabila assumed power the Lingala-speaking Ngbandi were replaced with Swahili speakers from Shaba – Kabila's region of origin. The use of Swahili on the national currency is representative of this shift. This overlapping is a very important dimension of 'being *Kinois*' and extends beyond ethnicity to all kinds of other networks, for example neighbourhood, professional or religious ones.

The construction of *Kinois* identity is based in large part on the cleavage between those who are *Kinois* and those who are not. *Mbokatiers* is a derogatory term used for people living in rural Congo – the 'country bumpkins'. This negative image can be explained in part by the centralised nature of Mobutu's Second Republic (1965–1990). It is also a universal phenomenon of constructed urban identities: *monter à Paris* is how the French describe having succeeded in 'making it to Paris', in the same way that folk from New Jersey view crossing the river over to New York as upward social mobility. On the opposite end of the spectrum is *Miguel*: the nickname given to Europeans or whites in general. Today, the world of *Miguel* is associated primarily with money – and the status, education, health care or technology it can provide (For a very interesting historical account of how Congolese perceived whites, see Jewsiewicki 1993:43–62). Two other interesting denominations used by the *Kinois* to describe the 'other' are: *bamapeka* (migrants who pretend they are 'real' *Kinois*) and *bawuta* (strangers). The *Kinois* have amalgamated these two worlds, syncretising the global and the local – what De Boeck (1996:100) describes as 'transitional spaces and interconnecting strategies'.

---

[16] *Evolués* were mainly urban Africans who had received some education, spoke French and had renounced polygamy. They were to constitute the emerging middle class encouraged by Belgian policy-makers in the late colonial period.

[17] Approximately 40% of people living in Kinshasa are members of the Kongo ethnic group.

Another identity cleavage that has taken form is that between *mwana-quartier* (neighbourhood kid) and *mwana-mboka* (son of the country). The latter epithet was used by Mobutu in the spirit of 'return to authenticity' (along with *citoyen* and *citoyenne)* and supplanted the 'unauthentic' titles of Mister and Missus. The valorisation of the neighbourhood as a vital social space, in contrast to the city at large *(mwana-kiri),* and in sharper contrast to the country as a whole, supports Devisch's hypothesis of the 'villagisation' of Kinshasa (Devisch 1995b;1996).

Kinois identity is also manifested across a broad cultural spectrum. Fashion, referred to as *la SAPE (Société des Ambianceurs et des Personnes Élégantes),* use of Lingala slang, popular painting and notably music are important forms of cultural and political expression. Music, for example, has contributed to the emergence of an urban civilisation and transethnic national conscience (Tsambu 2001). It also enhances the image of the *Kinois* well beyond their borders (White 2002). When a singer like Werrason *le roi de la forêt* fills the Bercy stadium in Paris, his success is appropriated by all Congolese.

The Congo state: what can you expect?

There are multiple levels of expectations from the Congo state. The international community, for example (represented by the World Bank, the United Nations or Belgium's 'Africanist' Foreign Affairs Minister Louis Michel), continues to invest in the post-colonial ideal of a legitimate central authority that will respect its commercial agreements and bilateral accords or establish a debt repayment schedule. The political establishment of Joseph Kabila – including of course its Angolan and Zimbabwean 'allies' – expects continued access to neo-patrimonialist forms of extraction and exploitation.

The *Kinois* themselves, however, expect very little from the state. The evolution of political discourse in the post-Mobutu transition has not improved their living conditions. The post-colonial state model that was designed to be a provider of social services has transformed into a social predator. Lack of progress in putting democratic institutions in place is considered by the people as a deliberate political strategy aimed at maintaining incumbency to the detriment of social and economic priorities. The state is perceived as having accommodated itself to the process of social cannibalisation, society being its own prey.

Under Mobutu, discontent was rarely voiced because anything closely resembling political contest was brutally silenced. In the wake of this situation, complaints and criticism are still rarely directed against political authorities by the *Kinois.* They are directed against society itself or God. A political implication of the dynamism and multiplication of solidarity networks is the 'protection' they provide to whatever group is in power, because reliance on solidarity has replaced reliance on government. While Western Africanists may have made some progress in the intellectual debate as to whether or not the post-colony has failed as a political entity, not enough attention has been given to the strategies invented by the people who live in these nation-states. As this article has attempted to demonstrate, the *Kinois* constitute an interesting case study for two primary reasons: one, they expect very little from political authorities, and two, thanks to their unique form of social organisation, they have already made significant progress in re-inventing the post-colonial nation-state model.

References

Allen, Chris. 1999. Warfare, Endemic Violence and State Collapse in Africa. *Review of African Political Economy* 26(81): 367–384.

Bezy, Fernand, Jean-Philippe Peemans and Jean-Marie Wautelet. 1981. *Accumulation et Sous-Développement au Zaïre: 1960–1980*. Louvain-la-Neuve: Presses Universitaires de Louvain (UCL).

Bierschenk, Thomas and Jean-Pierre Olivier de Sardan. 1997. Local Powers and a Distant State in Rural Central African Republic. *Journal of Modern African Studies* 35(3): 441–468.

Braeckman, Colette. 1992. *Le Dinosaure: Le Zaire de Mobutu*. Paris: Fayard.

Brunei, Sylvie. 2002. *Famines et Politiques*. Paris: Presse de Sciences Po.

Bruneau, Jean-Claude. 1995. Crise et Déclin de la Croissance des Villes au Zaïre: Une Image Actualisée. *Revue Belge de Géographie* 58(1–2): 103–114.

Bustin, Edouard. 1999a. The Collapse of 'Congo/Zaire' and its Regional Impact. In *Regionalisation in Africa: Integration and Disintegration*, ed. Daniel Bach. Oxford: James Currey.

Bustin, Edouard. 1999b. Après Moi le Déluge? The 'Transition Charade Comes Full Circle'. In *Africa Contemporary Record*, vol. XXIV, ed. Colin Legum. London: Rex Collins.

Chabal, Patrick and Jean-Pascal Daloz. 1999. *Africa Works: Disorder as Political Instrument*. Oxford: James Currey.

Callaghy, Thomas. 1984. *The State-Society Struggle: Zaire in Comparative Perspective*. New York: Columbia University Press.

Chomé, Jules. 1974. *L'Ascension de Mobutu: Du Sergent Joseph Désiré au Général Sese Seko*. Brussels: Editions Complexe.

DDK (Département de Démographie de la Faculté des Sciences Economiques de l'Université de Kinshasa). 1998. *La Question Demographique en République Démocratique du Congo*, Kinshasa: DDK/United Nations Population Fund.

De Boeck, Filip. 2004. On Being Shege in Kinshasa: Children, the Occult and the Street. In *Reinventing Order in Kinshasa: How People Respond to State Failure in Kinshasa*, ed. Theodore Trefon. London: Zed Books.

———— 1996. Postcolonialism, Power and Identity: Local and Global Perspectives from Zaire. In *Postcolonial Identities in Africa*, eds. Richard Werbner and Terence Ranger. London: Zed Books.

De Herdt, Tom and Stefaan Marysse. 1999. The Reinvention of the Market from Below: The End of the Women's Money Changing Monopoly in Kinshasa. *Review of African Political Economy* 26(80): 239–253.

De Heusch, Luc. 1985. *Sacrifice in Africa: A Structuralist Approach*. Manchester: Manchester University Press.

Delegation de la Commission Européenne en RDC. 1998. Rapport de Poste sur les Conditions de Vie en République Démocratique du Congo. Unpublished report. Kinshasa.

de Maximy, René. 1984. *Kinshasa, Ville en Suspens: Dynamique de la Croissance et Problèmes d'Urbanisme, Approache Socio-Politique*. Paris: ORSTOM.

de Villers, Gauthier and Jean Omasombo. 2004. When *Kinois* take to the Streets. In *Reinventing Order in Kinshasa: How People Respond to State Failure in Kinshasa*, ed. Theodore Trefon. London: Zed Books.

Devisch, René. 1996. 'Pillaging Jesus': Healing Churches and the Villagisation of Kinshasa. *Africa* 66(4): 555–586.

———— 1995a. Frenzy, Violence and Ethical Renewal in Kinshasa. *Public Culture* 7(3): 593–629.

———— 1995b. La 'Villagisation' de Kinshasa" *Revue Belge de Géographie* 58(1–2): 115–121.

De Witte, Ludo. 2001. *The Assassination of Lumumba*. London: Verso Books.

Dunn, Kevin. 2001. 'Madlib #32: The (Blank) African State: Rethinking the Sovereign State in International Relations Theory'. In *Africa's Challenge to International Relations Theory*, eds. Kevin Dunn and Tim Shaw. New York: Palgrave.

Durkheim, Emile. 1991,1893. *De la Division du Travail Social*. Paris: Presses Universitaires de France.

Emerson, Barbara. 1979. *Leopold II of the Belgians: King of Colonialism*. London: Weidenfeld and Nicolson.

Gondola, Charles-Didier. 1997. *Villes Miroirs. Migrations et Identités Urbaines à Kinshasa et Brazzaville 1930–1970*. Paris: L'Harmattan.

Hannerz, Ulf. 1980. *Exploring the City: Inquiries Toward an Urban Anthropology*. New York: Columbia University Press.

Herbst, Jeffrey. 2000. *States and Power in Africa: Comparative Lessons in Authority and Control*.

Princeton, NJ: Princeton University Press.

Hochschild, Adam. 1998. *King Leopold's Ghost: A Story of Greed, Terror, and Heroism in Colonial Africa.* Boston, MA and New York: Houghton Mifflin Company.

Jackson, Stephen. 2001. 'Nos Richesses sont en Train d'être Pillées!'': Economies de Guerre et Rumeurs de Crime dans les Kivus, République Démocratique du Congo. *Politique Africaine* 84: 117–135.

——— 2002. Making a Killing: Criminality and Coping in the Kivu War Economy. *Review of African Political Economy* 29(93–94):517–531.

Jewsiewicki, Bogumil. 1993. Moi, l'Autre, Nous Autres. In *Naître et Mourir au Zaïre: Un Demi-siècle d'Histoire au Quotidien*, ed. Bogumil Jewsiewicki. Paris: Karthala.

Legum, Colin. 1961. *Congo Disaster.* Baltimore, MD: Penguin Books.

Lemarchand, René. 2001. *The Democratic Republic of Congo: From Collapse to Potential Reconstruction.* Occasional Paper. Centre of African Studies, University of Copenhagen.

Leslie, Winsome. 1993. *Zaire: Continuity and Political Change in an Oppressive State.* Boulder, CO: Westview Press.

MacGaffey, Janet. 1986. Fending-For-Yourself: The Organization of the Second Economy in Zaire. In *The Crisis in Zaire: Myths and Realities*, ed. Nzongola-Ntalaja. Trenton, NJ: Africa World Press.

MacGaffey, Janet and Rémy Bazenguissa-Ganga. 2000. *Congo-Paris: Transnational Traders on the Margins of the Law.* Oxford: James Curry.

——— 1999. Personal Networks and Trans-Frontier Trade: Zairian and Congolese Migrants. In *Regionalisation in Africa: Integration and Disintegration*, ed. Daniel Bach. Oxford: James Currey.

Maractho, Angéline Mudzo Mwacan and Theodore Trefon. 2004. The Tap is on Strike: Water (Non)distribution and Supply Strategies. In *Reinventing Order in Kinshasa: How People Respond to State Failure in Kinshasa*, ed. Theodore Trefon. London: Zed Books.

Marysse, Stefaan and Tom De Herdt. 1996. *Comment Survivent les Kinois Quand l'Etat Dépérit?* Antwerp: Centre for Development Studies.

McNulty, Mel. 1999. The Collapse of Zaire: Implosion, Revolution or External Sabotage. *Journal of Modern Africa Studies* 37(1): 53–82.

Metela Shumb. 2000. Soutiens Institutionnels à la Créativité et Emergence de l'Identité Kinoise. Unpublished Doctoral Thesis. Université Libre de Bruxelles.

Ministère de la Santé Publique, République Démocratique du Congo. 1999. Etat des Lieux du Secteur de la Santé: Profil Sanitaire du Niveau Central, des Provinces des Zones de Santé et des Ménages. Kinshasa.

Newbury, Catharine. 1986. Survival Strategies in Rural Zaire: Realities of Coping with Crisis. In *The Crisis in Zaire: Myths and Realities*, ed. Nzongola-Ntalaja, Trenton, NJ: Africa World Press, Inc.

Nzeza, Athanase. 2004. The Kinshasa 'Bargain'. In *Reinventing Order in Kinshasa: How People Respond to State Failure in Kinshasa*, ed. Theodore Trefon. London: Zed Books.

Nzongola-Ntalaja. 1986. Crisis and Change in Zaire, 1960–1985. In *The Crisis in Zaire: Myths and Realities*, ed. Nzongola-Ntalaja. Trenton, NJ: Africa World Press, Inc.

Oxfam/Great Britain. 2001. Aucune Perspective En Vue: La Tragédie Humaine du Conflit en République Démocratique Du Congo. Unpublished report. Kinshasa.

Pain, Marc. 1979. Kinshasa: Ecologie et Organisation Urbaines. Unpublished Doctoral Thesis. Toulouse le Mirail.

Pourtier, Roland. 1997. Du Zaïre au Congo: Un Territoire en Quête d'Etat. *Afrique Contemporaine* 183: 7–30.

Schatzberg, Michael. 1991. *The Dialectics of Oppression in Zaire*, Bloomington: Indiana University Press.

Slade, Ruth. 1960. *The Belgian Congo.* London: Oxford University Press.

Stockwell, John. 1978. *In Search of Enemies: A CIA Story.* New York: Norton.

Tollens, Eric. 2004. Food Security in Kinshasa: Coping with Adversity. In *Reinventing Order in Kinshasa: How People Respond to State Failure in Kinshasa*, ed. Theodore Trefon. London: Zed Books.

Trefon, Theodore. 2000a. Population et Pauvreté à Kinshasa. *Afrique Contemporaine* 194: 82–89.

——— 2000b. Forest-City Relations. In *Les Peuples des Forêts Tropicales Aujourd'hui, Vol. II. Une Approche Thématique*, ed. Serge Bahuchet. Brussels: APFT-ULB.

Tsambu, Léon. 2001. Musique et Violence à Kinshasa. Unpublished Manuscript.

Tshilemalema, Mukenge. 1986. Societal Constraints and Adaptive Strategies: The Predicament of Dependent Business in Zaire. In *The Crisis in Zaire: Myths and Realities*, ed. Nzongola-Ntalaja. Trenton, NJ: Africa World Press, Inc.

Turner, Thomas. 1981. Mobutu's Zaire: Permanently on the Verge of Collapse? *Current History* 80(463): 124–127.

United Nations. 2001. *World Population Prospects: The 2000 Revision*, New York: United Nations.

———— 1997. *World Urbanisation Prospects: The 1996 Revision*, New York: United Nations.

Vanderlinden, Jacques. 1985. *La Crise Congolaise*, Brussels: Editions Complexe.

Weiss, Herbert. 1995. Zaire; Collapsed Society, Surviving State, Future Polity. In *Collapsed States: The Disintegration and Restoration of Legitimate Authority*, ed. William I. Zartman, Boulder, CO: Lynne Rienner.

White, Bob W. 2002. Rumba and Other Cosmopolitanisms in the Belgian Congo (1949–1999). *Cahiers d'Etudes Africaines*. spring/summer.

Widner, Jennifer. 1995. States and Statelessness in late Twentieth-Century Africa. *Daedalus* 124(3): 129–153.

Willame, Jean-Claude. 1986. *L'Epopée d'Inga: Chronique d'une Prédition Industrielle*, Paris: Harmattan.

———— 1972. *Patrimonialism and Political Change in the Congo*, Stanford, CA: Stanford University Press.

Wrong, Michela. 2001. *In the Footsteps of Mr. Kurtz: Living on the Brink of Disaster in Mobutu's Congo*. New York: Harper Collins.

Yoka, Lye Mudaba. 1999. *Kinshasa, Signes de Vie*, Tervuren: Institut Africain-CEDAF and Paris: L'Harmattan.

Young, Crawford. 1984. Zaire: Is there a State? *Canadian Journal of African Studies* 18(1): 80–82.

———— 1965. *Politics in the Congo: Decolonisation and Independence*. Princeton: Princeton, NJ: University Press.

Young, Crawford and Thomas Turner. 1985. *The Rise and Decline of the Zairian State*. Madison, WI: University of Wisconsin Press.

Zartman, I William. 1995. *Collapsed States: The Disintegration and Restoration of Legitimate Authority*. Boulder, CO: Lynne Rienner.

12

A City under Siege: Banditry & Modes of Accumulation in Nairobi, 1991–2004

MUSAMBAYI KATUMANGA (2005)

This is a study of the impact of political and economic liberalisation on modes of socio-economic engagement and accumulation in Kenya's capital city, Nairobi, subsequent to the introduction of multiparty 'democracy' in 1992.[1] On the one hand, economic liberalisation led to a diminished state-provisioning capacity and unwillingness to protect public interests. On the other hand, political conditionalities opened up political space but also spawned anomic tendencies within the regime and among social groups and individuals, with struggles in defence of economic position against each other at one level and against the state and local councils at another. This account focuses on the political economy underlying the resultant urban banditry in Nairobi. It seeks to demonstrate how a besieged regime facilitates the criminalisation of urban existence in a bid to ensure its survival.

The argument here is that beleaguered regimes survive through a twin strategy. They privatise public violence and appropriate private violence. The net effect is the perversion of social order and the emergence of bandit economies. Regime longevity may derive not only from lack of an alternative leadership and organising ideology, but also from the threat to perceived benefits accruing from such informal economies. The ruling elite respond to the possibility of losing power by using neo-patrimonial structures to selectively allocate public spaces to their cronies, thereby subverting social order and undermining democratisation, security and social harmony; this in turn spawns urban banditry. Urban banditry here denotes the unregulated deployment of instruments of coercion by the ruling elite and various elements within the citizenry in bids to facilitate acquisition of economic benefits and political leverage.

Withering state and the logic of urban banditry

The nature, role and survival of the state as an entity remain at the core of political debate. Realists, system theorists and political economists as well as Marxists have at one point or another predicted its demise. While liberal reformers

---

[1] In 1992 and 1997, the opposition lost the election due to a combination of tactics applied by President Moi and the ruling party, KANU. In 1992 extreme levels of political violence in the Rift Valley were accompanied by the bribery of voters using funds siphoned out of the Central Bank through the Goldenberg scandal (see below); whilst in 1997 fragmentation of the opposition in addition to violence in Mombasa delivered victory again to Moi. It was not until 2002 that an opposition united under Mwai Kibaki and the National Rainbow Coalition, NARC, took power.

179

expected globalising capitalism to diminish the state's national and international roles, Marxists foretold not only the disutility of its violence once exploitation was ended but also its disappearance.

A state's legitimacy rests on it fulfilling certain responsibilities such as security, the management of economic reproduction, the balancing of input and output roles and the construction of a national identity. Conversely, it is the increasing inability to deliver on these functions that diminishes the essence of stateness (Navari 1991). Indeed in the global South, contemporary predictions of the state's demise are anchored in what is perceived as its increasing irrelevance, given its diminishing capacity to rule and control society. States are rooted in a trinity of variables: the idea of State; its institutional framework; and its material base. Notwithstanding its abstraction, the idea of State is core to its legitimacy. Underlying its legitimacy are questions such as; what does the state intend or exist to do and what constitutes its political identity? For states grappling with deep-seated identity crises, the transformation of diverse ethnicities into a nation-state is incumbent upon the evolution of a dominant ideology around which politics can be organised. Facilitating and reinforcing the idea of State is the capacity of leadership to build institutions and evolve programmes critical to socio-economic reproduction.

Institutions are core to this process. They include the executive, administrative and participative infrastructures. A weak idea of State engenders recourse to coercion and patronage by ruling elites in a bid to maintain order which eventually leads to state demise. This is a *longue durée* process characterised by a decline in the state's institutional capacity to provide for society or to uphold the security of its citizens, paralysis in decision-making realms and social polarisation. If unchecked, the withering process engenders state collapse (Zartman 1995). State withering is not the monopoly of a predatory leadership. It can also emerge in a context where a regime, in a bid to co-opt certain social formations, allows them to access and privatise certain common public goods. While state capacity in a wide range of formal activities diminishes, its affinity to illegalities and repressive violence increases. Underlying this is the instrumentalisation of violence and patronage in the manipulation of social forces to the advantage of power wielders. As Navari notes (1991:151), the state is in a position to choose which restraints it imposes and 'the demand for new rules in a situation of social change increases both a state's substantive legislative rights and its political salience'.

In essence, it is the ruling elite's ability to act, manoeuvre and manipulate social formations against each other that enhances its freedom of choice in deciding who to back or displease. This fact is best understood when a conceptual distinction between the state and the regime is attempted. A state is an organised aggregate of relatively permanent institutions of governance (Duval and Freeman 1981:106), an instrument that serves the interests of certain social categories. Those who control its reins tend to make choices that highlight their interests and preferences. Its behaviour, and more so, that of the actors occupying its institutions, differentiates it from a regime. The latter refers to rules, principles, norms and modes of interaction between social groups and state organs, bringing into focus not only political relations between power wielders and social groups but also how these are continually re-composed or decomposed.

The neoliberal agenda of economic liberalisation and privatisation is promoted both by internally marginalised aspirant entrepreneurs and international capitalist forces with the aim of facilitating state integration into the global capitalist system. Ideologically rationalised as a means to good governance, it seeks to widen the internal economic space for international capital investment and market penetration by undercutting the bargaining power of post-colonial economic nationalism. It insists that the state abandons protectionism and instead privatises public goods such as parastatals (often meaning their sale to foreign investors) and removes tariff barriers while opening up trade. The state is also called upon to remove 'market distortions' such as subsidies (to health and education sectors), price controls and restrictions on the movement of commodities. Once its bureaucratic baggage has been reduced, the state is reduced to a 'watchman' role of securing property rights, providing effective legal, judicial and regulatory systems, improving civil service efficiency and protecting the environment (World Bank 1996:110–122).

Since the late 1980s, structural adjustment programmes (SAPs) have been presented as an economically rational means to roll back prebendal politics while implanting democratisation. What is striking is the assumption that such a shrunken state can then play midwife to the birth of a productive African entrepreneurial class, capable of profiting from the play of 'anonymous' market forces. Yet it is the control of sources of accumulation that allows the state to shape social forces and relations of production, class formation and struggle. The fact that international capitalist forces are not homogeneous enables the regime to play off one external faction against the other while creating an internal space within which readjustments for regime consolidation and survival are undertaken. The nascent nature of the domestic private sector ensures that, instead of distancing itself from the regime, it seeks to ensure its reproduction by appending itself to the regime; in the process it ends up giving the latter the opportunity to manipulate it. Bandit economies emerge out of the illegal privatisation of public goods and the distribution of these to those deemed to be regime-friendly.

If rivalry within the international capitalist system tends to engender anarchy at the international level, at the domestic level it spawns violence. Exploitation of vulnerabilities and self-interest at individual and group levels and the convergence of these material factors with ruling elite interests spawn multiple identities and particularistic tendencies. The pursuit of these tendencies constitutes the foundation upon which tyranny is constructed and sustained. As Etienne La Boetie noted in 1548, every structure of tyranny is founded on the voluntary submission of hundreds or thousands of men and women. When a few opt to serve a tyrant in a bid to realise their immediate gains, this creates a structure of patronage from which perks filter to lower-level quislings who in turn expect gains for 'little' services. The second, third and fourth level of obedience is enabled to flourish only because the first exists. In the end, people are made to believe that they are compelled to obey. It does not require troops on horse-back, or companies afoot; it is not even arms that defend the tyrant, for force would not be available in the first place unless many were willing to obey and to voluntarily wield military power. The power of tyrants depends on voluntary servitude sustained by multiple ladders of tyranny – what De Jouvenal (1948) calls the state's 'grammar of power'. Conversely, tyranny and corruption can also come to an end consequent on the withdrawal of consent.

Mobilisation and contestations over economic spaces, and the resultant voluntary servitude, have the effect of engendering instrumentalised violence

that tends to narrow associational space as variegated social groups turn
against each other at the behest of the state. This process entails the rolling
back of the logic of stateness, especially the state's need to dominate the means
of violence in society. Instead, various lumpen social formations are allowed
to arm themselves. When the need to contain oppositional forces arises, the
regime appropriates and deploys this private violence. These regime mari-
onettes are in turn rewarded through illegal access to common public goods.
This mode of engagement not only conceals state complicity but also allows it
to retain effective control of associational space away from the prying eyes of
external forces.

In Kenya's case the foregoing behaviour can be best conceptualised as triple
deviance: that is, the deviance of the state (manifested through its descent into
and encouragement of illegalities); group deviance (illegalities committed by
groups); and individual deviance (inclination to illegality by individuals). This
collective social maladjustment sustains both state banditism and predatory
violence. It equally engenders widespread violation of norms, a process that
erodes trust while threatening the foundation of social life. Social life requires a
degree of predictability based on people doing what is expected of them. Extensive non-conformity engenders social disorder, chaos, tensions and conflicts. It
is equally expensive to the individual and society at large. Underlying this is the
fact that it diverts resources such as security resources that could otherwise
have been used elsewhere.

The foregoing forms the basis of my argument that externally driven pressure for economic liberalisation engendered the construction of a logic of voluntary servitude that entrenched regime longevity and more particularly, the
de(re)composition of socio-economic and political spaces in Nairobi. This thesis
is based on a study I undertook in Nairobi on modes of accumulation in the
context of supposed political and economic liberalisation and the impact these
had on politics of change in Kenya.

Regime survival and the drift into collective social deviance

The decade of the 1990s created near-revolutionary conditions that spawned
atomisation and subjectivism in Kenya. IFI-imposed SAPs engendered hikes in
food prices, a decline in real wages and redundancies. Reduced public expenditure in education spawned high drop-out rates (three million by 2001) and
many of these drop-outs made the great trek from the rural into the urban frontier. There they constituted a pool of disaffected youth, open to recruitment by
opposition parties seeking to maximise the opening of associational space and
external support to acquire political power. Together, they evolved into a culture
of political revolt that emerged in the early 1990s.

Instead of spawning good governance, externally imposed political conditionalities laid the foundations for insecurities that would plague the state for
more than a decade. Conversely, the consequences of economic liberalism were
more ambiguous. It was not the nascent private sector but rather the regime
that had the last word on who accessed expanding opportunities under privatisation (what I describe as SAP sites of accumulation) – this fact enhanced
regime power. The regime responded to the situation accordingly, by minimising

the adverse effects of conditionalities as it maximised on the favourable ones of liberalisation.

The regime undertook minimum constitutional amendments. In July 1992, it passed a Bill which compelled prospective winning candidates to the presidency to garner at least 25% of the votes cast in five of the eight electoral provinces in addition to garnering the highest number of votes cast (Katumanga 1998:31). At the informal level, it resorted to the appropriation of private violence (violence organised by criminal social formations) and the privatisation of public violence (which sometimes involved informalising security agents by having them operate without formal uniforms before deploying them undercover alongside vigilante groups to wreak violence on those deemed enemies of the regime). The politically instigated ethnic violence that engulfed parts of the Rift Valley, Western and Nyanza provinces in 1992 (Ngunyi 1996:203–4; Africa Watch 1993) and in Likoni in 1997 should be seen in this perspective. The net effect was the containment of social formations opposed to the regime. Those displaced by this violence were unable to exercise their rights (see KHRC 1997). Demonstrations or public rallies organised by civil society associations were quickly dispersed, seemingly by agents of private violence.

Those who became agents of the regime were rewarded according to their class status. Those from the higher middle class were established bandit companies through which funds were ferreted from the Central Bank. A prime example was the Goldenberg scandal in which more than KSh100 billion (US$769.2 million) was siphoned out of the Central Bank on false pretences. KSh4.5 billion (approximately US$57.7 million) of this cash was allegedly given to the then ruling political party, KANU, to facilitate the buying of political support in the 1992 election.[2] By 2003, politicians and senior civil servants had set up their own modes of extraction from companies seeking to do business in Kenya. It is alleged that a contract worth KSh100 million would cost companies KSh7.5 million in bribes. In printing and publishing, companies were forced to part with an average of 11.5% of the total contract sum; in textiles, garments and furniture 8.9%; and in the metal sector 8.8% (Kimuyu, 2004). Such modes of extraction culminate in the estimated KSh300 billion (US$3.75 billion) stashed outside the country by former power wielders (*Daily Nation,* 17 December 2003).

In an attempt to detach unemployed urban youth from their 1992 alliances with the opposition, rewards were found, ranging from cash payments to the securing of access to spaces of socio-economic reproduction. The existential 'illegality' of urban lumpen elements, their precarious existence in informal habitations and livelihoods, could be manipulated to motivate them into compliance. If necessary, their economic reproduction sites or informal habitations could be destroyed or appropriated for politically compliant individuals who would then be free to dispose of the assets. Following violent eviction of previous tenants, the politically well-connected used their influence to have parastatals such as the National Social Security Fund (NSSF) or National Hospital Insurance Fund compelled to buy them in the name of acquiring assets. NSSF is said to have allocated KSh30 billion (US$384.6 million) over five years for acquisition of such plots. The new owners would subsequently resell, usually to rich Asian businessmen (*The Standard,* 2 November 2004). Conversely, in a bid to blunt opposition to the state, allocations of public land were granted to religious

---

[2] Proceedings of the Goldenburg Enquiry.

organisations, politicians, civil servants and foreign embassies.[3] Kenya Airports Authority, for instance, lost as much as 972.36 hectares of land distributed to private developers, who later set up illegal structures on flight paths posing a danger to aviation.[4] The fact that the ruling elite used the state to undertake this process, enhanced its powers. It became the major source of potential accumulation.

Patronage might also mean access to sites of accumulation such as drug growing and trafficking. A classic example is the Cannabis Sativa plantations allowed in the Mount Kenya forest whose produce was sold in Nairobi and illegally exported (Katumanga 2001:269). By 2004, Kenya had become a major transit point for drug traffickers as manifested by the discovery of a cocaine haul worth six billion shillings at the Mombasa port in December 2004 (*The Standard*, 1 January 2005). Others were given licences to import contraband goods from South-East Asia. By 2004, these were costing the state KSh40 billion annually (*Financial Post*, 15 November 2004). The diminishing capacity of law and order institutions (detailed below) had the effect of spawning other urban forms of predation such as motor vehicle theft and hijackings. The rise in crime has often been understood in terms of the 'deviant sub-culture' thesis, which attributes poverty and delinquency to individual failure (Lewis 1978), whereas the 1990s deviance in Kenya was state-encouraged for politico-economic ends.

What seemed constant was the drift into bad governance characterised by lack of accountability, trust and authority. In 1997 the ruling elite of KANU had recaptured power with less than 30% of the vote cast. It did not believe it was accountable to anybody. Instead of enhancing legitimate state penetration into society – an element critical to the evolution of social order, conflict management and resolution – the state was located at the centre of these conflicts. This crisis was exemplified in Nairobi.

Of self help, violence and differentiated bandit economies

Decades after independence, Nairobi remains a differentiated city. Unlike the simple citizen-subject racial dichotomy of the colonial period, in the 1990s the city was spatially divided not only in class terms but around both race and ethnic identities, especially among the urban poor who sometimes seemed to have merely relocated their villages into the city. New entrants from rural areas continued to flood into the city, their numbers augmented by refugees from collapsed states in the region (some estates like Eastleigh and Komarock were literally taken over by Somali, Ethiopian and Rwandan refugees). All sought survival in any way they deemed fit, in a city without any pretence to planned amenities and where corruption and outright incompetence abounded. By

---

[3] These included the Catholic Church, the Anglicans, the African Inland Church, Presbyterians, the East Africa Seventh Day Adventists, the Full Gospel, Pentecostal Independent Church of Africa, Pentecostal Assemblies, Holy Trinity (*Daily Nation*, 'Churches and MPs named in Land deals', 8 October 2004:1/4).

[4] Allottees included Manchester Outfitters Limited, Mechanised Cargo Systems, Kenya Airways, Mumbu Holdings Ltd, Dehasa Investments, NAS Airport Services, Signon Cargo Center, African Airlines, Kejpa Motors, Homegrown Kenya Limited, Skybird Executive Safaris, Pinnacle Development Limited, Oserian Development Co. Ltd, Ramco Investments, Uchumi Supermarkets, Makindu Growers and Packers Ltd, Markfirst Kenya Ltd (*The Standard*, 'How State Firms Lost Billions in Bogus Bills', 12 November 2004:1).

2003, new slums such as Soweto, Mukuru kwa Njenga and Maili Kayaba had emerged. Together they housed two-thirds of Nairobi's three million population. Those earning less than KSh15,000 found themselves in Dandora, Githurai, Zimmerman, Umoja II, Kayole, Mathare North, Ngong' and other neighbourhoods.

City residents responded to poor governance, the lack of services and regime-led predation on public utility spaces in diverse ways. These ranged from self-help to more direct forms of engagement. Middle-class groups often organised themselves into supportive networks that extracted additional 'taxes' from their members to pay for services such as security, garbage collection, street lights and road repairs which the local government no longer provided. In Karen-Langata, a 'settler' suburb (dominated by affluent whites), residents formed the Karen-Ngata Association in a bid to shield themselves (through legal means) from what they perceived as taxation without services or representation. These differentiated petty bourgeois responses were informed by perceptions of costs and benefits likely to accrue from any action undertaken and capacity to sustain the said action within the prevailing political context.

The urban lumpen element living in Nairobi's slums opted for limited direct resistance against forced dislocation of their abodes through mass demolitions. Poorly organised, ambushed in the night and overwhelmed by the naked violence of the state, their resistance tended to fizzle out as soon as it had begun. Unrestricted violence led to many deaths as was the case during the Muoroto demolitions of informal settlements near the city centre in the early 1990s. For most urban lumpen elements, direct resistance was a function of the fact that they had no fall-back position and everything to lose (Anderson 2002).

In the end, this class differentiation of response fragmented oppositional social forces while reinforcing the regime. Resistance failed to evolve into solidarity, greater political participation or effective pressure for good governance. An agenda for far-reaching reforms would have necessitated organisational initiatives led by a radicalised leadership, an ideology and methods of engagement against the state such as seeking to gain control of the mainstream structures of governance. Instead, economic liberalisation, regime deviance, and an ever-expanding urban population with its contradictory responses of co-option, withdrawal, defiance and resistance, converged in transforming urban engagements and modes of socio-economic reproduction into congruence with the regime's logic. The net effect was the decomposition and recomposition of social space. Four cases of engagement between the state and social forces are now addressed to evidence the assertion that a ruling elite forced to liberalise will tend to prioritise its survival to the detriment of the state as an entity capable of provisioning society and enhancing its legitimacy.

Conflict, co-operation and pavement spaces for economic production

The defiance that characterised the 1990s combined with state deviance to erode the institutional capacity of a corrupt city council to enforce its own by-laws. Hordes of hawkers took advantage of this to conquer and occupy city alleyways, before subsequently descending on pavements running parallel to main streets such as Tom Mboya and Ronald Ngala Streets and Moi Avenue. By

2002 there were around 10,000 hawkers on the streets of Nairobi. This behaviour set in motion violent modes of production-based contestations. The first contestations pitted licensed (mainly Asian) traders against hawkers. The second pitted the hawkers against the city councillors seeking to eject them from the city. The third pitted hawkers against regime-friendly beneficiaries of illegal land allocations.

Yet situationally defined alliances were also forged among these groups, rooted in their mutually reinforcing needs. For instance, hawkers who sold second-hand clothes and electronic goods were provisioned by some Asian businessmen and regime-friendly actors engaged in illegal importations of the same. Trade in counterfeit goods cost the state around KSh40 billion annually in the 1990s (see the *Financial Post*, 15 November 2004). Women hawking vegetables, on the other hand, paid bribes to city *askaris* (local government police) in exchange for 'permission' to sell their fresh vegetables and fruits to city dwellers heading home from work.

Understanding their voting potential, the President occasionally sought to intervene on behalf of these petty traders, promising to allocate spaces for them, only to reallocate the same to his political cronies when it suited him. In so doing, he was able to play off one group against another and in the process gain short-term advantage over his opponents. The moment hawkers identified once again with the opposition, the regime would initiate 'crack-downs' resulting in violence and loss of property, precipitating those with already meagre livelihoods into poverty.

By 2002, hawkers had invaded Harambee Avenue (which houses the seat of government). They eventually occupied Parliament Road, the famous Kenyatta Avenue and Koinange Street. Weakening state capacity to maintain order created what Durkheim (1964) calls anomie. Its net effect was a disorganised society and the existence of a situation where individuals lost any sense of shared values and norms. With the emerging discrepancy between culturally prescribed goals and legitimate (socially approved) means of obtaining them, more people drifted into deviance.

Hawker presence in the streets, for instance, constrained human circulation and spawned petty crime while negatively affecting retail trade (more so as hawkers sold similar items). Once in a while the City Council would engage them in disruptive and violent running battles. Whilst ruining the livelihoods of some, it reminded others of the value of social order. There was increasing pressure from businessmen in the Central Business District (CBD) and members of the public for a permanent solution to the hawker problem. Oppositional forces to the KANU government were able to capitalise on this discontent by promising to remove hawkers in the CBD, contain crime and offer a permanent space for established businesses and hawkers respectively, as well as free movement for members of the public. These promises became part of the platform of the National Rainbow Coalition (NARC), constituted after the bifurcation of KANU which in 2002 successfully ejected KANU from power.

By the time the Council was retaking its streets in 2003, the crime-infested Central Business District had been abandoned by Asian business in preference for more secure new and burgeoning shopping malls. A new crop of young merchants emerged from among the thousands of unemployed Kenyan college and school leavers. These new entrants rode in on the appeal of cheap South-East Asian products and successfully took over hundreds of spaces in the abandoned CBD areas. The post-KANU administration has so far failed to create job opportunities for high school or graduate youth; hence they continue to invade the commercial realm, creating precarious petty 'table shops'. This is a generational phenomenon, cutting across ethnicity.

'Militia' politics and the struggle for residential spaces

Edged on by the sheer need to survive, thousands of marginalised youths in Nairobi drifted into gangs, militant formations under labels such as *Talibans*, *Baghdad boys*, *Jeshi la Mzee* (the elder's battalion), *Jeshi la Embakasi* (the Embakasi battalion) and *Mungiki*, a millenarian group that derived its name from the word *muingi* (meaning masses in Kikuyu). These groups could be hired by politicians for around KSh250 (US$4) to unleash violence on their opponents. *Jeshi la Mzee* was used to beat up civil society activists such as the Reverend Timothy Njoya, whilst *Jeshi la Embakasi* was deployed in land disputes in Nairobi, with the most notable incident being an invasion of the 818-acre piece of land that sits between Umoja II, Kayole and Komarock Estates in Nairobi. Some provided vigilante security in working class estates. What was notable about the operations of these groups was their mobilisation around ethnic identities within which class difference was obscured. Politicians sought to borrow their violence by playing down their own class interests and instead appealing to ethnic solidarity.

Underlying these formations in some cases is the ownership of land and houses in low class settlements. In a settlement like Kibera, with a population of more than 700,000 for instance, houses are mainly owned by Nubians and Kikuyu, yet the majority of the tenants are Luo, Luhya and Kamba. Conflicts emerged following attempts by the regime to construct a new power base to cement a national alliance between KANU and the Raila Odinga-led National Development Party (NDP). In a *Harambee* meeting (public exhortation and fundraising), held in Kibera on 31 October 2001 and presided over by the then President Daniel arap Moi, the District Commissioner was instructed to have local rents reduced by 50% – a move designed to appeal to the ethnic solidarity of those most likely to support the new alliance (*Daily Nation*, 1 November 2001). The decision met stiff resistance from the private landlords who were then set upon by the *Talibans* – a predominantly Luo militia. Armed with whips, stones, *rungus* (knobkerries) and machetes, the *Talibans* invaded Kibera (*Daily Nation*, 6 March 2002). By the time the violence was contained, many had lost their lives, women had been raped and property destroyed (*The People*, 27 November 2001). Poverty, unemployment and lack of political consciousness have engendered a situation where political entrepreneurs can instrumentalise ethnicity to mobilise political constituencies.

Kariobangi (another sprawling informal settlement) was 'ruled' by *Mungiki*. Ideologically this appeals to the broadly marginalised of Kenyan society, even to 'the public' (*East African*, 15 November 2000). *Mungiki* advocates a return to cultural values, the right to land and opposition to neo-colonial control of Kenya's economy. Its spread in the 1990s can be attributed to the uprooting of the Kikuyu masses from the Rift Valley, parts of Ole Nguruoine, Elburgon, Subukia, Laikipia and Nyahururu following widespread clashes over land. It began its career in opposition to the regime, while assuring its members' livelihood through provision of security in estates inhabited by lowly-paid workers such as Kariobangi North, Kahawa West and Dandora (*Daily Nation*, 3 April 2001).

In the mid-1990s, *Mungiki's* leaders claimed to have an enrolled membership of between 3.5 and 4 million people, with branches across the country. With each member paying KSh3 per month, it claimed to raise as much as KSh4.5 million per month (US$58,000) in subscriptions. In March 2002, *Mungiki* murdered 23 people and injured 31 others in the sprawling slums in Kariobangi North when 500 of them took revenge on the *Taliban* for the murder of two of their members (BBC, 4 March 2002).

To the extent that *Mungiki* was perceived to be aligned to the opposition, it was often confronted by state security. But by late 2002, the regime's relation with *Mungiki* was transformed from one of confrontation to overt tolerance. This change was apparently informed by Mungiki's decision to back the regime's new presidential candidate, Uhuru Kenyatta. Subsequently it was allowed to take over certain transport routes (a fact that allowed it to raise cash which it used to pay its adherents), hold public processions and threaten opposition opponents with impunity.

The transport spaces

Transport spaces stand out as one of the most contested realms in Kenya. Contestations revolve around the *matatu* – cheap private minibuses and taxi-cabs competitively plying for business. An informal transport system, the *matatu* industry was estimated in 1993 to employ 80,000 people directly countrywide, and an equivalent number indirectly. Its activities were said to earn the economy an estimated KSh60 billion, with KSh1.9 billion reaped in taxes (*Economic Survey*, 1993).

Liberalisation of the Kenyan economy in the 1990s animated not only growth in this industry but also struggles for its soul. Two factors underlay its growth: a relaxation on the import of second-hand cars (mainly Urvan Nissans and Toyotas) which were immediately converted into *matatus*; and the importation of vehicle chassis which enabled faster assembly of minibuses (christened *manyangas*). The availability of these vehicles expanded accumulation for owners, their drivers, traffic police, and thousands of urban youth hardened by opposition politics who worked on these vehicles as touts. Profits in the industry were predicated on extortion. Vehicle owners expected to receive up to KSh7,000 a day from the drivers working their *manyangas*, whilst drivers and touts took home an average of KSh1,500 and 1,000 per day respectively (*Daily Nation*, 17 July 1996). There was also protection money, extorted by poorly remunerated and highly demoralised police officers from both the owners and the touts lest they were arrested for frivolous reasons. This led to the arbitrary raising of commuter costs. The involvement of some police officers as owners as well as extortionists seemed to encourage the bandit logic among touts, providing a visa for violence and disregard for the law.

There was cut-throat competition, even wars fought over routes and terminal points among these new petty capitalists. Nairobi has a total of 100 *matatu* routes. Cartels emerged to monopolise routes and launch a booming business by setting high entry barriers for their use. Vehicle owners paid an average of KSh20,000–50,000 (depending on potential return) to have their vehicles ply certain routes, as well as an average KSh300 per day to various route-manning cartels. They also paid parking fees of KSh250 to the City Council, and there was KSh20 to be paid by the owner every time the vehicle left a given estate with passengers (*The Standard*, 21 November 2003, p.13).

Enlivening the *matatu* subculture was the blaring hip hop music played with impunity in these vehicles, transforming them into moving discos in total disregard of the tastes of their clients. Clad in baggy trousers and American baseball caps, the *khat*-chewing *matatu* touts were easily identified by their foul language, disregard for passenger safety and rudeness towards their clients. They would arbitrarily raise the fares or stop the vehicles in the middle of roads in total contempt of traffic rules and regulations.

By the mid-1990s, vigilante groups like *Mungiki* and *Kamjeshi* entered into this fray. Given the high returns in the *matatu* industry, its profits could be converted with ease to financing the tools of violence. The control of *matatu* routes became a battleground as *Mungiki* and *Kamjeshi* began fighting for physical occupation of the routes and termini: 'between July and September 2001 about 15 people were hacked to death consequent to engagements between *Mungiki* and *Kamjeshi* gangs over control of Dandora route' (*Daily Nation*, 20 February 2002).

By November 2001, *Mungiki* had taken over the Kayole, Babadogo and Kikuyu routes while the Transport Licensing Board sat on the fence and failed to support the Matatu Welfare Association's (MWA) demand that they keep out. MWA is the successor of the Matatu Vehicle Owners Association (MVOA) which had been banned by the Moi regime in 1980. The Government in most cases remained a bystander as these pro-opposition groups fought for supremacy, the police seemingly unable to contain their activities (*The Standard*, 5 November 2001). To the extent that the violence involved opposition-linked groups, the regime was disinclined to intercede. Yet it would selectively rush to intervene whenever the conflict threatened the interests of regime-friendly interests.

Later, the inability of the Government to demonstrate its monopoly over violence for the common good saw *Mungiki* successfully take over fifteen out of one hundred routes in Nairobi. This coincided with their new modes of collaboration with the regime in late 2002. It was not until 2004 that a serious attempt was made by the new NARC government to bring order in the transport sector. This entailed the imposition of new rules that limited the numbers of passengers that could be ferried by vehicles and the compulsory fitting of seat belts. They also attempted to remove the self-imposed stage managers. After a brief resistance by various gangs, the rules were operationalised. *Mungiki* went underground, only to re-emerge in January and February of 2003 with the killing of several people in Nakuru and security officers in Nairobi's Dandora area.

Lumpen banditry

The 1990s saw increased forms of banditry with roots among urban lumpen elements. Their audacious behaviour was shadowed by the diminishing institutional capacity of the police force. Constraints on government recurrent expenditure imposed by the IMF and the World Bank had the net effect of freezing not only the salaries of security forces but also their complements. By

1996, there were 30,000 police officers compared to a population of about 30 million, translating into one police officer for every 1,000 Kenyans. By 2002 it had grown to 1:1400. Worse still, the security forces suffered from lack of infrastructure and institutional capacity, poor leadership and corruption in recruitment, promotion and operational matters. Poor pay combined with favouritism to engender demoralisation and lethargy in the force. This was reflected in the absence of adequate supervision with respect to gun handling, to the extent that some began hiring out their guns to others for robbery and other criminal activities.

In the late 1990s the state created the National Intelligence Service. The core of this service was recruited from the best cells of the police force. Little effort was made to retrain and improve the welfare of those who remained. Young graduate recruits to the police force ended up frustrated due to poor pay and lack of promotion opportunities. As the frontiers for primitive accumulation increased, the security forces jumped on the bandwagon. Many doubled up by extorting bribes and collaborating with bandits. Special units created to combat crime became a source of the same. Some police officers went to the extent of leaking operational plans (*The People's Daily*, 13 October 2004). Before long, security frameworks become fragile, lacking effectiveness and legitimacy. State institutions were engaged in what Crawford Young calls 'self-cannibalisation'. Citizens experienced state rule as simple predation instead of protection (Young 1997:2).

By 2004, the very survival of urban economic activities had come under serious threat from lumpen banditry, exacerbated by the collapsing formal economy and the influx of small arms. One of the more recent developments is the hijacking of vehicles and robbery of their passengers, including *matatus*. Drivers have been shot, conductors and passengers robbed of their money, cell phones and other personal effects. In some extreme cases passengers and drivers have been robbed, assaulted and stripped naked. Women have also been subjected to rape ordeals.[5]

In a survey[6] on incidents of *matatu* hijacking carried out in Nairobi and its suburbs between 7 and 19 June 2004, 46 (or 25.5%) confirmed having experienced hijacking incidents during the year. Routes with high rates of hijacking tend to have certain characteristics. These include density of population (and by inference daily rates of collection) and the availability of accessible escape routes for thugs. These routes are also characterised by poorly lit pick-up points from which thugs can access the vehicles.

A total of KSh576,350 (US$7389) and 398 mobile phones valued at KSh1,173,000 (US$15,038) were expropriated at gunpoint in these hijackings. The total value of assets stolen in the course of the 46 reported incidents of *matatu*-jacking amounted to KSh2,168,350 (US$27,799.4). If this survey were projected to the total number of *matatus* in Nairobi, this would translate to approximately 2,550 *matatus* hijacked annually. The value of this economy thus translates to approximately KSh120 million for the six months period and approximately KSh240 million (equivalent to US$3 million) per year. The actual

---

[5]   Interviews with Senior Security and Administrative Officers engaged in urban anti-bandit operations.

[6]   The data in this section are extracted from a survey undertaken on a cross-section of routes in Nairobi, courtesy of the University of Bradford Study on Impacts of Violent Crime and Conflict on Poverty. Nine routes were surveyed and a total of 817 vehicles sampled.

cost of the bandit economy is a function of the estimated cost of lost assets plus value gained by bandits after resale.

Those operating in this highway bandit economy are basically young unemployed lumpen elements for which it reaps returns far greater than employment. Their victims are equally Kenyans of lesser means who rely on public transport. On average, poor Kenyans live on less than a dollar per day. It is the poor who end up paying more for services/goods due to the increased costs of living engendered by thuggery. For instance, on Routes 32/42 (Dandora), and 19/61 (Kayole, Komarock), *matatus* tend to hike their fares by 25% from 8 p.m. as a premium for the risk to owners and franchisees of hijacking. The effects of the bandit economy continue to marginalise the already disadvantaged poor. Given this state of affairs, and the dangers of *matatu* transport, many are forced to trek long distances to work.

Given the magnitude of losses, it is worth speculating how this money could have been better spent. The actual value of this capital could have facilitated the tarmac of 10 kilometres of road, or upgraded 32 kilometres of murram road. Such a road could facilitate peasant access to markets. In a bid to respond to highway banditry, *matatu* proprietors have had to purchase security screening handsets. Those without them often drive their vehicles to police stations for body searches. Most *matatus* now avoid picking up passengers en route at night. The net effect of all this is a loss in earnings as well as anxiety and insecurity when travelling that continue to impact negatively on the formal economy. In a bid to combat this mode of banditry, the new police commissioner, General Hussein Ali, has set up a new police unit to deal with banditry in *matatus*. There has also been an increase in the number of roadblocks and motor vehicle inspections aimed at flushing out gun-carrying bandits.

Bourgeois banditry

Nairobi has also been experiencing high levels of predation on personal vehicles. While urban lumpen youth are again at the core of this urban banditry, they are here basically puppets of organised syndicates. The godfathers seem to be individuals involved in 'respectable' businesses that act as fronts to camouflage their real activities. Those involved are alleged to include renowned industrialists and businessmen.[7]

Like the *matatu* banditry this mode is also characterised by high levels of impunity that have seen motorists who hesitate to hand over their vehicles killed. In the early 1980s it was only parked vehicles that were stolen; currently one is as likely to lose one's vehicle while driving it. An interesting phenomenon of the current thefts is the apparent organised and powerful networks that lie behind them and that make the one-man 'jobs' of the 1980s pale into insignificance. While the latter were basically focused on the city centre, the current predatory activities are web-organised to serve regional bandit markets. During the four-year period from 2000 to 2004 the scale and value of this trade has increased dramatically.

Of the total of 2,300 vehicles stolen in 2000, only 693 cars were recovered, representing an average recovery rate of 30%. At an estimated value of

---

[7] Amongst the major arrests were Fai Amario, a wine manufacturer and politician from Naivasha, and members of the Akasha family with huge businesses in Mombasa.

KSh500,000 each (US$6,250), 1,607 vehicles unrecovered had a staggering total value of KSh803,500,000 (US$10,043,000).

By 2004, the situation had worsened. For instance, in the first five months of 2004, a total of 1,127 vehicles had already been recorded stolen; another 857 cars had been reported hijacked. The law enforcement agencies had so far recovered 513 vehicles, representing a recovery rate of 45.5%. Net stolen vehicles for the period under review were 614 units. At an estimated value of KSh500,000 each (US$6,250), 614 un-recovered vehicles are worth a total of KSh307,000,000 (US$3,837,500).

Between 2000 and 2003, the total value of the vehicles stolen was over KSh3 billion (US$38.6 million). Aside from vehicle theft, examination of figures given by a local daily (*The Standard*, 1 October 2004) notes that there was a total of 2,349 cases of reported carjacking up to October 2004. The cars were snatched from motorists in a total of 1,061 cases, while in 797 cases motorists and/or passengers were robbed. In 491 incidents, there were attempts to steal a parked car; 45% (1,091) of the vehicles were recovered in that period. 90% of the vehicles recovered had been used by criminals as getaway cars. Musa Yego of the special crimes prevention unit notes that 70% of incidents occur in upper-class estates in Nairobi. The level of sophistication of the process is discernible by the tactics deployed. Reconnaissance is undertaken on the victims and on ambush spots. The most popular points are black spots: busy roundabouts, T-junctions, pothole points, feeder roads and gates.

It takes an average of one day to plan and steal a vehicle, another day to either dismantle it prior to selling the spare parts or arrange to have new but fake papers, new number plates and the re-spray needed to drive the car across the border. Stolen cars are driven across the border using what are referred to as 'panya routes' (unofficial 'rat' routes). This is how the vehicle of Kenya's Chief of General Staff was 'siphoned' out of the country into a local garage at Singa in Tanzania after his wife and escort had been carjacked (12 October 2004).

Out of the 10,993 vehicles stolen in the four and a half years under review, 8,129 units were taken at gun-point, representing 74% of the vehicles stolen. The implication here is that a motorist is at three times the risk of being robbed of the vehicle than when the same is parked. An owner-occupied vehicle is likely to be in good shape and with fuel. In any case, one can also threaten the victim for the cash needed for petrol. More importantly, parked vehicles are likely to be under surveillance.

Insecurity and the economic base

Between 1999 and 2002, a total of 140 foreign investors pulled out of Kenya, citing corruption, poor infrastructure, bureaucratic bottlenecks and the increased crime rate (*East African*, 16 October 2002; Habitat–ITGD.EA 2001). Direct foreign investment dropped from KSh26 billion to KSh22 billion between 1996 and 1998. It has been estimated that the bandit economy averaged KSh1.5 billion (US$19.2 m.) and KSh6.2 billion (US$79.5m.) annually for vehicle theft and hijacking and predation on forests respectively between 1990 and 1998, whilst government corruption averaged KSh127.4 billion between 1990 and 1999 (Ngunyi 1999). The Kenyan regime literally sustained a bandit economy that ran parallel to the weak formal economy. There were some key beneficiaries of crime rates such as the owners of security firms. The top 20 security companies earned KSh20 billion (US$250m.) in 1999. A conservative estimate of a 10% increase would put their earnings at KSh32 billion (US$400m.) today. More of these firms continue to mushroom, whilst security guards are among the most poorly paid and hardly earn enough to send their children to school.

Coupled with an increasing sense of insecurity at the personal level, Kenya's economic recovery, and by inference people's standards of living, will continue to be undermined. Local industrialists and multinational corporations represented in the Eastern African Association point to crime as their second main concern after poor telecommunication infrastructure. Of the 100 companies sampled, insecurity scored 87.8% compared to communication at 90%. The UN Habitat and Intermediate Technology Development Group-East Africa (2001) survey carried out in March-June 2001 indicated that 40% of Nairobians had been victims of robberies, and 22% had been victims of theft at least once in 2000; 18% claimed to have been physically assaulted. Most respondents intimated that they had been victims in broad daylight (*East African*, 16 October 2002; Habitat–ITGD.EA 2001).

It is notable that increases in crime have the net effect of creating a siege mentality that has seen Kenyans leave their places of work very early, in the process generating heavy traffic jams which in turn erode productive time. Most are afraid of accessing cash machines for fear of being attacked, a factor that has led to plans by the Kenya Bankers' Association to install closed circuit surveillance cameras along Nairobi's main streets.

Shopping complexes in Nairobi like the Village Market and Sarit Centre have invested heavily in security (Kariuki 2005:4). Village Market spends an average of KSh500,000 (US$6,250) per month on 24-hour patrols and security gadgets. Alongside this are insurance premiums which have also increased by between 5 and 10% annually. Sarit Centre incurs a security bill of KSh800,000 (US$10,000) per month. The cost of hiring regular police patrols has also gone up from KSh200 (US$2.5) to KSh1,000 (US$12.5) per day. More critical is the increasing despondency amongst business elements that the state cannot guarantee their rights to property, a factor that constrains commitment to hard work and encourages the drift towards informal economies as the cheap way out of a marginalising formal economy. Informalisation is boosted every time they purchase cheap goods which are probably stolen. Conversely, criminals operate with an increasing sense of impunity.

Nairobi remains a city under constant de(re)composition. It continues to be characterised by vicious struggles over spaces for socio-economic reproduction. The exclusivist logic of the formal political economy ensures that thousands in the slums (especially hawkers and self-employed artisans, unemployed youth and women) remain marginalised. There is an informality that characterises socio-economic reproduction in the city which follows from the weakening capacity of a state under siege from global forces of liberalisation and privatisation. The net consequence is a drift towards urban banditry. It is this informal economy that may explain the survival of Kenya, despite aid embargoes from IFIs and the poor physical and communications infrastructure and diminished institutional capacity to guarantee law and order.

To extricate the city from the morass in which it finds itself, there is the need to re-establish a governance realm within the state as a whole. This calls for a developmental state to grapple with questions of access to means of production and enhanced state penetration in the society and provision of education services to stem the supply side of candidates for crime. The increasing rate of crime will not be contained without a concerted attempt to resolve the crisis of more than four million young Kenyans ejected out of the formal system by the IMF/World Bank-driven logic of a minimalist state. A national youth service under the military that can help build infrastructure, housing units, and schools and in the process enhance skills at one level (or opportunities to return to school at another) is one way out. The foregoing is an argument for state-building animated by internal dynamics and needs, rather than externally driven neo-liberal projects that call for a 'watchman state'. Externally imposed liberalisation and privatisation do not midwife a democratic, secure or harmonious society; they initiate the distribution of spoils as a desperate means to retain power.

References

Africa Watch. 1993. *Divide and Rule: State-Sponsored Violence in Kenya*. New York: Human Rights Watch.

Anderson, David M. 2002. Vigilantes, Violence and the Politics of Public Order. *African Affairs* 101(405): 531–555.

BBC World Service, Broadcast, 4 March 2002.

De Jouvenal, Bertrand. 1948. *Power: The Natural History of its Growth*. London: Hutchinson.

Durkheim, Emile. 1964. *The Division of Labor in Society*, New York: The Free Press.

Duval, Raymond and John Freeman. 1981. State and Dependent Capitalism. *International Studies Quarterly* 25(1): 99–118.

Habitat (UN) and Intermediate Technology Development Group (ITDG-EA). 2001. *Strengthening Partnership for a Safer Nairobi*. Nairobi.

Kariuki, John. 2005. The Cost of Fear: Security Firms' Turnover Tops $400 Million. *East African*, 25–31 October.

Katumanga, Musambayi. 1998. *The Political Economy of Constitutional Amendments in Kenya, 1895-1997*. SAREAT-IPAR Collaborative Paper 005/98.

———— 2001. *Moral Imperatives of Conflict*. Nairobi: IEA/SID.

Kenya Human Rights Commission (KHRC). 1997. *Violence, Ethnicity and State in Coastal Kenya*. Nairobi.

Kimuyu, Peter. 2004. *Corruption, Firm Growth and Export Propensity in Kenya*. IDS (University of Nairobi) and Kenya Institute of Public Policy Research and Analysis, Nairobi.

La Boetie, Etienne. 1969, [1548]. *Discours de la Servitude*. Paris: Réed Payot.

Lewis, Oscar. 1978. *The Study of Slum Culture*. New York: Random House.

Navari, Cornelia. 1991. On the Withering Away of the State. In *The Condition of States: A Study in International Political Theory*, ed. Cornelia Navari. Buckingham: Open University Press.

Ngunyi, Mutahi. 1999. The Bandit Economy, Corruption and Crime as the Fourth Factors of Production In Kenya. *East African Alternatives*, Sep/Oct, Nairobi: SAREAT

———— 1996. Resuscitating the Majimbo Project: The Politics of Deconstructing the Unitary State in Kenya. In *Challenges to the Nation-State in Africa*, eds. Adebayo O. Olukoshi and Liisa Laakso. Uppsala: Nordiska Afrikainstitutet.

Young, Crawford. 1997. Reflections on State Decline and Societal Change in Zaire. Unpublished Manuscript.

World Bank 1996. *From Plan to Market*. Washington, DC: World Bank.

Zartman, William. 1995. *Collapsed States: The Disintegration and Restoration of Legitimate Authority*. Boulder, CO and London: Lynne Rienner Publishers.

13

Côte d'Ivoire: Patriotism, Ethno-Nationalism & other
African Modes of Self-Writing

RICHARD BANÉGAS (2006)

Ever since the outbreak of war in September 2002, Côte d'Ivoire has been floun-
dering in a poisonous morass of identity politics. The most obvious sign of this
is the affirmation by a certain section of the population of an ultranationalist
and extremely violent 'patriotism', to use the term favoured by its proponents.
In the south of the country, which remains under government control, this
particular brand of nationalism, aggravated by the radical rhetoric of the ruling
party and its allies, is the expression of a three-pronged rejection. The first rejection is of the former colonial power, France, which retains a strong presence in
the country. The second is of immigrants from neighbouring countries. The
third, and most damaging, is a rejection of the many Ivorian citizens whose
geographical origin, ancestry, religion or family name makes them second-class
citizens, of doubtful nationality, in the eyes of southern 'patriots'.

This article aims to investigate both the historicity and the novelty of this
ultranationalist mobilisation, best understood within the longer history of the
formation of the Ivorian state and its political economy. At the same time,
however, it also has to be understood within the shorter-term perspective of
political struggle, most obviously the extended succession dispute that followed
the death of President Félix Houphouët-Boigny in 1993, and as a reflection of
the generational conflicts at the heart of the country's political elite. Beyond
the political aspects of these struggles for power, we hope to show that the
violence of the self-styled 'young patriots' in Ivorian public space stems from
two related tendencies. One of these is the claim made by the 'patriots' to champion a second independence from the former colonial power, France, and to
contest the nature of national sovereignty. This is a debate that is highly necessary but that has been postponed constantly ever since Côte d'Ivoire's formal
accession to independence in 1960. The second tendency is towards a redefinition of the relations between communities and generations. This is the result of
a substantial cohort of the country's younger generation claiming its purported
rights, through violence and the discourse of liberation. Many Ivorian youths
who have enlisted in the 'patriot' militias experience the current conflict as a
struggle for independence. For them, it is both a war of national liberation and
a daily struggle to assert their autonomy as individuals. It would be a mistake to
underestimate the interconnectedness of these intertwined elements, even
though the 'patriot' militias represent only a minority of Ivorians and are
controlled by the presidency.

However, in this article, we argue that the nationalist mobilisation represented
by the young 'patriots' cannot be reduced solely to its political aspect. It is a

phenomenon with a deep social or sociological significance that must also be understood. Policy-makers, particularly those intent on integrating youth into society and in redefining Franco-African relations, must draw the appropriate conclusions. At stake in Côte d'Ivoire's war of rival patriotisms[1] is the redefinition of the contours of the political community as well as the content and modes of citizenship. As some of the protagonists themselves say, it is a war of modernity; at bottom, it concerns the fundamentals of nationality and citizenship. The questions are deceptively simple: who is Ivorian, and who is not? What is the nation? Who is included in the nation? More prosaically, it is a conflict about the rights – political, economic, educational, cultural, matrimonial, concerning property, etc. – that are conferred by possession of a national identity document. Pitted against each other are two different conceptions of citizenship – one orthodox and the other based on a political ideology of autochthony and exclusion. In other words, this is a war of identification,[2] with deep historical roots. To appreciate its historical resonance, it is not sufficient to limit oneself to a study of the actors' discourse and points of symbolic reference. It is also necessary to take account of the social and political structures erected by the current government with a view to controlling territory and imposing its message of 'patriotism'.

Finally, Ivorian 'patriotism' and its radical offshoots must be placed in a perspective that is continental or even global. Only in this way is it possible to understand the ultranationalism expressed in speeches at the Sorbonne, the informal meeting place in Abidjan's central business district favoured by political activists, or in the bars of the popular Abidjan district of Yopougon. These discourses are neither more nor less than the echo of other African modes of self-writing (Mbembe 2000; 2002) that, from Dakar to Johannesburg, via Addis Ababa, Kampala and Kinshasa, aspire to establish a new politics of Africanness.

From *Ivoirité* to ultranationalist patriotism

Many authors have noted that the war that broke out in September 2002 and the subsequent nationalist mobilisation are more than a matter of coincidence (Banégas and Marshall-Fratani 2003). On the contrary, they emerge from rivers that are deep. Politics has burst out of its usual channels as a consequence of the ideology of *Ivoirité*. The forms of political regulation that formerly allowed indigenes and *allogènes*[3] to co-exist in peace are henceforth obsolete.

During his more than three decades in power, President Houphouët-Boigny (1960–1993) established a system of politics that was based on the use of rents derived from extraversion. The most obvious form of this external orientation was the sale of coffee and cocoa for export, but rents were also generated by Côte d'Ivoire's strategic position at the hub of the Franco-African relationship sometimes known as *la Françafrique*. Three key relationships formed the sinews

---

[1]   Both sides in the military and political contest claim to be motivated by patriotism, as witnessed, for example, by the name of the main opposition movement, the *Mouvement patriotique de Côte d'Ivoire* (MPCI or Ivorian Patriotic Movement), or the title of the main opposition newspaper, *Le Patriote*, close to the *Rassemblement des Républicains* (RDR) party.

[2]   An expression used by a petty trader in the Koumassi district of Abidjan. Interview, September 2003.

[3]   There is no exact English equivalent to this word. The nearest translation would be 'foreigner'.

of this political system: alliances with the former colonial power, with local planters and with the migrant workers who were welcomed in large numbers as labourers on Côte d'Ivoire's plantations. This post-colonial compromise was translated into an institutionalised system of clientelism greased by money from cocoa sales that was handled by the government's agricultural product purchasing office, the *Caisse de stabilisation des produits agricoles*, or *Caistab*. The bases of the Houphouët-Boigny system of clientelism were eroded by economic crisis, the rise of new generations of both civilians and soldiers and, above all, the political ambitions of the politicians who aimed to succeed the founding father after his death.

Some commentators go as far as to claim that the current war is, at bottom, the result of a crisis of succession, pitting the two putative heirs of the Houphouët system (Henri Konan Bédié and Alassane Dramane Ouattara) against its historic opponent, Laurent Gbagbo. Like many other autocrats, Houphouët-Boigny was wary of any potential successor who risked accumulating enough power to challenge him during his own lifetime. When he appointed Alassane Ouattara as Prime Minister in 1990, it was certainly because the latter was a technocrat, a former deputy director of the International Monetary Fund, who could help the country emerge from its economic crisis by cementing relations with the international financial institutions. But it was also no doubt because Houphouët-Boigny calculated that, because of Ouattara's northern background and his close association with Burkina Faso, he could never become head of the Ivorian state. The man whom Houphouët-Boigny most consistently presented as the crown prince of his government was the notably uncharismatic Henri Konan Bédié, whose key qualities were his loyalty to the regime, an intimate knowledge of the ruling *Parti démocratique de la Côte d'Ivoire* (PDCI), and membership of the Akan group, and especially the Baoule, who had held the reins of power since independence. Elected as president of the National Assembly, Bédié became the official number two of the state. According to the constitution, it was he who succeeded to the presidency when Houphouët-Boigny died in December 1993. But this did nothing to resolve the crisis of succession. On the contrary, the struggle for power became more intense in the run-up to presidential elections in 1995 that saw Ouattara leave the PDCI and establish his own party, the RDR. The whole opposition bloc, consisting of the RDR and Gbagbo's *Front populaire ivoirien* (FPI), allies in those days, boycotted the polls. Thus, the PDCI retained power, but with little legitimacy. The two opposition groups gained ground. Gbagbo's FPI had the prestige of being the first party openly to defy the Houphouët-Boigny system and of having struggled for democracy. A party of the left, a member of the Socialist International, the FPI traditionally gained support from marginal social categories, including unemployed, workers, small farmers and youth from the urban townships, such as Abidjan's Yopougon area. At the same time, the FPI had roots in the indigenous population of the west, Gbagbo's own region of origin, where there was a strong feeling of resentment against *allogènes*, 'outsiders' who had come from the north as agricultural labourers or in the form of the Dioula petty traders, or from the east, in the shape of the Baoule planters who had established cocoa farms in the region. The RDR, in contrast, was more inclined to gain support in the north of the country but also in the cities, notably among traders. It gained support from anyone who, like the party's own leader, Ouattara felt threatened by the policy of *Ivoirité*

('Ivorianness') espoused by the Bédié government. This electoral sociology was to be profoundly disturbed by Gbagbo's assumption of power in October 2000, at the end of a period of military rule under General Gueï, who had overthrown the Bédié government in December 1999 (Le Pape and Vidal 2002). Above all, the older patterns were upset by the war that broke out in 2002, with the appearance of new political actors such as the *Forces nouvelles*, the group led by Guillaume Soro that emerged from the rebellion of that year, and the radicalisation of political conflict around the theme of nationality.

Coinciding with this period of political tumult, Côte d'Ivoire has for some 15 years been undergoing an unprecedented economic and financial crisis. Liberal reforms, notably in regard to coffee and cocoa marketing, have served only to make matters worse. There was more at stake in the liberalisation of the export marketing channels than the success or failure of structural adjustment policies. Also at issue was a mode of regulating political tensions that had previously legitimated a highly unequal social division of labour. The scrapping of the *Caistab* and the opening of the agricultural sector to international competition effectively dismantled the machine for regulating political disputes through clientelism that formerly guaranteed the country's stability. The traditional social base of national power, notably Baoule planters and the urban middle classes, has been profoundly destabilised during this process. The Henri Konan Bédié government that lasted from 1993 to 1999 was an early victim of these changes. Laurent Gbagbo, President since 2000, has not only been unable to re-establish the post-colonial compromise created by Houphouët-Boigny but has actually aggravated tensions among different communities through his aspiration to refound the nation and modernise the state. He has pursued this programme without creating any viable new socio-political alliance to replace the one that has been lost.

The gradual erosion of the former system of political regulation based on the plantation economy has brought into question one of the fundamentals of the Ivorian 'miracle' of the 1960s and 1970s, namely the warm welcome that the government in those days extended to the foreigners and *allogènes* who were the real artisans of the country's economic growth, and who today represent perhaps one-third of the total population of Côte d'Ivoire. This process was already visible in the 1970s and 1980s, when a policy of Ivorianising the civil service was implemented. The tensions among different segments of the population were aggravated above all under the Bédié presidency, when, partly for purely electoral reasons, the Head of State himself opened the Pandora's box of *Ivoirité* (Dozon 2000). Conceived and used by the organic intellectuals of the ruling PDCI as a means of excluding Alassane Ouattara as a rival for the presidency, the theme of *Ivoirité* rapidly became a formidable instrument of exclusion, adaptable for a range of techniques of stigmatisation and discrimination at every level of society. Laurent Gbagbo, who was one of the first people to use the discourse of *Ivoirité* to denounce the political use that Houphouët-Boigny had made of immigrants, went on to employ *Ivoirité* for his own ends. So effectively has he done this that his party, the FPI, and its media organs have become in the space of six years the main channels for a vision of citizenship that could be described as radically nativist. Since the outbreak of war in 2002, the language of autochthony has taken a strongly xenophobic and ultranationalist turn, directed against strangers and northerners.

Any explanation of the diffusion of this ultranationalist ideology within a population previously reputed for its tolerance must encompass the role of the media, politicians and the 'patriot' groups. But this is not enough. We should recall that behind the image of Côte d'Ivoire as a land of welcome, social relations were for many years in reality more tense than they seemed. The country was not a melting pot. Rather, there was a cohabitation and a division of labour among communities, each group occupying what Dembélé (2002) calls an 'ecological niche'. Moreover, we need to understand how nationalist mobilisation has been fuelled by the crisis of urban unemployment and by the serious land disputes that have long divided rural areas. The liberal land policy followed by Houphouët-Boigny – who famously declared that 'the land belongs to whoever cultivates it' – had the effect of encouraging migration both from abroad and from region to region within the country. These movements increased the tensions generated by claims to land and by disputes between newcomers and the earlier occupants of specific areas. Generally speaking, the first-comers were steadily losing possession of the most fertile areas of the country. In the 1990s, these land problems reached a breaking point, with the result that there were numerous more or less open conflicts even before the outbreak of a nationwide war in 2002 (Chauveau 2000; Chaveau and Bobo 2003). Finally, all of these problems need to be seen in the longer-term context of the formation of the Ivorian state and its history of agrarian colonisation. *Ivoirité* and its ethno-nationalist variants have historical roots. Relations between 'autochthones' and 'strangers' have been a constant theme of political debate since the 1930s, leading to violent outbreaks of xenophobia on various occasions. In the past, however, this problem was never politicised and radicalised to the extent that is now evident.

Since the outbreak of the present conflict, inter-community relations have become radicalised at both national and local levels under the influence of the ultranationalist mobilisation of the Gbagbo presidency. Intercommunity tensions have changed in nature, with disputes grounded in problems of land and economics becoming political and cultural. Today, the motives for hatred are not only socio-economic but have acquired political, military and religious aspects. The perception of strangerhood has become ethnicised; criteria based on area of origin, culture and religious affiliation have become the prime markers of identity, replacing the economic and social criteria that were most prominent in the affirmation of difference in earlier periods. This change is pregnant with meaning. It means that henceforth the category of 'stranger' consists not only of immigrants but also of Ivorians considered to be 'Dioula' and virtually anyone with an identity as a northerner or a Muslim. This category now includes all people considered allochtones, even neighbours. Thus, inter-community tensions have changed in scale, creating geopolitical blocs (north versus south) and collectives (northerners versus southerners). Despite their history of co-existence and their internal divisions, members of these two groups now think of themselves in terms of a radical difference between themselves and anything external to their own frame of reference. In other words, the ethno-nationalist discourse, apart from being a mode of denouncing foreign interference in the affairs of Côte d'Ivoire, is first and foremost an internal language of discrimination and stigmatisation of 'the enemy within'.

Becoming Ivorian: the politics of identification

It is clear that at stake in the conflict in Côte d'Ivoire are not only the boundaries between groups but also the response to such questions as: What is the nation? Who is part of it?

In part, the conflict concerns the technical arrangements for printing new national identity cards. Far from clarifying the debate on citizenship, the formal process of identification has aggravated the fracture between communities. There have been arguments for years about identity cards and the alleged usurpation of citizenship, but these remain central to an understanding of the current war and nationalist radicalisation. The controversy came to a head in the 1990s when Alassane Ouattara, during his years as Prime Minister (1990–1993), introduced residents' cards for immigrants. Thereafter, the debate became more poisonous under the Presidency of Henri Konan Bédié (1993–1999) and the military government of Robert Guéï (1999–2000), each of whom tried to resolve the problem of *vraies-fausses* national identity cards (i.e. cards issued by a government authority but to people not qualified to receive them) and to resolve the question of 'real' and 'fake' Ivorians. The debate took a further twist when the governing FPI in 2001 tried to implement a new identification process based on the political ideology of autochthony. Here, the problems were less in the wording of the new legal texts, which were rather conventional, than in the way these were interpreted by the functionaries charged with their implementation. With the consent of the political authorities, including the then Minister of the Interior, Emile Boga Doudou (who was killed during the coup attempt of 19 September 2002), the administrators of the *Office national de l'identification* (ONI) – a creation of the Gbagbo government) in effect created their own jurisprudence. Anyone requesting an identity document was required to prove their nationality by obtaining a statement of origin issued by a committee from their village of origin.[4] More precisely, village committees were established to decide on the nationality of any person applying for an official identity document. Each applicant was required to prove birth in a given locality. The local notables and village chiefs who sat on these committees thus acquired formidable power. It is not difficult to imagine the type of conflicts encouraged by such a system, and especially the abuses inflicted on any applicant for an identity document whose surname did not accord with received ideas about which groups were indigenous to which areas (Zoro-Bi 2004). The village committees were formally abolished as part of the changes required by the *Marcoussis* accords of January 2003, but the administrative procedures used by such committees remain current in debates about indigeneity and the politics of locality. An example is the 'aliens' hearings' ('*audiences foraines*') inaugurated in May 2006 as part of a new process to identify formally people who do not have papers. These hearings give credence to the same principle of testimony by local notables to establish whether an applicant was indeed born in a given locality.

---

[4]   According to the ONI's management, 'anyone claiming to be an Ivorian must have a village. Anyone who takes pains to forget the name of his or her village or who is incapable of attaching himself or herself to a specific locality in Côte d'Ivoire is a person without roots and is sufficiently dangerous that it is necessary to determine the origins of a person in such a condition' (Sery Wayoro, deputy director of the ONI, quoted in *Notre Voie*, 27–28 July 2002).

The identification procedures created by the FPI government have had the effect of privileging the notion of an 'ancestral territory', a 'village of origin', considered as the prime location for the production of identity and the proof of citizenship. In a highly urbanised society, where links with a village of origin have become strained at the very least, and where individuals and groups are used to being socially and geographically mobile, these administrative procedures are clearly inane. It is easy to see some of the unintended consequences of such measures, which push to the margins of the national community anyone who is not able to produce local-level proof that they belong to a national community. This has had a particular effect on anyone with a typically northern surname who is also recorded as having been born in a southern village. Official discourse and everyday administrative procedures have combined to create a 'nativist' concept of citizenship, founded on roots in a micro-territory, which has rapidly become the central principle in a process of national refoundation. Henceforth, nationalism and autochthony have become identical, both founded on the same argument concerning legitimation and rights.

In this context, even minor changes in the semantics of political discourse can have an exaggerated importance. Thus, from the start of the war, talk of *Ivoirité* has been replaced by mention of 'patriotism' by both government and rebel forces. This 'patriotism' consists of the defence of an imagined community that is formally contiguous with the national territory but that, historically speaking, is constituted by demonstrating allegiance to the micro-territory that constitutes the motherland. In other words, war and the rhetoric of ultranationalism are steadily contributing to the creation of a citizenship of a micro-territory (*'terroir'*) that is considered to be imbued with qualities of autochthony, excluding anyone external to the village community. To break out of this ethnonationalist logic and refound an open concept of citizenship and nationhood will be no easy task. Rewriting the legal texts concerning nationality, as required by the *Marcoussis* accords, and revising the electoral register are necessary preconditions: necessary, but not sufficient.

For many Ivorians, most notably the FPI ideologues or *refondateurs* who aspire to refound the nation on new principles, the process of identification is much more than a simple administrative procedure that, carried out in the right way, would also bring election victory to their party. The revision of the electoral register, as with that of the population register, is at the heart of their project of national refoundation. Since the mid-1990s, the FPI has been insisting that the administrative procedure of formal identification is essential for eliminating the informality that is the legacy of the system operated by Houphouët-Boigny, where almost anyone could obtain Ivorian nationality documents if they were able to pay for them. FPI ideologues propound a vision of a national revolution that involves building a new state and a modern nation, its administration modelled on the Weberian notion of legal-bureaucratic norms. In their view, careful enumeration is necessary to achieve these goals. The state must rigorously investigate who is who – exactly – and who may become what. In short, what they are calling for is a population register, an *état civil*, that is appropriate to a modern state. According to them, this alone will permit Côte d'Ivoire to become a state of law able to take its rightful place in the family of nations.

The modernisation of the nation-state and the need for administrative rationalisation are classic arguments that have been voiced by nationalist movements throughout recent history. In the Ivorian case, however, this aspiration, further bolstered by arguments on the virtues of good governance, covers an exclusivist ideology of citizenship, founded on the principles of autochthony and adherence to a micro-territory.

Militaristic patriotism and the pentecostalist politics of deliverance

Some readers may respond with the thought that this is rhetoric, and that behind the words are the real social, economic and political interests of actors who use the vocabulary of ultranationalism in the interests of a politics of the belly (Bayart 1993). Such interests certainly exist. In both town and country, it is easy to see how the discourse of ultranationalism serves to justify strategies aiming at the acquisition and capture of resources. In the west of Côte d'Ivoire, there have been numerous cases of agricultural land being expropriated under the cover of autochthony and nationalism. In villages throughout the region, groups of self-styled 'young patriots', generally organised into associations, have no compunction in taking over the land of villagers deemed to be 'foreigners', on the grounds that the land does not belong to them. The young 'patriots' represent themselves as the guardians of local tradition, accusing their own parents of having sold their ancestral land to outsiders. It is easy to see how the various registers of autochthony, nationalism and tradition (invented or otherwise) combine in the service of local strategies of power that fuel conflicts between alleged first occupants and allochtones, but also between generations. The same tendency to generational conflict is perceptible at the national level, where the lifestyle of a Blé Goudé, a Konaté Navigué or a Eugène Djué ('the only patriots we have left'[5]) shows how the ultranationalist discourse has become, in the space of just a few short years, a redoubtable vector of economic accumulation and social ascension by a new elite, these days known in Abidjan as *ventriotes*.[6]

An everyday sight in Abidjan is of squads of young militiamen in uniform under the command of a group leader. The growth of militias is contributing to the militarisation of a part of the country's youth, which sees in paramilitary structures a means of escaping from the misery and anonymity of their lives and also – a factor not to be underestimated – a space of collective organisation and socialisation where personal values are formed and reinforced. In a society eroded by violence and years of economic crisis, and where education no longer fulfils its former role as a means of social ascension, the social role of militias is a crucial factor that no doubt explains some of the influence of these groups. Youth organisations formed by groups of young 'patriots', whether in the city or in the village, are more than a means of defence in the face of a precarious existence: they are places where young people can become actors, recognised in public space. This too is an important factor.

The ultranationalist mobilisation of 'patriotic' youth can also be seen, then, as a means for social juniors to take power by imposing themselves in the public sphere as a political category in their own right. Although this is a process replete with ambiguity, it contributes to the reformulation of relations between generations and the affirmation of a new political generation that is claiming

---

[5]   These terms are borrowed from a song 'coupé/décalé', entitled *Marcoussis*.
[6]   This neologism is a play on words, deriving from *patriotes* and those who engage in *la politique du ventre*.

its place. This is having a steadily greater effect on public affairs. The young 'patriots' who aspire to power, without having 'spent their time in the waiting-room', as Yacouba Konaté (2003:67) expresses it, in many cases have been marked by a political culture of violence honed in student politics, where for years differences were settled by force of arms (*Ibid.*). The rank and file of the young 'patriots', recruited mostly among the streetwise youth of the popular quarters and urban ghettoes or the unemployed youngsters of the suburbs, use violence as a means of taking revenge on society.

The latter tendency is well illustrated by the looting that accompanied the patriotic mobilisation in November 2004, when 'patriot' organisations, frustrated in their hopes of invading the north of the country, turned on French troops and French citizens. The discourse of ultranationalism and the exhilaration of looting combined in a single matrix of appropriation and the affirmation of rights. Combined, these two are part of what Achille Mbembe calls 'an unprecedented culture of liberty as a mode of domination' (Mbembe 2000:42) and accumulation. 'Here, the course of life is assimilated to a game of chance, a lottery, in which the existential temporal horizon is colonised by the immediate present and by prosaic short-term calculations. The freedom to trample over another person and over what belongs to him is not only a matter of strength. It also has a certain aesthetic quality' (Mbembe 2002:271). In the absence of any statistics or precise data on the composition of the young patriot groups, it is difficult to say just how widespread this political culture of youth has become. Nevertheless, the lifestyle of the young 'patriots' has been quite visibly successful and is spreading throughout Ivorian society, at least in the southern part of the country.

This last remark concerning lifestyles requires further precision of a point that is vital for comprehending the nature of Ivorian nationalism, too often analysed simply as the artificial varnish that covers a logic of predation and power. As we have suggested, considerations of predation and power are by no means negligible. It is common knowledge that the leaders of the 'patriot' groups are not motivated exclusively by deep conviction, to put it mildly. But there is more to it than this. Interviews in the popular areas of Abidjan suggest that aggressive 'patriotism' cannot be reduced solely to its instrumental dimensions, whether political, economic or administrative. Like every mobilisation in the name of nationalism, it draws its strength from a social imaginary which, in this case, has been deeply affected by the general spread of violence. If the nationalist and patriotic repertoire has the power to mobilise, it is because it is a register that lends itself to the explanation of misfortune, in a context of generalised crisis, violence and the erosion of the norms and values of earlier times. In Côte d'Ivoire as elsewhere, the language of ultranationalism can provide a narrative framework useful for interpreting problems that afflict the whole of society, with the added advantage of designating scapegoats. In this sense, it fulfils some of the anthropological functions of a witch trial or witch hunt, with which other comparisons are also possible. It makes further search for people responsible for Côte d'Ivoire's crisis unnecessary: external aggressors and the former colonial power and its local collaborators are the obvious scapegoats for a general malaise. In the lexicon of Ivorian ultranationalism, the enemy is often described in such satanic terms as 'evil', 'a devil' or 'a vampire'. The analysis of the language used by popular newspapers that are close to the government, as well as by some popular orators, underlines the importance of this rhetorical register (Chabasseur 2004).

It is easy to see in this vocabulary the influence of a movement that has gained greatly in importance in Africa in recent years, namely the discourse of the new pentecostalist churches that have based their appeal on the need to struggle against the forces of evil and on the promise of a better future.[7] For present purposes, it is necessary to observe only that Ivorian ultranationalism, fed by the FPI's language of revolutionary socialism, is also situated within a religious imaginary of deliverance as articulated by the numerous evangelical churches (and it is notable that both the Head of State and the first lady are known for their adherence to evangelical Christianity). In a country with a long tradition of prophetism that plays a role in politics, there are very important reverberations between the political register of national liberation and a second independence, on the one hand and, on the other hand, the idiom of deliverance that insists on 'the power of the Spirit and the war "against the forces of evil"' (Mary 2002:92), in order to hasten the arrival of the earthly Jerusalem. In this symbolic economy of deliverance, salvation cannot come only from the eradication of evil forces or the healing of the ills that infect the body of society.[8] It is a fight to the death, with aspects of a total war against an enemy who is both within and without. There is no place for compromise.

France in the face of anti-colonialism and new 'African modes of self-writing'

This warlike eschatology, a combination of national liberation and religious deliverance, is all the more effective in that it is associated with two other registers of legitimation, this time concerning international affairs. The first of these is the global war on terror, and the second is the old theme of anti-colonial struggle. Further explanation on the first of these two themes is hardly necessary, as it is easy to see how the pentecostalist discourse of struggle against the forces of Satan resonates with the American neo-conservative notion of struggle against an axis of evil. Laurent Gbagbo and his aides (some of whom, including notably his wife, have a close relationship to churches in the United States and to the United States Right more generally) operate in these two registers with skill, without ever having succeeded in receiving backing from Washington.

The theme of anti-colonialism, on the contrary, plays well both in Ivorian society at large and throughout Africa. To be sure, few Ivorians are fooled by the anti-French diatribes that have become standard fare among different players in the Ivorian conflict. It is generally understood that the tirades regularly launched by Mamadou Koulibaly, the president of the National Assembly,[9] or of other FPI dignitaries against the former colonial power, are part of a political-diplomatic ritual. In Paris, New York and elsewhere, these sentiments provoke little more than a shrug of the shoulders except in cases where the virulence of these verbal attacks is translated – as in November 2004 and January

---

[7]   Among many publications on this theme, see the Special Issue of *Politique Africaine* entitled 'Sujets de Dieu', 87 (2002).

[8]   Compare the frequency with which Laurent Gbagbo uses in his speeches metaphors drawn from illness and healing, for example in regard to the notion of the 'bitter medicine' of *Marcoussis*.

[9]   The author of a pamphlet entitled *La Guerre de la France contre la Côte d'Ivoire* (La Refondation, Abidjan, 2003).

2006 – into physical threats and attacks against French nationals. For the rest, anti-French rhetoric seems to be accepted as part of the political game. To French officials, it is just one more constraint on a diplomatic position that is already difficult. For the Ivorian government, the rhetoric of anti-colonialism provides a valuable source of legitimacy, a precious commodity otherwise in short supply. This interpretation provides an explanation for the wave of violence that followed the failure of Operation Dignity, the Ivorian government's attack on the northern fief of the *Forces nouvelles* in November 2004. By turning public opinion against France, whose troops had opened fire on a crowd in Abidjan, and in exploiting the martyrdom of young 'patriots' who had fallen in the struggle, the government was able at least temporarily to turn a military failure into a political victory.

It is possible to remain at this level of analysis, going no further than an instrumentalist interpretation. However, the argument in the present article is that an instrumentalist reading, linked to the idea that anti-French feelings are shared by only a tiny minority of the population (which is no doubt true, although difficult to prove), amounts to a superficial analysis of anti-colonialist mobilisation, underestimating its social roots and its influence on Franco-African relations generally. In order to go further, it is useful to place Ivorian anti-colonialism in both a historical and a continental perspective.

The current violent wave of ultranationalism expresses an alienation that is both of long standing and has deep roots in Ivorian society. Furthermore, there is a comparable situation in some of Côte d'Ivoire's francophone neighbours who have never cut the umbilical cord that links them to their former motherland. To be sure, the relationship with France has been more pronounced in Côte d'Ivoire than anywhere else as a result of the political, economic and strategic choice made by President Houphouët-Boigny to remain within the ambit of the former colonial power. Faced by advocates of Pan-Africanism, Houphouët-Boigny defended the idea of a francophone community and the maintenance of a privileged relationship with Paris even after independence. In marked contrast with his neighbour Nkrumah, he built his country's prosperity by reinforcing the former colonial relationship in every sphere, including military, economic, political and cultural affairs. If there is one country where, in effect, independence involved hardly more than the raising of a new flag, that country is Côte d'Ivoire, where for decades the functions of sovereignty were exercised by French personnel and where even the country's security was guaranteed not by a national army but by the *43ème Bima*, the permanent French garrison in Abidjan. The commanding heights of the economy too were in French hands. The vigour of the current wave of nationalism is clearly linked to this history of alienated sovereignty, and in this sense, the call for a second independence is real. This much is well known, but what is less widely appreciated is that, at the same time as they enjoyed their economic rents and their political alliance with Paris, Houphouët-Boigny and his colleagues deliberately suppressed any reference to local history that could have served to underpin any rival version of nationalism. The current violent wave is also related to this suppression of national memory, as witnessed, for example, by the importance in public discussion of certain painful episodes, such as the repression of the Guébié revolt in 1970. During a critical phase in the formation of the Ivorian state and economy, the strategic choice made in favour of extraversion and Franco-African partnership is the reason that many Ivorians today suffer from what has been called 'a lack of self-representation'.[10] In classic fashion, this may be rectified by a war of liberation.

This line of enquiry can be extended further. Paradoxically, perhaps, it may be argued that the current brand of aggressive ultranationalism is the product of an essentially democratic debate concerning the question of who constitutes 'the people' and on the nature of sovereignty. Jean-Pierre Dozon, in his analysis of Ivorian nationalism, has correctly noted that during the long period of single-party rule, these questions were conspicuous by their absence:

> ... during these years, in effect the Ivorian people was no more than an emanation of the individual who, in the absence of any democratic mechanisms ... to a large extent assumed personally the role of the sovereign power. In endowing the latter with a political-religious dimension or a charismatic legitimacy, Houphouët-Boigny developed a conception of the people solely in regard to himself ... Consequently, insofar as sovereignty was not located in the people and, from Houphouët-Boigny's point of view, he could fashion it as he deemed fit, the question of immigration from outside the country or the distinction between 'foreigners' and 'nationals' simply made no sense (Dozon 2000:60).

In this light, it is not surprising that debates on sovereignty and the identity of citizens accompanied the call for an end to single-party politics and that the FPI, the party in the forefront of the struggle for democracy, should have made of sovereignty and identity its leading demand under the euphemism of 'civic nationalism'. The subsequent history of this issue is well known, and notably how the political struggles to assume the succession to Houphouët-Boigny, the war and the FPI's search for a source of legitimation have gradually pushed debate towards an ethnic definition of nationalism and a nativist concept of citizenship.

The complex history of Ivorian nationalism needs to be taken into account by anyone who seeks to understand the current conflict and contribute to its eventual resolution. If the fundamental question at issue is that of sovereignty and citizenship, it is hard to see how an externally imposed arrangement could provide a solution – not to mention the logic of trusteeship that has become steadily more apparent since the Security Council's adoption of Resolution 1633 in October 2005.

Conclusion

Whatever happens next, France in particular, and the international community in general, will have to take note of the fact that the Ivorian conflict represents a new page in the history of the Franco-African relationship. The crisis in this relationship, now of several years' duration, is reaching a climax, for better or for worse. The virulent anti-French diatribes heard in Abidjan certainly have a purely instrumentalist dimension and may well not reflect the sentiments of a silent majority of Ivorians who would be content to see the resumption of the long-standing relationship with France. But, even among this sector of the population, people express a deep-seated wish to redefine the relations of cooperation. If they want to leave the current confrontation behind

---

[10] An expression used by Ousmane Dembélé, personal communication.

them, it is not in order to return to the past, but to establish a more normal type of relationship, shorn of the unwholesome aspects implied by references to *la Françafrique*.

Such an aspiration is not new, to be sure, but it is gaining ground all over the continent of Africa, increasingly often in violent form. Anti-French demonstrations in Lomé or N'Djamena are further evidence of the wish of the public in various parts of francophone Africa to break free from old patterns of intrusion. Here, as elsewhere, the theme of anti-colonialism is accompanied by demands for a more meaningful democracy, an aspiration that has received too little support from Paris since the early 1990s. Confusingly, perhaps, other political, ideological and intellectual currents may also be detected in the same movement, expressed with renewed vigour, and not only in countries that were once colonies of France. In Congo, South Africa, Ethiopia and even in Senegal, new political and nationalist movements are gestating in various forms, all aspiring to forge a new Africanist political identity. In regard to what he calls 'African modes of self-writing', Achille Mbembe notes that 'philosophical inquiry into the conditions of access of the African subject to a sense of fulfilment has historically been couched in the liturgical mode of victimisation. Two main ideological currents have, on this basis, aimed to establish a politics of Africanness: a Marxist current and a nationalist one, that may be labeled "nativist"' (Mbembe 2000:16). Mbembe regrets that these philosophical currents, based as they are on a polemical relationship with the outside world and a self-abasing concept of the self, have led to the constitution of a 'metaphysics of difference' that exalts the condition of nativism and an identity based on exclusion. In this paradigm, 'there can be no more radical utopian vision than the one suggesting that Africa disconnect itself from the world – the mad dream of a world without Others' (Mbembe 2002:252). One may respond by pointing out that the logic of an exclusionary identity is espoused by only a small minority in Africa, generally in intellectual circles. Nevertheless, it remains the case that, as Mbembe writes:

> A more significant development has been an emerging junction between the old anti-imperialist thematics – 'revolution', 'anticolonialism' – and the nativist theses. Fragments of these imaginaries are now combining to oppose globalization, to relaunch the metaphysics of difference, to reenchant tradition, and to revive the utopian vision of an Africanity that is coterminous with blackness (*Ibid.*: 263–264).

The Ivorian case is only the most dramatic example of this fusion between the registers of anti-colonial revolution and autochthony. Other traces of the same element can be found elsewhere, notably in Zimbabwe, or in Congo, which is also home to a persistent contest pitting the "original" population against others deemed to be non-originals. In more complex form, the same tendency is present in the discourse of the African renaissance or, on another level, in an Afrocentric epistemology that makes nativism a prerequisite for scientific knowledge and legitimacy.

Fortunately, the meta-narrative of exclusionary identity is not the only mode in which the contemporary history of African societies may be related. Claims also exist for another major paradigm – that of an Africanness that is fully part of the world and of a universal politics. The latter idea contains within itself a certain notion of citizenship that is in harmony with the reality of societies in today's Africa, which are fundamentally cosmopolitan in nature.[11] Africans themselves will determine which of these two utopian visions guides their political future. However, the attitude of external powers, especially France and the rest of Europe, will certainly have an influence on the outcome. If the northern powers – especially the signatories of the Schengen Accord that imposes such strict limits in immigration to its member-states – continue to regard Africa as being on the fringes of the world, the condition of regarding the rich world through a window, as the Comaroffs have written (2001), could eventually contribute to an Afrocentrism that is still more aggressive than anything that may be witnessed at present.

[11]   See on this theme the Special Issue of *Politique Africaine* entitled *Cosmopolis. L'Afrique dans le monde* 100 (2005).

References

Banégas, Richard and Ruth Marshall-Fratani. 2003. *La Côte d'Ivoire en Guerre: Dynamiques du dedans et du dehors,* Special Issue of *Politique Africaine* 89.

Bayart, Jean-François. 1993. *The State in Africa: The Politics of the Belly.* Cambridge: Polity Press.

Chabasseur, Eglantine. 2004. La construction des figures de l' 'assaillant' et du 'patriote' dans la presse ivoirienne depuis le 19 Septembre 2002. Unpublished Master thesis, Etudes Africaines, University of Paris 1.

Chauveau, Jean-Pierre. 2000. Question Foncière et Construction Nationale en Côte d'Ivoire: Les Enjeux Silencieux d'un Coup d'Etat' *Politique Africaine* 78:94–125.

Chauveau, Jean-Pierre and Samuel Bobo. 2003. La Situation de Guerre dans l'Arène Villageoise: Un Exemple dans le Centre-Ouest Ivoirien. *Politique Africaine* 93:12–32.

Comaroff, Jean and John L. Comaroff. 2001. *Millennial Capitalism and the Culture of Neoliberalism.* Durham, NC: Duke University Press.

Dembélé, Ousmane. 2002. La Construction Economique et Politique de la Catégorie 'Etranger' en Côte d'Ivoire. In *Côte d'Ivoire, l'année terrible – 1999–2000,* eds. Marc Le Pape and Claudine Vidal. Paris: Karthala.

Dozon, Jean-Pierre. 2000. La Côte d'Ivoire entre Démocratie, Nationalisme et Ethnonationalisme. *Politique Africaine* 78:45–61.

Konaté, Yacouba. 2003. Les Enfants de la Balle: De la Fesci aux Mouvements de Patriotes. *Politique Africaine* 89:49–70.

Koulibaly, Mamadou 2003. *La Guerre de la France contre la Côte d'Ivoire.* La Refondation, Abidjan.

Le Pape, Marc and Claudine Vidal. 2002. *Côte d'Ivoire, l'année terrible – 1999–2000.* Paris: Karthala.

Mary, André. 2002. Prophètes Pasteurs: La Politique de la Délivrance en Côte d'Ivoire. *Politique Africaine* 87: 69–94.

Mbembe, Achille. 2000. A propos des Ecritures Africaines de Soi. *Politique Africaine* 77: 16–45.

——— 2002. African Modes of Self-writing. *Public Culture* 14(1):239–273.

Zoro-Bi, Eglantine. 2004. *Juge en Côte d'Ivoire: Désarmer la Violence.* Paris: Karthala.

14

Beyond Civil Society: Child Soldiers as Citizens in Mozambique

CAROL B. THOMPSON (1999)

The conditions match any of the most terrifying and depraved suffered by past generations afflicted by war. Yet the victims are not only soldiers. At the beginning of this century, 90% of war casualties in the world were military; today about 90% are civilian. Yet even this sobering UNDP (1994) figure does not name the problem, for the term 'civilian' obfuscates the vulnerability and innocence of child victims. The conditions for children who are forced to bear arms erase the traditional analytical categories of military, civilian and child. An estimated 300,000 children under 18, some as young as five years old, are currently serving in 36 wars around the world (Brett and McCallin 1998:19, 24).

In some of the wars, traditional gender distinctions have also been erased, as girls are forced to bear arms and boys are forced to render sexual service. Both have been used as cannon fodder (for example, Liberia, Uganda) advanced as the first wave of infantry-style assaults with the purpose of inhibiting the enemy, who may be reluctant to fire at children.

By employing the case of Mozambique, this study first raises the question of why children face this new technique of abuse. The military answer is easy: in the last 20 years, modern technology has provided weapons which weigh less than seven pounds, cost about US$6, and can be stripped, reassembled, loaded and fired by an illiterate child of 10. The social, political and economic answers are more difficult.

Second, throughout this paper, questions will be raised about current theorising, suggesting that our theories are still lacking in concept formation and explanatory power to elucidate the destruction of community caused by the use of child soldiers. The social reconstruction necessary is much more difficult than rebuilding roads or schools. This study proposes that the use of child soldiers and their reintegration into communities may require displacing theories of civil society as a corollary to democracy.

Third, the study analyses why the reintegration of boy soldiers and other 'children under difficult circumstances' (traumatised by war, exploited, displaced) was relatively successful in Mozambique, offering a beacon for humanity. UN Deputy High Commissioner for Refugees, Sergio Viera de Mello, stated there was 'no form of recrimination or hatred' among Mozambicans and praised this as 'the culture of reconciliation, the culture of peace' (Mozambique News Agency 1996:14). As will be discussed, community values and community organising are reintegrating Mozambican children, not the formal institutions of the state, nor of opposition parties, nor of the economy.

Boy soldiers and girl 'slave wives'

The origins of Renamo (Mozambique National Resistance) are well documented and only need brief reference here to remind us of the history that forms the background for the use of child soldiers. During the final years of the war against Zimbabwean guerrillas, the Rhodesian secret service recruited and trained Mozambicans, hostile to the ruling party of Frelimo in Mozambique, to locate and eliminate the Zimbabwean guerrillas finding sanctuary in Mozambique; they were also to terrorise Mozambicans who were supporting the Zimbabwean combatants and refugees. Just before the independence of Zimbabwe in 1980, Rhodesian intelligence transferred these Mozambicans to apartheid South Africa.

The apartheid regime turned this small group of 'counter-revolutionaries' into an army for the systematic destabilisation of the Mozambican state and economy by attacking not the Mozambican army, but civilians and infrastructure (Gorongosa Documents 1986; Hanlon 1984; Minter 1994). Apartheid commanders armed, trained and led Renamo. As the destabilisation expanded, Renamo commanders became more independent, but never autonomous, from their external patrons (Nilsson 1990; United Nations 1995; Vines 1991). Therefore, many scholars refer to the war (escalated in 1981 until the peace accord in 1992) as a war of destabilisation, not a civil war.

Documentation over more than a decade concludes that Renamo systematically recruited boys to train as soldiers; girls became personal servants, including sexual services, with some remaining with one man or boy for years, later to be designated as 'wife'. Documentation also shows that the government of Mozambique forcefully conscripted some unemployed urban youth (14–16 years). Yet international agencies conclude that the use of boy soldiers for transport of goods and for armed combat was overwhelmingly Renamo, not government, practice.

The leadership of Renamo consistently denied they were even using boy soldiers, let alone forcefully recruiting them. In February 1994, however, Renamo agreed with UNICEF (1994:3) to transfer child soldiers to non-military transit centres, which took almost a year to accomplish. The very first soldier demobilised at the end of the war in 1992 submitted his gun and then told the press he was 16 years old, was kidnapped in Gaza at the age of 9 and had been fighting ever since (UNICEF 1994:37). Many accounts of the war document Renamo's recruitment of boys by capture (Gersony 1988; Magaia 1988; UNICEF 1994).

Renamo engaged in a 'pillage economy', by living off the fruits of others' labour, goods which they stole as war booty, and therefore required porters for logistical survival. It appears that the military did not generally practise agriculture or other productive activities. Although varying widely depending on whether the zone was a 'tax area', a 'destruction area' or a 'control area' (Gersony 1988), tactics were generally predatory for labour, food, and energy. When production occurred around Renamo camps, it was by the captured civilians (most often women), who were kept in different parts of the camp from the military. Even where 'taxes' were collected, such 'support' must be seen in relative terms, for recruitment of combatants was still primarily by capture (Roesch 1992).

During an attack, Renamo often forced boys to kill parents or relatives by the soldiers beginning to cut off a finger, a limb until the parent begged the child to finish him/her off. Some had to hold down their mothers or sisters while the soldiers raped them. Others were forced to kill or be killed. Renamo's tactics earned the movement a 'well-deserved reputation for savagery'. Renamo was feared for its policy of 'mutilating civilians, including children, by cutting off ears, noses, lips and sexual organs' (Human Rights Watch 1992:27 and 1998:26). Children were taken from the village to act as porters to carry the booty; those who faltered on the trail were killed (loads up to 60 kg reported, Machel 1996:18). Beatings and near starvation became initiation.

Complete obedience was required, to the extent that the boys depended on their commanders for any decision such as when to eat, bathe and sleep. Rewards included some use of drugs (marijuana) and being given a girl as a 'wife', sometimes for a few hours, sometimes more permanent. In the South, only commanders were allowed to bring women into temporary bases, the rest were 'attaching themselves' to the civilian population.[1] In the North, large bases included more girls (UNICEF 1994:40). Rank and responsibility were given as rewards for doing something special, and usually it was some kind of atrocity. Referring to the same reward system for boys in Liberia, a UN commander pointed out, 'it's the only competition they have' (Human Rights Watch 1994:30).

Recruitment of children is considered desirable because of children's energy levels. Second, they are more susceptible to propaganda and, therefore, more readily obey. Third, their moral values are still in formation so they can more easily than an adult suspend moral judgments. Right becomes one with obedience: commanders say child soldiers are 'more obedient, do not question orders and are easier to manipulate than adult soldiers' (Machel 1996:16). Fourth, with fewer skills and less knowledge about the area, they are less likely to escape successfully. Finally, they don't demand pay.

The females never advanced in authority, remaining totally subordinate to the males with whom they were 'attached'. There is no record of girl soldiers in Mozambique (Muianga 1995:68; interview, Ruth Ansa Ayisi, UNICEF-Maputo, 26 June 1996). Renamo reinforced the gender division of labour, with women cooking, cleaning and growing crops for the men. They could also be passed around from soldier to soldier. Kenneth Wilson (1992a:536) describes Renamo's exploitation of women as a reward for combatants:

> Rape and the use of slave-wives is rather seen by Renamo soldiers as simply their right of access to women, and a key 'perk' of the job, not a direct tactic of war... Renamo commanders repeatedly stress their special rights to women and girls, along with the status and prowess that this confers upon them as men of power relative to the Renamo rank and file... The almost ritualised allocation of women to Renamo soldiers after their initiation has also been reported.

---

[1] Much has been made of the idea that Renamo used different tactics in different parts of the country, for example, raping women less frequently in northern Mozambique than in southern. While not doubting that military tactics required different approaches in 'zones of control' vs. territory through which Renamo passed, the destruction, brutality and rape were systematic policies of Renamo. The Jeichande (1990) survey documents the degree of brutality against women in northern Mozambique, even where Renamo was interested in instilling allegiance among the population, Wilson (1992a: 529–31) documents the contradictory variation of Renamo tactics. See also Gersony (1988).

The strategy and tactics used in the war relate to the goals. There was no interest in defeating the Mozambican army, but the targets became whatever symbolised the state – from schools and clinics to anyone bringing services from the state (for example, teachers, health workers, railway workers). Atrocities occurred to separate the victims and perpetrators from their social context, their future. For boy soldiers, it rendered them totally dependent on the commanders. For others, the degree of violence was to destroy the social fabric of communities which were relating to the central state or just trying to remain neutral. Sergio Viera, a member of parliament, stated that the aim of the war was to create a 'nonsociety' (Nordstrom 1997: 130).

Socio-economic impact of the war

This pillage economy – of structures, people and psyches – brought productive capacity to a stand-still in many areas. Whole parts of the countryside were emptied of people, as villagers fled to urban areas, to foraging in the bush, and to neighbouring countries. For those in the war zones, including the more remote towns, many services were disrupted, from literacy classes to access to safe drinking water, to health care.

A few statistics denote the overall extent of suffering: 30% of the population were displaced from their villages (5 million) and 47% of the primary schools became dysfunctional (some estimates give over 50% of the schools). About 1 million died, out of a population of 16.6 million. After the war, student-teacher ratios were estimated at 80:1 (Ansa Ayisi 1996). In 1991, 62% of the population had no formal education, a statistic that dramatically demonstrates the difficulties reconstruction still confronts. The war also created a high rate of urbanisation (national: 6%; Zambezia province: 15%), increasing the urban sprawl of unemployed and destitute (Governo de Moçambique 1995).

Health care delivery, which won international awards in the early 1980s, was crippled. During the height of the war, women were delivering in the bush in the dark, fearing to light even a candle. The statistics show the results: an estimated of 1 in 9 in northern Zambezia province risked death during pregnancy or childbirth; in Maputo province 1 in 18; in North Europe, the ratio is 1:10,000. Under 5 mortality rates were almost five times that of neighbouring Botswana and over four times of recently post-apartheid South Africa (Governo de Moçambique 1994; world comparison given by World Bank 1994).

What these social conditions indicate is that the first community (and national) agenda is to recreate production and exchange networks to guarantee food supply, for they cannot rely on commercial markets, which do not exist without roads, telecommunications, warehouses or capital. Rebuilding infrastructure is especially hazardous in many areas, for an estimated 2 million land mines were laid, with some 10,000 victims; a legacy that will continue to maim not only the individuals but handicap the communities who depended on them for productive activities.

Rebuilding schools and health clinics has been a priority, with some success. In 1997 the government increased the number of functioning primary schools by 12%, with pre-war levels reached by 1999. But staffing them takes much longer, with the goal being a teacher/student ratio of 1:50 (from the post-war

1:80). Human resource development is much more difficult to redeem than mud walls and desks.

Socio-political impact of the war

Peace was brokered in Mozambique in 1992, during the worst drought of the century in southern Africa and as the transition from apartheid was under way. National elections were held in 1994, with Renamo running as a political party, heavily financed (including its own radio transmitter) by foreigners who wanted to ensure 'multi-party' elections, considered a necessary, if not sufficient, condition for democracy. Speaking of democratisation under the above socio-economic conditions, however, gives scholars pause (Huber et al. 1993; Macamo 1995). A right to equal justice entails not only the responsibility of the state to ensure formal equality before the law. More fundamentally, it requires that citizens have the capacity (health, skills, literacy, resources) to take advantage of the processes of representation and justice. If equal protection before the law is improbable, because of the thoroughness of destruction of social resources in the community, participation in formal state institutions becomes formidable. Only a very few villagers have the time, physical energy, health, or education to participate. Conceptualisations of liberal democracy, which focus on the technical exercise of holding periodic elections, demonstrate the worst case of 'grand theory' modelling imposed on local sites (Ake 1996; Shin 1994). David Held, long-time scholar of democratic transformations, laments:

> no current conceptualisation of liberal democracy is able adequately to specify the conditions for the possibility of *political participation by all citizens...* the structure of civil society (including private ownership of productive property, vast sexual and [ethnic] inequalities), which is misunderstood or endorsed by liberal democratic models, does not create conditions for effective participation, proper political understanding and equal control of the political agenda (1990:16, emphasis added).

Approaches (theoretical and applied) to democratisation which ignore the local conditions of deprivation that preclude 'effective participation' will be meaningless to the local communities. Indeed, inequality is so severe in Mozambique that many question whether 'stability', with or without democratic participation, can endure. Deputy Minister of Social Welfare Filipe Mandiate reported that poverty is deepening (25 February 1998): 'the data currently available show that... the scale and intensity of poverty and social exclusion are reaching intolerable and unacceptable levels'. Economic gains can 'only be preserved through the guarantee of a basic social peace' (Mozambique News Agency 1998: 20). In addition to the socio-economic conditions which challenge democratisation, Mozambican Jamisse Taimo (1995:149) raises the cultural difference: the concept of democracy as it is understood and elaborated in the West will encounter problems of application as does a pot of flowers replanted without considering climatic conditions or the environment.

One might expect that theories of civil society, of its interaction with the state, would correct the above contradictions. Theories of civil society address discourses of social and religious associations, cultural groups and other non-state activities encouraging participation and cooperation. Yet the appropriateness of this concept in the Mozambican context is also questioned.

Civil society

Gaining popularity during the theoretical and policy offensive against the state in the 1980s, the concept civil society generally refers to that segment of society that interacts and influences the state but remains distinct from it. It addresses the dynamic, complex and ambivalent relation between state and society. For neoliberal theorists, civil society is to complement private enterprise, to curb the power of the state; antistatist, this approach to civil society privileges private property (for elaboration, see Harbeson et al. 1994; Hyden 1997). Another approach, the associational school, focuses on the importance of autonomous associations in promoting the role of citizenship. The current appeal of creating non-governmental organisations (NGOs) in post-war societies is based on the principle of advancing active popular participation. While the first approach entitles private property, this view of civil society may also entitle the very few who have resources (for example, education, communication) by which to organise and pursue their interests (for debate, see Beckman 1993; Ndegwa 1996; Marcussen 1996; Allen 1997).

A third approach criticises the power and domination embedded in formal organisations of civil society: 'By generally reflecting the lopsided balance of class, ethnic and sexual power, the organisations of civil society tend inevitably to privilege the privileged and marginalise the marginalised' (Fatton 1995:72).

Researchers, for example, find that African women network informally more than in civic organisations, because the formal organisations marginalise women; agreeing with Fatton, they call for the redefinition of the political, not simply of civil society (for example, Tripp 1994:153, 162). This approach defines civil society not so much as a public arena of politics, but as a terrain for struggle where social forces compete to delineate the national ideology, to define legitimacy, and to gain power.

After independence in 1975, Frelimo used the single-party state to build national consciousness and local participation, first through 'dynamising groups' and then through mass organisations. However, the agenda was often directed by the central state and, in attempting to inculcate a national identity, often promoted values antithetical to local cultures. Many, for example, have written about how the OMM (Organisation of Mozambican Women) was constrained in improving women's condition; few have analysed how extraordinary the OMM message was in a patriarchal village setting (Harrison 1996; Kruks and Wisner 1989; Sheldon 1994). Renamo took advantage of this clash of values, reviving traditional norms and roles, reasserting patriarchy and chieftaincy. To the extent that Renamo had support from local villagers, their leaders denounced Frelimo's disrespect for local traditions. Mozambicans freely joining Renamo cited the denigration of traditional values and the replacement of traditional family compounds with communal villages as the primary reasons for rejecting Frelimo (Geffray 1991; Wilson 1992a, b).

What is passing now in Mozambique as key for (re) creating civil society is nongovernmental organisations (NGOs), local and international; they build 'capacity' by offering chances to practise local organising. Most local and foreign NGOs view a quantitative increase in the number of voluntary associations as a sign of the growing strength of civil society to delineate legitimacy.

Using the associational approach discussed above, these NGOs see the this formation of civil society as 'filling the empty spaces in African politics' (Abrahamsson and Nilsson 1995:266). However, as Sogge (1997:45) points out, NGOs are 'the smallest, youngest and perhaps weakest type of actor in the civil sector, despite being the most sought-after by aid agencies'. And they are not always as neutral as they appear, often ignoring rural social relations, often reinforcing the agenda of a rapidly emerging business class. Some NGOs, more neoliberal in their approach, as well-documented by Hanlon (1991), are directly assisting this class formation in Mozambique, seeing the 'private sector', no matter how large the corporations or how foreign, as a necessary control on the state.

Jeannette Hartmann explains the difficulty of formulating civil society in Africa through its origins: both state and national societies are artificial entities created first by colonialism and consolidated by external economic linkages, but remaining transient (1994:221): 'The processes (bringing state and society together) were transposed in time, collapsing many multi-ethnic nations and concentrating them into the formation of a state and society... a transformation, which would have taken years and probably centuries to evolve and develop, was instead carried out within less than a century.'

Hartmann also points out that African political alliances and discourse are often mediated through ethnicity. Strong ethnic loyalties and consciousness translate the meaning of allegiance to a state. If the state falters in providing security or distributing resources, primary political allegiances can quickly return to ethnic or religious patterns, even if the distinctions of who belongs to which group were long ago blurred by marriage or migration. Hartmann was not reductionist in her explanation of the mediating role of ethnicity, and the Mozambican experience confirms both the importance of ethnic identity and pervasive inter-community assistance. As will be demonstrated shortly, Mozambicans came to the aid of those beyond the borders of their villages, their districts and their languages.

Mozambican traditions have many non-economic means for exchange, such as reciprocity and redistribution (Abrahamsson and Nilsson 1995:178; Sulemani 1995). Families accept mutual or social responsibility for long-term survival, such as sharing food and fields. Most relevant here, the up-bringing of children is accepted as a social, reciprocal responsibility. Children belong to the extended family and to the whole clan.

Redistribution most often refers to food, where the chief and elders have enough information and moral authority to know which families are in need and to allocate goods from the collective surplus. Those in trouble received assistance through shared labour. Especially in times of war or drought, the social fabric depends as much, or more, on this reciprocity within the collectivity, than on market exchange of commodities. Non-economic control mechanisms often did ensure survival.[2] Actual practices, of course, are open to abuse, with various hierarchies (gender, age, local chieftaincies) creating disparities.

Several African theorists, therefore, agree with Hartmann that the concept of civil society seems inappropriate for explanation of participation, loyalty, or the

---

[2] During the worst drought in the century in 1992, 20 million people were at risk of starvation in the southern Africa region, but no one starved. In the post-drought evaluations by numerous international relief agencies, much credit was given to the extended families who shared what they had, from urban to rural, from the 'wealthy uncle' to the poorest.

mobilisation of social resources (Osasghase 1994; Sulemani 1995). Most poignantly expressed are the questions of Mamdani:

> For what indeed is that vast sea of humanity that falls outside the parameters of 'civil society'? What is that inexhaustible reserve of 'tradition' that state-centrists see as the hotbed of 'particularism'? Is it not the original community from which 'society' is supposed to have emerged? That natural habitat that 'modern man' is supposed to have left behind as he (and she) entered 'civil society'? Is 'community' not the silent residual term in the polarity of which 'civil society' is the lead term? (1995:613)

The concept appears to be too narrowly confined by Western traditions to explain social relations, where extended families and communities, not commodities, still define rural life: 'It is not so much the state-civil society opposition but rather the capital-community opposition that seems to be the great unsurpassed contradiction in Western social philosophy... Community, which ideally, should have been banished from the kingdom of capital, continues to lead a subterranean, potentially subversive life within it because it refuses to go away' (Chatterjee 1990:130).

In order to discuss rebuilding a polity, with active citizens setting norms for government behaviour, community practices and symbols (familial, economic, cultural) need to be incorporated into political analysis, not treated as a relic for academics to marvel at or as a 'residual' to ignore. At the very least, 'civil society' (interpreted as 'behaviour by which cultures define rules', Harbeson et al. 1994:299) as a concept must incorporate informal and sporadic, as well as formal, associations and networking.

Renamo employed tactics of severe violence to destroy familial identity and attachment to community. Requiring children to commit heinous acts, such as killing family members or torturing another child, alters identity; the children must then look to the commanders for survival, no longer the community nor the clan. Therefore, while Renamo propagandised to chiefs and religious leaders against the centralising culture of Frelimo, it also violated traditional values by its methods of conscription. Reports recount that local spiritual leaders had allied with Renamo because of Frelimo's ideological hostility but, by the late 1980s, they became alienated by Renamo's tactics and began to accept Frelimo's increasingly conciliatory position toward traditional leaders (Wilson 1992a: 548; Pitcher 1996:27).

Reintegration and cultural affirmation

Both the soldiers and victims understood that savage use of violence was to destroy both personal integrity and family relations; as one victim stated, 'They have not just killed my family and taken my home, they have killed my soul' (Nordstrom 1997: 114). Yet it is these very norms, resilient and adaptable to new demands, which have promoted and nurtured reintegration of traumatised children. In 1983 and 1984, provisional centres were set up for traumatised children who were severely afflicted by the destabilisation war, but this policy of separate centres with mainly medical personnel proved not successful (Kanji 1990:108; interview, Eunice Mucache, Mozambican Red Cross, 28 June 1996). By 1987, when the first boy soldiers began returning from Renamo territory, Mozambican welfare officials decided that Western individualistic psychology had only limited insight to offer for healing. Modern techniques were employed, but alongside of traditional ones, with the latter proving to be more effective.[3] At certain stages, psychologists have been involved to classify the degree of trauma, but healing has generally not occurred through psychoanalysis.

This local policy has been verified cross-nationally in six regions (Europe, West and Central Africa, Eastern and Southern Africa, Asia and Pacific, and Latin America) by a UN study on the impact of war on children. A combination of approaches is best, with 'normalcy' and engaging in community life essential for healing:

> Psychotherapeutic approaches based on western mental health traditions tend to emphasise individual emotional expression... While many forms of external intervention can help promote psychosocial recovery, experience with war trauma programs has shown that even those designed with the best intentions can do harm... In-depth clinical interviews intended to awaken the memories and feelings associated with a child's worst moments risk leaving the child in more severe pain and agitation than before ... Rather than focusing on a child's emotional wounds, programs should aim to support healing processes and to reestablish a sense of normalcy... including community life (Machel 1996:51, 53).

From the mid-1980s, Mozambican policy has centred on the community – first, to give material assistance to vulnerable families so they could sustain their children and second, to reunite children with families as quickly as possible (Muianga 1995). Traditional healers *(curandeiros)* provide psychosocial intervention which builds on the strengths of families, rather than on the concept of pathology. Whole families were affected by the war, with adults feeling guilty for not protecting the child who was captured (Interview, Criancas e Familias Desenvolvimento, CFD, 27 June 1996). Many ways were found to reintegrate the child who was lost.

Muslim, Christian and traditional religious leaders adapted purification rituals for cleansing and reintegrating those returning. Traditional purification ceremonies, for example, often isolate the returned child for a few days to re-establish communication with the ancestors. Herbs are used to cleanse; harmful spirits are exorcised. The child discards his/her identity and becomes as a different person. Further, ceremonies call on the ancestral spirits, who are all-knowing; no one can hide what s/he did, what atrocities committed. Reconnection with the ancestors is the first acceptance back into the community. Thus, the child is absolved of the behaviour of the previous, discarded identity. Children emerging from purification have been able to recount their experiences, considered by Western psychology as basic to the healing process. In contrast, many of those treated by Western psychoanalysis were never able to recount their stories (UNICEF 1994: 46).

To give one concrete example, in Xai Xai a family decided a daughter could move in only after a house purification ceremony was held, normally performed only when a member of the family has passed away. She was kidnapped when only 11 and forced to serve as a soldier's wife; she became pregnant but the child was still-born. After the ceremonies, her family accepted her as a 'new'

---

[3] South Africa has also used a combination of the traditional with modern techniques to reintegrate their 'lost generation' of township youth. For one excellent account, see Robertson and de Kiewit (1998).

daughter, totally different from the one who left (Save the Children 1995: 12). Bonding can begin again. Anthropologist Carolyn Nordstrom (1997:210) quotes at length a group of older women from a village devastated by the war who explain:

> 'We ask that everyone who arrives here be taken to a *curandeira* or a *curandeiro* [healer] for treatment. The importance of the *curandeiro* lies not only in her or his ability to treat the diseases and physical ravages of war, but in their ability to take the violence out of a person and to reintegrate them back into a healthy lifestyle. You see, people who have been exposed to the war, well, some of this violence can affect them, stick with them, like a rash on the soul... (the *curandeiros*) work with the whole family, they include the community. They cut the person off from any holds the war has on him or her, they scrape off the violence from their spirit,.... they make them alive again, alive and part of the community.

In contrast to Western cultures, responsibility for injustice is not an individual concern. Responsibility is a social issue. Families of the perpetrators of violence performed ceremonies to placate the spirits; often a community paid compensation, showing up even during the war to bring an embattled village cows, goats, seeds. Nordstrom concludes (1997:215): 'The message was clear: Nothing justifies this violence, even the actions of our kin. This is not a war about villagers and we will do what is in our power to stop it.'

Two programmes devised in Mozambique – one for healing traumatised children and one for tracing children separated from family members – build on Mozambican traditions and cultures. They de-emphasise the negative legacy of war and build on the strongest community resources: familiarity and reciprocity. For example, traumatised children are not viewed as pathological, but as family members who need nurturing. The programmes affirm and engage indigenous knowledge that is valued by the communities, rather than rely on highly technical 'expertise' or equipment.

Brincar curando (healing through play) originated in 1993 and has been promoted in six provinces by the Mozambican Red Cross (Draisma 1995; Fleming 1995). Volunteers have been trained to conduct games which encourage children to concentrate and participate. Group games, story-telling, theatre, and songs reinforce Mozambican cultures and increase social interaction among all children in groups of about 40. The volunteers can then distinguish the ones who might need additional attention, for they exhibit contrary behaviour, such as not joining in the play, inability to focus, or hostility. The activities stimulate the entire community and help everyone to deal with their own war experiences. The community joins in to help the child become less aggressive. Gradually, by rebuilding trust, the child may be able to go to school and to learn productive skills.

The volunteers are women of the village, who receive a few hours of training. Many have accepted children in their own homes, acting as foster parents until the birth parents were located; many have accepted children in their homes permanently. Most of the women were illiterate and suffering from their own war experiences, including loss of family members, dislocation for years from the home village, and physical deprivation (Interview, Eunice Mucache, Mozambique Red Cross, 28 June 1996). Yet they had the strength to assist the little ones with their own trauma, often patiently seeking out a child who would not join the play group. A woman might daily for months go and sit quietly near a child, simply to offer a human, non-threatening, presence. Only slowly would the child begin to trust the adult enough to accept a drink of water or exchange a few words with her. Later the child may join the play group. Only much later would the story emerge.

The lessons which Mozambicans say they have learned from this success is to trust their own cultures' ability to heal (Honwana 1995). Their traditions offer effective means for social and psychological integration.[4]

The second programme of tracing children who had been captured or lost during the long war was only partially successful until traditional networks were mobilised. After the peace accord in 1992, NGOs used computer lists and airplanes to trace children who had been separated from their families; they placed about one child per week. As Mozambican volunteers, male and female, organised via their traditional networks, in coordination with the NGOs, the success rate became very high.

In the cities and at centres, posters were made from pictures of 21 displaced children per poster. Mass meetings were then held in villages where details of the displaced child were given, such as the surname, name of grandfather, village names, places named after events – any detail the child shown in the picture could remember. Quickly, the word would spread among chiefs, traditional healers, traders, and travelers; relatives would be located (Interview, Criancas e Familias Desenvolvimento, 27 June 1996; Boothby 1991; da Silva 1995). The UNDP now estimates that 95% of the estimated 250,000 affected children have been reunited with a family member (Interview, UNDP, Maputo, 26 June 1996). In other post-war societies, family tracing programmes are now being implemented using traditional knowledge and community networks (Bonnerjea 1994).

Yet this Mozambican success story has a somber refrain. Neither demobilisation nor tracing seems to have occurred for the girls, who were forced sexual partners – now women with their own children. There is no data about how many were 'linked to' soldiers, how many went home with them during demobilisation to their districts, how many were simply abandoned. UNDP (Interview, Maputo, 26 June 1996) reports Renamo soldiers boarding the vans to return to their home districts, simply leaving the women standing in the road. Women's welfare organisations also reported women and their children being dumped or in other cases being forced to accompany the man. During the exercise to return the demobilised soldiers to their home districts, women were seen trying to get out of the vehicles, screaming, 'I want to go to my home!' (Jacobson 1996:19). About 91,000 male soldiers were demobilised from both sides. How many women/girls were abandoned? How many were coerced into remaining sexual objects? A Mozambican NGO (Interview, CFD, 27 June 1996) stated that some women requested assistance to be reintegrated with their parents but then frequently would not show up to finalise the reunion. If their own families had not endorsed the union with the father (or fathers) of their children, the women could be hesitant to return to their original villages.

One UNICEF study gives a glimpse of the conditions suffered by captured women. In 1990 Ivelte Jeichande interviewed 132 *mulheres dislocadas* ('displaced women', all captured by Renamo) in Maputo province, 83 in Zambezia and 76

---

[4] Foreign psychologists working in Angolan war conditions found that reconstructing a sense of family and using healing rituals were necessary to process the trauma (McIntyre and Ventura 1998: 5).

in Inhambane. Their period of captivity ranged from a few days to over three years; some were moved to as many as six different locations in three years, and over 50% from all three provinces attempted to escape more than once. Of those from Maputo province, 67.5% had experienced death of family members, 63.9 % from Zambezia and 77.6% from Inhambane. Some were forced to have sex with their own children, 'one of the most serious trauma produced by the armed bandits on Mozambican society' (Jeichande 1990: 73). From Zambezia, 26% reported being raped, in Inhambane 1.3%. In Zambezia, 44.6% reported being tortured, 18.4% in Inhambane.

The women stated reasons for husbands rejecting returning wives included her being infected with a sexually transmitted disease (STD), loss of ability to bear children, or her bearing children during the captive period. Returning before the end of the war (1992), they cited the most serious impediments to recuperation as lack of land or materials for artisan activities. They also saw health care as inadequate for their convalescence. Many exhibited some of the same conditions as traumatised children: headaches, irritability, tremors, digestive problems, and difficulty with sleeping.

A UN study covering many more conflicts than Mozambique, also documented the difficulty of girls returning to their homes: 'Reunification may be particularly difficult for girl soldiers who have been raped or sexually abused, in part because cultural beliefs and attitudes can make it very difficult for them to stay with their families or to have any prospects of marriage. With so few alternatives, many children have eventually become victims of prostitution' (Machel 1996:19).

Given the Jeichande study was completed in 1990, it is quite astonishing that Mozambican girls and women still accompanying soldiers at the time of demobilisation in 1994 were not counted, addressed, nor cared for. It appears that no one among either the international or national agencies knows exactly what happened to them. They and their scars remain invisible.

Occasionally we have received reports that the young women may be enduring sexual slavery under new auspices. Human Rights Watch and Anti-Slavery International have reported several cases of Mozambican women being sold to South African men as 'wives'. A South African reporter, exposing the illicit trade, stated he 'purchased' two young Mozambican women, aged 14 and 17, as 'wives' (Human Rights Watch 1998:43; Vines 1991; McKibbin 1992, quoted in Wilson 1992a:6).

This non-finding ('where are the young women?') is not extraordinary for Mozambique, however. The international agencies conducting campaigns to censor the use of child soldiers have not raised the issue of the girls 'given' to the boys as a reward, although the practice appears to occur in every conflict where there are child soldiers. Although both are traumatised, the experiences of boy soldiers differ from the girls. Theories and policies that ignore such a social group cannot claim to be strengthening civil society.

As a way of conclusion – tasks ahead

This analysis suggests that most mainstream definitions and approaches to civil society are too narrowly confined by Western traditions to explain Mozambican social relations, where extended families and communities, not commodities, still define rural life. Yet formulating a new concept will not be unproblematic, for its complexity would need to theorise not only the reciprocity of social relations, but their inequity. Mozambican villages have proven their capacity to heal, but at the same time many perpetuate patriarchy which disadvantages girls and women. The new concept could neither assume the business class dominance inherent in the concept of 'civil society' nor the patriarchy enshrined in many traditional practices. The following quote, from an Argentine psychologist working for 12 years in Mozambique, summarises the complexity of the theoretical tasks ahead: 'While Western culture affirms positivism, free markets, capitalism, individualism and reason; in Africa, the social fabric, extended family, lineage, mutual help, the collective and emotions are central' (AIA 1996).

Second, in addition to the theory-building, the policy tasks ahead are equally consequential. International experience has proven that reintegration of boy soldiers takes more than turning in the guns. In Mozambique, the UN provided 18 months of support to former soldiers to assist their reintegration, giving them time to find jobs or most often, land for farming. Yet the children need schools and training, and families must have basic necessities. The economic prerequisites for reintegration of boy soldiers and other traumatised children are fundamental as the two-year world-wide UN study concluded: 'The field visits and research... repeatedly stressed the importance of links between education, vocational opportunities for former child combatants and the economic security of their families. These are most often the determinants of successful social reintegration and, importantly, they are the factors that prevent re-recruitment' (Machel 1996:20).

Peace must bring basic economic survival, or there will be no peace. Only with the basic means for economic survival can one then begin to speak of political participation, not simply staging elections:

> The elections had made no difference to the oppressive and precarious social position of women in the villages that were visited. Women in Namaua were not centrally concerned with the elections... they were concerned with the fact they had to walk for hours to bring water to the village; they were concerned with the fact that the hospital in Mueda district capital had no medicines... For those women with no husbands, all efforts were focused on bringing up children with no support whatsoever – no welfare state, no NGO support (Harrison 1996:11).

As Harrison points out, one cannot be more marginalised than this – economically and politically. One cannot talk of inclusion or participation of these women in political processes. With few skills and no literacy, they are trying to survive until the next morning, and then the next (see Tripp 1994:155).

Third and finally, this case study demonstrates why the international community needs to support UNICEF's call for children to be 'zones of peace'. The goal is to outlaw adults from using children as targets or as instruments of war. Since 1996, a new effort is being launched to designate rape as a form of torture, to make it unacceptable as a tactic of war, punishable by imprisonment. What these international campaigns have not highlighted, however, is the sexual slavery of girls and women, treated as 'war booty' and quite like property to be used or distributed by the highest-ranking male. Not exactly new, in fact as old as war itself, it is time that this practice is named and condemned as enslavement. The abuse of 'boy soldiers' has attained international notoriety (Coalition to Stop the Use of Child Soldiers 1998). It is time to focus attention on the girls, who may not be 'soldiers', but who are sexually enslaved.

Many children (estimates are as high as 500,000 traumatised or killed) in Mozambique did wither as flowers during the war of destabilisation. But President Samora Machel's maxim is not without hope, for Mozambique is successfully reclaiming most of its traumatised children, offering many lessons to other post-war states. Reintegration of traumatised children and the demobilisation of boy soldiers remain unusual; the first global overview of the use of child soldiers (Brett and McCallin 1998: 140) concluded: 'Because we know so little about what happens to children after demobilisation, the issue of justice as a factor of influencing social reintegration was not documented in the research. It requires further study... to promote reconciliation...'

Perhaps the people in this extremely impoverished economy can also lead the world in directing attention to the young women, who now have their own children from forced concubinage – children that also deserve to be flowers that never wither.

References

Abrahamsson, Hans and Anders Nilsson. 1995. *Mozambique: The Troubled Transition*, London: Zed Books.

Africa Information Afrique (AIA). 1996. Mozambique: Rituals Help Heal Child Soldiers. aiacan@web.apc.org, 24 January.

Ake, Claude. 1996. *Democracy and Development in Africa*, Washington, DC: The Brookings Institution.

Allen, Chris. 1997. Who Needs Civil Society? *Review of African Political Economy* 24(73): 329–337.

Ansa Ayisi, Ruth. 1996. *Moçambique*, Maputo: UNICEF.

Beckman, Bjorn. 1993. The Liberation of Civil Society: Neoliberal Ideology and Political Theory. *Review of African Political Economy* 20(58): 20–34.

Bonnerjea, Lucy. 1994. *Family Tracing*, London: Save the Children.

Boothby, Neil. 1991. Reuniting Unaccompanied Children and Families in Mozambique: An Effort to Link Networks of Community Volunteers to a National Programme. *Journal of Social Development in Africa* 8(2): 11–22.

Brett, Rachel and Margaret McCallin. 1998. *Children: The Invisible Soldiers*. Stockholm: Radda Barnen.

Chatterjee, Partha. 1990. A Response to Taylor's "Modes of Civil Society". *Public Culture* 3(1): 119–132.

Coalition to Stop the Use of Child Soldiers (1998), *Stop Using Child Soldiers!*, London: International Save the Children Alliance.

Draisma, Frieda. 1995. *Psycho-Social Support for Children Healing Through Play*. Maputo: Mozambique Red Cross.

Fatton, Robert. 1995. Africa in the Age of Democratisation: The Civic Limitations of Civil Society. *African Studies Review* 38(2): 67–99.

Fleming, John. 1995. *Brincar Curando*: Healing through Play. In *Transcending the Legacy: Children in the New Southern Africa*, eds. Jeffrey Balch et al. Amsterdam: African-European Institute.

Geffray, Christian. 1991. *A Causa das Armas: Antropologia da Guerra Contemporânea em Moçambique*. Porto: Edições Afrontamento.

Gersony, Robert. 1988. Summary of Mozambican Refugee Accounts of Principally Conflict-Related Experience in Mozambique. Report submitted to Chester A. Crocker, U.S. Department of State, April.

Gorongosa Documents (Documentos da Gorongosa – extractos). 1984. Captured and Released by the Mozambican Government after the Fall of a Renamo Camp in Gorongosa, August 1986.

Hanlon, Joseph. 1991. *Mozambique: Who Calls the Shots?* London: James Currey.

——— 1984. *Mozambique: The Revolution Under Fire*. London: Zed Books.

Harbeson, John, David Rothchild and Naomi Chazan. 1994. *Civil Society and the State in Africa*. Boulder, CO: Lynne Rienner.

Harrison, Graham. 1996. From the 'Global' to the 'Local': Democratisation as 'Inclusion' in Mozambique. Paper presented to the African Studies Association Conference, San Francisco.

Hartmann, Jeannette. 1994. The State in Tanzania. In *African Perspectives on Development: Controversies, Dilemmas and Openings*, eds. Ulf Himmelstrand and Kabiru Kinyanjui. London: James Currey.

Held, David. 1990. The Contemporary Polarisation of Democratic Theory: The Case for a Third Way. In *New Developments in Political Science*, ed. Adrian Leftwich. London: Edward Elgar.

Honwana, Luis Bernardo. 1995. Politica Cultural e Identidade Cultural: Cultura de Paz e Democracia, UNESCO Conference Papers: 67–73.

Huber, Evelyne, Dietrich Rueschemeyer and John D. Stephens. 1993. The Impact of Economic Development on Democracy. *Journal of Economic Perspectives* 7(3): 71–85.

Human Rights Watch. 1998. *Prohibited Persons: Abuse of Undocumented Migrants, Asylum Seekers and Refugees in South Africa.* New York: Human Rights Watch.

—— 1994. *Easy Prey – Child Soldiers in Liberia*, New York: Human Rights Watch.

—— 1992. *Conspicuous Destruction – War, Famine and The Reform Process in Mozambique.* New York: Human Rights Watch.

Hyden, Goran. 1997. Civil Society, Social Capital, and Development: Dissection of a Complex Discourse. *Studies in Comparative International Development* 32(1): 3–30.

Jacobson, Ruth. 1996. Mozambique: Women in the Reconciliation Process. *African Topics* 14: 18–19.

Jeichande, Ivette. 1990. *Mulheres Deslocadas em Maputo, Zambezia e Inhambane.* March, Maputo: UNICEF.

Kanji, Nazneen. 1990. War and Children in Mozambique: Is International Aid Strengthening or Eroding Community-based Policies? *Community Development Journal* 25(2): 102–112.

Kruks, Sonya and Ben Wisner. 1989. Ambiguous Transformations: Women, Politics, and Production in Mozambique. In *Promissory Notes: Women in the Transition to Socialism*, eds. Sonya Kruks, Rayna Rapp and Marilyn B. Young. New York: Monthly Review Press.

Macamo, Eugenio. 1995. War, Adjustment and Civil Society in Mozambique. In *Democracy, Civil Society and the State: Social Movements in Southern Africa*, ed. Lloyd Sachikonye. Harare: Sapes Books.

Machel, Graça. 1996. Impact of Armed Conflict on Children: Report of Expert to UN Secretary-General Submitted to the UN General Assembly. A/51 /306, dated 26 August, released 8 November.

Magaia, Lina. 1988. *Dumba Nengue: Run for Your Life.* Trenton, NJ: Africa World Press.

Mamdani, Mahmood. 1995. A Critique of the State and Civil Society Paradigm in Africanist Studies. In *African Studies in Social Movements and Democracy*, eds. Mahmood Mamdami and E. Wamba-dia-Wamba. Dakar: Codesria.

Marcussen, Henrik Secher. 1996. NGOs, the State and Civil Society. *Review of African Political Economy* 23(69): 405–423.

McIntyre, Teresa Medonca and Margarida Ventura. 1998. Angolan PTSD Study Refocuses. *Psychology International* 9(2): 1–5.

Minter, William. 1994. *Apartheid's Contras: An Inquiry into the Roots of War in Angola and Mozambique.* Johannesburg: Witwatersrand Press.

Moçambique, Governo de, Ministério do Plano e Finanças, Direcção Nacional de Estatistica. 1994. *Anuário Estatistico.* Maputo, May.

Mozambique News Agency (AIM) (1996 & 1998). *Mozambiquefile*, various issues.

Mucache, Eunice, Freida Draisma and Cecilia Bilale. 1995. Ways of Helping Children Affected by Violence and War: The Experience of Mozambique. Maputo: Mozambique Red Cross Society.

Muianga, Elisa. 1995. Mulheres e Guerra: Reintegração Social das Mulheres Regressadas das 'Zonas da Renamo' no Distrito de Mandlakazi. *Arquivo*, October, 18: 47–92.

Muianga, Lucena. 1995. Rehabilitation and Empowerment of Children in Difficult Circumstances: The Experience in Mozambique. In *Transcending the Legacy: Children in the New Southern Africa* Jeff Balch ed. Amsterdam: African-European Institute.

Ndegwa, Stephen. 1996. *The Two Faces of Civil Society: NGOs and Politics in Africa.* West Hartford, CT: Kumarian Press.

Nilsson, Anders. 1990. *Unmasking the Bandits: European Involvement with Apartheid's Tool of Terror.* London: ECASAAMA.

Nordstrom, Carolyn. 1997. *A Different Kind of War Story.* Philadelphia, PA: University of Pennsylvania Press.

Osaghase, Eghosa. 1994. Between State and Civil Society. In *Africa: Prospects on Development.* Dakar: Codesria.

Pitcher, M. Anne. 1996. Chiefs, Companies and Cotton: Observations from Nampula. *Southern Africa Report* November: 26–30.

Robertson, Gavin and Steven de Kiewit. 1998. Wilderness Therapy with Militarized Youth in Traumatised Communities. *Journal of Social Development in Africa* 13(1): 53–58.

Roesch, Otto. 1992. Mozambique Unravels? The Retreat to Tradition. *Southern Africa Report* May: 27–30.

Save the Children Federation. 1995. *Children and War: The Mozambique Experience*. Maputo: Save the Children Fund.

Sheldon, Kathleen. 1994. Women and Revolution in Mozambique: A Luta Continua. In *Women and Revolution in Africa, Asia and the New World*, ed. Mary Ann Tetreault. Columbia, SC: University of South Carolina Press.

Shin, Doh Chull. 1994. On the Third Wave of Democratization: Review Article. *World Politics* 47(1): 135–170.

da Silva, Terezinha. 1995. Disaster Preparedness in Mozambique: Family Tracing and Reunification Project. In *Children Separated by War*. London: Save the Children.

Sogge, David. 1997. The Civil Sector. In *Mozambique: Perspectives on Aid and the Civil Sector*, ed. David Sogge. Oegstgeest: Gemeensohappelijk Overlag Medefinanciering.

Sulemani, David Aloni. 1995. Experiéncia Democrática na Tradição Africana: Cultura de Paz e Democraçia. UNESCO Conference papers, May 1994: 5–63.

Taimo, Jamisse. 1995. Cultura de Paz e Democracia em Mozambique: Cultura de Paz e Democracia. UNESCO Conference papers, May 1994: 145–52.

Tripp, Aili Mari. 1994. Rethinking Civil Society: Gender Implications in Contemporary Tanzania. In *Civil Society and the State in Africa*, eds. John Willis Harbeson, Donald S. Rothchild and Naomi Chazan. Boulder, CO: Lynne Rienner.

United Nations Development Programme (UNDP). 1996. Preliminary Results of the Quantitative Analysis of Data obtained during Interviews with 1000 Demobilized Soldiers', 28 May, Maputo: UNDP.

——— 1994. *Human Development Report*, New York: UNDP.

UNICEF. 1994. *An Assessment of Children and Youth in Renamo Zones: Strategies and Recommendations – Final Report*. Maputo: UNICEF.

United Nations. 1995. *The United Nations and Mozambique, 1992–1995*. New York: United Nations.

Vines, Alex. 1991. *Renamo: Terrorism in Mozambique*. Bloomington, IN: Indiana University Press.

Wilson, Kenneth. 1992a. *Internally Displaced, Refugees, and Returnees from and in Mozambique*. Oxford: Oxford University Press.

——— 1992b. Cults of Violence and Counter Violence in Mozambique. *Journal of Southern African Studies* 18(3): 527–582.

World Bank. 1994. *Population and Development: Implications for the World Bank*, Washington, DC: World Bank.

Index

Printed and bound by CPI Group (UK) Ltd, Croydon, CR0 4YY

13/04/2025

14656514-0004